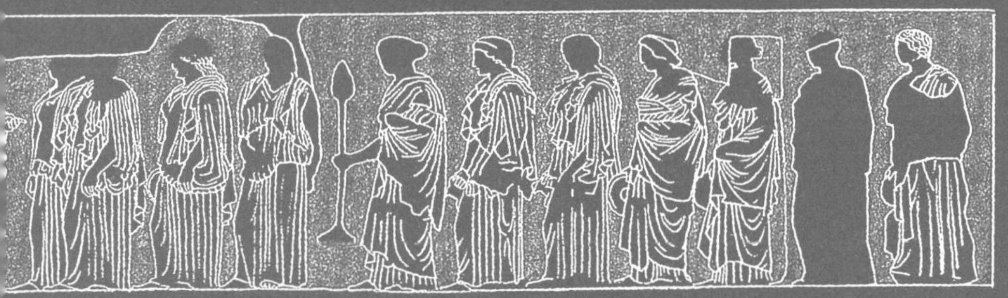

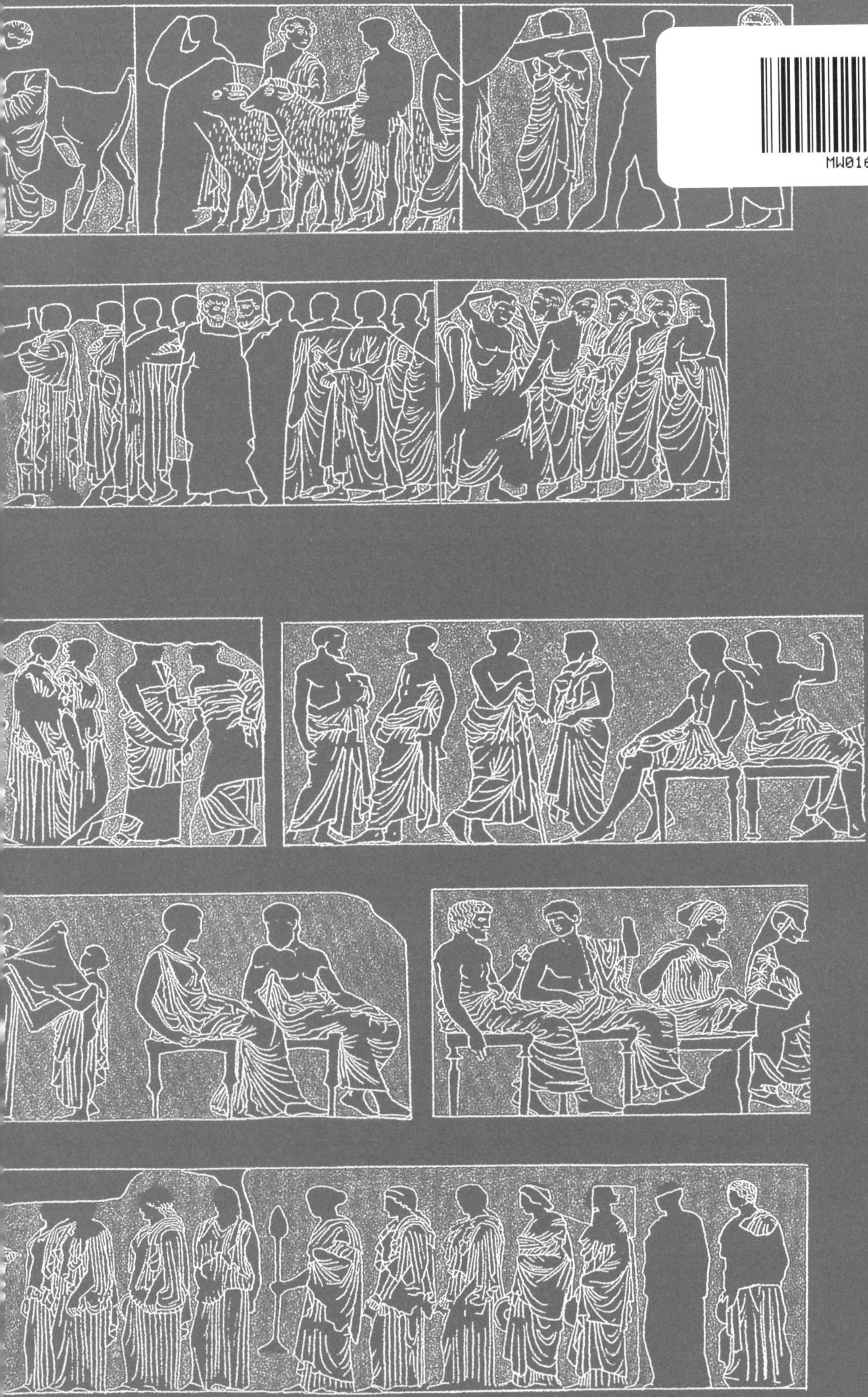

CLASSIC GREEK MASTERPIECES
OF
SCULPTURE

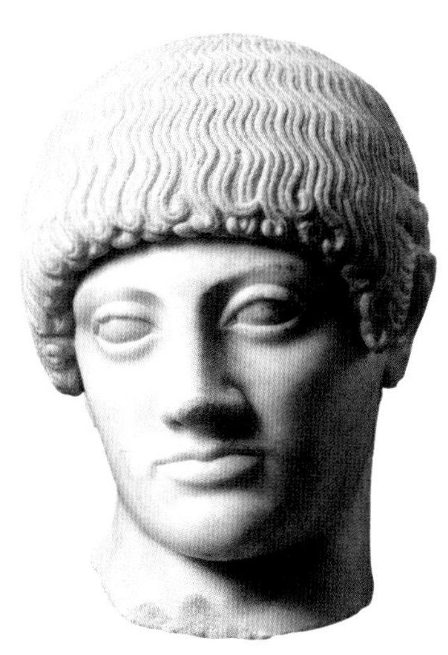

CLASSIC GREEK MASTERPIECES OF SCULPTURE

Photini N. Zaphiropoulou

FOREWORD
Stelios Lydakis

PHOTOGRAPHS
Elias Eliadis
Sokratis Mavrommatis

Abrams, New York

CONTENTS

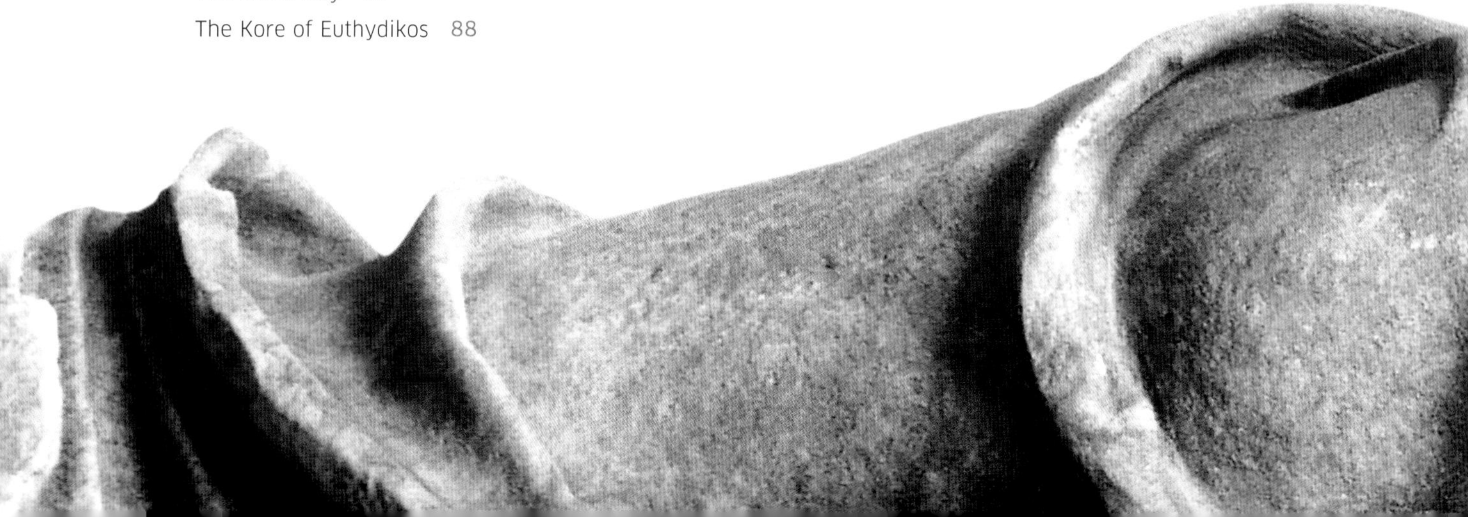

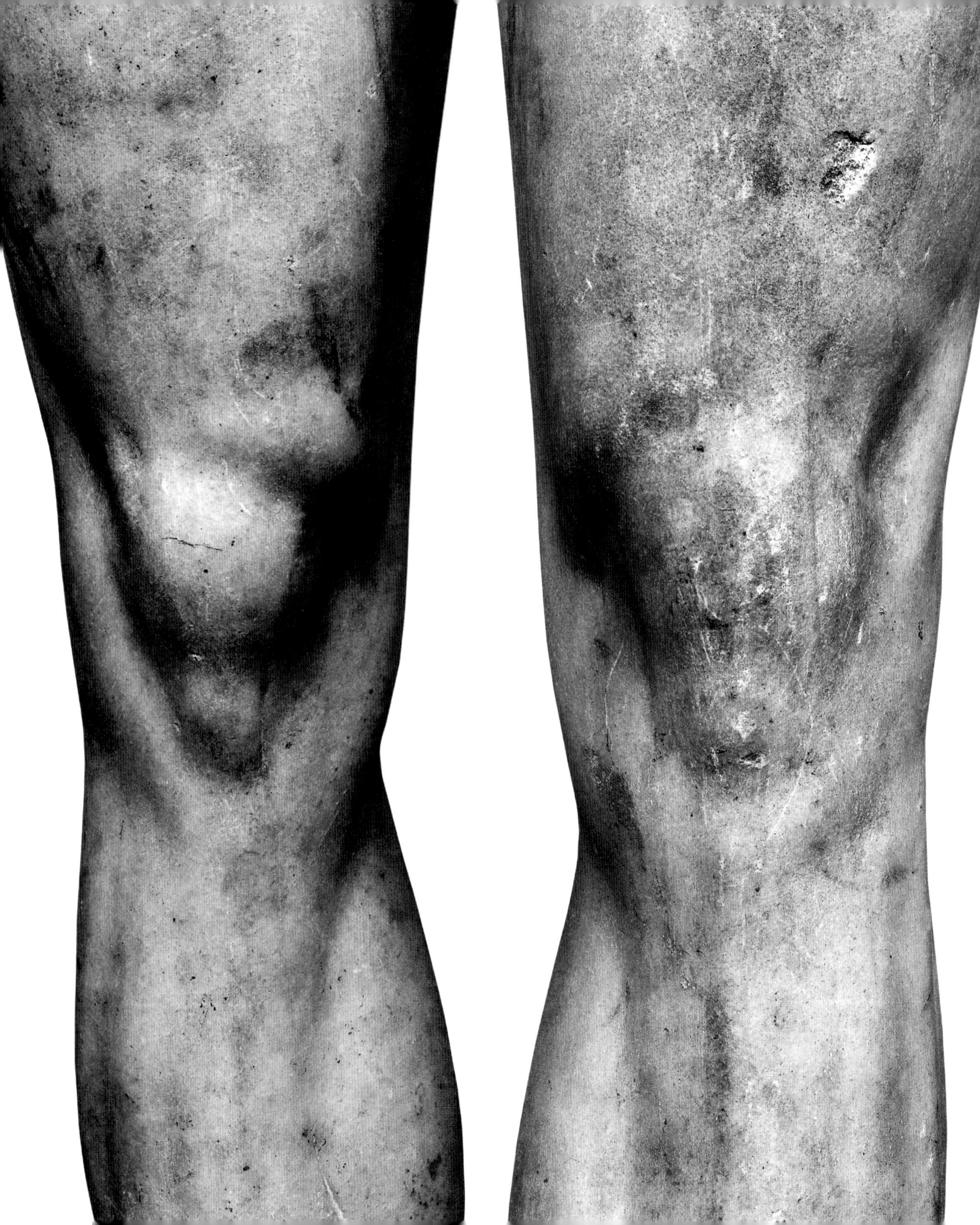

PUBLISHER'S PREFACE

Ancient Greek sculpture, the anthropomorphic art par excellence, constitutes an essential chapter in human expression. Each period approaches sculpture of the human form with its own cultural repository and vision. For modern viewers, ancient Greek sculpture is only high art, having been emptied of its religious character. Yet until the end of the classical period, sculptures–images of gods, heroes, mythical beings, and the dead–adorned *loci sancti*, places of worship, and cemeteries.

This book celebrates the beauty of ancient Greek sculpture. Brief descriptions of select works from museums in Greece, Europe, and the United States introduce the reader to the milieu–geographical, historical, social, and religious–in which the sculpture was created and that contributed to its development. The illustrations take a different approach, consciously avoiding the whole in favor of details. These details both highlight aspects of sculpture and reflect the eye of two exceptionally talented Greek photographers, Elias Eliadis and Sokratis Mavrommatis. Thus, this history of ancient Greek sculpture proceeds as a visual quest to breathe life into staid museum exhibits.

This project would have been impossible without the contributions of Photini Zaphiropoulou, who enthusiastically agreed to support it as both its author and as the technical editor of the texts, which illuminate diverse aspects of ancient Greek sculpture.

We give our warm thanks to Professor Stelios Lydakis, whose foreword introduces the reader to significant art historical concerns of ancient Greek sculpture.

We are grateful to the National Archaeological Museum, the Acropolis Museum, and the archaeological museums of Kerameikos, Delphi, Olympia, Paros, and Delos for granting permission for photography. For providing photographs for the book's illustrations, we are grateful to the British Museum; the Louvre Museum; the J. Paul Getty Museum, in Los Angeles; the Metropolitan Museum of Art, in New York; and the French School at Athens. We owe special thanks to the German Archaeological Institute at Athens for its unstinting collaboration and for permitting us to publish excellent photographs from its archives.

Melissa Books

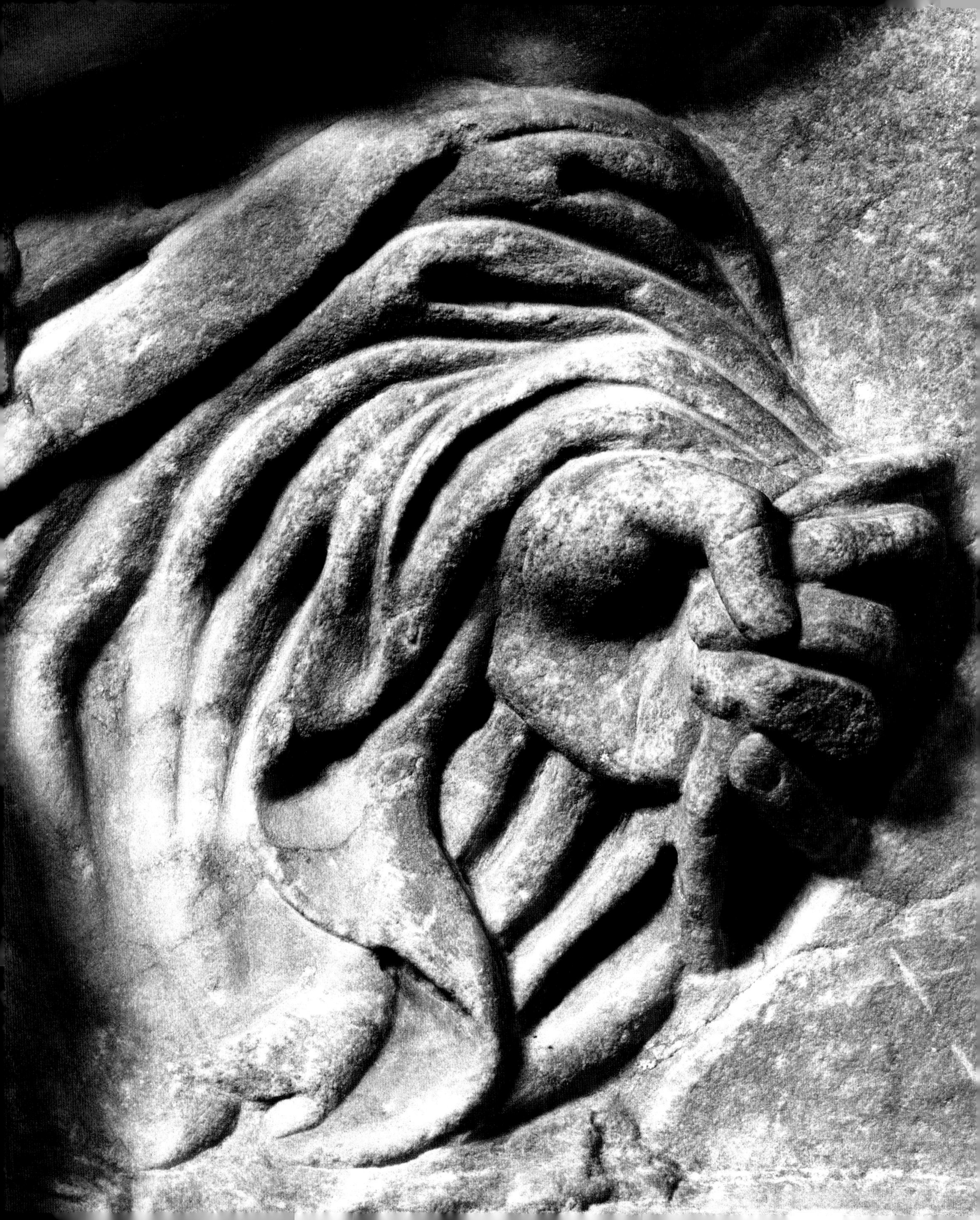

"MEN CREATED WITH WISDOM A BEAUTIFUL STATUE"

"Du mußt dein Leben ändern" [You must change your life]

Rilke, on beholding a torso of a kouros in the Louvre Museum, Paris

As modern viewers admire the original masterpieces of ancient Greek sculpture, many will wonder what factors informed this great art. The search for these factors must begin in the second half of the seventh century BCE, when the creation of monumental sculpture in stone began. By the sixth century BCE, Greek sculptors had gained sufficient experience to produce, in tandem with monumental architecture, larger-than-life works. These sculptors also mastered the clothed female figure and the nude male figure. While workshops differed depending on their locale, the general characteristics of the art remained the same. The naturalistic rendering of the human figure was at first abstract and stylized, but over time sculptors mastered the anatomy, movement, and pathos of the physical model; beauty and virtue remained important, and the youthful figure was the ideal. Of particular interest here are the views of the artists, poets, and philosophers, expressed primarily during the final decades of the fifth century BCE, that help us to understand the Greeks' relationship with their art in the Archaic period. A seminal text in this respect is the succinctly written "The statue is beautiful because it was made by someone who was not incompetent" (*Περικαλλές ἄγαλμα ἐξεποίησ' ούκ ἀδαής*), a concise yet comprehensive work by the great Greek archaeologist Christos Karouzos that was published in the *Philologist's Library* (*Βιβλιοθήκη του Φιλολόγου* 1946, no. 5). The ancient Greeks appreciated a work of art conceived with wisdom and knowledge. They esteemed someone with wisdom, someone who knew what he was doing. This appreciation is evident in an analogous inscription: "Men created with wisdom a beautiful statue" (*ἄνδρες ἐποίαισαν σοφίαισιν καλόν ἄγαλμα*).

Wisdom and knowledge are apprehended in how the work is structured, set up, carved, and so on. The technique—the craftsmanship—was admired first, just as the material was admired in the Daedalic works. The inscription on the gold statue of Zeus dedicated at Olympia by either the tyrant of Corinth, Kypselos (657–627 BCE), or his son, Periander (627–585 BCE), for example, declares, "If I am not a full, all-gold colossus, let the line of the Kypselids be lost forever" (*εἰ μή ἐγώ ναξός παγχρύσεός εἰμί κολοσσός ἐξώλης εἴη Κυψελιδῶν γενεά*). The size, material, and value impress and surprise, as another colossal statue attests: The torso of the marble statue that the Naxians dedicated to Apollo on his sacred isle of Delos, in 600 BCE, alone is 7 feet (2.20 m) high. It declares, "I am from a single stone, statue and base" (*τό αὐτό λίθο εἰμί ἀνδριάς καί τό σφέλας*). The material's contribution to the beauty of the statue never lost its importance.

That said, the phrase "beautiful statue" (*περικαλλές ἄγαλμα*) carries with it a judgment. The Greek word for "statue" (*ἄγαλμα*) derives from the verb *ἀγάλλομαι* (to rejoice, to delight) and at first did not refer solely to statues but to "all things that delight" (*πᾶν ἐφ' ᾧι τίς ἀγάλλεται*). In the sixth century BCE, because the god was understood as the subject of the rejoicing, every votive offering was called a "beautiful delight, a beautiful statue" (*περικαλλές ἄγαλμα*). This association continued until at least 530 BCE.

The phrase "*περικαλλές ἄγαλμα*" was later replaced by "*καλόν ἄγαλμα*," which also means "beautiful statue," as evident in inscriptions from Ptoon, Olympia, and elsewhere. These statues that the ancient Greeks admired as beautiful, lovely, or good could be made of wood, as was common in the early phases of Greek sculpture, in the *xoana* (wooden cult effigies), or could be a mixture of materials, as with the chryselephantine statues whose flesh parts of ivory and garments of gold were attached to a wooden frame. The most famous examples of the latter were by Pheidias: the statue of Zeus at Olympia, one of the Seven Wonders of the Ancient World, and the statue of Athena in the Parthenon. Sculptors also used, and often preferred, metals, including iron, copper, and most commonly bronze. Clay was used for sculptures of relatively small dimensions, such as those produced in Corinthian workshops and figurines from Tanagra, except in Cyprus, where we have monumental terra-cottas. Porous stone and various kinds of marble also appear in statues. Bronze, however, seems to have been held in higher esteem, and attempts were made to achieve coloration in this material through additives (e.g., the lips of the so-called Benevento Youth, in the Louvre Museum, are rouged). Nevertheless, polychromy was of interest mainly where it could be applied easily, such as on terra-cotta and stone statues. Indeed, Praxiteles is said to have been particularly fond of those of his works that the painter Nikias had colored.

Polygnotos, according to Pliny in his *Natural History* (33.160), invented ochre, which when mixed with other pigments mutes the general coloration, in earlier times rather garish. Although Johann Joachim Winckelmann, founder of the field of archaeology, considered polychromy "barbaric" and maintained that the whiter a statue the lovelier it was, by the nineteenth century the investigation of polychromy, by architects such as Antoine Quatrèmere de Quincy, Jakob Ignaz Hittorff, and Gottfried Semper, had made significant strides. Today archaeologists such as Vinzenz Brinkmann and Ulrike Koch-Brinkmann, in Munich, promote polychromy in their studies and experiments, as in the exhibition "Bunte Götter" (Gods in Color) in the Glyptothek. Certainly the famous kore at the Acropolis Museum (inv. no. 675), dating to the last quarter of the sixth century BCE, was and remains, with its well-preserved polychromy, one of the most important sculptural documents of this practice. More indicative is the polychromy on some terra-cotta sculptures, which, owing to a special surface treatment, is in places preserved. The group of Zeus and Ganymede (Archaeological Museum of Olympia) and the head of the Sphinx from Thebes (Paris, the Louvre Museum) also contribute to our understanding of polychromy in ancient Greek sculpture.

The ancient Greeks admired a sculpture's material, the knowledge and wisdom the artist brought to its making, its polychromy, and, more generally, its color, which they also admired in painting. This admiration for color explains why painting moved the ancient Greeks more than sculpture did, but the great works of ancient painting have been lost, and our knowledge of them derives from pottery (vase painting) and more generally from the arts that are resilient to time (like mosaics and engravings on metal). Our knowledge of ancient sculpture is better supported. However, here too, in most cases the largest original works are missing. Very few pieces in wood have survived; a remarkable exception is the statuette of a goddess (h. 8 inches [20 cm]; c. 630 BCE) in the Samos Archaeological Museum. The chryselephantine statues were dismantled for the preciousness of their materials. The value of the material also accounts for the destruction of original works in bronze, relatively few of which have survived. The Charioteer remained safe buried in the earth at Delphi, while the God of Artemision, the Youth of Antikythera, the Boy from the Sea of Marathon, the Heroes of Riace, and the Lady of Kalymnos were recovered from sunken ships on the seabed. Most exceptional, of course, are the chryselephantine works, which, because of their prized materials, are rare. The bronzes come next, followed by the wooden works, and finally the marmoreal sculptures. Renowned artists like Praxiteles chiseled their most important works in marble; Pliny relates that Praxiteles was more proficient in the technique of sculpting marble than of bronze.

Humans are the predominant subjects in ancient Greek sculpture. But mere mortals are not distinguished from heroes, nor the living from the dead. Thus, a statue may represent a god, a living mortal, or a deceased one. Only the place—be it a sanctuary, cemetery, or public space—and the signature (if one existed) allowed the ancient Greek (and even more so the modern viewer) to make the identification. If, for example, Kroisos or Phrasikleia had not been found with their inscribed bases, we would not have been able to say for certain that they were funerary statues set up on tombs.

Despite the central position the human figure occupied in ancient Greek art, animals were represented, too. The figure of a dog, in the Acropolis Museum, is a masterpiece of sculpture, while the bronze Cow by Myron was so famous it is referenced with wonder in more than fifty literary sources and numerous epigrams. Alongside the Lions of Delos, we know that lions adorned tombs at Chaironeia and Amphipolis, and there is the Bull from the Kerameikos cemetery. But it is the horse more than any other animal that evidently appealed to the aesthetic of the ancient Greek. Its association with deities such as Athena and Poseidon and with heroes undoubtedly derives from its intrinsic valor and free spirit, which is why it appeared so frequently, from the dawn of Greek sculpture to its twilight years. The little stylized "Geometric" bronze horse from Olympia in the Peloponnese (Berlin, State Museums), dated to the second half of the eighth century BCE, is one of the "greatest and loveliest works of art of its kind" (Reinhard Lullies, 1960). There are numerous masterpieces that reveal the Greeks' love of one of the most important and valuable domesticated animals: the horses on the frieze of the Siphnian Treasury; the horses on the east pediment of the Temple of Zeus at Olympia; the horses on the Parthenon frieze, culminating in the superb quality and beauty of the horse head from the Parthenon's east pediment (Chariot of Selene, London, the British Museum); the horse from the so-called Alexander sarcophagus (Istanbul Archaeological Museums, no. 68 [370], fourth century BCE). The horse had entered religious worship even earlier, and we could argue that the horse expresses the heroic nature deeply embedded in the epic-idealistic discourse of the Hellene in general.

This book presents masterpieces of ancient Greek sculpture from all the historical periods in which this great art, so characteristic of Greek spirituality, found its lofty expression. The kouros and the kore, the male and female figures, respectively, that express the vigor of youth, dominate the anthropocentric art of the Greeks. The kouros may derive from a type created in Egypt, but it was the Greek sculptor who promoted and developed it into a free-standing figure with the left leg slightly to the fore and the arms extended down the length of the torso and ending in clenched fists. In the beginning, the format was small, but by the sixth century BCE the monumental figure of the by-then-standardized kouros had appeared in all regions of the Hellenic world: the Peloponnese, the Cyclades, Thera, Samos, and Crete. By the sixth century BCE Attica took the lead, with kouroi such as those of the Dipylon and of Sounion reaching 10 feet (3 m) tall and featuring stylized bodies in dynamic, geometric schemas and frontal poses. As the Greek archaeologist Constantinos Romaios perceptively observed, these figures are characterized by a latent movement, which differentiates them from analogous works of the East and of Egypt.

After the Kroisos from Anavyssos (530–520 BCE), the tendency to cast off stylization and latent movement in favor of overt motion and striking vitality reached its apotheosis in the Aristodikos. This superb kouros, one of the last Attic kouroi, dated c. 500 BCE, is the work of an important sculptor from the circle of Antenor. In it the naturalistic, vivid conception of the sculpted figure reaches its climax while heralding classical art.

The wealth of late Archaic art includes the korai, which appear in strictly frontal poses and elegant attire. In general the female figures of the period display a penchant for refined fashion, including elaborate coiffures and colorful garments. An excellent example is the kore by the sculptor Antenor, now in the Acropolis Museum, an *ex-voto* (votive offering) made for the vasemaker Nearchos, dedicated c. 525 BCE.

The relief friezes on treasuries and temples enabled the continuous narrative flow of a subject and the rendering of figures in a multiplicity of positions and poses, often in complex interlacement. The high point is the late Archaic frieze from the Siphnian Treasury in the sanctuary of Apollo at Delphi. The subject is the Gigantomachy. Although no foreshortenings are discernible in this fluid composition, crossings and gradations extend to three superimposed layers. The dynamism of the conflict between the gods and the giants lends itself to the depiction of vigorous movement and to antithetical axes.

The classical period (490–323 BCE), in which form was harmonized with content, boasts works of supreme maturity and integrity. A preliminary phase, conventionally known as the "Severe Style," includes sculptures from the pediments of the Temple of Zeus at Olympia, which number among the greatest masterpieces of sculpture (Heinrich Bulle). The east pediment presents a tragedy, in the form, as it were, of a *tableau vivant*. This is the preparation for a chariot race between Oenomaos and Pelops that was to bring about the fall of the old royal dynasty and the beginning of a new one. The spirit of the tragic poetry of Aeschylus informs the splendor of the protagonists, who are at the mercy of the gods and fate. Despite the different positions and poses of the figures, the effect of the ensemble is both majestic and serene.

The majesty continues on the west pediment, at least as far as the central figure of the god Apollo is concerned. But the serenity is undone by a concatenation of motion between battling centaurs and Lapiths to the right and left of the god. The element of movement supports the flow of the composition and offers bold solutions to the positioning and entwinement of the bodies. The sculpting is unprecedentedly dynamic, increasing opportunities to exploit the plasticity of the figures. The dynamism turns the sculptures into actors in a drama in which mercy and fear lead to catharsis.

The Charioteer of Delphi belongs to the same stylistic framework as the sculptures of Olympia and is close to them in date (c. 470 BCE). The verticality of the wonderful figure, confident of victory, contributes to its expression of calm and self-assurance. The work, cast in seven separate pieces, is attributed to the sculptor Pythagoras from Rhegion. Both the general profile and the details reflect a concern with the essentials, while the inlaid eyes, which fortunately have been preserved, emphasize the dynamism of the expression. To the same framework belongs another masterly original work, the Zeus or

Poseidon from Artemision (c. 460 BCE), now housed in the National Archaeological Museum. This statue departs from strict verticality and ventures an audacious opening of the figure within space, which it dominates. The factor of time—here, the moment the god is on the verge of hurling the thunderbolt or trident—vivifies the figure. At the very next moment, the target would have been hit and the pose changed. The work heralds an ideal that was to reappear in its full range in the Hellenistic baroque: the temporality, or moment of action, that energizes the figure.

These developments reached their maturity in the sculptures of the pediments and the frieze of the Parthenon. Behind these sculptural designs lies a great mind, an artist with a feeling for plasticity and a sense of the monumental: Pheidias. On the east pediment of the Parthenon, as on that of the Temple of Zeus at Olympia, the figures are rendered with formal austerity, whereas on the west pediment, in the contest between Athena and Poseidon to win the land of Attica, the energetic element was more pronounced. The reclining figures of Dionysus from the east pediment, the wonderful head of a horse from the Chariot of Selene (the goddess of the moon) possess a unique sculptural quality. Superb too is the personification of the Kephissos River, from the west pediment, which begs comparison with the conceptions of Michelangelo. The frieze features a clear flow of figures, each with a distinct outline. The minimal height of the relief (2.5 inches [6 cm] at most), the probably blue ground, and the appropriate polychromy would have given the scene a painterly quality, with the foreshortening of perspective and the graduation of planes. The dynamism of the movements and the play of the horses' legs create a continuous undulation, while the pedestrian figures disrupt the monotony of the flow with backward turns, which create opposing axes.

The grave reliefs and statues are unique artistic masterpieces. Greeks considered it their sacred duty to render honors to the dead. One manifestation of these honors is the tomb monument. The kouroi or relief stelai from the Archaic period, and the subsequent grave *naiskoi* (small temples) enclosing a relief composition or one in the round, were set up on the tomb. One of the best-known funerary monuments is now kept in the Villa Albani in Rome. It presents a young warrior who has just dismounted from his horse and is poised to strike his vanquished opponent. This monument comes from the funerary monument for the Athenians who fell in the first year of the Peloponnesian War and was apparently taken to Rome by Sulla in 86 CE. Discovered in 1761, it is the largest known funerary relief (5.90 x 7.81 feet [1.80 x 2.38 m]) and dates to c. 431 BCE. It recalls the Parthenon workshops and draws on the Pheidian mastery of synthesis. The grave relief from Aegina, of a youth holding a little bird in his left hand, is of a comparable caliber. Splendid too is the grave relief of Hegeso, daughter of Proxenos. Seated on a chair, she looks at her jewelry for the last time, brought to her in a casket by her maidservant. This masterpiece is suffused with dignity and restrained grief.

But the grave relief, without a doubt, acquires its unprecedented psychological profundity in the example found in the bed of the River Ilissos. The high quality and style of this work suggest the sculptor Skopas from Paros, and it dates to c. 430 BCE. In the time of Plato and of Aristotle, the deceased was considered the strongest, highest being (Fuchs). He is the hero, the complete, the perfect one. On the Ilissos relief he appears nude and in a frontal pose, leaning against a pillar upon which he has placed his cape. The *lagobolon* (a throwing stick for catching hares) hanging from his left arm and the hound indicate that he is a hunter. On the stepped base of the *cippus*—which corresponds to the grave marker of the deceased—is curled a small naked child with half-open eyes. Opposite the deceased is his elderly father, whose hand is brought to his chin in a gesture of pensiveness over his dead son. The viewer of the stele, in effect, sees the father's thoughts given visual form. The composition is calculated to the minutest detail. The two vertical axes of the figures in the upper part are related to the old man's intense gaze; in the lower part the dog sniffs at his foot, creating another relationship. The unfocused gaze

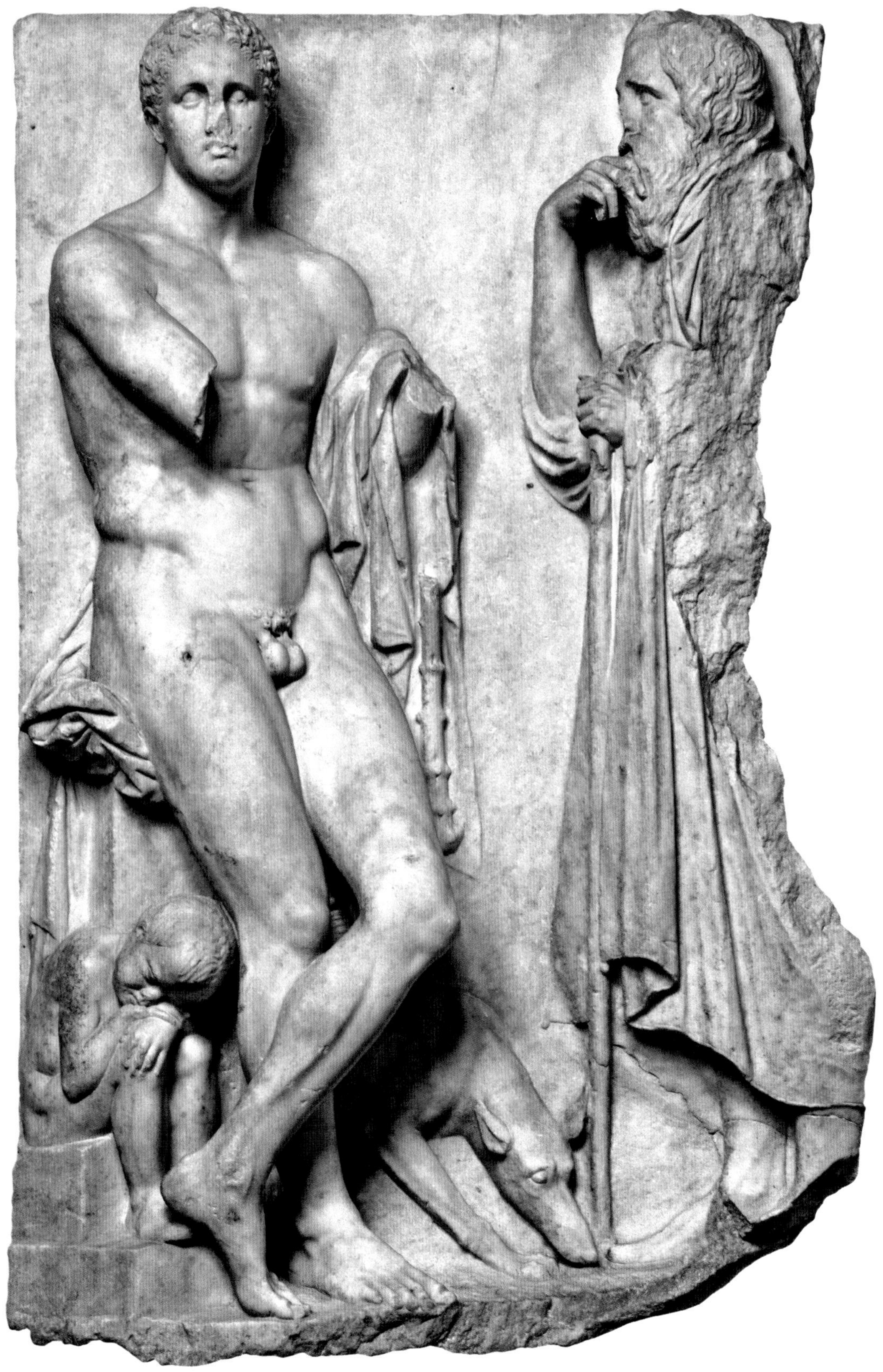

of the deceased and the old man's concentration on the image his thoughts create invoke both introspection and reverie. This is without a doubt one of the most important works of ancient Greek sculpture.

From the same period, 340–330 BCE, is the statue of a Youth, recovered from the seabed off the island of Antikythera. Some believe it to be the Paris created by Euphranor, which Pliny mentions (33.77), while others feel it represents Perseus holding the head of Medusa. This athletic figure with its youthful face embodies the same ideal of the hero evident on the funerary stele from the Ilissos. In the case of the Youth from the Antikythera shipwreck, the synthesis acquires a baroque element, as the figure appears to "spread" freely in space. All of the youth's weight falls on the stable left leg, to which the raised right arm corresponds, while the relaxed right leg barely touches the ground on tiptoe and the left arm is totally inert. Beyond these morphological observations, however, what is of more interest is the facial expression of goodness and virtue, and the statue's radiance of human fulfillment.

This baroque element is evident also in the marble statue of Hermes by Praxiteles, which corresponds to the Irene (peace) and Pluto by his father, Kephisodotos (374–370 BCE; copy in the Munich Glyptothek). Here, a new aesthetic ideal is also expressed: the conquest of space, the third dimension. Nonetheless, the gentleness of the volumes and the sfumato based on the lustrous surface treatment, create a sense not of strength, as in earlier pieces, but of affectation and refinement, which is characteristic of the late classical manner.

From the Rhodes School, which developed in parallel with the Pergamon School, comes a baroque work par excellence: the Nike (Victory) of Samothrace. This work, which dates to c. 190 BCE and is now housed in the Louvre Museum, translates the achievements of the late classical style into a monumental style. Body and *chiton* (a garment of fine cloth) are in a dialogical relationship. The movement and the opposing axes energize the figure, the monumentality of which is enhanced by its huge size (the extant part alone, without the head, is 8.04 feet [2.45 m] tall).

From the middle of the first century BCE comes another important work of the Rhodes School: the Laokoon group. Pliny mentions its creators and believes it to surpass all works in sculpture and painting. This work, which was discovered in 1506 and had a profound impact on the Renaissance, is the creation of three sculptors: Agesandros, Polydoros, and Athenodoros. The composition of the three figures of Laokoon and his two sons, with snakes coiling and entwining their bodies, is aligned frontally. Interesting here is the expression of pathos, which reaches an exaggerated theatricality. Comparable tendencies are evident in the famous frieze from the great altar of Pergamon (180/160 BCE, Berlin), in which the pathos leads to dynamic movements, positions, and poses of bodies in a chain succession. The subject, the Gigantomachy, lends itself admirably to the hyperbole of the baroque, while the ambitious conception and execution of the frieze, which is almost 400 feet (120 m) long and 7.55 feet (2.30 m) high, must belong to one of the great, yet unknown, artists of the ancient world.

In general it is difficult to appraise ancient Greek sculpture as a whole, because the vast majority of works have been lost and because the sculptures were so numerous that they constituted "a second population of marble and metal," as Jacob Burckhardt remarked. But those original works that have survived—occasionally enriched by new discoveries on the seabed, such as the Riace Heroes and others, as well as by indications of the originals in Roman copies—give a clear picture of an art that will astonish us "*überall und immer*" (above all and always) (Thassilo von Scheffer) and will proclaim its spiritual grandeur for all eternity.

STELIOS LYDAKIS
Professor Emeritus of History of Art
University of Athens

INTRODUCTION

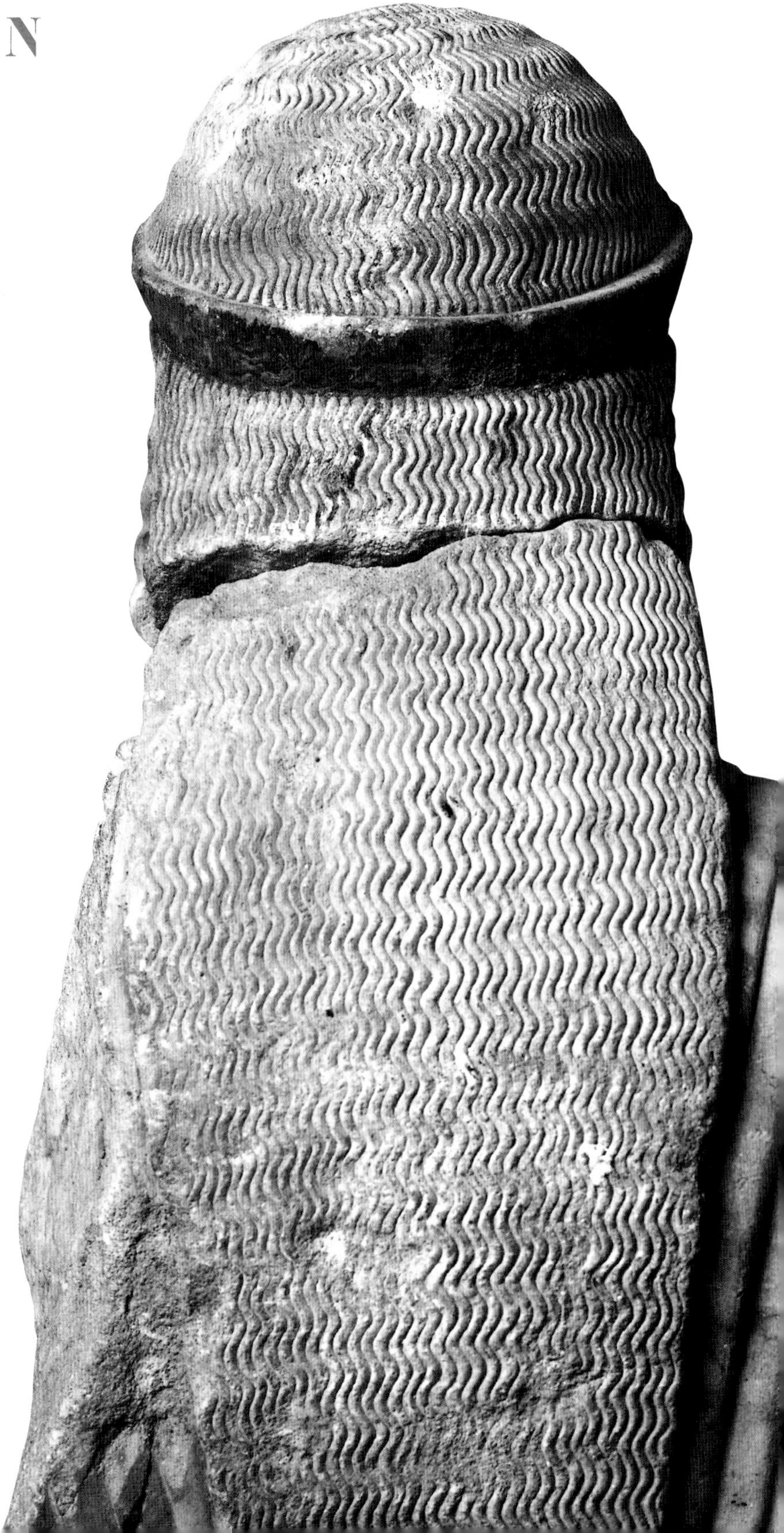

In the ancient Hellenic world, the region formed around the Mediterranean Basin (including the west coast of Asia Minor, the islands and mainland of Greece, and southern Italy) in the early first millennium BCE, Zeus, father of the gods, and his omnipotent consort, Hera, were for centuries the most revered couple of divine worship. The prevailing Hellenic tribes and, primarily, the domination of the Olympian Pantheon, expressed the new era. Their most important sanctuary was Olympia, in the western Peloponnese, where temples and monuments, most of them creations of great artists, such as Pheidias, adorned the sacred Altis (as the site of the sanctuary was known). Foremost among these temples and monuments were the venerable Heraion, the Temple of Hera, dating to the early sixth century BCE; and the magnificent Temple of Zeus, dating to the first half of the fifth century BCE. The founding of the first Olympic Games, in 776 BCE, added to the widespread fame the sanctuary acquired over the centuries. Likewise, the banning of the Games, in 393 CE, was essentially the death knell for the sanctuary.

The renowned daughter of Zeus, the august Athena Parthenos, who gifted wisdom to mankind, enjoyed no lesser honors, especially from the Ionian tribes. Paramount among the Ionians were the Athenians, who glorified their guardian goddess with a unique architectural and artistic achievement: the resplendent Parthenon, jewel of the most important sanctuary of the land, the Acropolis. It was on this sacred rock that all the artistic history of Athens developed, and the various monuments founded there also marked the historical events that had set their seal on the numinous site.

However, principal expresser of the Olympian spirit was the beloved son of Zeus: the blond god of light, Apollo. This old deity, in a new form in the Pantheon of the Olympian gods, came to bring humanity the joy of life, with his love of music as well as his knowledge of "measure" or moderation, which should govern every human action. With these two different hypostases, Apollo, like Christ who succeeded him, was worshipped in two places, each one characteristic of the corresponding persona of the god. The god who most clearly expresses the munificence of the Hellenic spirit could only have been born where shadows and darkness have no place. This was Delos, where the

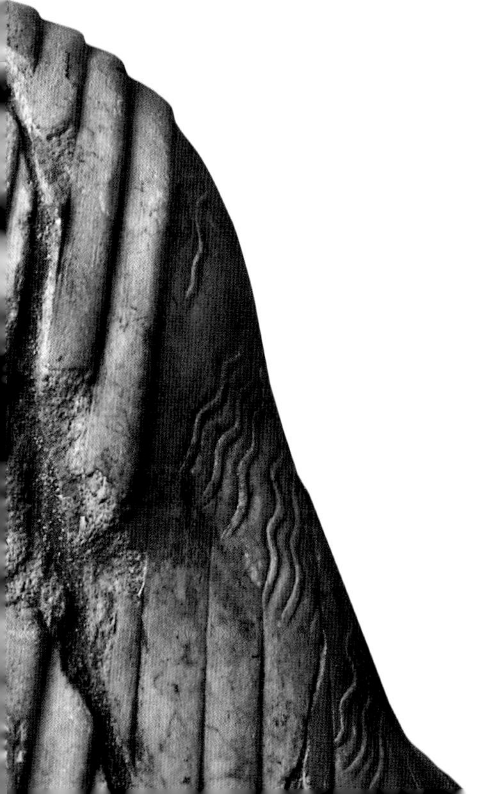

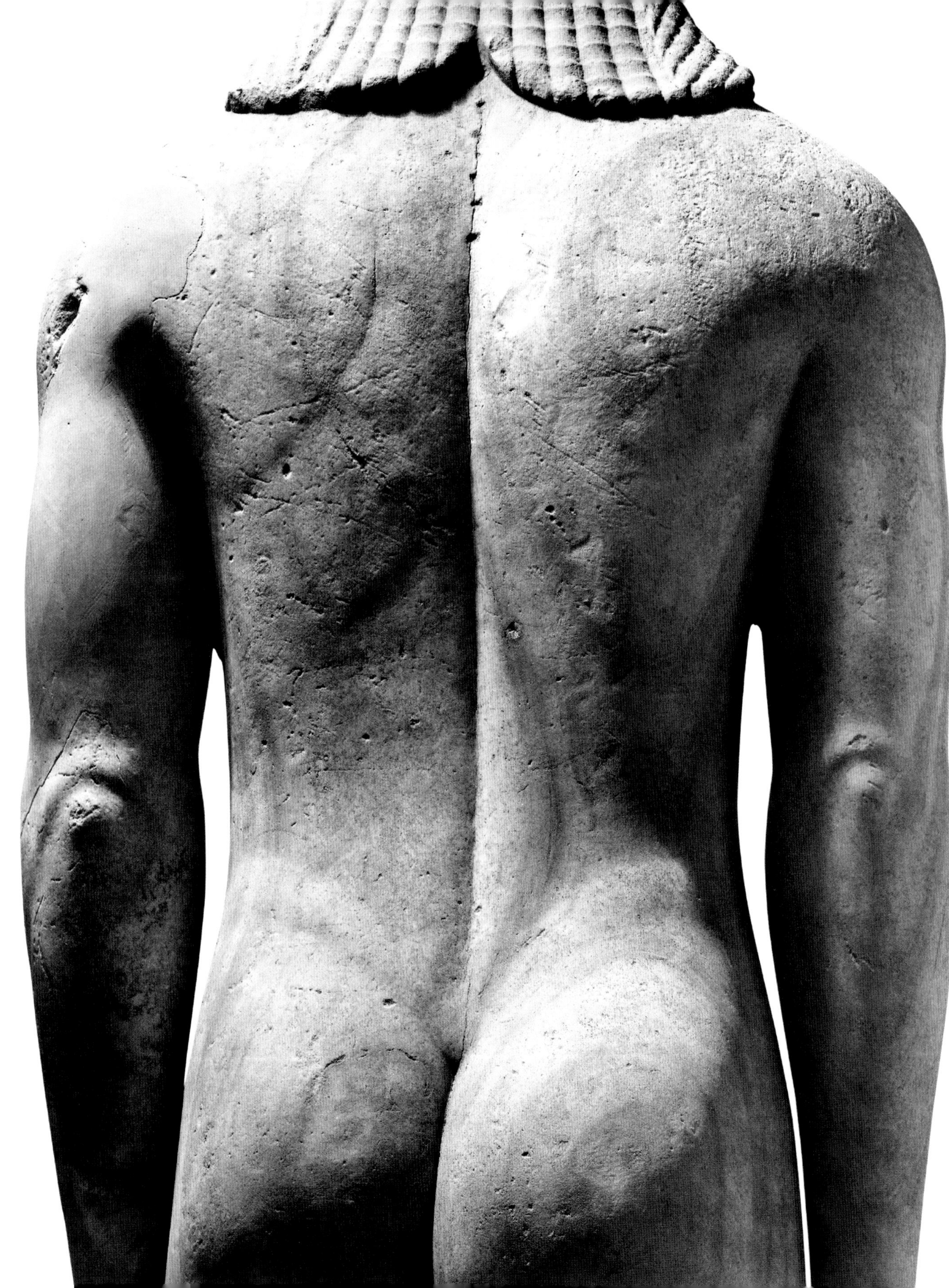

newborn god immediately acquired traits absolutely in keeping with the bright limpid atmosphere of the Cycladic island, which, as early as 700 BCE, was referred to in the sources as the sacred center of the Ionians. There they held their gatherings and their famed great assembly, under the enlightened patronage of Apollo, for their common interests. Delos was adorned not only with temples—three dedicated to Apollo, one to his mother, Leto, and one to his twin sister, Artemis—but also with important sacred edifices and monuments, the majority ex-votos of powerful cities or rulers who wished to display their might and wealth in a place not only hallowed but also renowned. In the festivals organized in Apollo's honor, music and dance had pride of place. Delos, in Hellenistic times (third–second century BCE), developed into one of the major ports of the Mediterranean, a cosmopolitan commercial center that thrived until its destruction in 69 BCE.

By contrast, we find Apollo also at remote, mountainous Delphi. There, Apollo was the just judge of human actions and determined the fate of mortals—an austere deity who made his divine presence and will known in a landscape whose majesty and ruggedness invoked in the visitor a supernatural awe. There, too, Apollo slew the dragon Python, to which feat is owed his epithet Pythios, to establish his sanctuary with the oracle-shrine, which developed into a *locus sanctus* of global fame, respected even by the barbarians. The *temenos* (sacred precinct) of the god, with the temple and host of monuments all around—here, as on Delos, chiefly comprising ex-votos of cities or rulers—grew upon a relatively precipitous slope of Mount Parnassos in Phocis, in western central Greece, below the imposing, magnificent Phaidriades rocks. At Delphi, as at many other major sanctuaries, games were held in honor of the god—in this case the Pythian Games—and votive offerings, such as the famous bronze statue of the Charioteer, were also dedicated by victors in the contests.

Apollo had many sanctuaries throughout the Hellenic world, particularly in the Aegean islands, close to his birthplace. In these insular sanctuaries, especially on Paros and neighboring Naxos, he was worshipped as Apollo Delios, even though on Paros there was also a sanctuary, of lesser importance, of Apollo Pythios. Also on Paros, on a hill north of the present capital of Paroikia and directly opposite Delos, was an old sanctuary known as the Delion, where Delian Apollo was worshipped together with his sister, Artemis, as on Delos itself. There were other sanctuaries, too, one of which was dedicated to the patron deity of the city, Athena, in the vicinity of the ancient city of Paros, whose ruins lie under modern Paroikia.

The centuries rolled by and social structures changed, and in the Hellenistic period important monuments of remarkable artistic creation appeared. But these were no longer dedicated to gods but to mortals who considered themselves representatives of the forces of good in the world, ordained to help humanity. One such case is the altar erected on the acropolis of the city of Pergamon in Asia Minor by the all-powerful monarch Eumenes II, a monument with which he sought, through art, to proclaim his omnipotence for posterity.

Finally, a few remarks about the world that inspired these works for the delight of gods and mortals are appropriate. After all, the Greek word for statue, *άγαλμα* (agalma), derives from the verb *αγάλλομαι* (agallomai), meaning to rejoice and to glorify, two verbs that clearly convey the character of these sculptures. And, as is commonly acknowledged, sculpture is the pinnacle of ancient Greek artistic expression.

The jubilant statues, whether standing in the bare landscapes of Greece—their rocks brought to life in the Apollonian light and scant vegetation, landscapes attuned absolutely to the ancient sculptures' solemnity and passion—or exhibited in museums, to this day and despite their fragmentary state hold a boundless fascination for the discerning viewer, awakening those humanist values that edify the soul and bring spiritual exaltation and exultation—*αγαλλίαση*!

PHOTINI N. ZAPHIROPOULOU
Archaeologist, Ephor Emerita of Antiquities

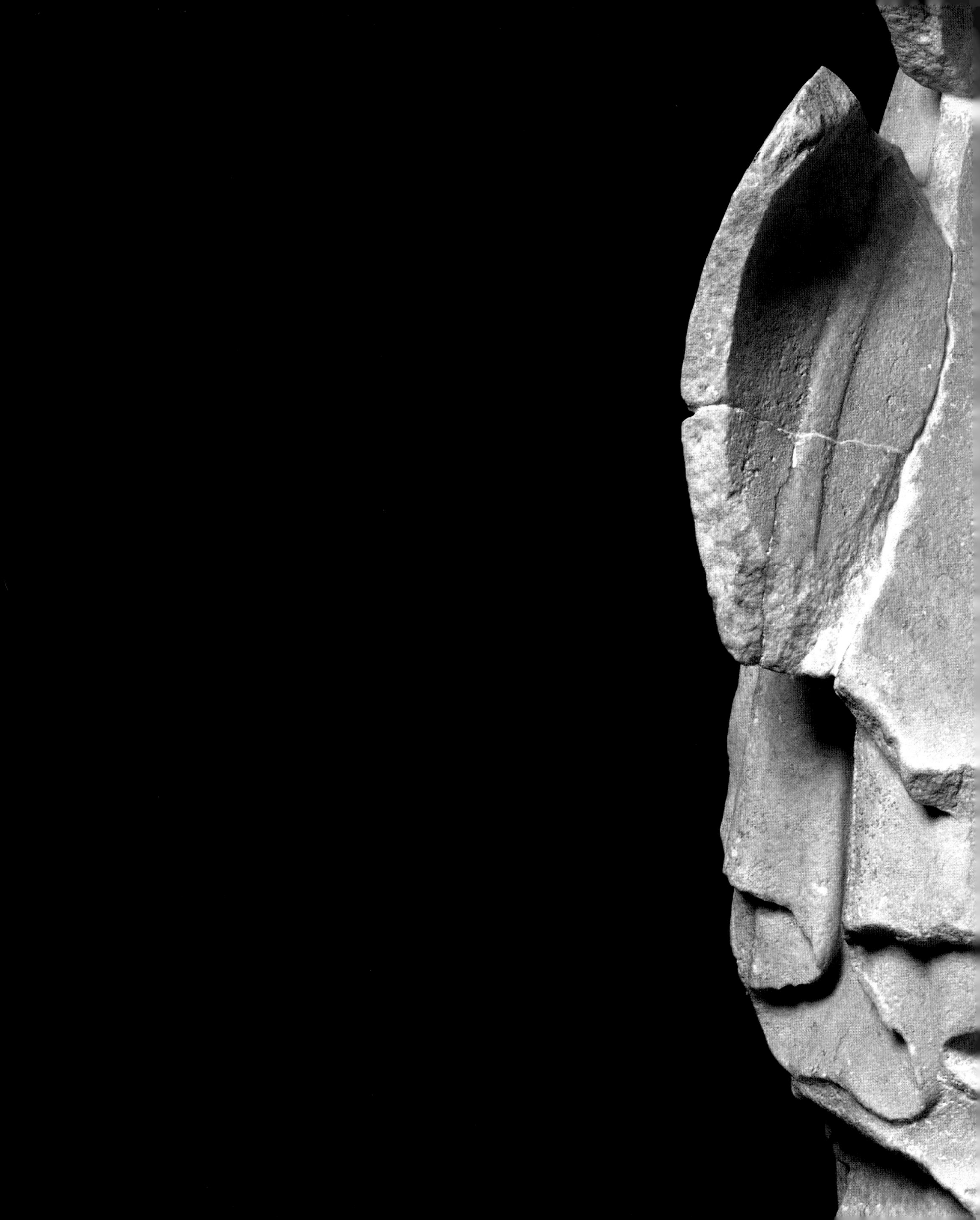

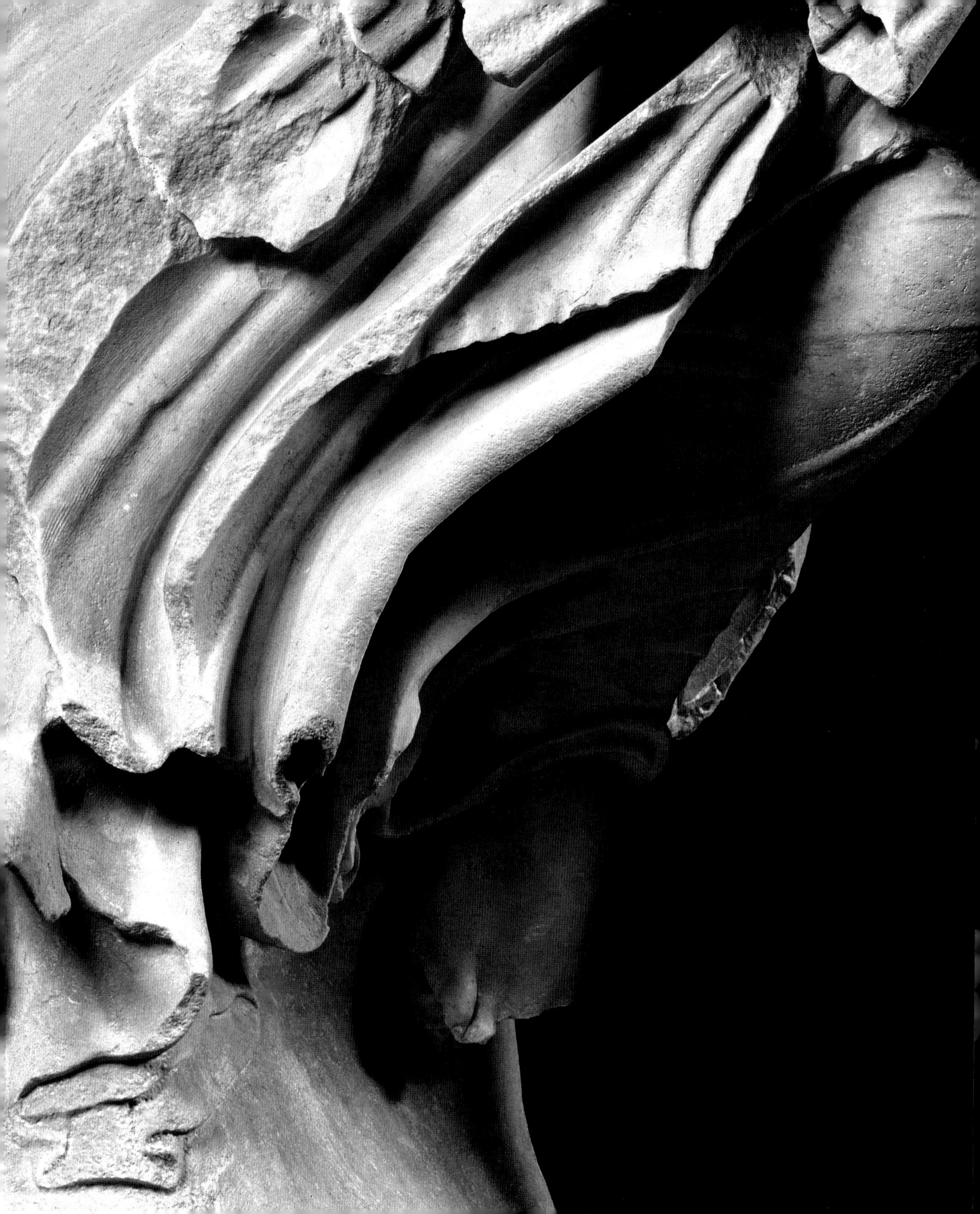

THE SOUNION KOUROS

ATTICA, SOUNION
C. 600 BCE
NAXIAN MARBLE. HEIGHT 10 FEET (3.05 M; AFTER RESTORATION)
ATHENS, NATIONAL ARCHAEOLOGICAL MUSEUM

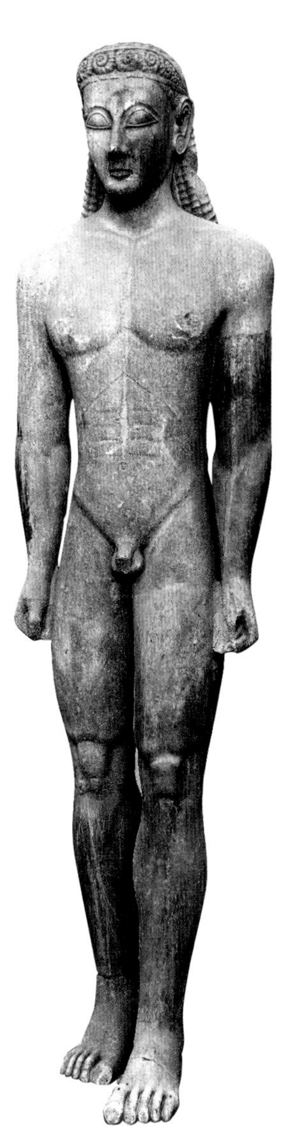

The Sounion Kouros is one of the most impressive kouroi, a series of statues of the Archaic period (sixth century BCE). These statues display Egyptian influences and represent young men in what is known as heroic nudity. The arms hang against the body, and the left leg is set forward in a suggestion of movement that disrupts the otherwise rigid frontal pose. Kouroi were usually placed on tombs, although examples have been found in sanctuaries, too. The latter, which were *ex-votos* (votive offerings), represented Apollo and accordingly were named Apollos.

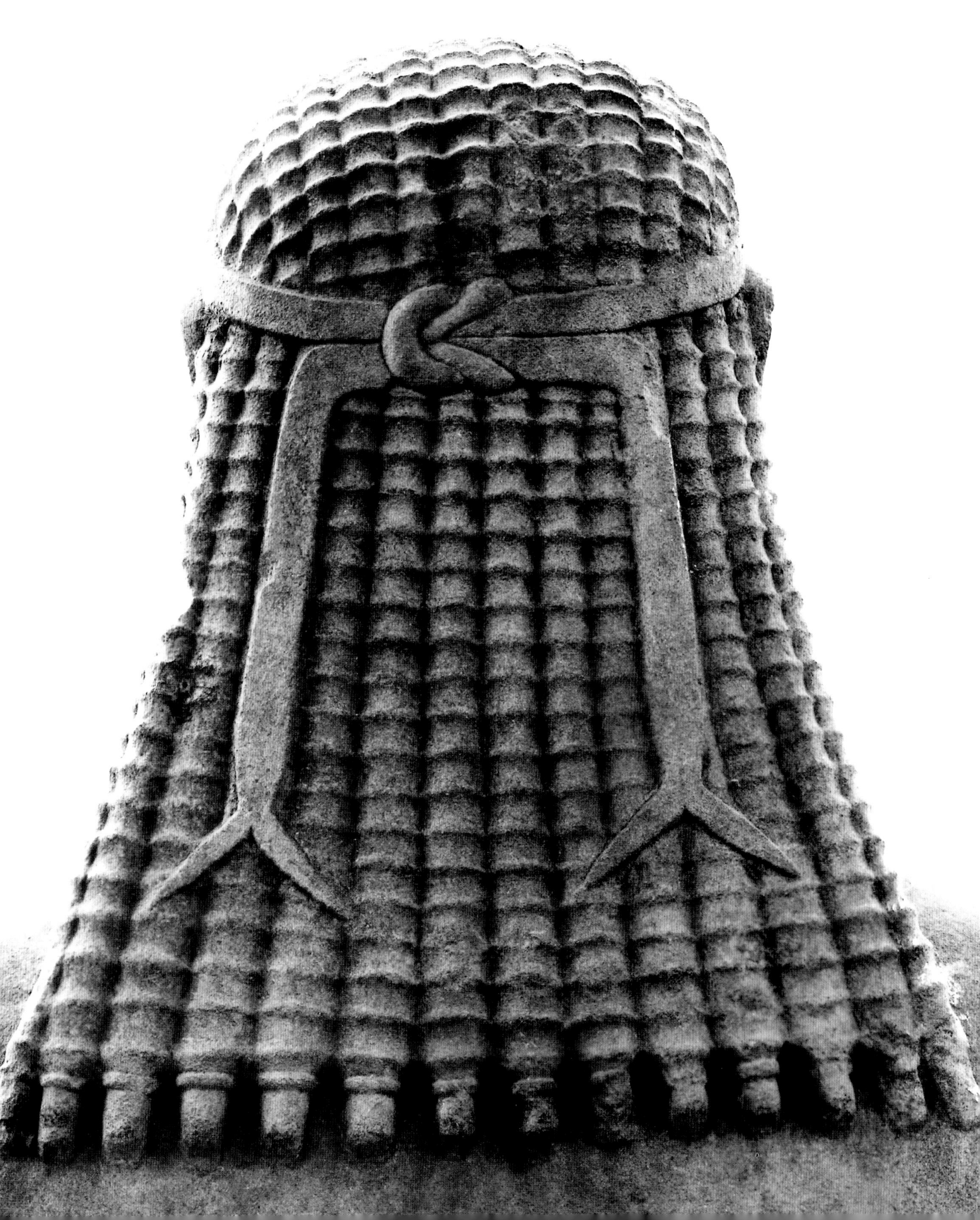

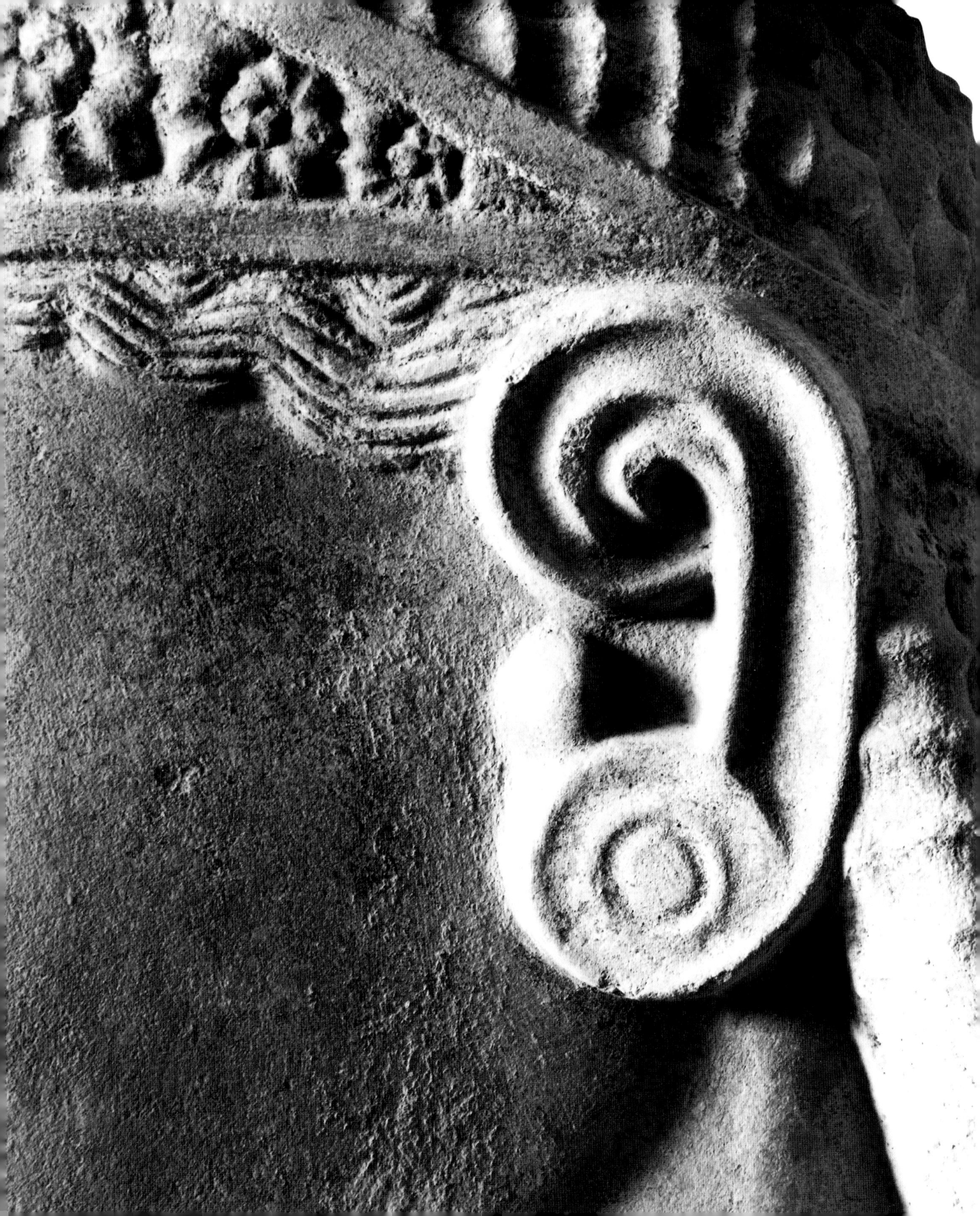

The sculpture's anatomical details are dynamically modeled, if on the schematic side; the knees, for example, are rendered as small, trapezoidal volumes below the swollen quadriceps of the thigh and verge on the decorative. The ears, too, formed as a pair of volutes, appear decorative, as do the spiraling curls, which are reminiscent of snail shells on the forehead. Although this kouros has only a rudimentary three-dimensionality and preserves traits of earlier *xoana*, its robust construction, together with the modeling of its larger-than-life volumes, endows the figure with a divine majesty that inspires the believer and impresses the beholder.

THE KERAMEIKOS KOUROS

ATHENS, KERAMEIKOS, CLOSE TO THE SACRED GATE
C. 600 BCE
NAXIAN MARBLE. PRESENT HEIGHT 4.75 FEET (1.45 M; ORIGINAL APPROX. 7.48 FEET [2.28 M])
ATHENS, KERAMEIKOS MUSEUM

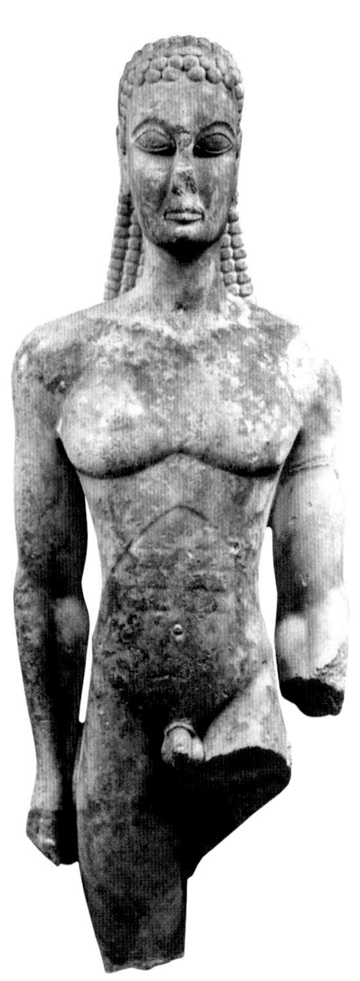

The greater part of this original work survives, extending from the head down to the top of the left thigh and to about the middle of the right; the left arm is missing below the elbow. Two enormous, almond-shaped eyes with heavy eyelids dominate the elongated oval face, which is strongly reminiscent of figures by Modigliani. The shadow of the eyes extends across the width of the face below the high, broad forehead, which is crowned by two rows of large spherical curls. The long beaded hairstyle is fixed by a fillet tied at the back in a reef knot (the *herakleion amma*, or Herakles knot), the two long ends of which slant outward. The determined chin and pursed, fleshy lips imbue the figure with a tension and energy uncharacteristic of other

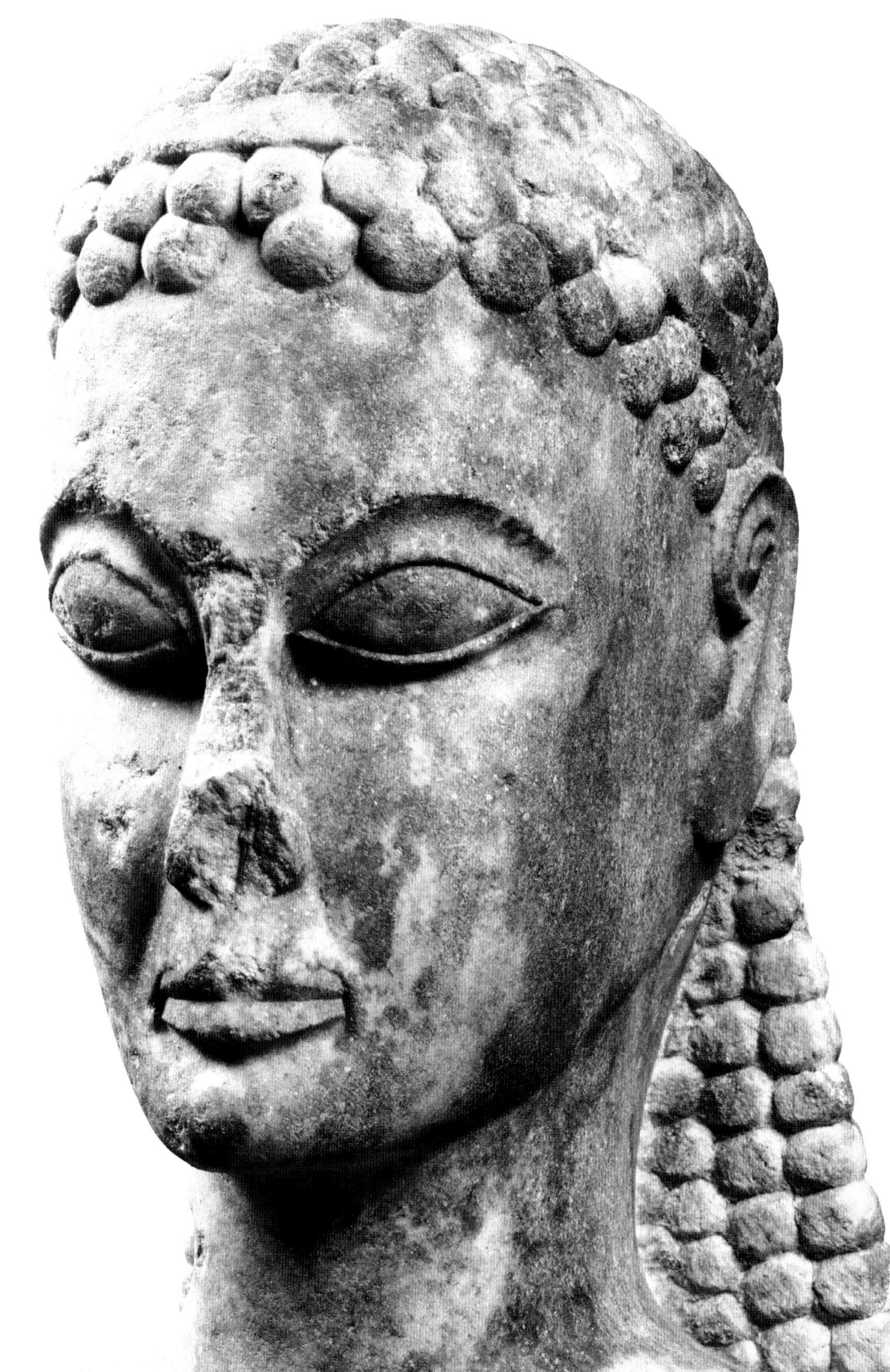

works of the period. The body parts are modeled with the robustness typical of kouroi; the volumes are treated as autonomous elements and are not developed in depth. The result, in some cases, is schematic, purely decorative forms, such as the nipples, or the elbow. The nipples are encircled by a zone of incisions that give the impression of a floral rosette, while the elbow is plastically rendered as a triangle with a diamond in the middle.

This kouros is undoubtedly the work of an accomplished sculptor. His avant-garde ideas, for his time, are evident in another oversize statue, of which only the head survives. This head—which displays the same unique features—was also found in the Kerameikos, close to the Dipylon. One scholar of the newly discovered kouros from the Sacred Gate has suggested, with some reservations, that both works belonged to a funerary enclosure and represented members of one or more high-ranking families.

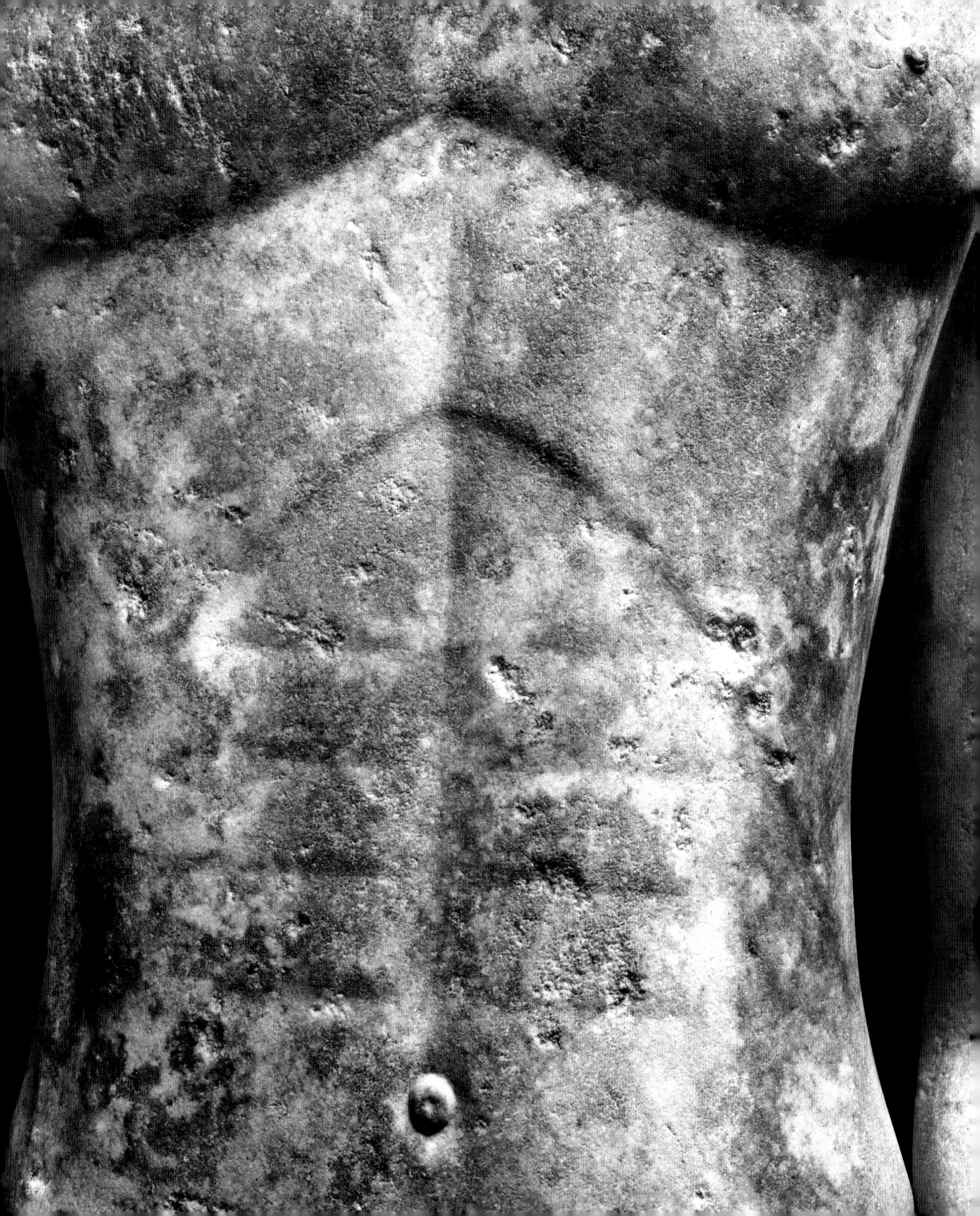

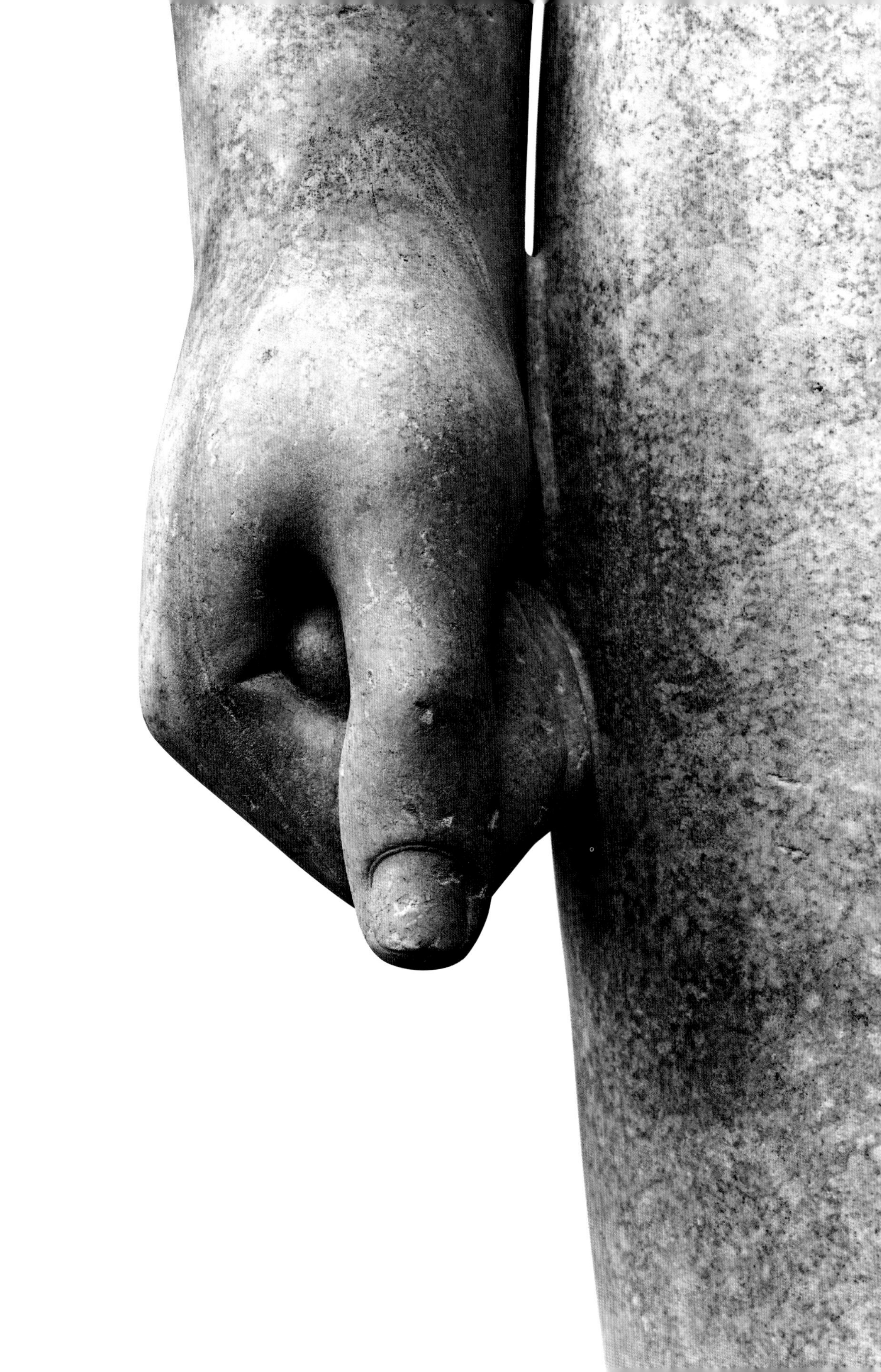

THE SAMOS KOUROS

SAMOS, SANCTUARY OF HERA (HERAION), EAST SECTOR TOWARD THE SACRED WAY
C. 580 BCE
SAMIAN MARBLE WITH BLUE-GRAY VEINS. ORIGINAL HEIGHT 15.75 FEET (4.80 M)
SAMOS, VATHY MUSEUM

As indicated by the inscription that runs virtually the entire length of the figure's left thigh, this colossal kouros was dedicated by Isches for the "delight" of Hera, the great goddess, in her sanctuary. The youthful male figure represented the ideal type of young man in East Greek-Ionian society: large, almond-shaped eyes, pronounced cheeks, thin, determined lips, thick hair flowing to the shoulders, and a tensed yet fleshy body.

In the major sanctuaries, the ex-votos expressing respect for the deity, whether architectural monuments or sculpture, were intended primarily as proclamations of the economic status and social class of the dedicator, be it a city, *demos* (the common people of a Greek state), or private citizen.

In this case the dedicator was without doubt wealthy and from a leading family in Samian society. His ability to establish a statue of this size and quality in a conspicuous position in the sanctuary—both close to the Sacred Way and only a short distance from the monumental temple of the goddess—proves this status.

All that remains of this likely powerful man are his name and the artistic masterpiece he dedicated, which continues to delight all who see it: *Hic jacet gloria mundi* (Here lies the glory of the world).

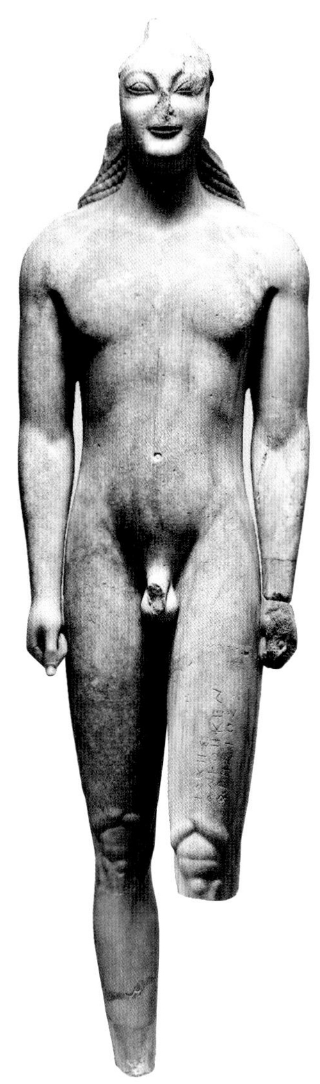

GORGON

PAROS, PAROIKIA, OPEN-AIR SANCTUARY
C. 580 BCE
PARIAN MARBLE. PRESENT HEIGHT 4.43 FEET (1.35 M; ORIGINAL APPROX. 5.25 FEET [1.60 M])
PAROS, ARCHAEOLOGICAL MUSEUM

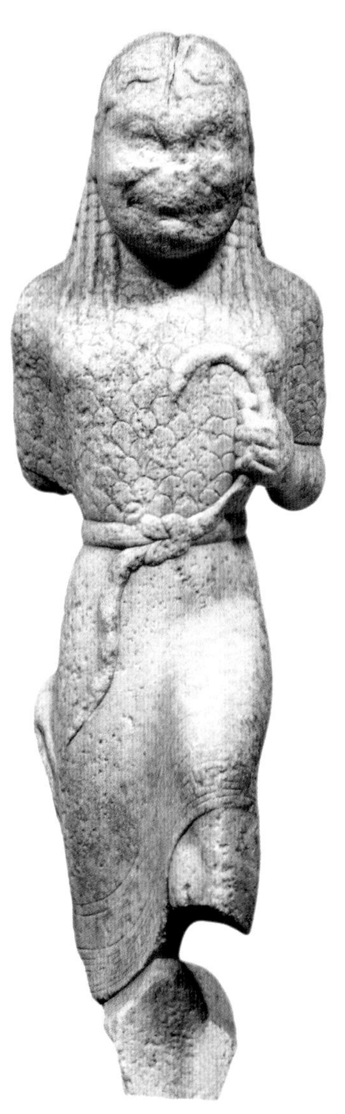

This Parian representation of the mythical monster Gorgon, who turned to stone all those who beheld her terrifying figure, most likely crowned a tall monument set in a sacred place. She is portrayed at the instant she descends from the heavens to alight on a roof tile.

This is a unique representation of Gorgon in the round. All other surviving sculptures of her are in relief and show her with enormous teeth protruding from her mouth like those of a wild beast, snakes instead of locks of hair, and other hideous features. The Parian sculptor has removed all of these elements except the fangs, which are also smaller, in an effort to arouse fear in the viewer through the size of the face and its expression. Rendered as a young female, the figure's upper body, covered in scales to denote her savage nature, contrasts with its lower body, to whose gentle curves the garment clings, owing to her rushing movement. Enormous wings appear mid-beat at the back and sweep upward. Noteworthy is the figure's depth: The whole body is turned in the direction in which it runs. The artist has captured the sense of motion, and the figure seems to pulsate with its violent descent and landing.

This groundbreaking statue from a Parian workshop of the Archaic period is among the most important achievements of ancient Greek sculpture.

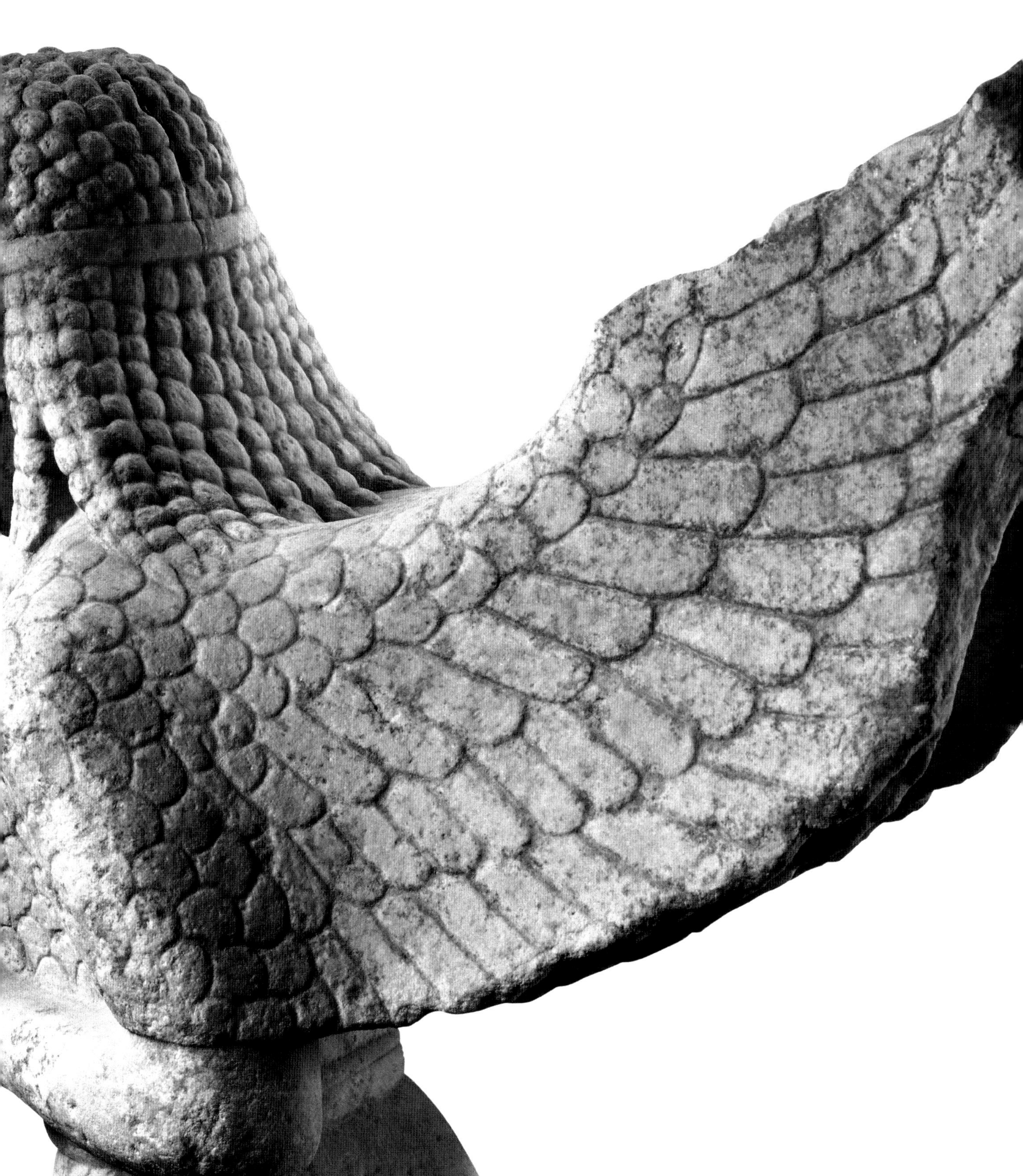

PART OF A GRAVE STELE OF A DISCUS-BEARER

ATHENS, KERAMEIKOS, CLOSE TO THE DIPYLON
C. 550 BCE
PENTELIC MARBLE. PRESENT HEIGHT 1.15 FEET (0.35 M); PRESENT WIDTH 1.44 FEET (0.44 M)
ATHENS, NATIONAL ARCHAEOLOGICAL MUSEUM

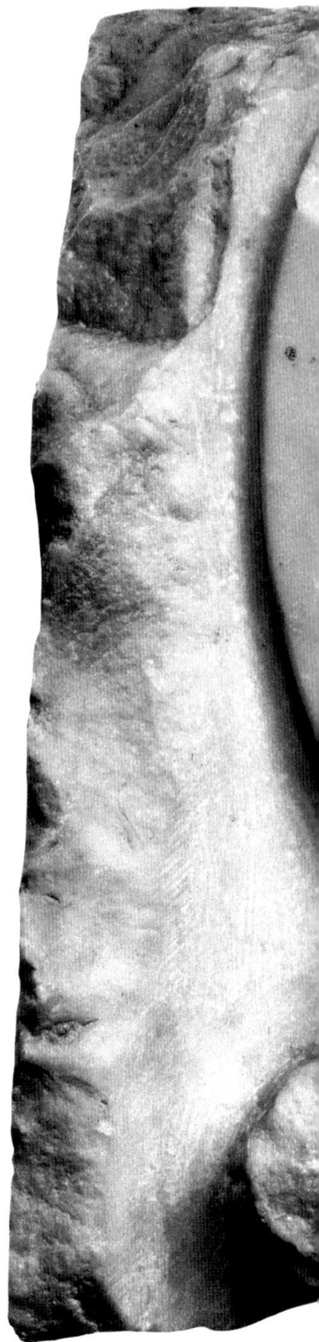

This fragment is from the upper part of the stele, which features a youth in profile, facing right. He holds in his left hand a discus, against which his head is projected. His hair is pulled back in a large twisted braid, which falls heavily on the nape of his neck and is tied tightly at the end. The remarkable plasticity of the volumes on the cheekbones, nose, and lips, parted in a barely perceptible "Archaic" smile, places this work among the masterpieces of Archaic Attic sculpture.

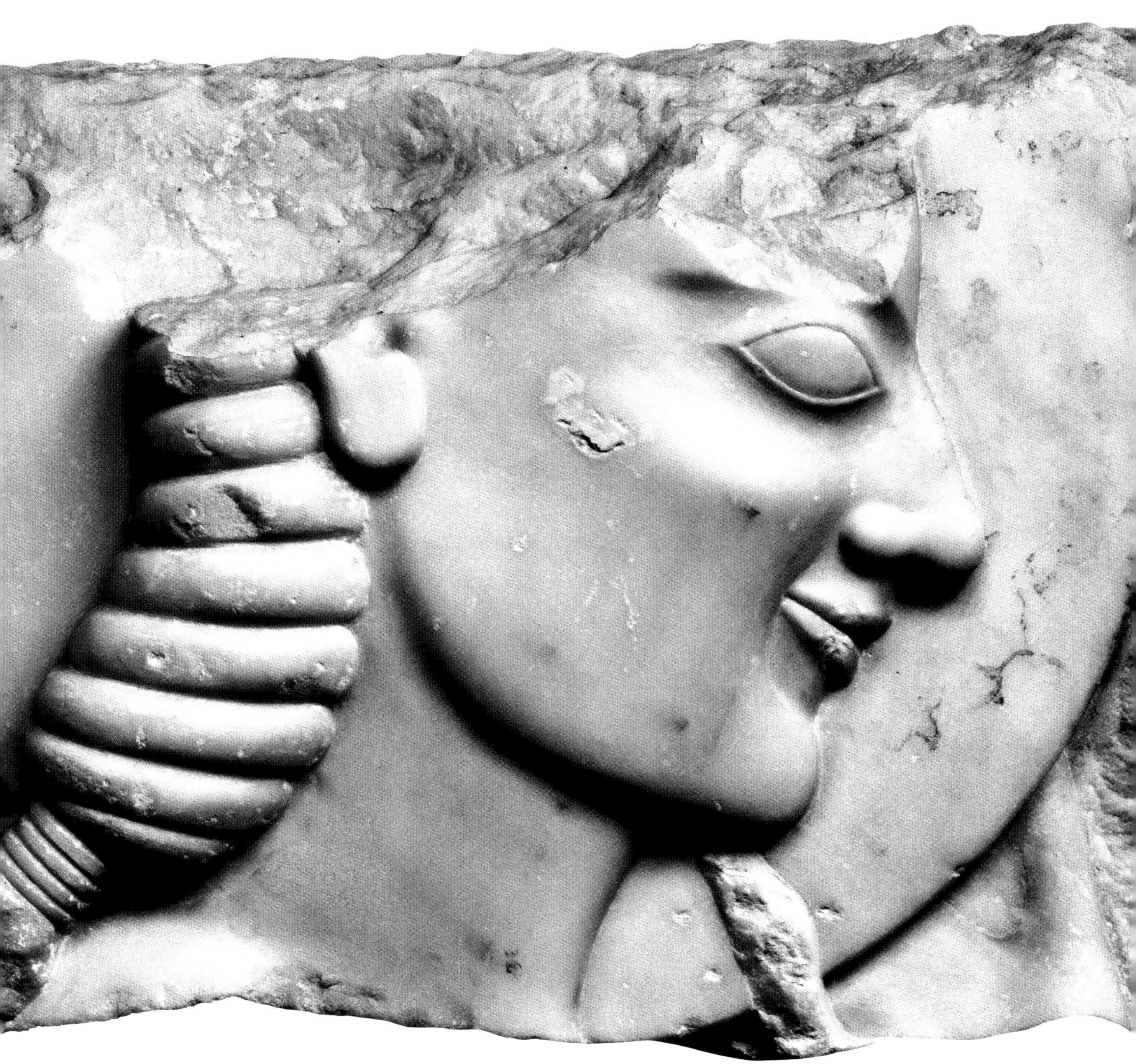

GRAVE STELE

ATHENS, CLOSE TO THE THEMISTOCLEAN WALL
550–540 BCE
PARIAN MARBLE. PRESENT HEIGHT 3.81 FEET (1.16 M); WIDTH 1.71 FEET (0.52 M)
ATHENS, NATIONAL ARCHAEOLOGICAL MUSEUM

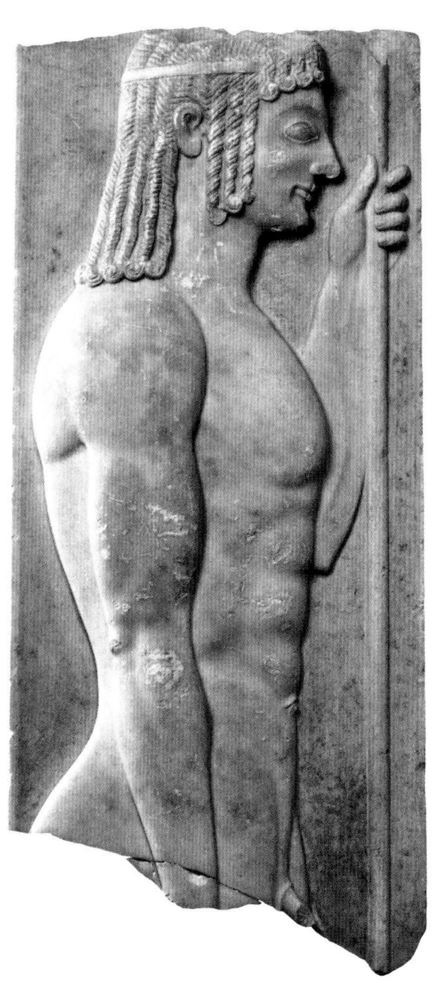

Both the upper and the lower part of this stele are missing. Represented on the truncated surviving section is a young nude athlete in profile, facing right. His left arm is bent upward and holds a javelin to the fore. His long hair, originally painted red, falls on his shoulders, to the sides of his temples, and on his forehead in ringlets that end in spiral curls. The upper part of his head is dressed in braids and tied with a narrow fillet that passes under the curls on his brow.

The robust modeling of his musculature and the dynamic outlines emphasize the figure's individuality and endow him with an austere introspective character, which expresses the disciplined physical control required of an athlete if he is to achieve his goal.

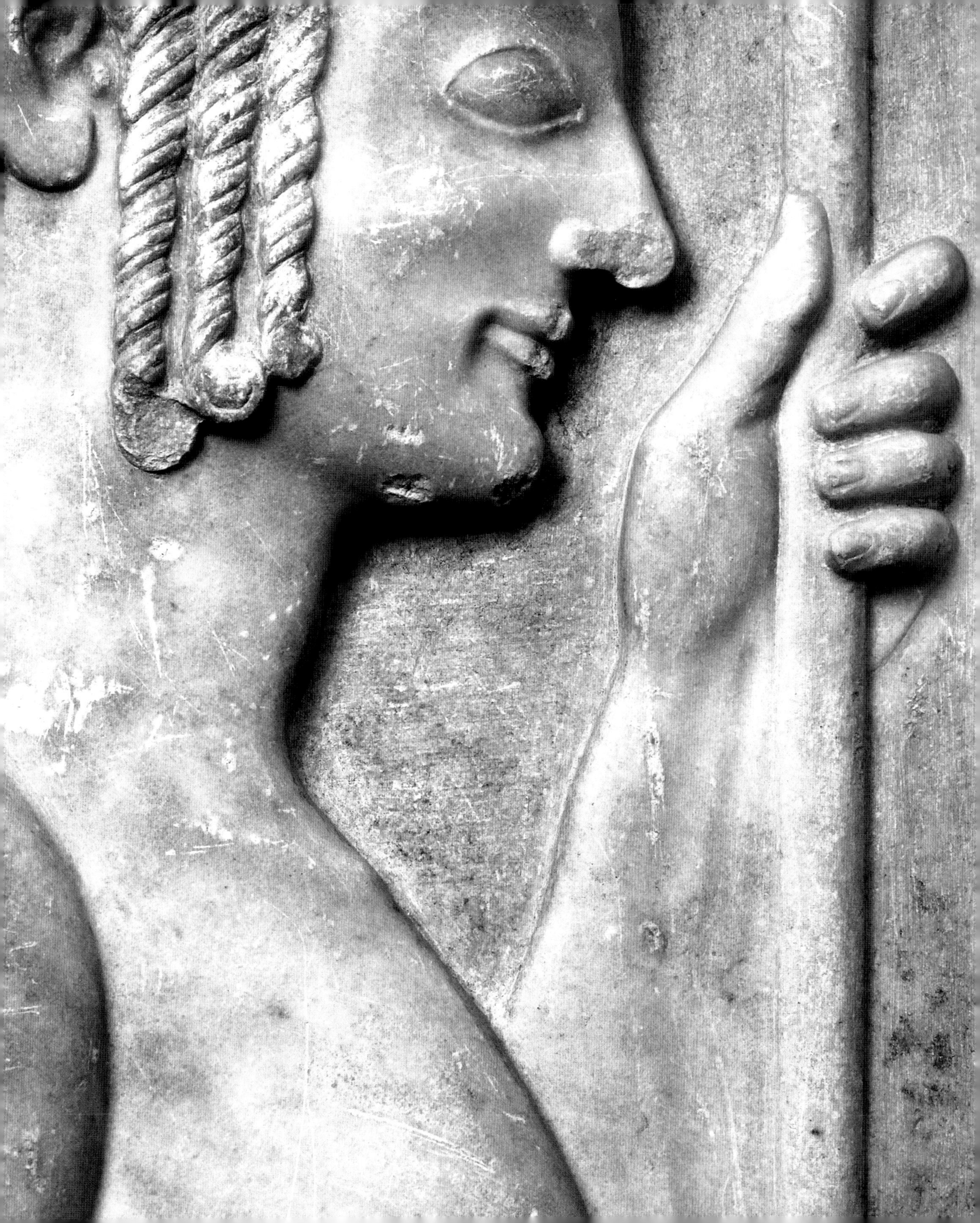

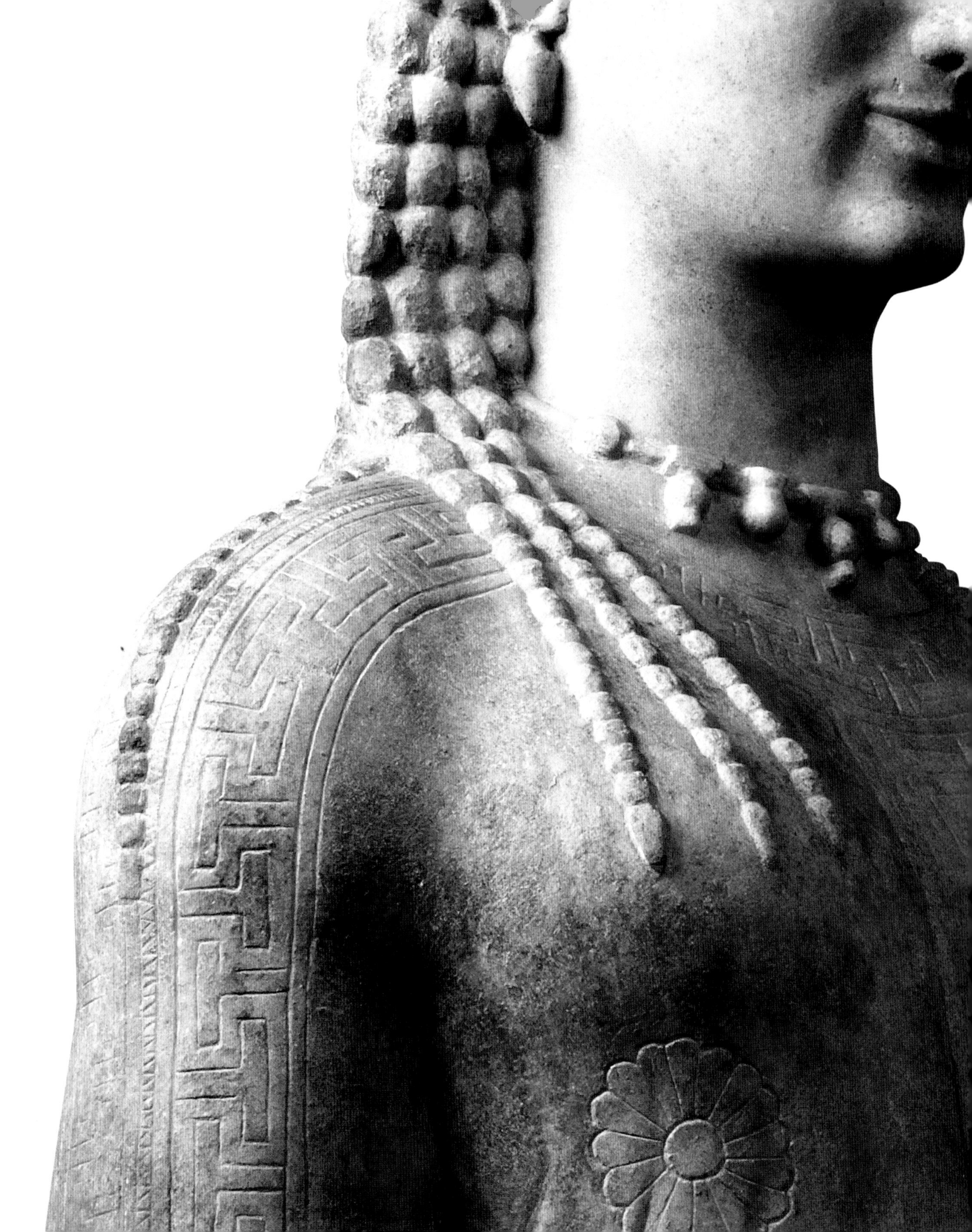

PHRASIKLEIA

ATTICA, MERENDA (ANCIENT MYRRHINUS)
550–540 BCE
PARIAN MARBLE. HEIGHT 5.87 FEET (1.79 M); INCLUDING BASE 6.96 FEET (2.12 M)
ATHENS, NATIONAL ARCHAEOLOGICAL MUSEUM

This funerary statue, by Aristion of Paros, depicts a kore standing in a frontal position and dressed in a long, sleeved *chiton* (a garment of fine cloth) girdled at the waist. She draws up the garment on her thigh with her right hand, and she presses the calyx of a lotus flower against her chest in a gesture of offering. Her long hair, falling in waves on her forehead, is rendered in beaded locks. Her head bears a high wreath of lotus flowers and calyxes, her ears pendant earrings, her throat a necklace, her wrists bracelets, and her feet sandals with a modeled button where the thongs are held in place. The red chiton is decorated with carved rosettes, meander crosses, and stars. Down the middle of the front, beginning below the neck, runs a broad band of meander pattern that continues on the neckline and sleeves. Around the hem of the chiton is a broad band of colored foliate motifs. An epigram inscribed on the pedestal of the statue indicates that this is the tomb of Phrasikleia, who died unwed.

Such statues of young girls, known as korai, were among the most characteristic ex-votos in sanctuaries during the Archaic period. Dressed in lavish garments and bedecked with jewelry, these figures were the most

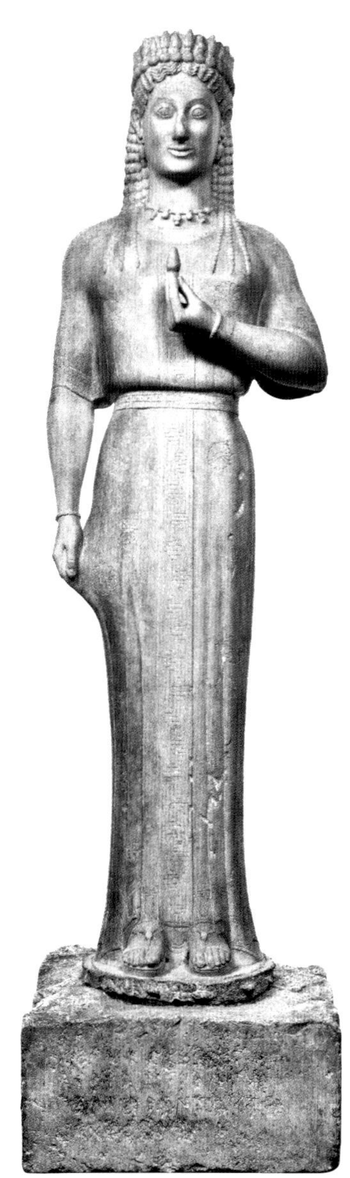

popular dedications to the deity and were usually made by women devotees. More than two hundred korai once stood on the Athenian Acropolis, where, after the Persian destruction in 480 BCE, they were buried as sacred heirlooms in hollows in the rock. There they remained for posterity, to be unearthed in the excavations conducted in the late nineteenth century. The statue type of kore had already been elaborated in Greece by the mid-seventh century BCE, and the earliest kore recovered from the Acropolis dates to c. 570 BCE.

There are many hypotheses about what the korai represented: mortals or statues of the goddess, priestesses of Athena or Athena herself? Some suggest that they were *arrephoroi* or *arretophoroi*, girls between the ages of seven and eleven from leading Athenian families who took part in the Arrephoria ritual, celebrated in honor of Athena sometime between mid-June and mid-July. This celebration was essentially a rite of passage from puberty to womanhood in which participants carried *arreta* (unspoken, secret) sacred objects. Perhaps the daughters of noble families dedicated their statues to Athena to enhance the splendor of her sanctuary.

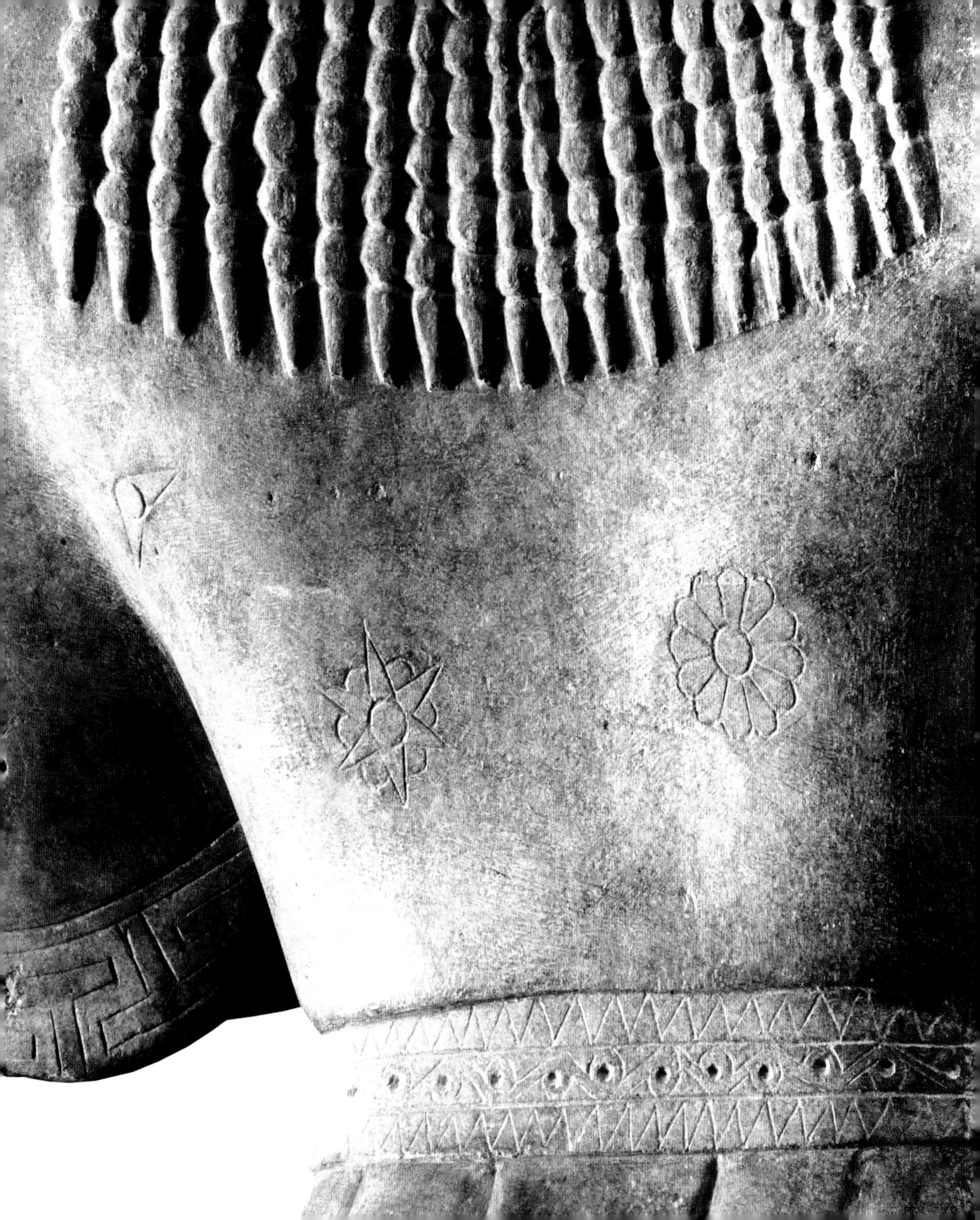

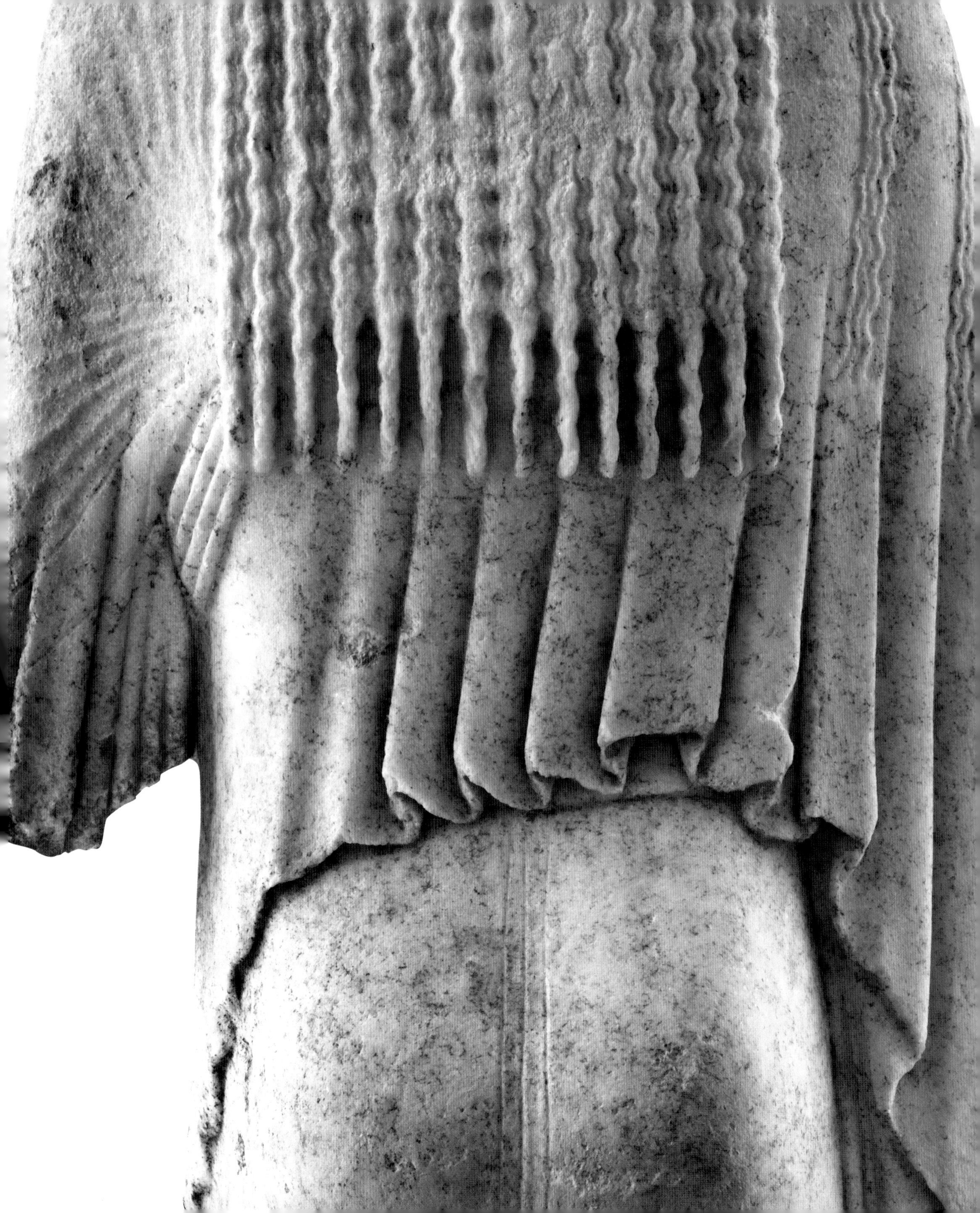

KORE

PAROS
C. 530 BCE
PARIAN MARBLE. PRESENT HEIGHT 2.36 FEET (0.73 M)
ATHENS, NATIONAL ARCHAEOLOGICAL MUSEUM
(REPATRIATED FROM THE J. PAUL GETTY MUSEUM, LOS ANGELES)

Preserved is the torso of a kore, from the neck to the knees. The figure is dressed in a chiton, which she drew out on her thigh with her left hand, and a heavy diagonal *himation* (mantle or wrap), held in place on the right shoulder and leaving the left breast exposed. Her long luxuriant hair falls in beaded locks down her back almost to the waist, and tumbles in waves over her shoulders and bosom. A row of vertical relief eight-petaled rosettes decorates the edge of the himation, which drapes over her right upper arm and below the inset right forearm (now missing), which was bent at the elbow and outstretched to the front.

The superb treatment of the marble's surface—the young, supple body with its soft outlines provocatively visible through the gossamer chiton—together with the studied folds in the drapery of the two garments of different textures produce a harmonious ensemble that places this work among the highest achievements of the Parian artistic circle in Archaic times.

Hanging from the relief rosettes on the forearm are the same number of small tassels, each with three undulating threads. These rosettes are an unprecedented decoration on this part of the himation of an Archaic kore.

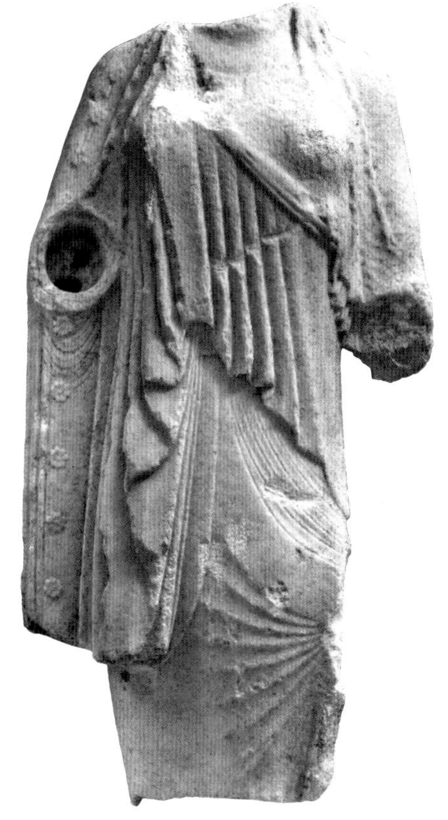

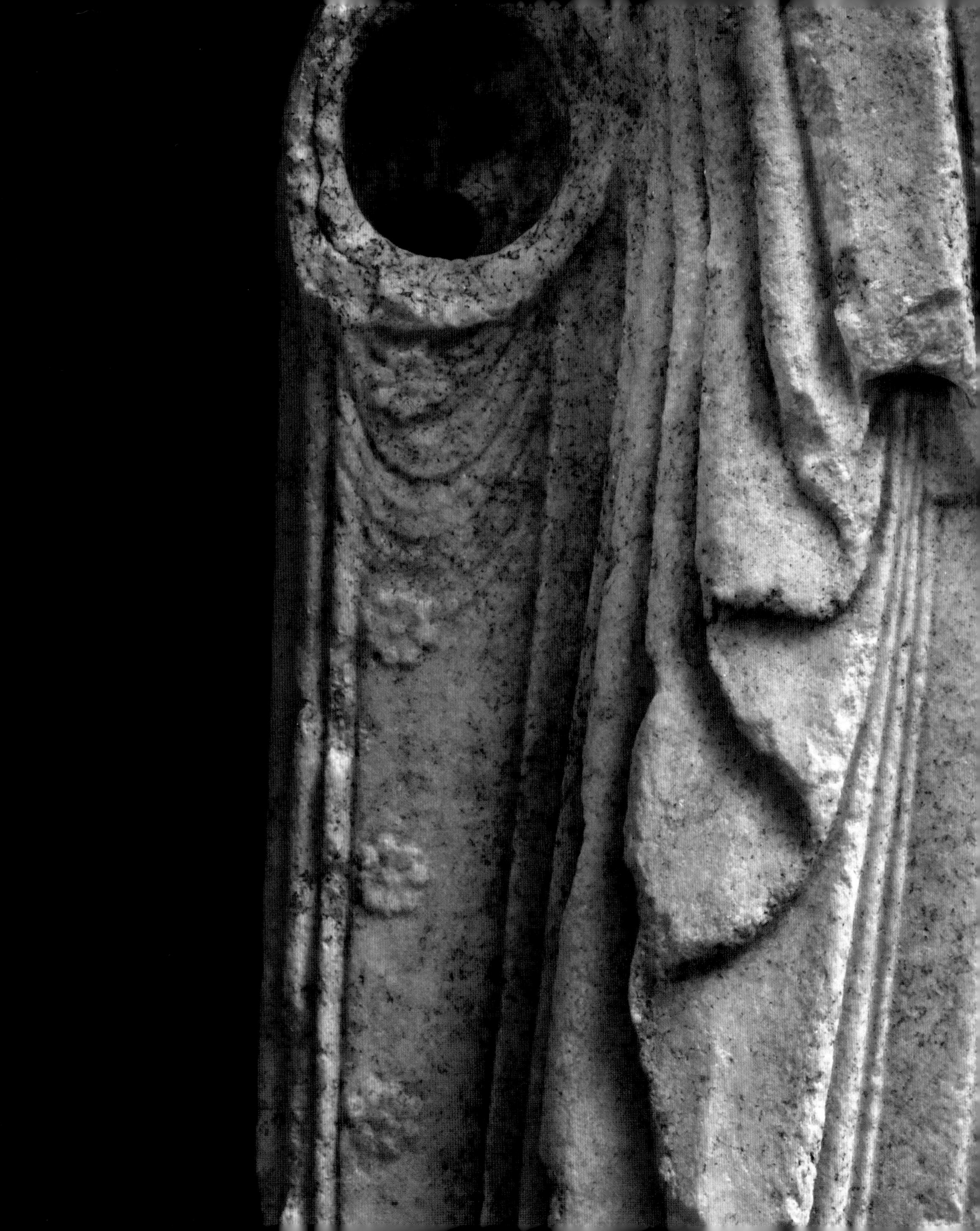

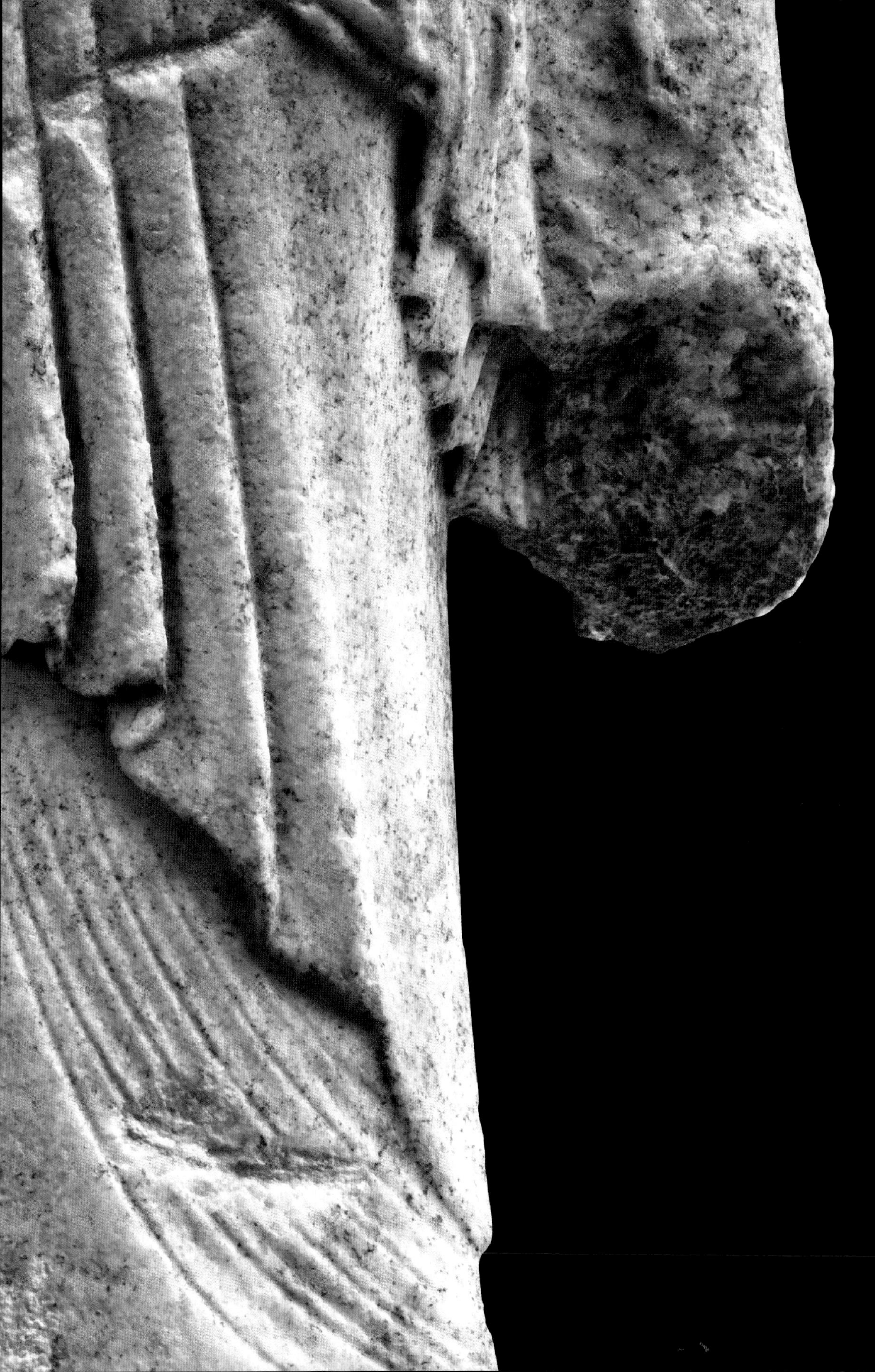

THE SIPHNIAN TREASURY AT DELPHI

530–525 BCE

From the time of Herodotus, the Siphnian Treasury at Delphi was considered the most imposing of all such edifices, mainly because of its magnificent sculpted decoration. The treasury, an ex-voto of the citizens of Siphnos (considered the wealthiest of the islanders because of their silver–and reputedly gold–mines) was paid for by the Siphnians through the practice of tithing.

This small building in the Ionic order stood on the left of the Sacred Way, shortly before the first turn in the upward course toward the Temple of Apollo and just in front of the Treasury of the Athenians. It was constructed of Parian marble, c. 525 BCE, upon a crepis of 27.46 x 19.49 feet (8.37 x 5.94 m). On its front, the narrow west face, two korai upheld the entablature, in place of the usual two columns *in antis* (between pillars) that adorned the entrance. Most notable, however, was the frieze, whose wonderful relief representations ran round the building, above the epistyle, reaching 28.31 feet (8.63 m) on the long sides, 20.51 feet (6.25 m) on the narrow sides, and 2.13 feet (0.65 m) high. The frieze was bordered by an ***Ionic cymatium*** (egg-and-tongue molding) below and by a ***Lesbian cymatium*** (leaf-and-dart molding) above.

The sculptures of the frieze were evidently executed by two different artists, the more gifted of whom worked on the east and north sides. Research suggests that the sculptures on the west and south sides are associated with the Smyrna region in Greek northern Ionia, whereas those on the east and north sides are linked with Parian art. The lively, narrative style of the latter is expressed in the clear, rounded outlines and impressive chiaroscuro effects of the relief. The ground of the frieze was painted blue; the garments of the figures, their weapons, and their hair preserve traces of red and green pigments; and all representations include appliquéd metallic elements. Inscriptions of their names are painted close to many figures.

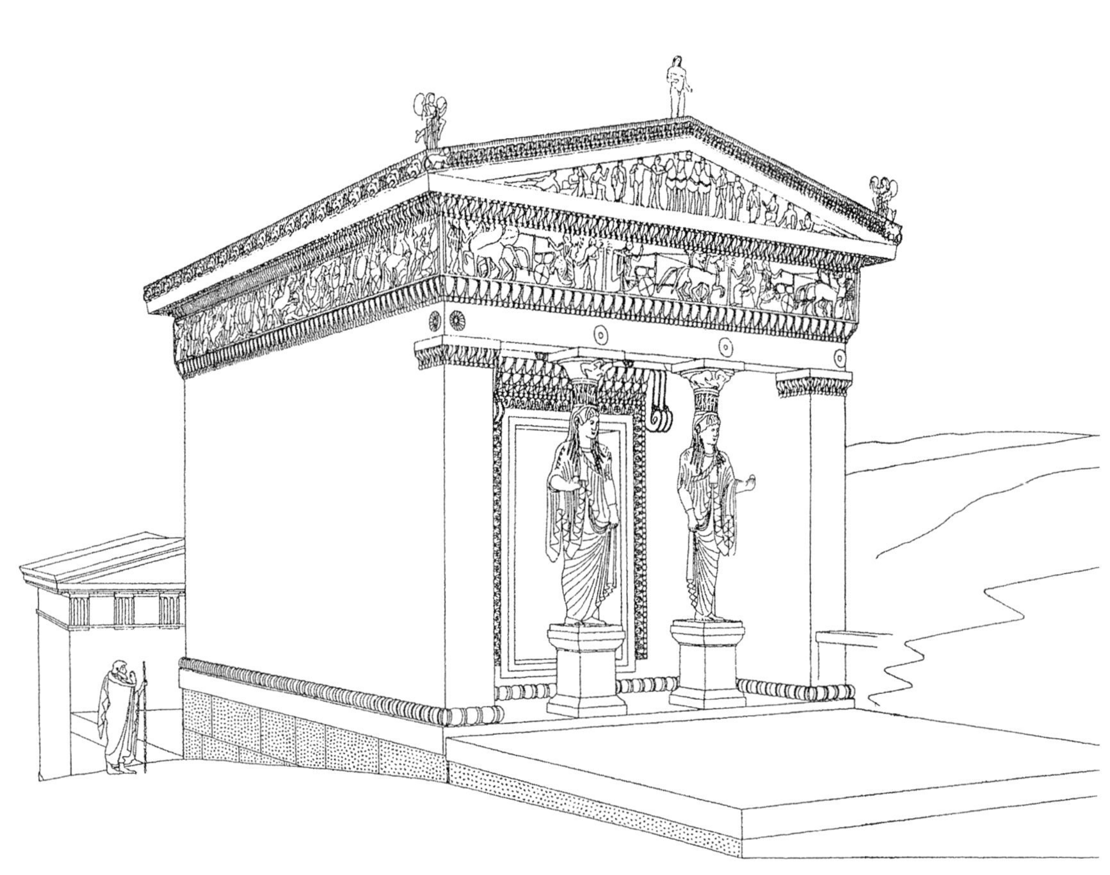

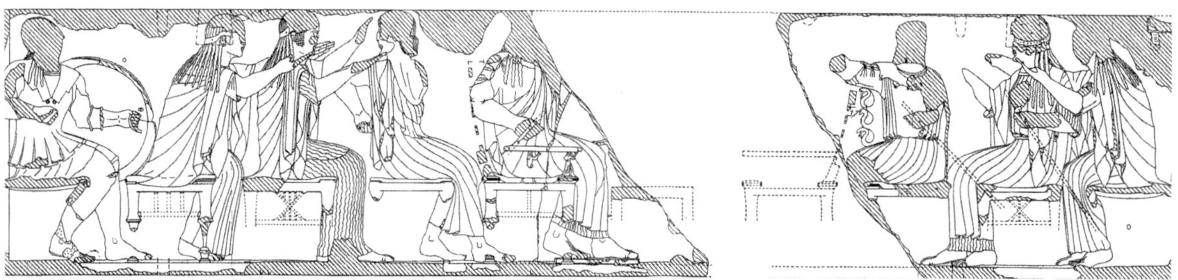

ASSEMBLY OF THE GODS

DELPHI, SIPHNIAN TREASURY, EAST FRIEZE
530–525 BCE
MARBLE. HEIGHT 2.09 FEET (0.64 M)
DELPHI, ARCHAEOLOGICAL MUSEUM

The sculptor who worked on the narrow east side of the Siphnian Treasury was inspired by the Homeric epic *The Iliad*: In this depiction, a gathering of gods watches the progress of a battle fought, before their eyes, in the Trojan War. Ares sits alone at the edge, cut off from the other deities, three of whom are represented conversing and gesticulating in a most human manner: Aphrodite and Artemis, lively and talkative, stretch out their hands to Apollo, who sits behind Zeus.

The scene is appealing and possesses warmth and immediacy owing in part to the figures' spontaneous gestures and poses: Aphrodite bows slightly toward Artemis, touching her on the shoulders, and Artemis in turn animatedly addresses Apollo, who is seated in front of her and has turned his upper body to hear her and participate in the discussion.

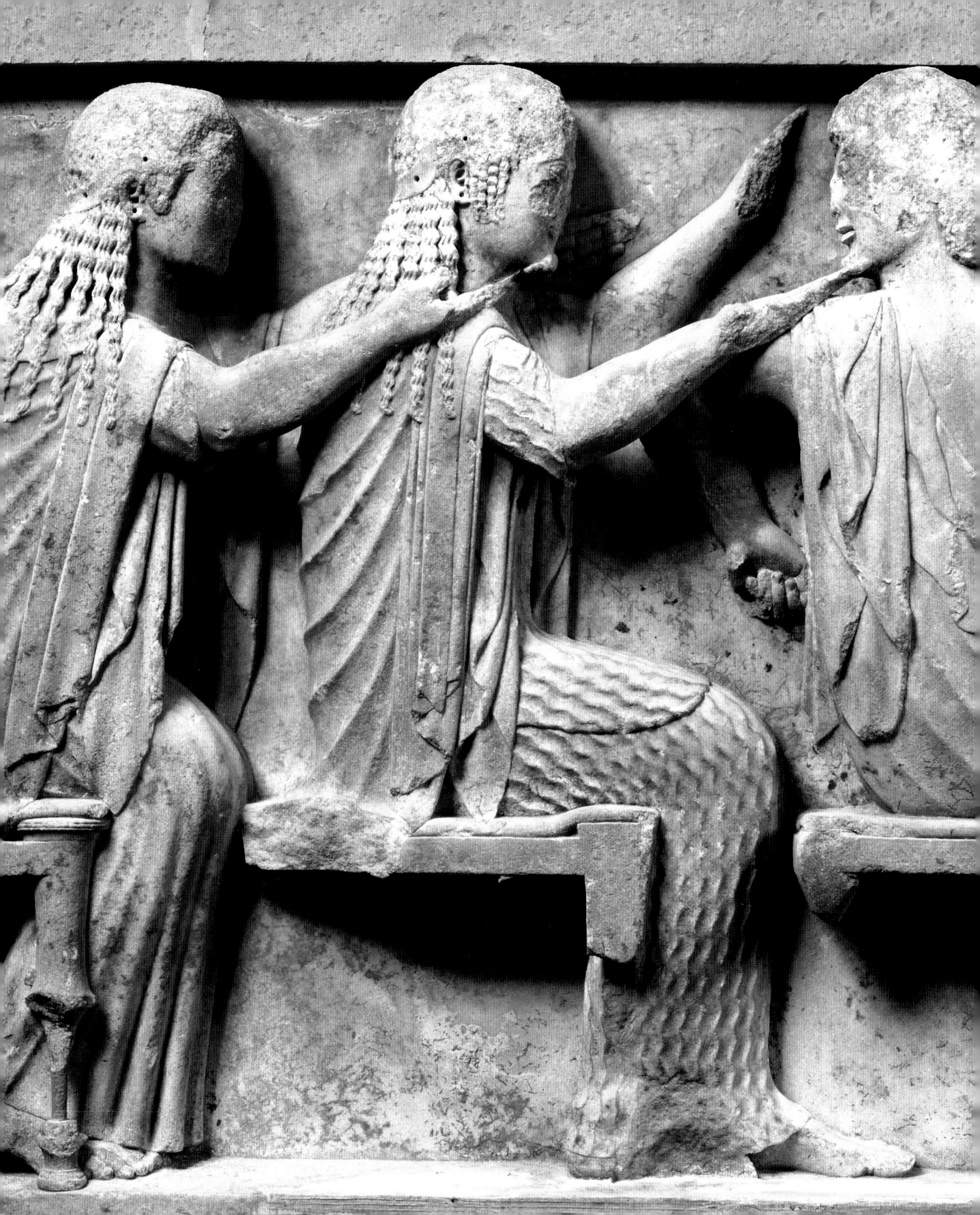

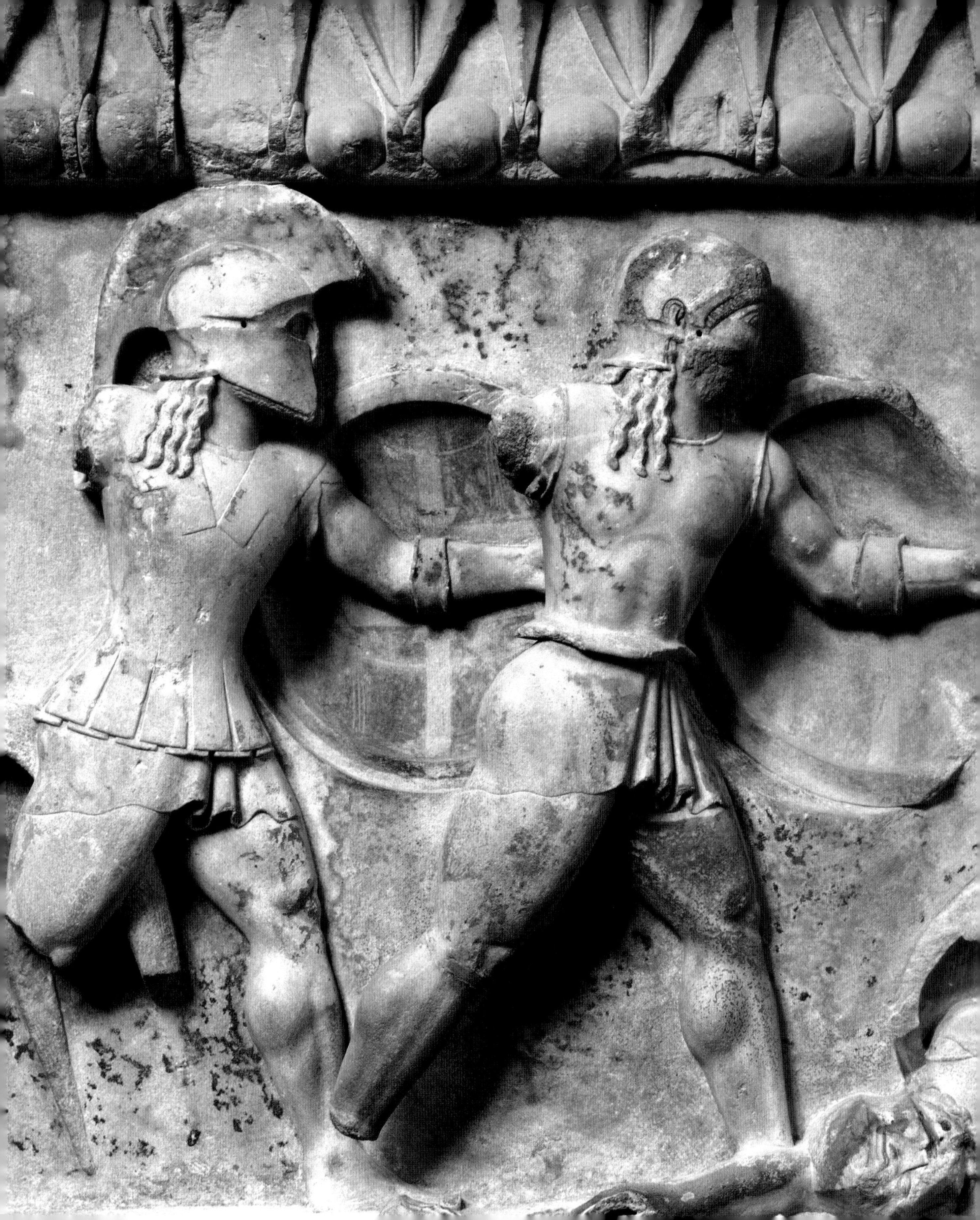

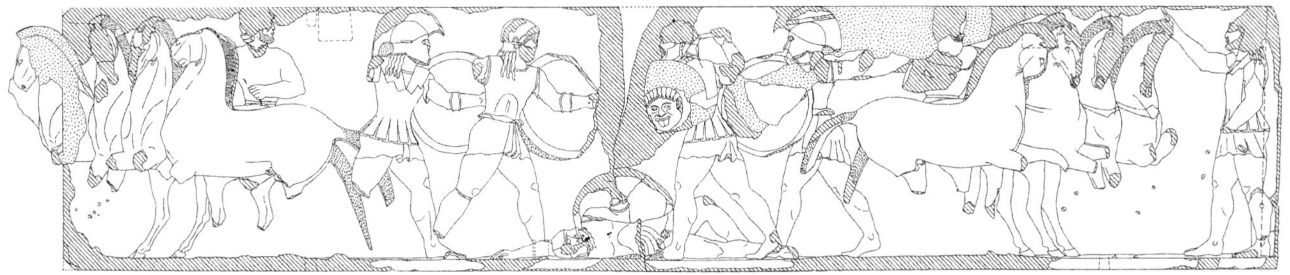

BATTLE BETWEEN GREEKS AND TROJANS

DELPHI, SIPHNIAN TREASURY, EAST FRIEZE
530–525 BCE
MARBLE. HEIGHT 2.09 FEET (0.64 M)
DELPHI, ARCHAEOLOGICAL MUSEUM

This half of the east frieze is occupied by martial scenes inspired by the epic cycle of the *Aethiopis*. Two fully armed warriors have dismounted from their ***quadriga*** (a four-horse chariot), behind which stands the watchful charioteer. The charioteer turns his head toward his masters, who advance with wide strides to confront their adversaries over a dead body. The corpse is that of Antilochos, son of Nestor, and the battle for its possession was to be fought between Achilles and Memnon, king of Aethiopia, in the presence of their respective mothers, Thetis and Eos. On the one hand, there is the horror and savagery of war, and on the other, carefree moments from daily life, even if these belong to the world of the gods, which mirrors that of the humans.

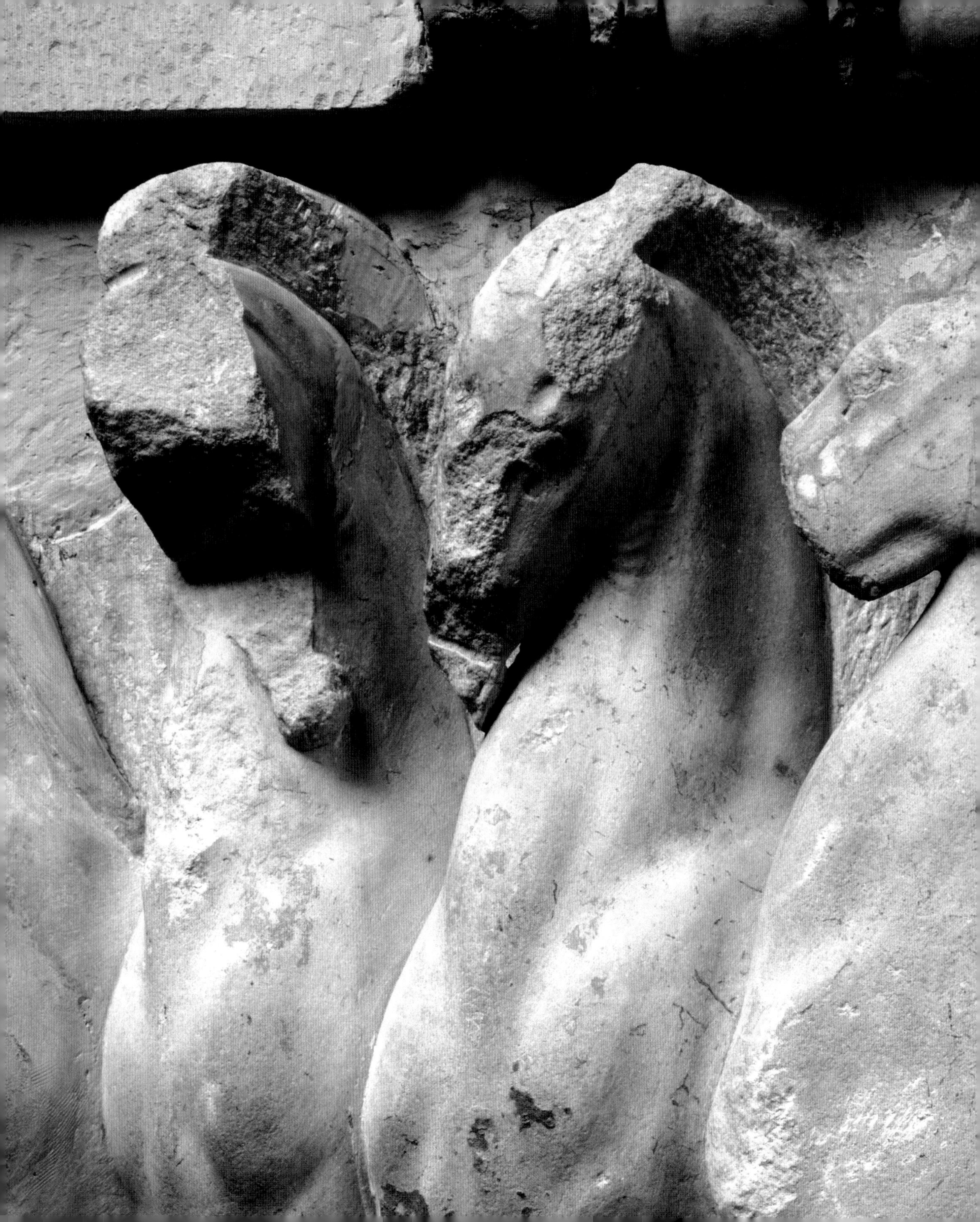

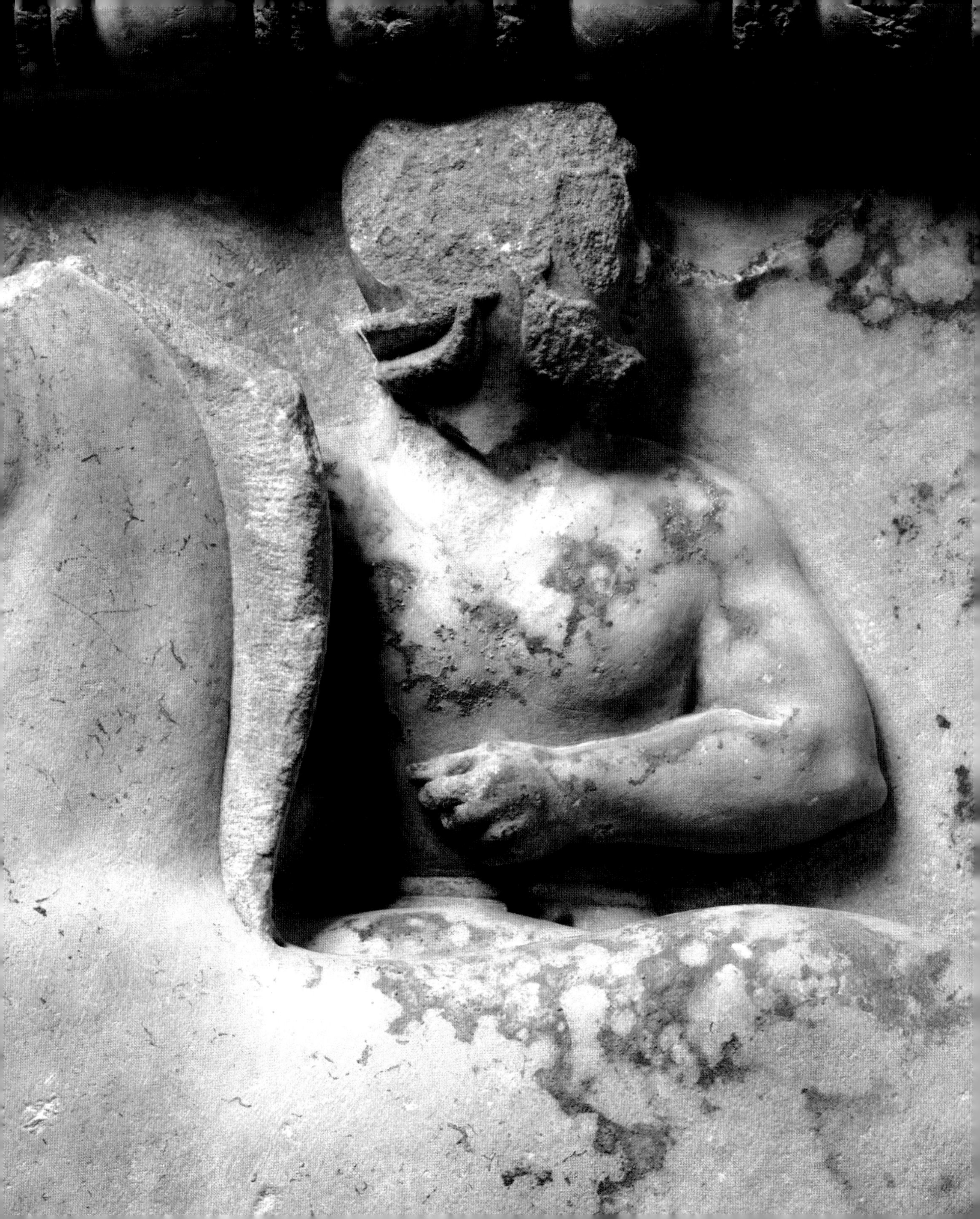

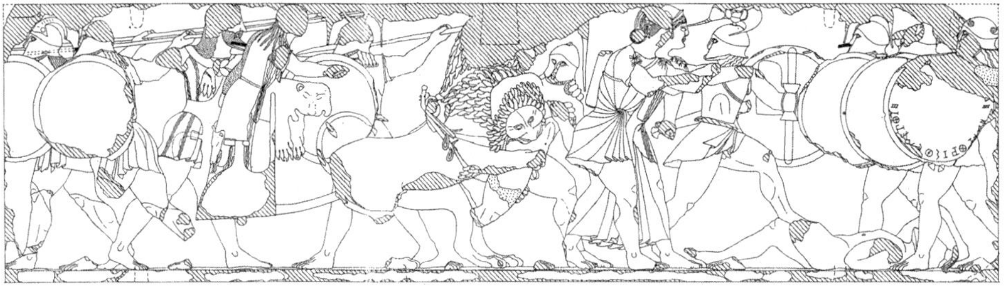

GIGANTOMACHY

DELPHI, SIPHNIAN TREASURY, NORTH FRIEZE
530–525 BCE
MARBLE. HEIGHT 2.09 FEET (0.64 M)
DELPHI, ARCHAEOLOGICAL MUSEUM

The north frieze takes its subject from mythology: the famous Gigantomachy, in which the Olympian gods fought and exterminated the pre-Olympian daemons, the giants, to secure their cosmic supremacy. The scenes here are more turbulent than those on the east frieze. The parties clash in violent combat, a melee of humans and beasts. The giants are depicted as hoplites with helmets, round shields, spears, and, in many cases, breastplates and greaves. Some of their names, incised on the rims of their shields, have a barbaric ring: Berektas, Astartas, and so on. The giants attack from the right, while the gods rush into battle from the left. According to the painted inscriptions, Dionysus, with a lion skin tied around his neck, advances behind the chariot driven by Themis and drawn by lions, one of

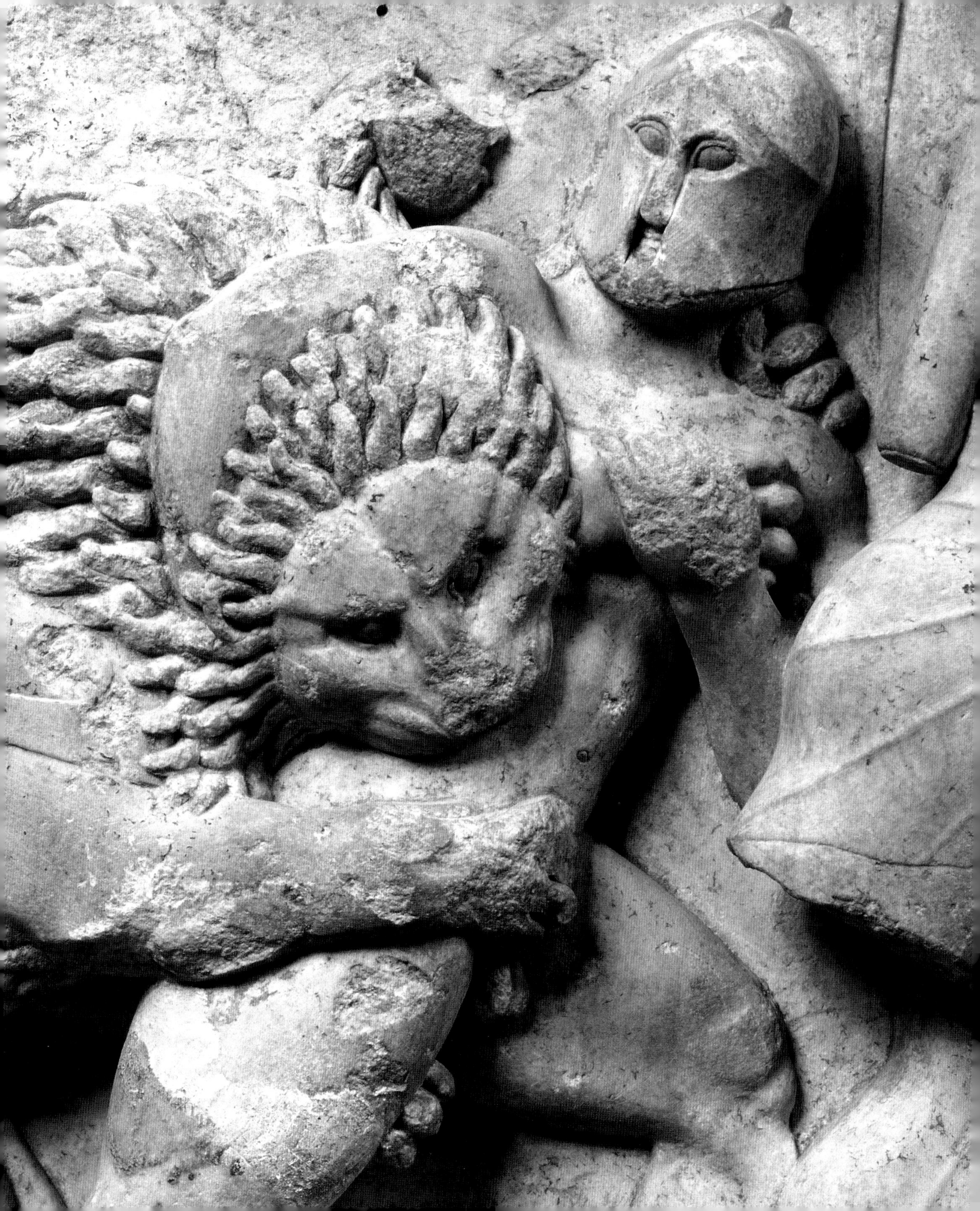

which lacerates a giant. Another giant is poised to strike Dionysus with his spear. In front of Themis' chariot, the twins Artemis and Apollo proceed in step side by side, shooting arrows at a giant who flees right but looks backward toward the two gods, who have already caught up with him and will prevent him from escaping.

As a whole, the scene, with its exceptional plasticity, individual graphic details, and complex narrative, could not have failed to capture the pilgrim's attention as he wended his way up to the Temple of Apollo. For here he beheld the struggles of the Olympian gods to eliminate evil and to impose the order that should govern the human world.

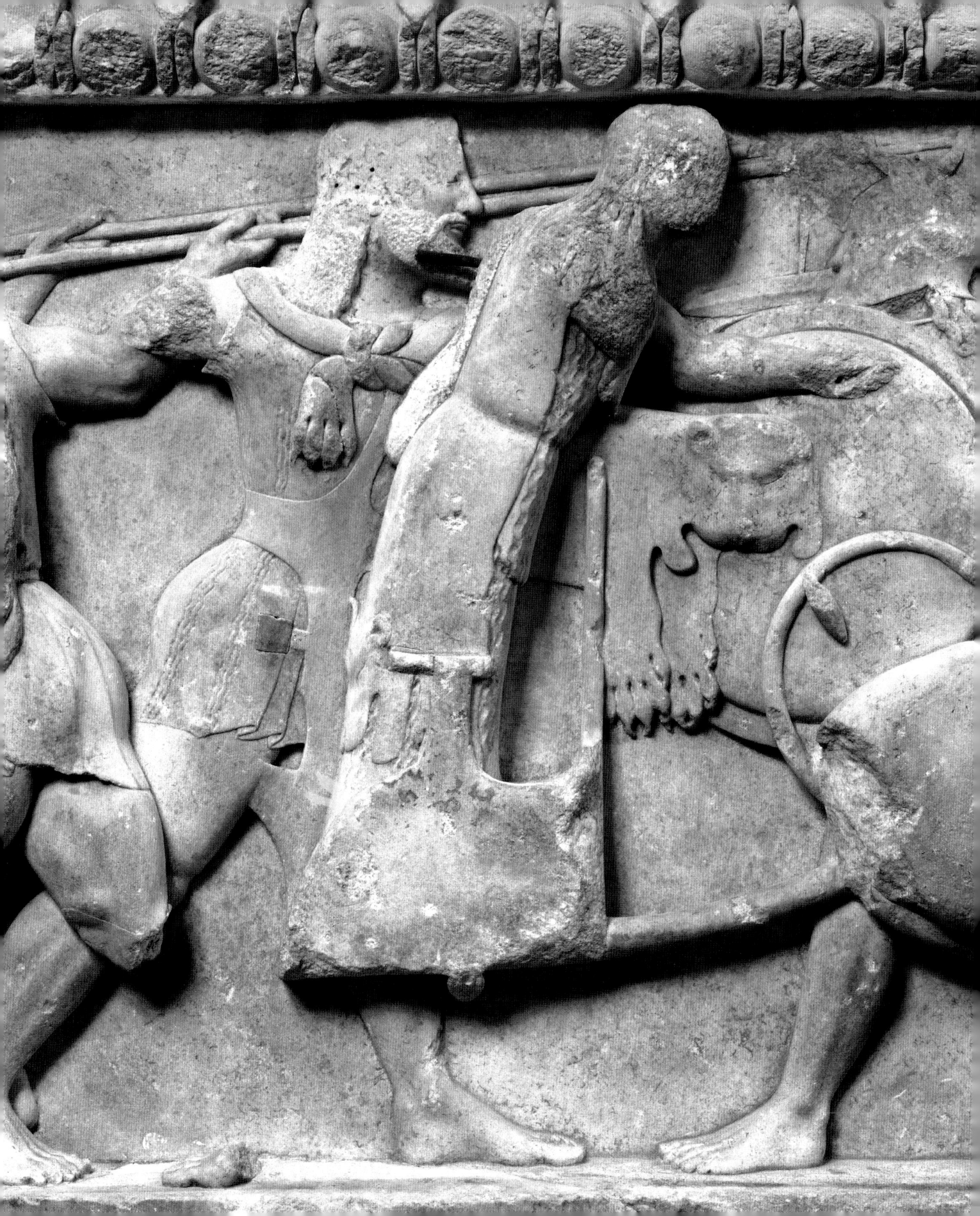

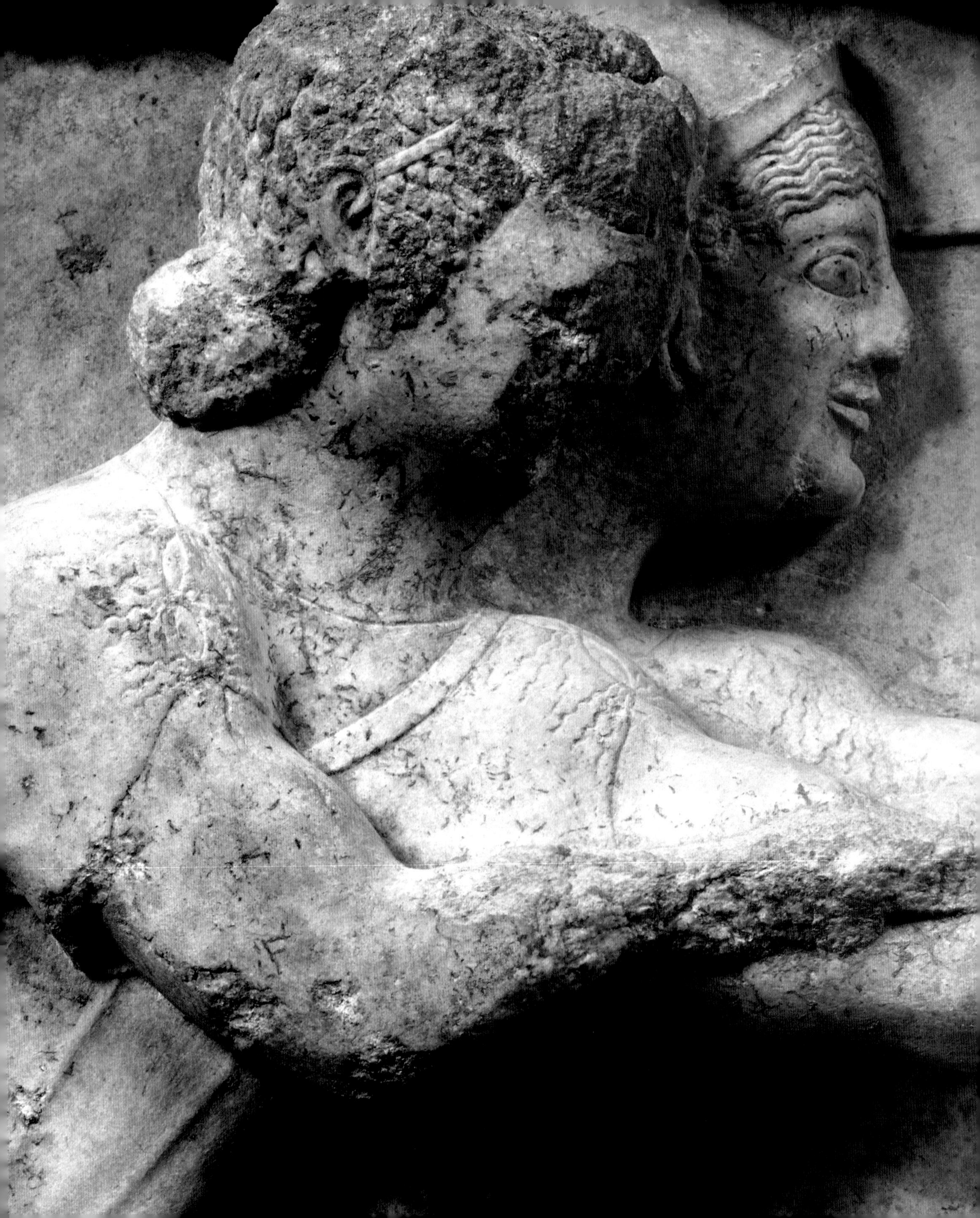

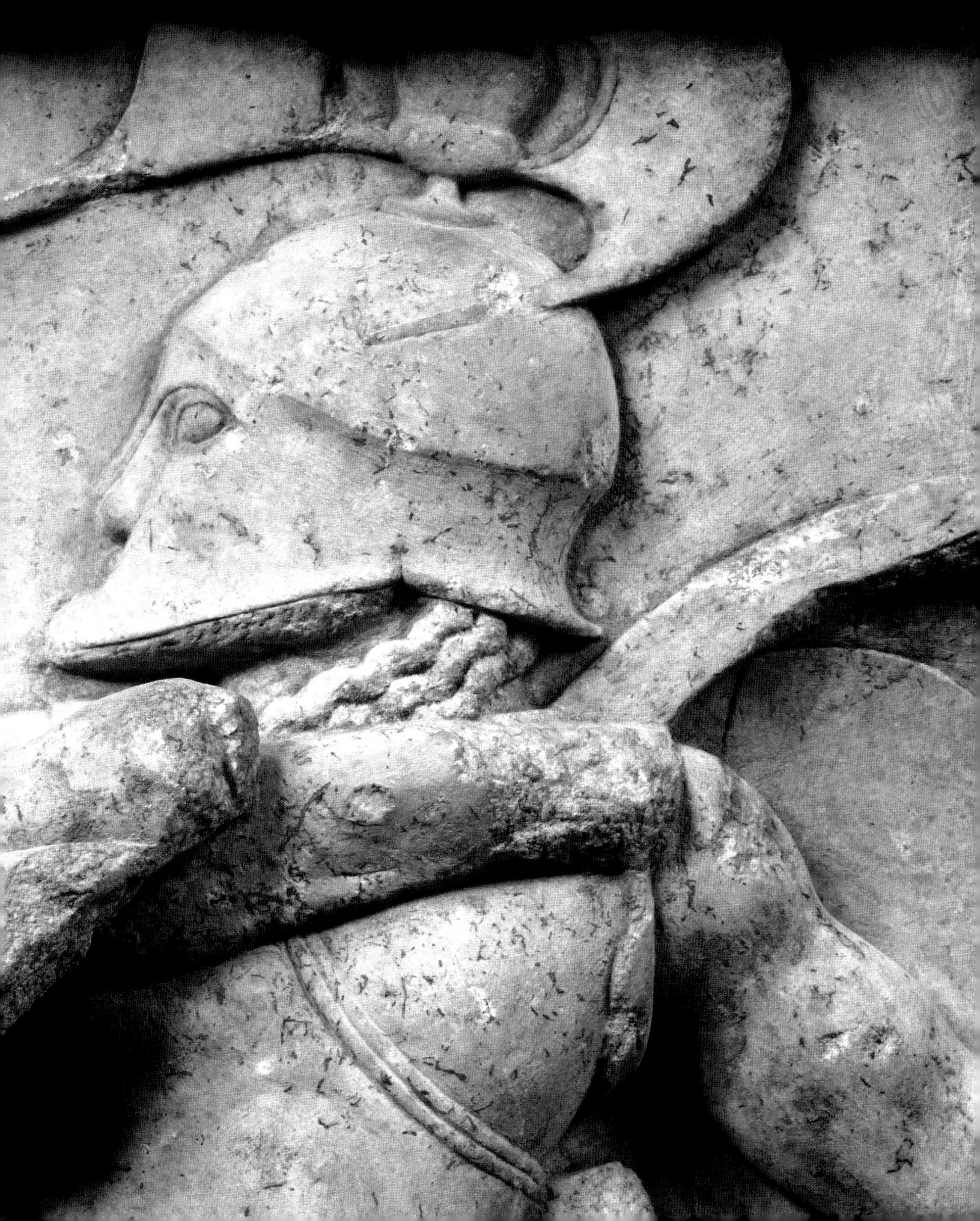

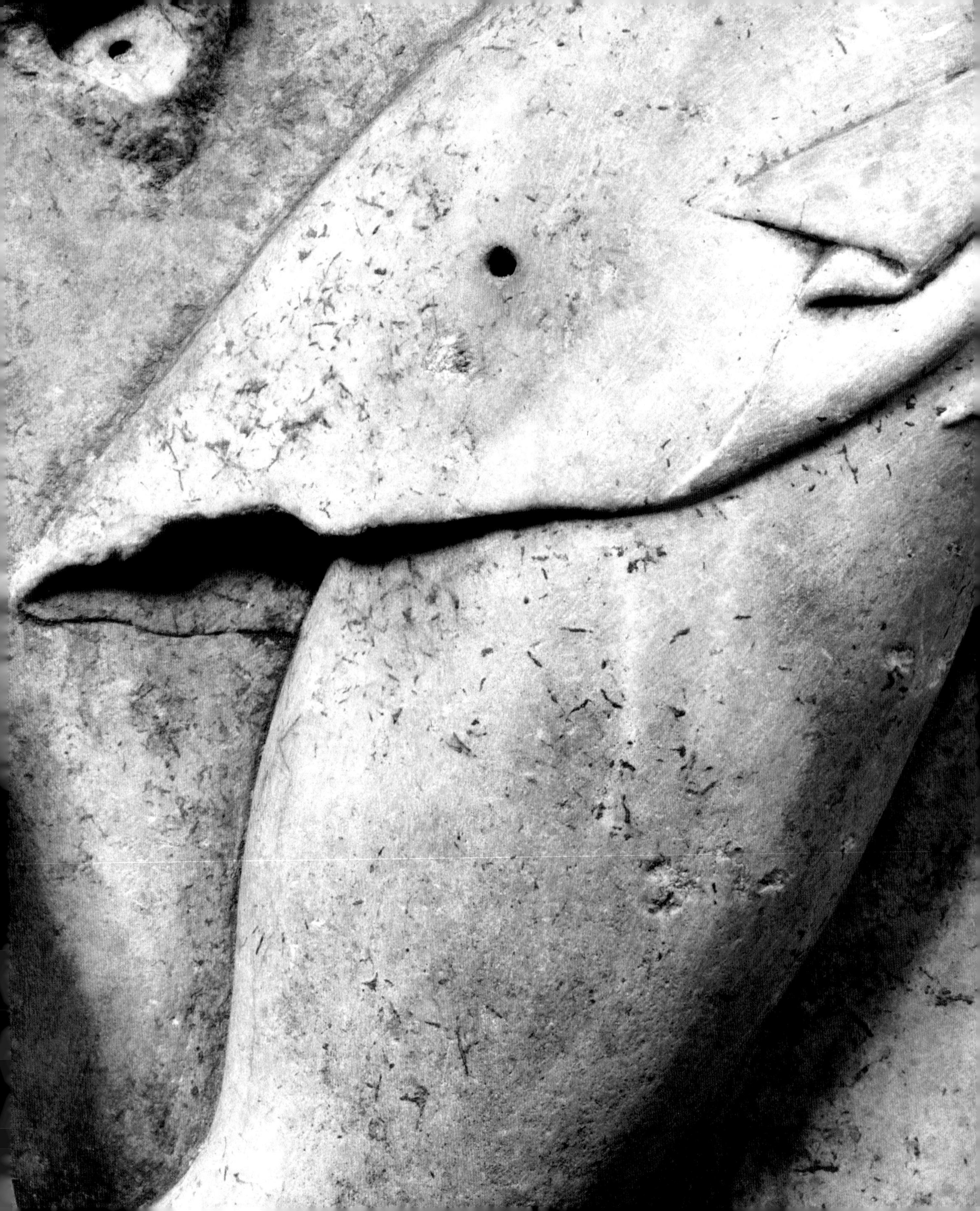

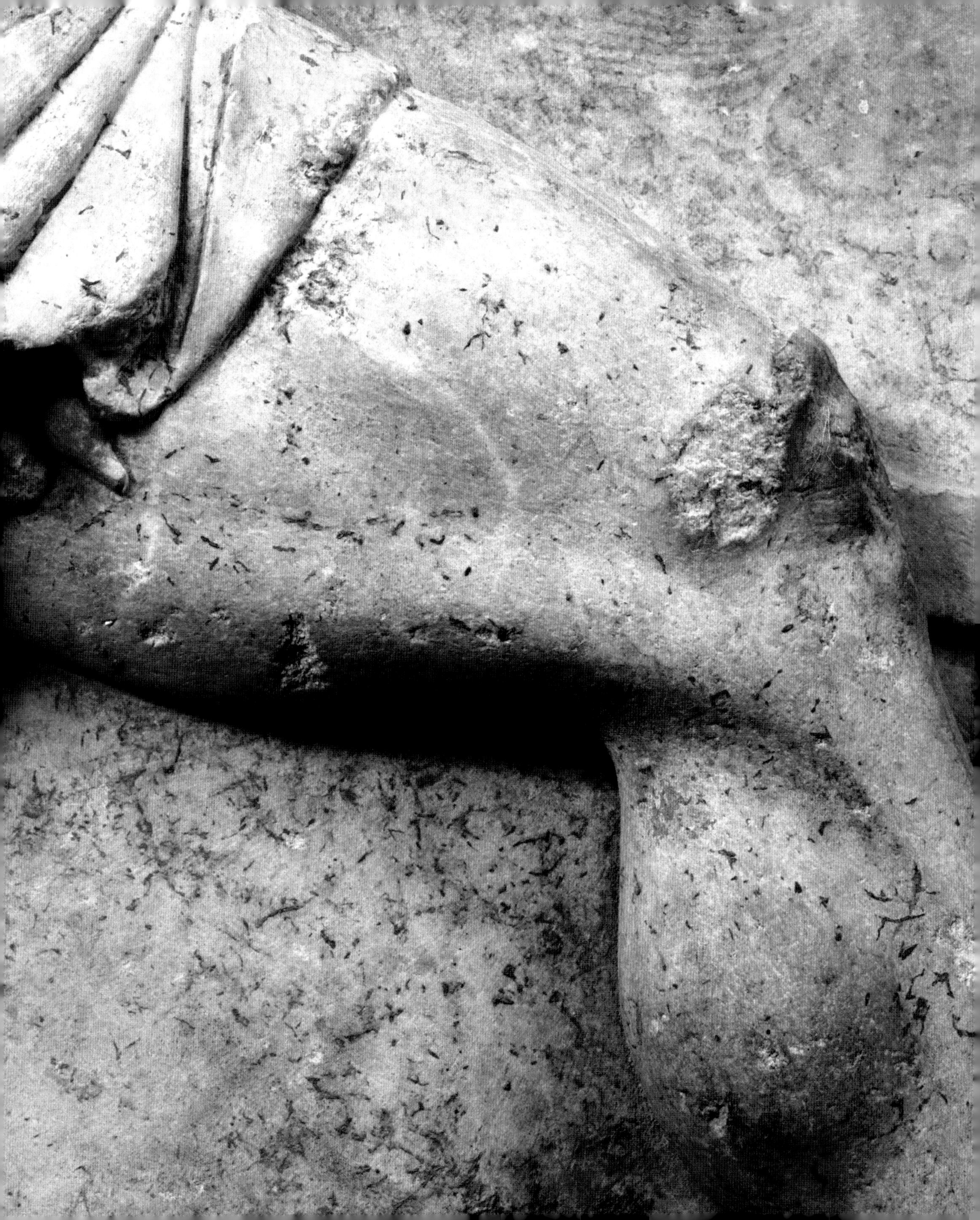

THE PEPLOS KORE

ATHENS, ACROPOLIS, WEST OF THE ERECHTHEION
C. 530 BCE
PARIAN MARBLE. HEIGHT 3.87 FEET (1.18 M);
HEIGHT INCLUDING PLINTH 4.46 FEET (1.36 M)
ATHENS, ACROPOLIS MUSEUM

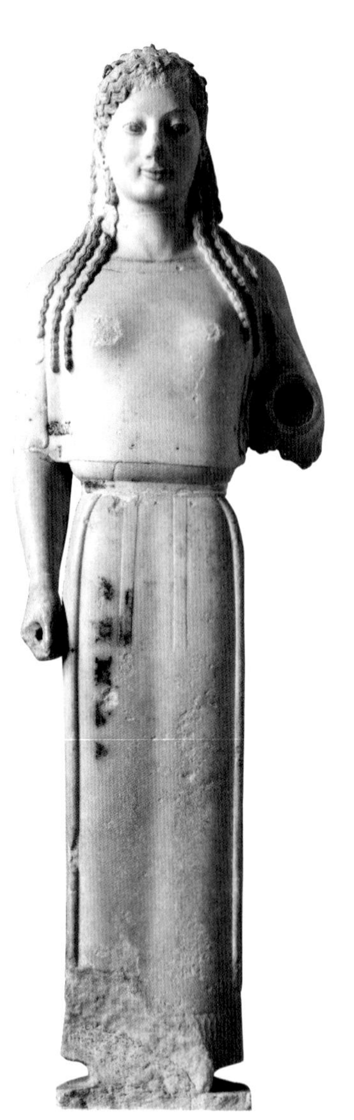

This kore, known as the Peplophoros (wearing a *peplos*, or garment worn by women that hangs in loose folds at the waist), differs from other korai: She is an adolescent girl with a slender, pubescent body. Her "old-fashioned" style of dress emphasizes the tender age of the figure (the small breasts and the body's lack of curves), which needs no further embellishment. Her chiton, barely visible on the left elbow and beneath the plain Doric peplos, which girdles the waist, is pinned over the shoulders and folded over, forming an *apoptygma* (an overfold). Her long, luxuriant hair with wavy curls extends to the middle of the back and to almost below the breasts in front. It is held in place by a ribbon at the nape of the neck. The kore would have worn a metal wreath on her head and metal earrings in her ears. On the neck there was a necklace, painted in green. Although her garment is without pleats, its painted

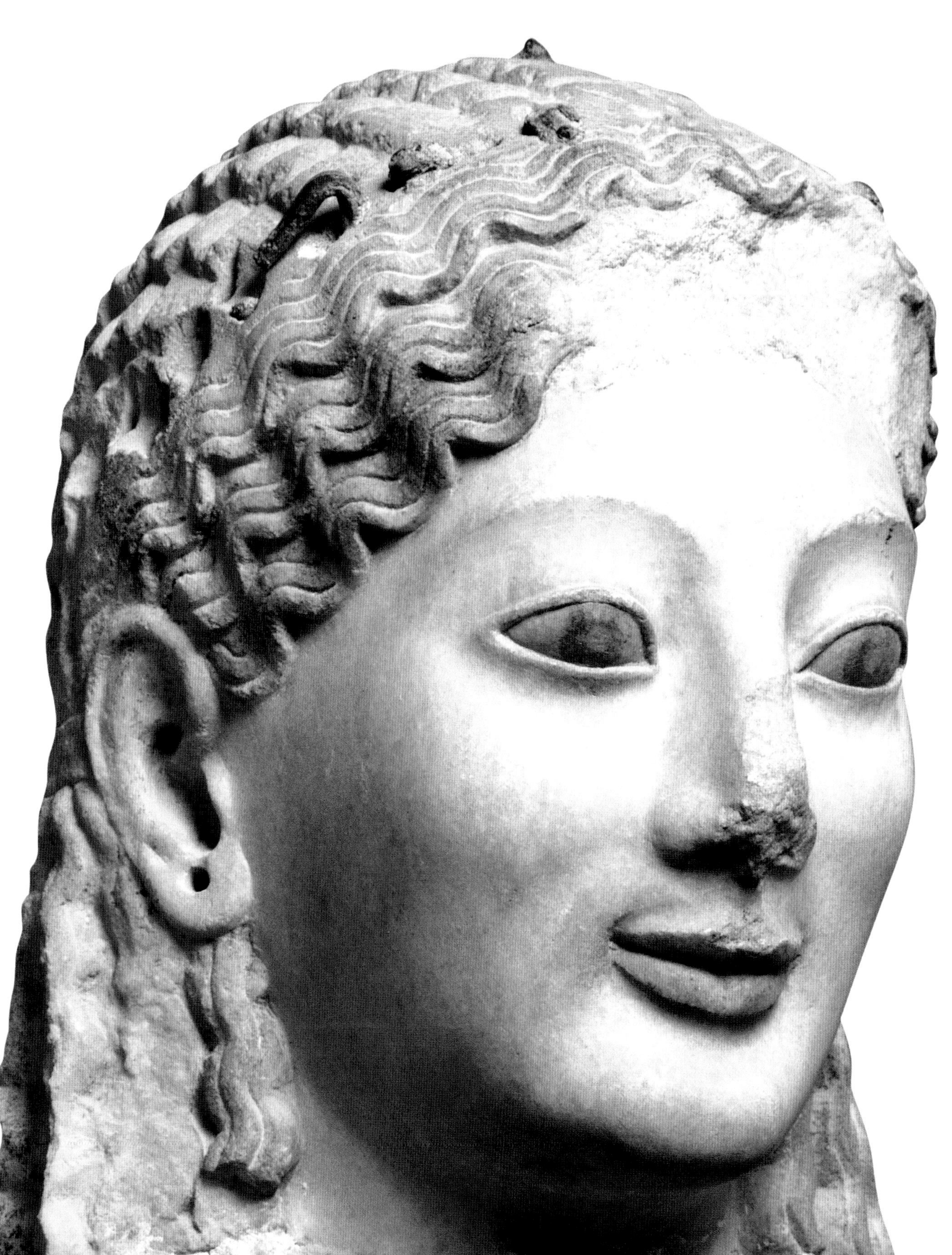

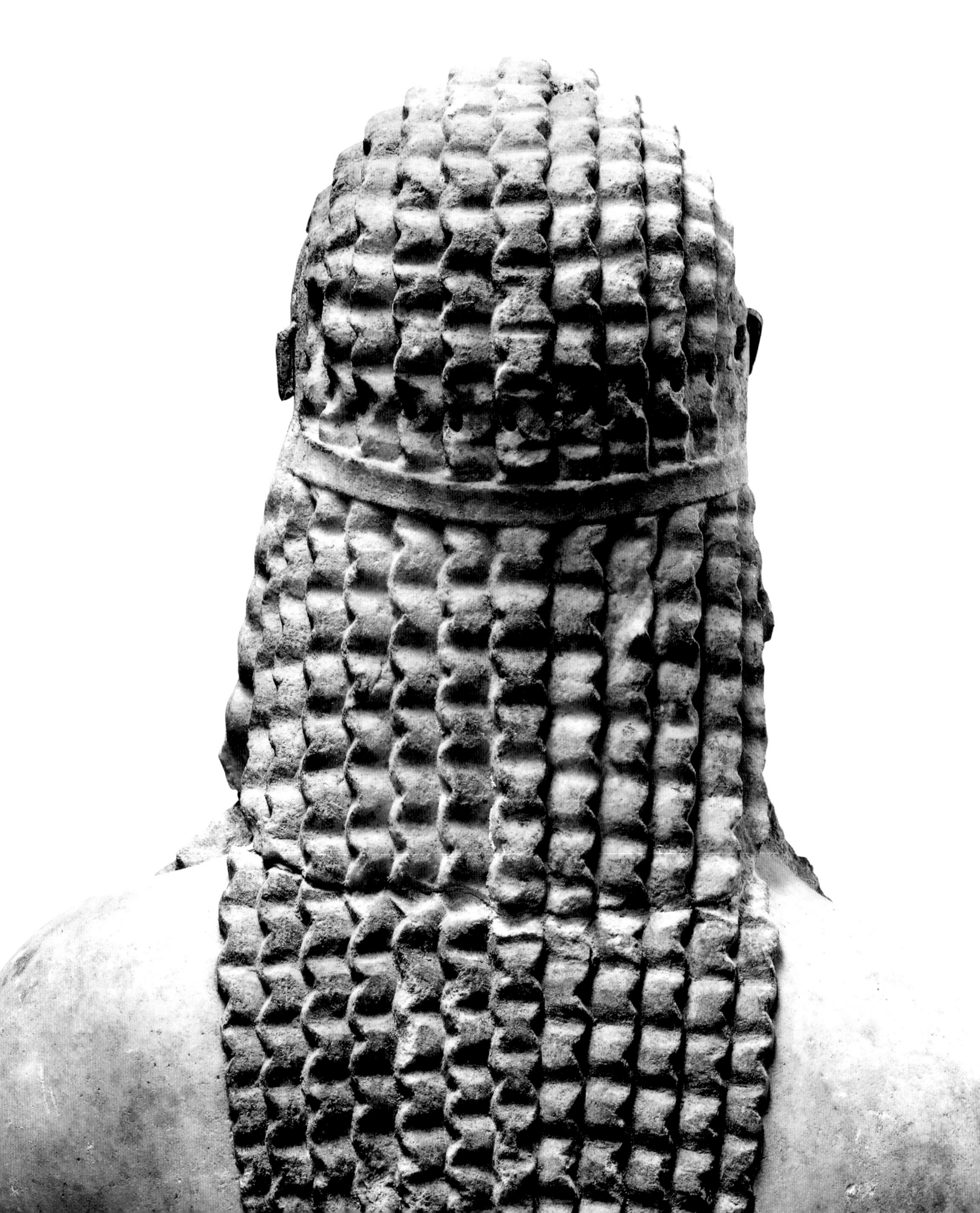

decoration gives the impression of a handwoven woolen textile; there are S-shaped bands on the neckline; sigmoid motifs and volutes with palmettes on the lower edge of the apoptygma and the peplos; and single ornaments, mainly rosettes, on various points of the Doric peplos. The hair, the pupils of the eyes, and the lips were painted red. The girl held offerings to the goddess in her lowered right hand and in her left, the arm bent at the elbow.

The relative youth of the figure is rendered with special sensitivity in the delicacy of the marble's surface and in the modeling of the volumes on the nose, the cheeks, and the chin. The incipient smile on the parted lips and the large almond-shaped eyes, which gaze eagerly on the world opening before her, add to her air of youthfulness.

THESEUS

ATHENS, ACROPOLIS, EAST OF THE PARTHENON
C. 530–520 BCE
PARIAN MARBLE. PRESENT HEIGHT 2.07 FEET (0.63 M)
ATHENS, ACROPOLIS MUSEUM

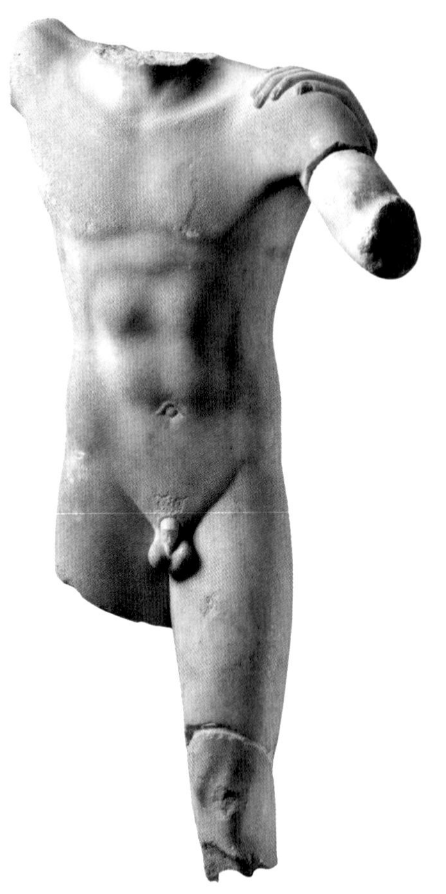

Preserved from a two-figure statue is the torso, including the left upper arm and the left thigh, of a youth, perhaps an *ephebe* (a young man undergoing military training). This statue, smaller than life-size, is interpreted as representing Theseus combating the brigand Prokrustes. The young man's right arm, missing from the shoulder, was raised to strike a blow to his opponent, whom he held with his left hand. All that survives of Prokrustes is his hand on Theseus' shoulder. The movement of the hero's slight but supple body is strange: He stands with his legs apart and his torso torqued almost three-quarters to the right, toward his adversary. The sensitive surface treatment of the marble, the fluidity of the outlines, and the clarity of the anatomical details compose a most charming work.

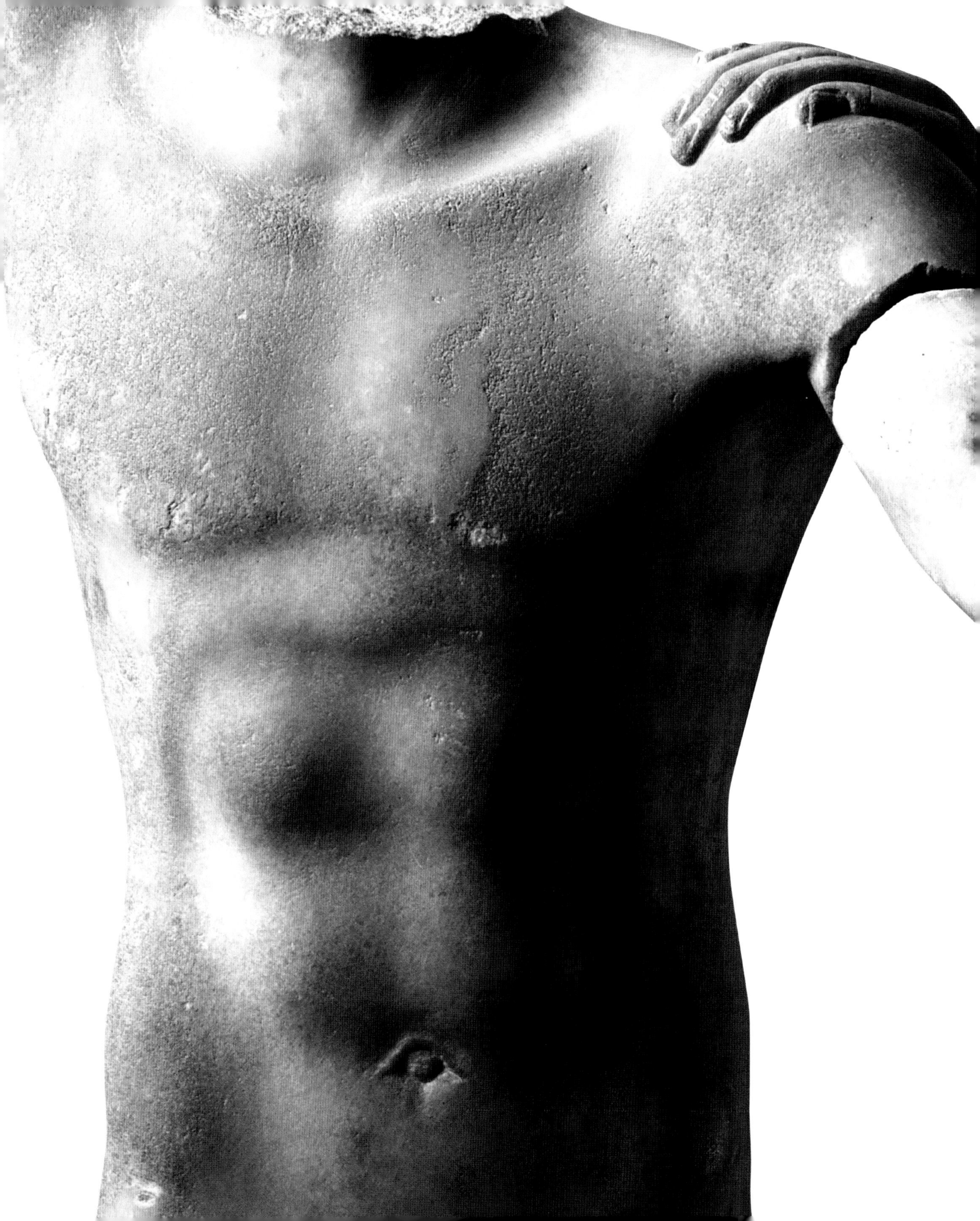

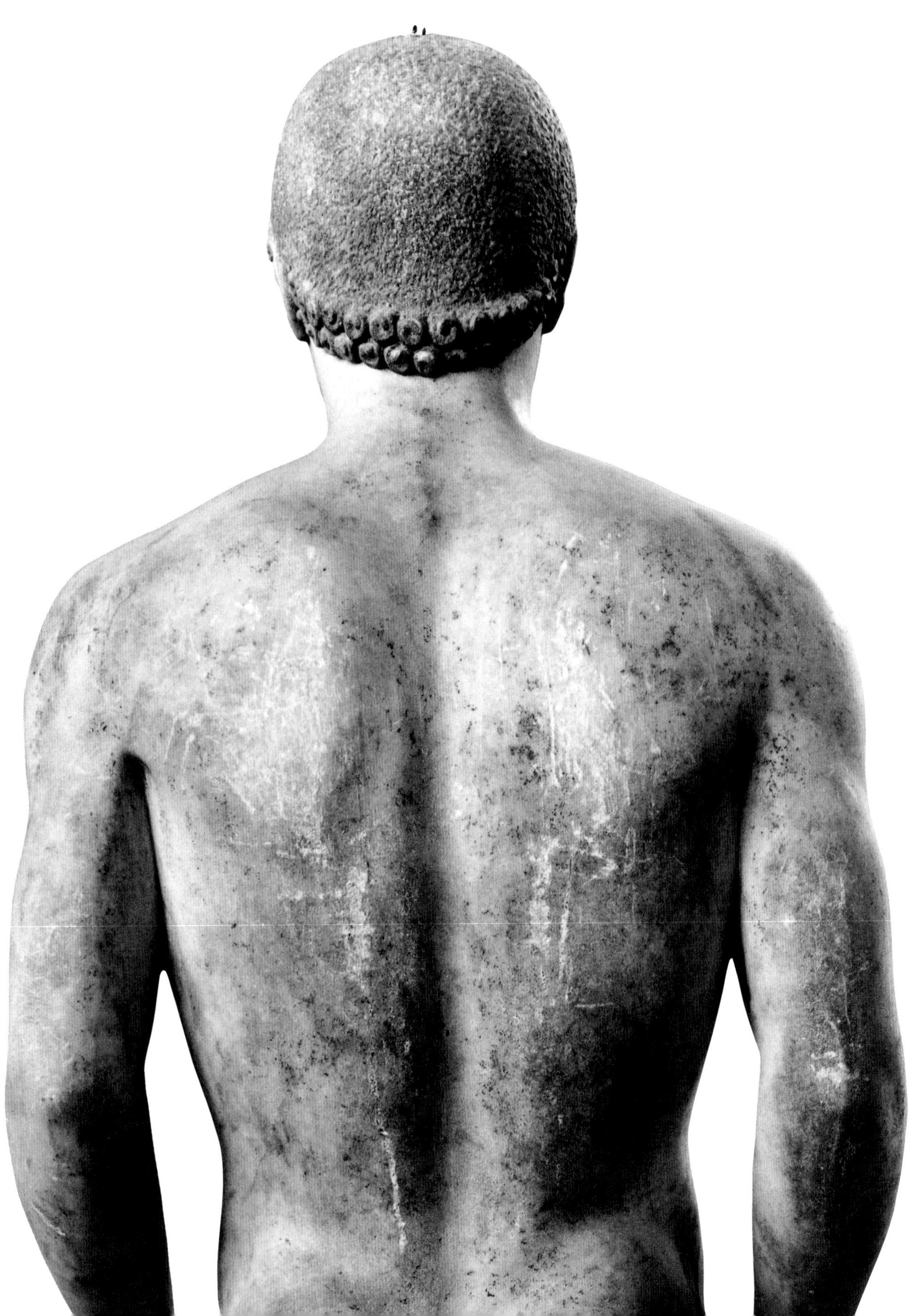

ARISTODIKOS

ATTICA, MESOGEIA
C. 510–500 BCE
PARIAN MARBLE (PENTELIC MARBLE BASE). HEIGHT 6.50 FEET (1.98 M)
ATHENS, NATIONAL ARCHAEOLOGICAL MUSEUM

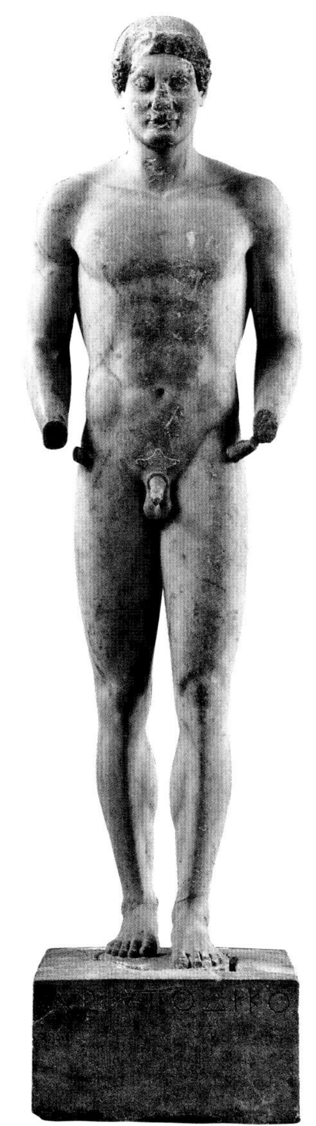

This funerary statue of an upper-class Athenian named Aristodikos is carved on a low rectangular base. The work is characteristic of the development of the kouros type from its appearance in the early sixth century BCE through its final years. The hair is now short and there are spiral curls on the forehead. The arms are no longer stuck to the torso and are bent slightly to the fore, reflecting the sculptor's attempt to place the figure more freely in space. This sense of space is further heightened by the position of the legs, which are set apart and in a more natural walking pose. The body has acquired a certain plasticity, and the muscles are rendered in a more naturalistic manner, while the proportions and structure of the figure in general place it among the most harmonious works of Attic sculpture in the late Archaic period. The dawn of a new era, in the fifth century BCE, is imminent.

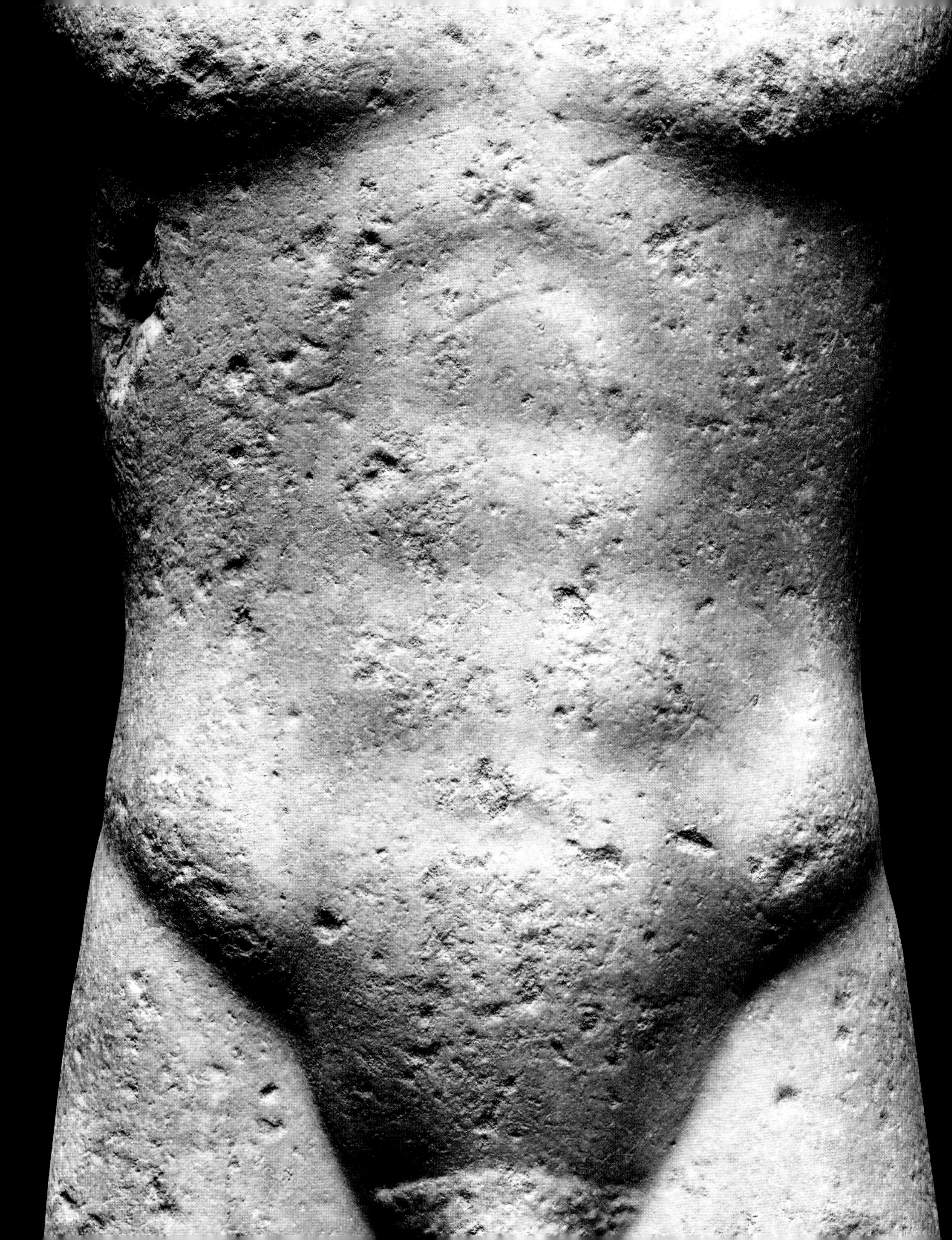

TORSO OF A KOUROS

PAROS, PAROIKIA
C. LATE SIXTH CENTURY BCE
PARIAN MARBLE. PRESENT HEIGHT 3.05 FEET (0.93 M)
PAROS, ARCHAEOLOGICAL MUSEUM

Paros, along with Attica and other major Greek cities of the time, was an important center of marble sculpture workshops. The raw material was available in abundance, and Parian marble was renowned for its quality and translucence.

Parian kouroi, with their solid yet slender outlines and their movement-filled corporeal planes, number among the comeliest of their kind. This torso, preserved from the neck to the mid-thighs, features harmonious proportions and the correct alternation of horizontal and vertical axes. The soft volumes on the surfaces recall the freshness and vitality of a youthful body.

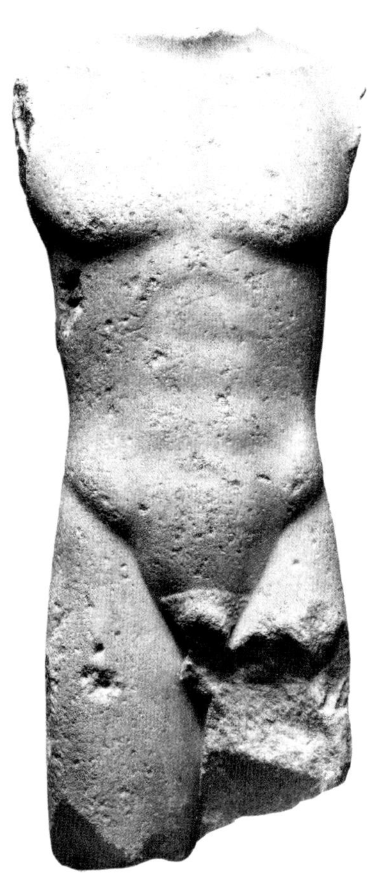

KORE

ATHENS, ACROPOLIS, PARTHENON
C. 490 BCE
ISLAND MARBLE. PRESENT HEIGHT 3.90 FEET (1.19 M)
ATHENS, ACROPOLIS MUSEUM

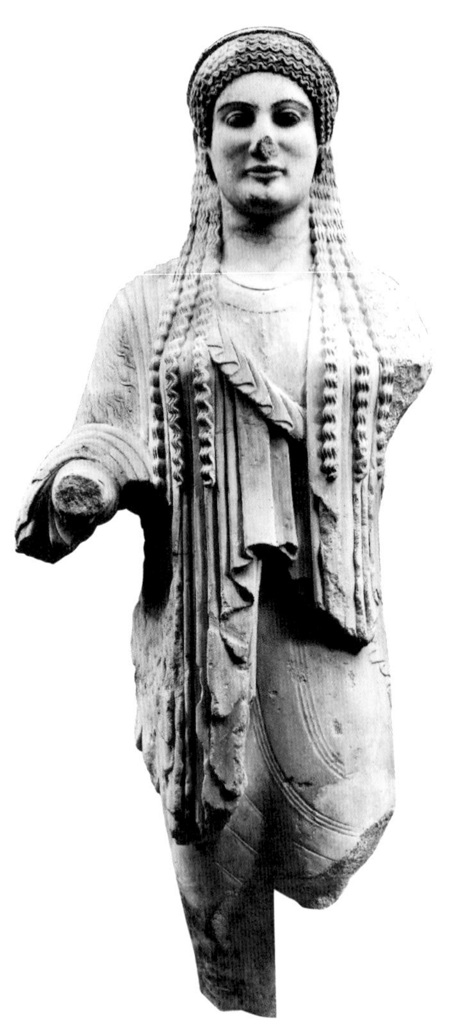

This kore stood in solemnity in the sanctuary of the goddess Athena, for whom she held an offering, now lost, in her outstretched right hand. She wears a chiton, an oblique himation, and an *epiblema* (a shawl worn by Greek women). With her left hand, held at the height of her buttock, she slightly draws up her fine, multipleated chiton. The himation hangs obliquely from the left shoulder and folds over on the right arm, while the epiblema, cast over the shoulders, falls in successive curves to the buttocks and in deep vertical pleats in front. The himation is embellished with painted ornaments. The luxuriant hair falls in fine, dense waves down the back, while three groups of curls sit on either side of the bosom. A relief fillet forming a close circle with painted white flowers crowns the elaborate coiffure, disc-shaped earrings with painted rosettes adorn the ears, and a bracelet is painted on the right wrist. The well-drawn eyebrows, the pupils of the eyes, and the lips were painted red.

Despite her Archaic features, this kore heralds radical changes in the art. The square structure of the body, the "weight" of the garments, and, primarily, the serious expression, devoid of the slightly playful character of the "Archaic" smile, reflect the Severe Style, which was to lead to the miracle of classical times.

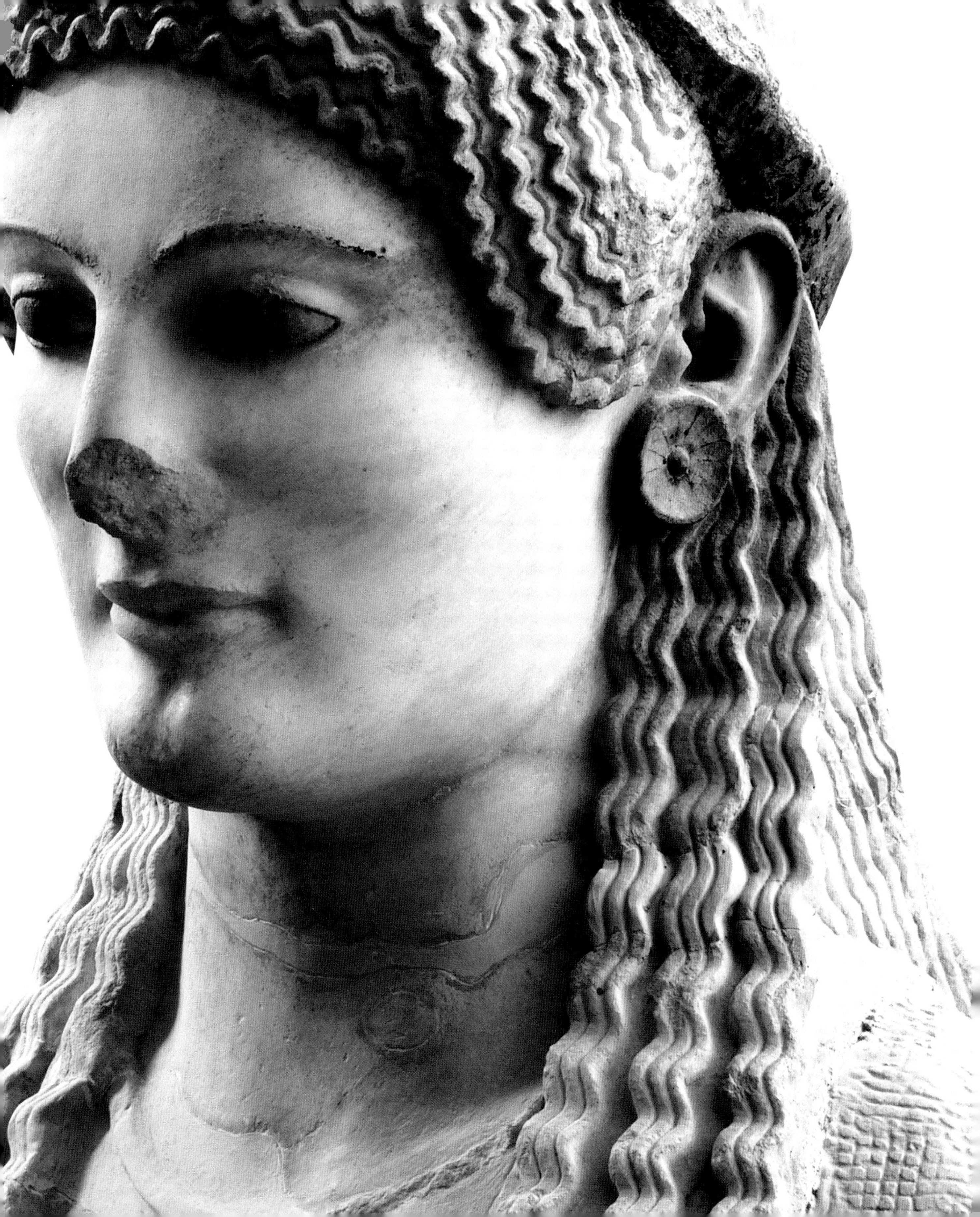

FRONT PART OF A HORSE

ATHENS, ACROPOLIS, EAST OF THE PARTHENON
C. 460 BCE
MARBLE. HEIGHT APPROX. 3.90 FEET (1.20 M)
ATHENS, ACROPOLIS MUSEUM

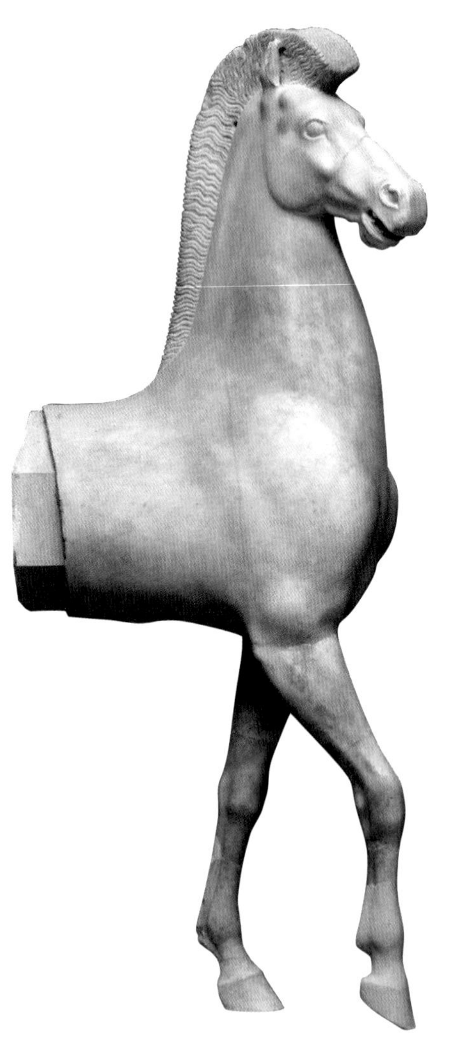

With its head held high, its small ears, and its pronounced cheeks, this horse is impressive. Its mane of small, wavy curls standing on end in the wind follows the movement and slight turn of the head, and only the warm breath of the proud steed is missing from the throbbing nostrils and half-open mouth. The dynamically modeled chest and neck, together with the fore part of the almost cylindrical body, are supported by slim legs whose hooves lightly touch the ground. The animal appears to move forward in an easy, flexible manner, perhaps toward victory. Truly a delight for the sanctuary of Athena Parthenos, this work, which represented only the horse, possibly commemorated a victory in a horse race. The details indicate that it is the creation of a highly skilled sculptor in marble.

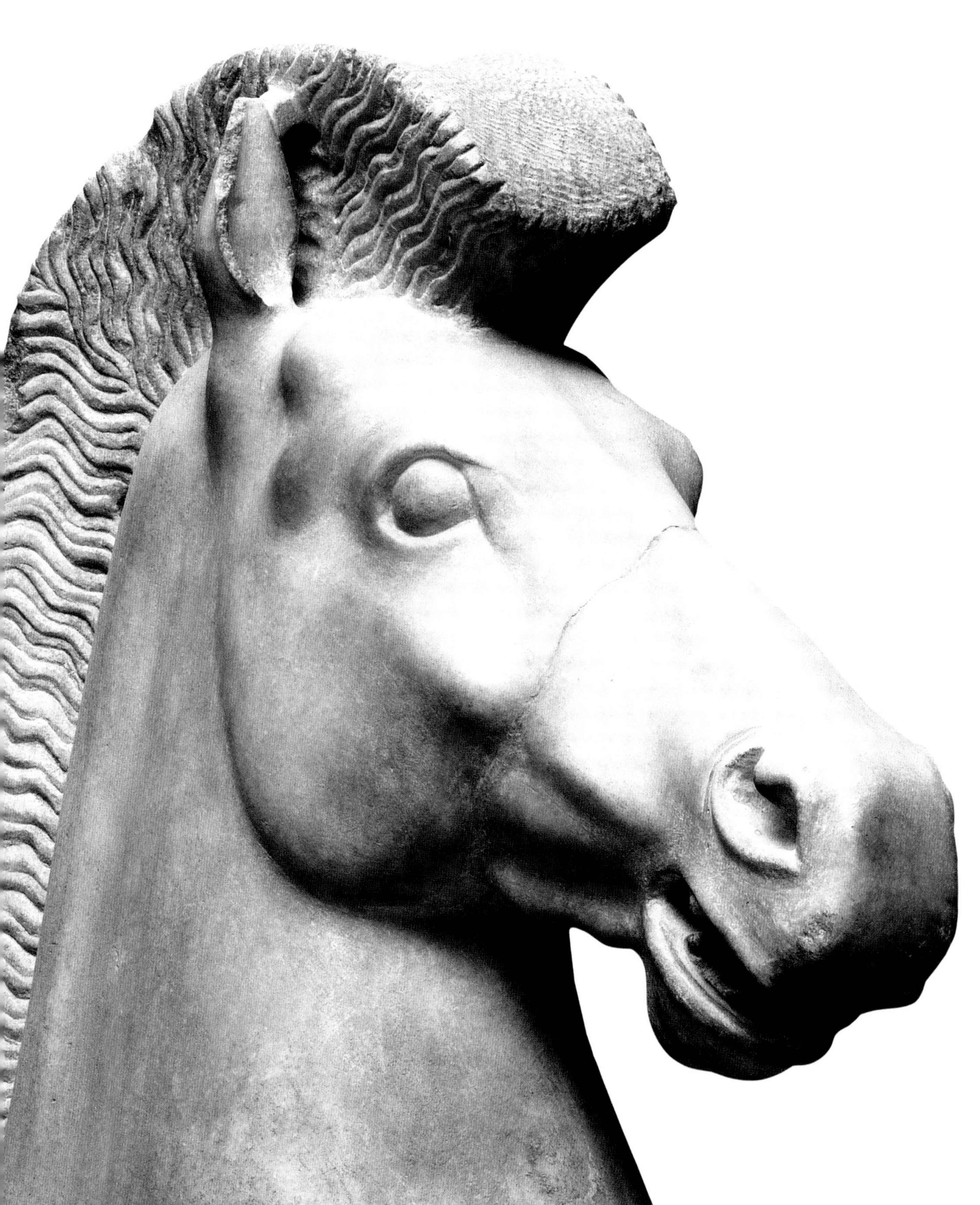

THE ATHENIAN TREASURY AT DELPHI

In the major sanctuaries of ancient Greece, cities (in the early years) and rulers (later on) built, in addition to the movable ex-votos offered to the tutelary deity, entire monuments, usually called treasuries. These treasuries often commemorated a victory in warfare but also allowed the cities and rulers to which they belonged to display their power and wealth in a renowned and often highly influential place in the Hellenic world. Among the best examples are the treasuries of the Syracusans, Sikyonians, Megarians, and so on at Olympia; the treasuries of the Sikyonians, Knidians, Siphnians, Athenians, and more at Delphi; oikos of the Naxians and the Archaic-classical treasuries of various cities on Delos; and the stoas of Antigonos and of Philip in Hellenistic times.

The Athenian Treasury occupied a conspicuous position, just after the first northward bend in the Sacred Way, leading from the lower part of the sanctuary of Delphi up to the Temple of Apollo. According to the second-century CE traveler Pausanias, a seminal source of information on antiquity, the Athenians built this treasury to commemorate their victory at Marathon, in 490 BCE. However, many scholars consider the sculptures and architecture to date to much earlier, and the possibility that the treasury was erected immediately after the restoration of democracy in Athens, in the time of Kleisthenes (507–500 BCE), cannot be ruled out. Restored by the Municipality of Athens between 1903 and 1906, the treasury was a small edifice (31.82 x 21.72 feet [9.70 x 6.62 m]) in the Doric order, constructed entirely of Parian marble. It was adorned with thirty metopes, six on each narrow side and nine on each long side, that took as their various subjects the Amazonomachy, the Labors of Theseus, and the Labors of Herakles. As pilgrims walked up the Sacred Way, they beheld mainly the south side and the east side (which included the entrance), and for this reason the Athenians depicted on these sides scenes from their local mythology and history. Represented on the south side, close to human scale, were the labors of the Athenian hero, king, and founder of the democracy, Theseus, whose feats cleansed the land of villains and wild beasts; represented on the east side were the victories over the Amazons, who had campaigned against Athens and whom the Athenians vanquished, again with the aid of Theseus. Presented on the west and north sides were the Labors of Herakles, a Panhellenic hero who embodied the Doric ideal and its myths. Through these labors, Herakles used his superhuman power to defeat everything daemonic. At the time the treasury was erected, however, these ideas represented an old-fashioned spirit.

These metopes feature a perfect harmony of design and sculptural execution, which together with the vigor and solidity of the Attic figures creates a captivating ensemble, its fresh rendering of vibrant details enriching new subjects of bold conception. These sculptures are also the most characteristic surviving examples of the Attic School's transition from the Archaic to the classical period.

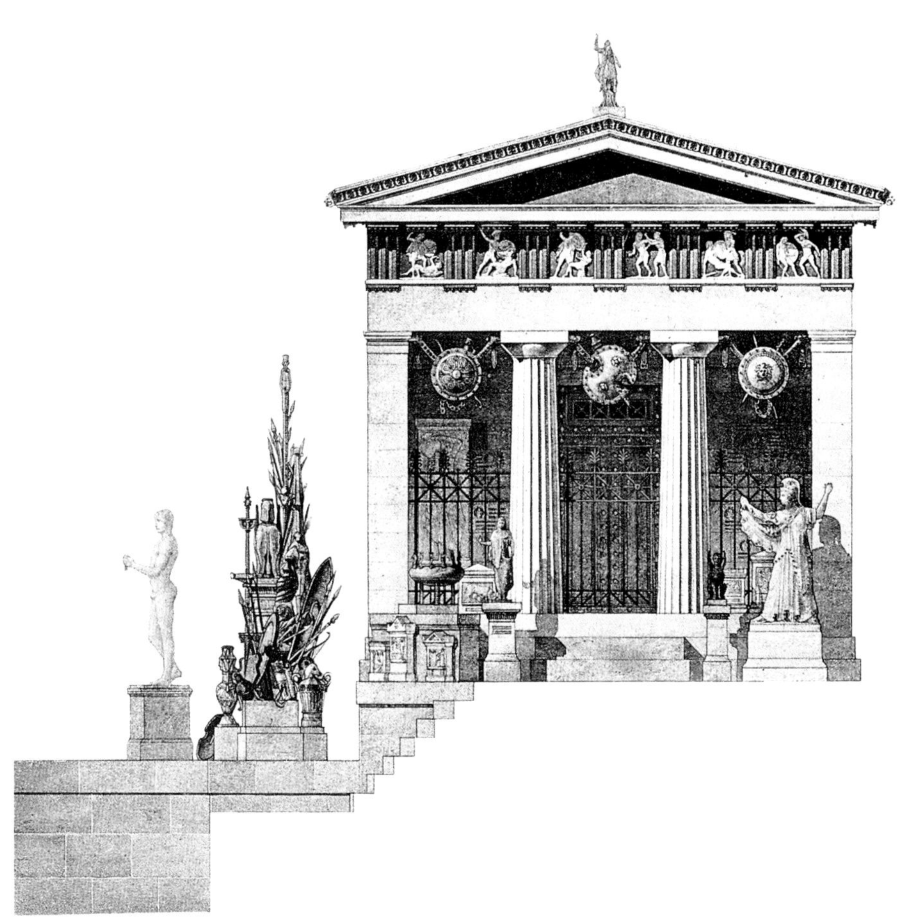

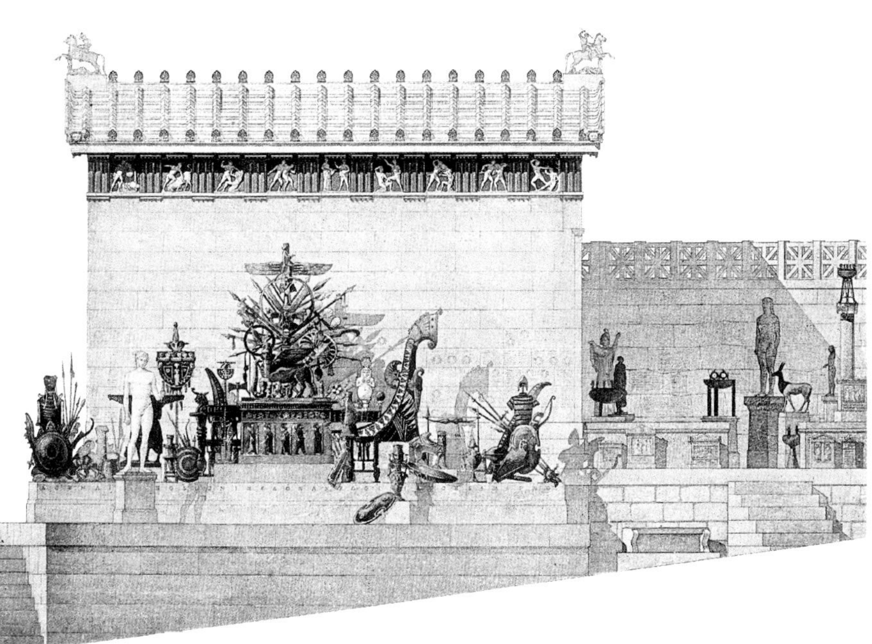

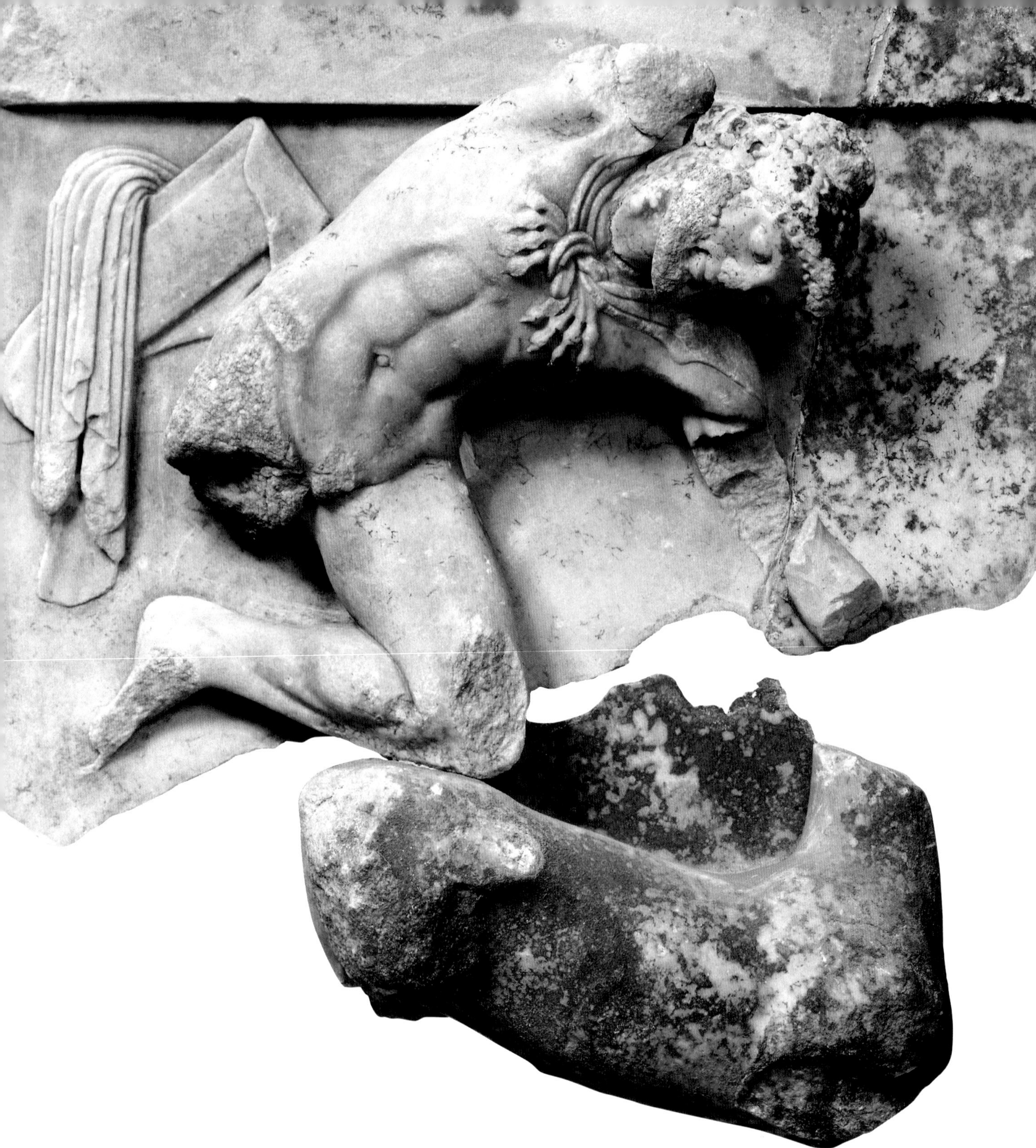

HERAKLES AND THE KERYNEAN STAG

DELPHI, TREASURY OF THE ATHENIANS, METOPE FROM THE NORTH SIDE
LATE SIXTH CENTURY, OR 490–480 BCE
PARIAN MARBLE. PRESENT HEIGHT 2.20 FEET (0.67 M); PRESENT WIDTH 1.97 FEET (0.60 M)
DELPHI, ARCHAEOLOGICAL MUSEUM

The hero, naked save for the lion skin around his neck (instead of on his head as usual), is represented from the left, jumping ferociously upon the stag, which he has caught by the antlers, while digging his left knee into its back. The curved body of Herakles and of the half-fallen deer trace the diagonal of the metope, while the two left corners below and above were filled, respectively, with the animal's crumpled legs (which, myth has it, were of bronze) and the hero's hanging himation.

One of the boldest compositions in ancient Greek sculpture, this figure of Herakles—vigorous but roughly rendered compared to the almost gentle dignity of the figure of Theseus—appears to be flying through the space in a pose at once unreal and full of movement and vitality. This is despite the fact that the metope is considered to reflect not the spirit that presages the classical miracle but that of Archaic art.

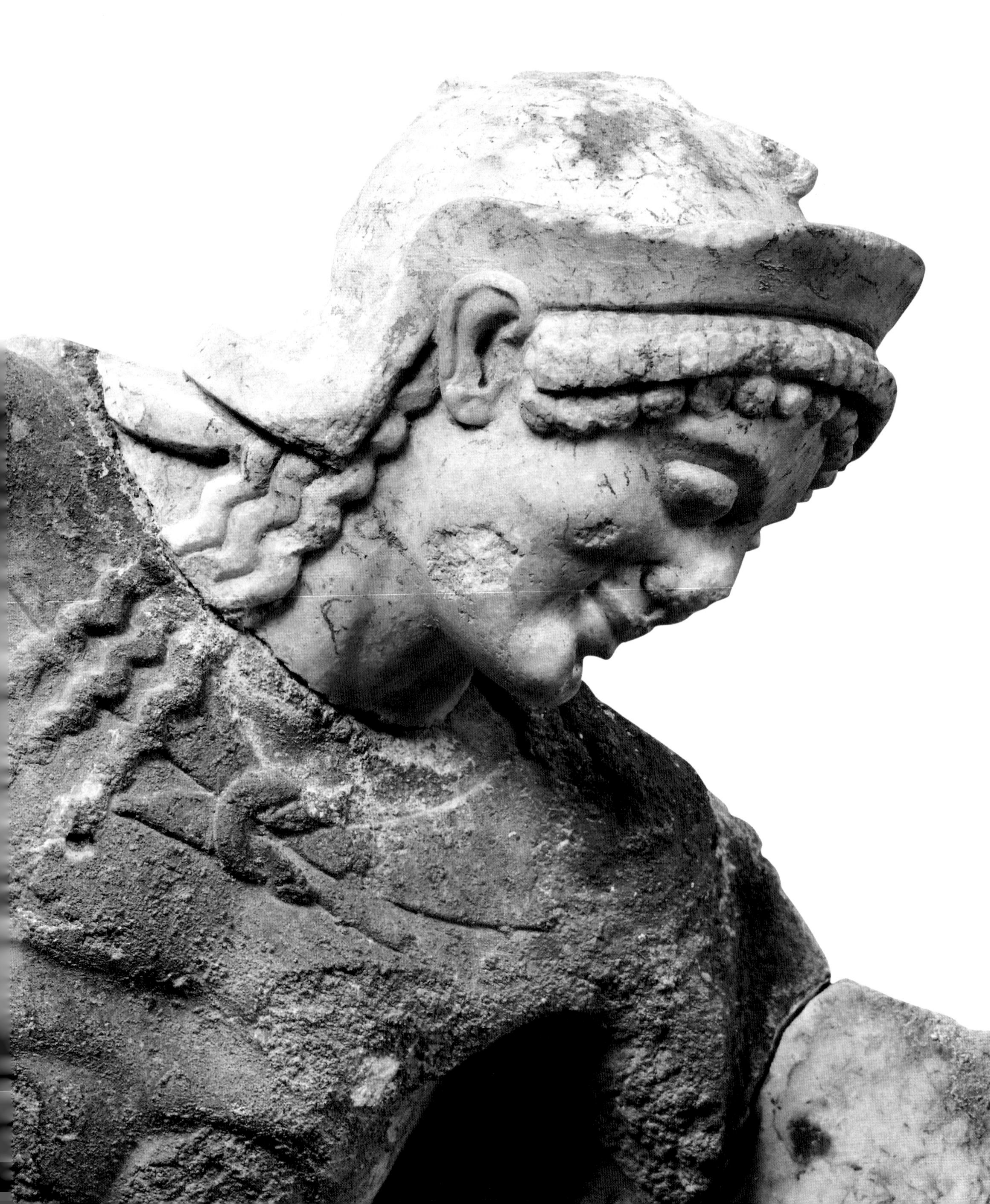

THESEUS AND AN AMAZON

DELPHI, TREASURY OF THE ATHENIANS, METOPE FROM THE NORTH SIDE
LATE SIXTH CENTURY, OR 490–480 BCE
PARIAN MARBLE. PRESENT HEIGHT 2.20 FEET (0.67 M); PRESENT WIDTH 1.97 FEET (0.60 M)
DELPHI, ARCHAEOLOGICAL MUSEUM

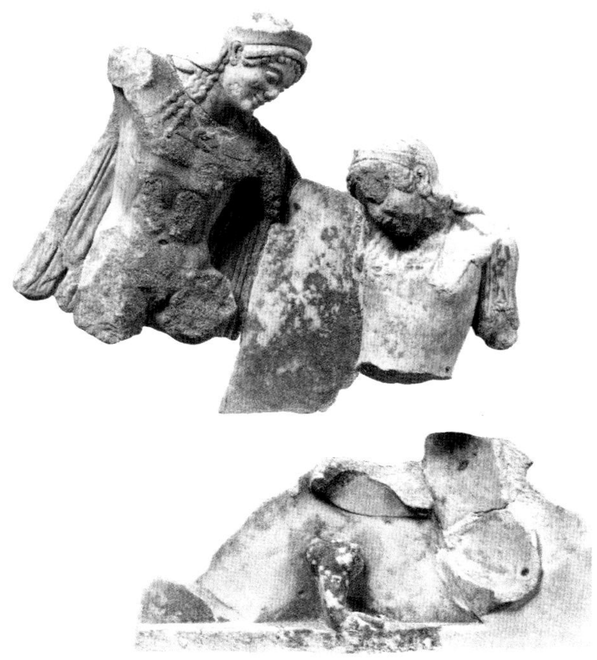

Theseus, from the left, overpowers one of the Amazons, presumably their queen, Antiope, who falls backward. The long-haired hero wears a helmet on his head and a short himation that spreads out on his back and is tied with a knot in front, high on the chest. The abdominal muscles are clearly described on Theseus' naked torso, denoting the pressure of his turn toward his adversary, who collapses under his blow. The Amazon, also long-haired and helmeted, wears a cuirass over her short-sleeved tunic.

HERAKLES AND KYKNOS

DELPHI, TREASURY OF THE ATHENIANS, METOPE FROM THE NORTH SIDE
LATE SIXTH CENTURY, OR 490–480 BCE
PARIAN MARBLE. PRESENT HEIGHT 2.20 FEET (0.67 M); PRESENT WIDTH 1.97 FEET (0.60 M)
DELPHI, ARCHAEOLOGICAL MUSEUM

Herakles, from the right, attacks Kyknos, son of Ares, who in myth was a villain who ravaged sanctuaries. The hero wears not only the distinctive lion skin on his head but also a large helmet with a plume. In contrast to the impulsive violence of the metope of Herakles and the Kerynean Stag, here we have two flexible nude bodies presented in three-quarter pose and opposing each other in an oblique arrangement. Each figure holds a shield in his left hand, creating an impressive interplay of the two surfaces, the inner shield on Kyknos' left and the outer shield on Herakles' right. This metope is an unusual representation of Herakles as an ordinary warrior, with helmet and shield but without his club. With its harmonious composition of differentiated planes, the metope reflects the movement of Attic art toward classical perfection.

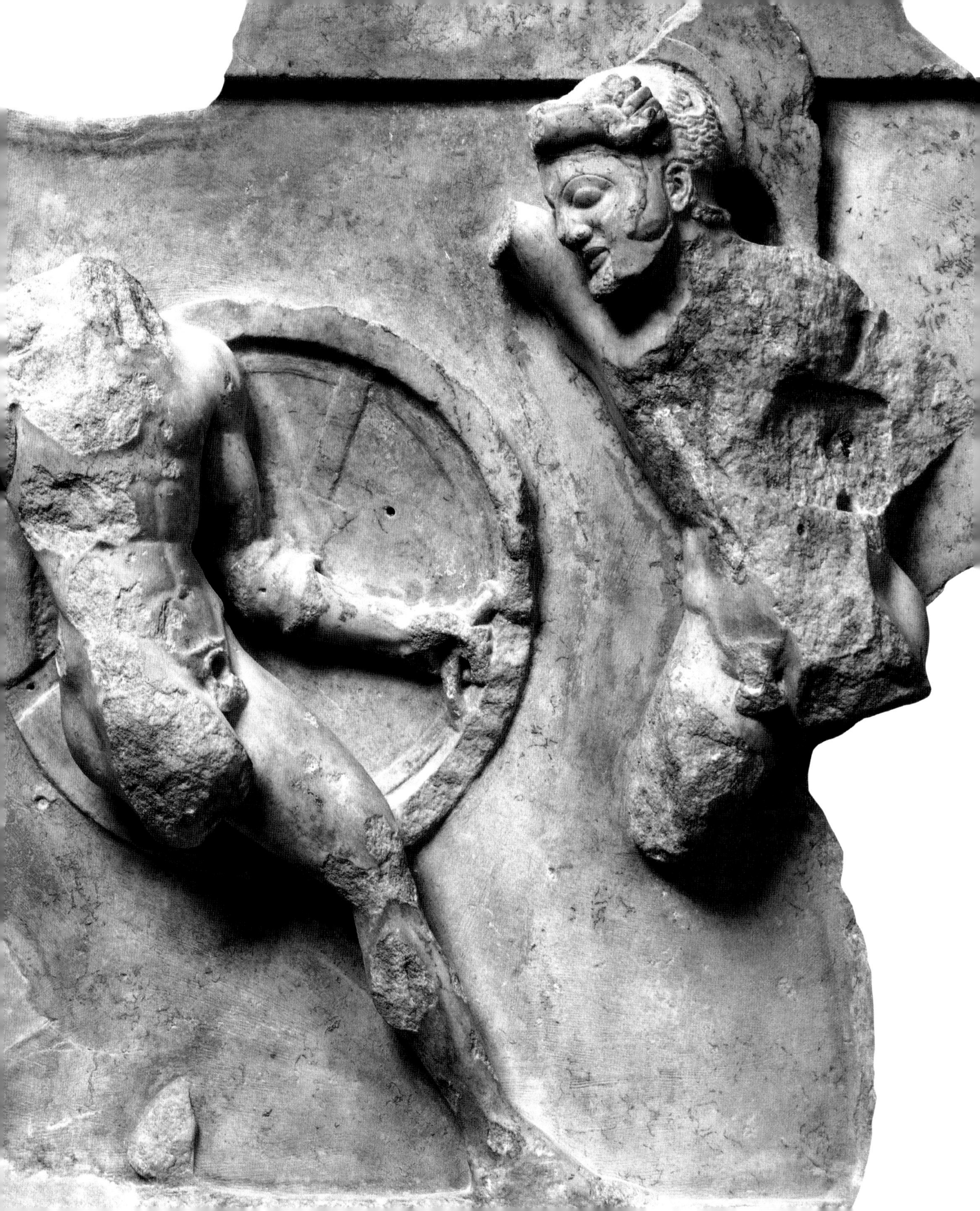

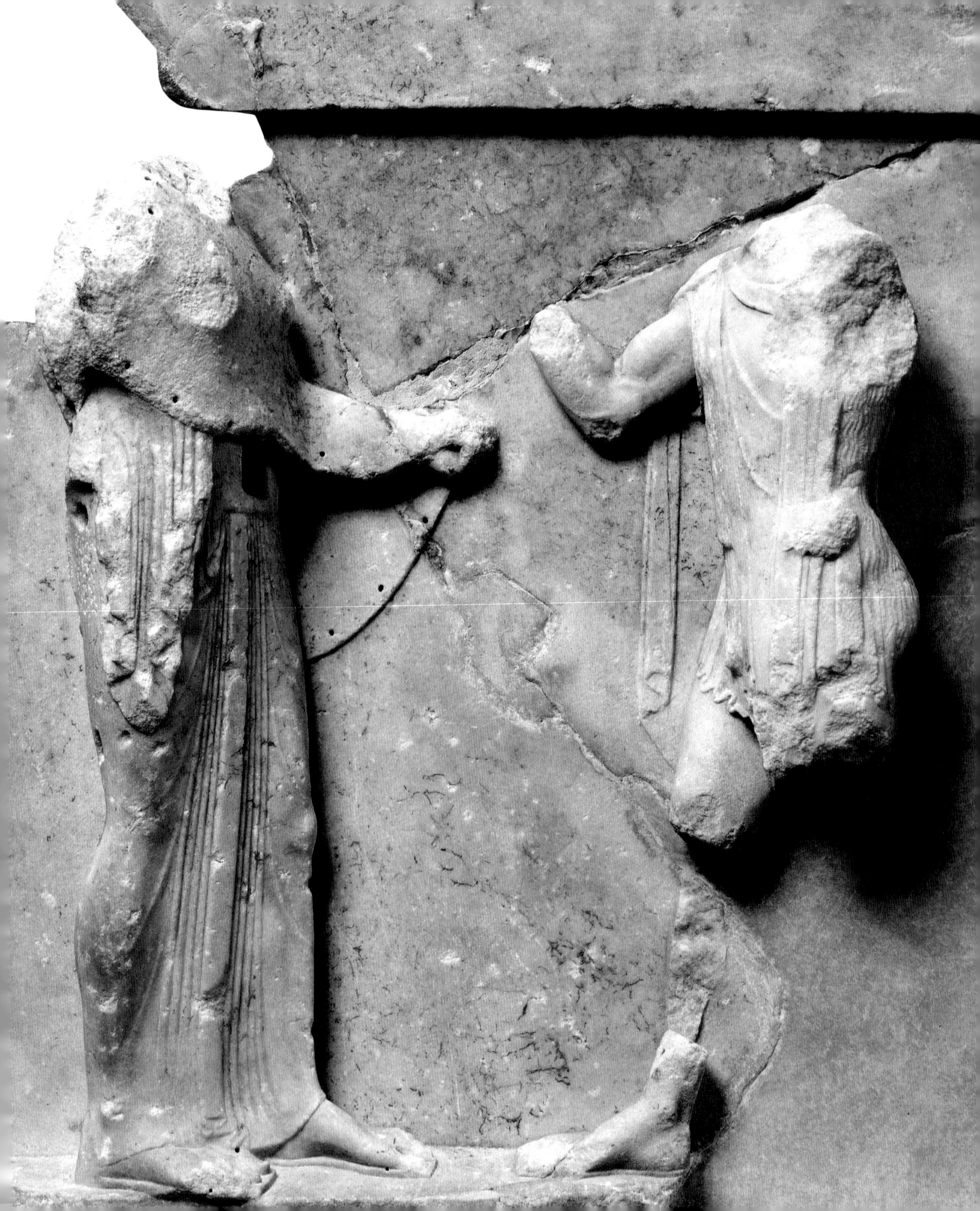

THESEUS AND ATHENA

DELPHI, TREASURY OF THE ATHENIANS, METOPE FROM THE SOUTH SIDE
LATE SIXTH CENTURY, OR 490–480 BCE
PARIAN MARBLE. PRESENT HEIGHT 2.20 FEET (0.67 M); WIDTH 1.97 FEET (0.60 M)
DELPHI, ARCHAEOLOGICAL MUSEUM

The two figures move antithetically toward each other, Athena from the left and Theseus from the right. The goddess wears a chiton, a himation, over which lies her *aegis* (a cloak characteristic of Athena) with its bronze snakes, and sandals with bronze thongs. Theseus wears a short, fine chiton that clings to his body, and a short himation hangs from his shoulders. His left hand is on his waist, while his right is extended to greet the goddess. Her divine presence is emphasized by her solemn, rigid pose and the almost vertical Doric pleats of her chiton, which contrast with the lightness and agility of the hero.

In this, one of the loveliest and most important compositions in the sculpted decoration of the Athenian Treasury, the patron goddess of the hero-king's native city declares her support.

THE BLOND BOY

ATHENS, ACROPOLIS, PERSIAN LEVEL
C. 485–480 BCE
PARIAN, OR PERHAPS PENTELIC, MARBLE. HEIGHT 0.80 FEET (0.245 M)
ATHENS, ACROPOLIS MUSEUM

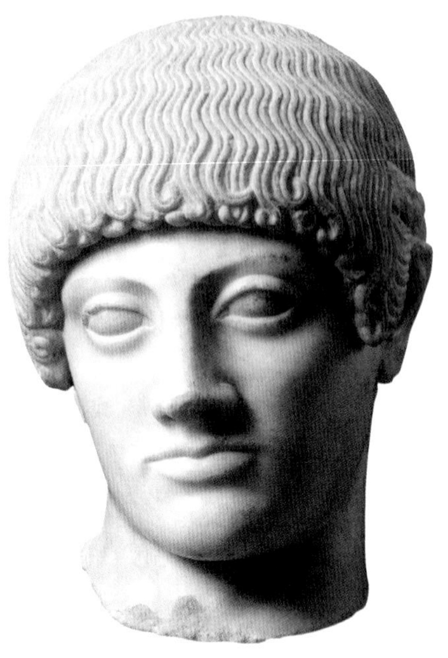

This head of a youth was dubbed the "Blond Boy" because when it was found, the hair was golden in color. The figure inclines slightly to the right and has heavy eyelids, a straight nose with dilated nostrils, and almost pursed lips, which heighten the slightly melancholy expression of the face. The wavy hairstyle ends in spiral curls set low on the forehead that cover the greater part of it. On the back of the neck, two large braids cross and then disappear into the mass of hair below the ears.

The work is one of the finest and most characteristic examples of sculpture in the Severe Style, that is, work from the first half of the fifth century BCE, when the art passed from the relatively standardized gaiety of the figures in the late Archaic period to a more realistic rendering of human features. This realism was part of an endeavor to enhance the inner dignified demeanor, or *ethos*, through an appropriate severity of expression.

Some scholars attribute this work to a Peloponnesian artist. However, the introspection of the face and the almost perfect execution point instead to a great Athenian artist. Others suggest Hegias, mentor of Pheidias, as the artist; indeed, Hegias' name appears in an inscription found on the Acropolis.

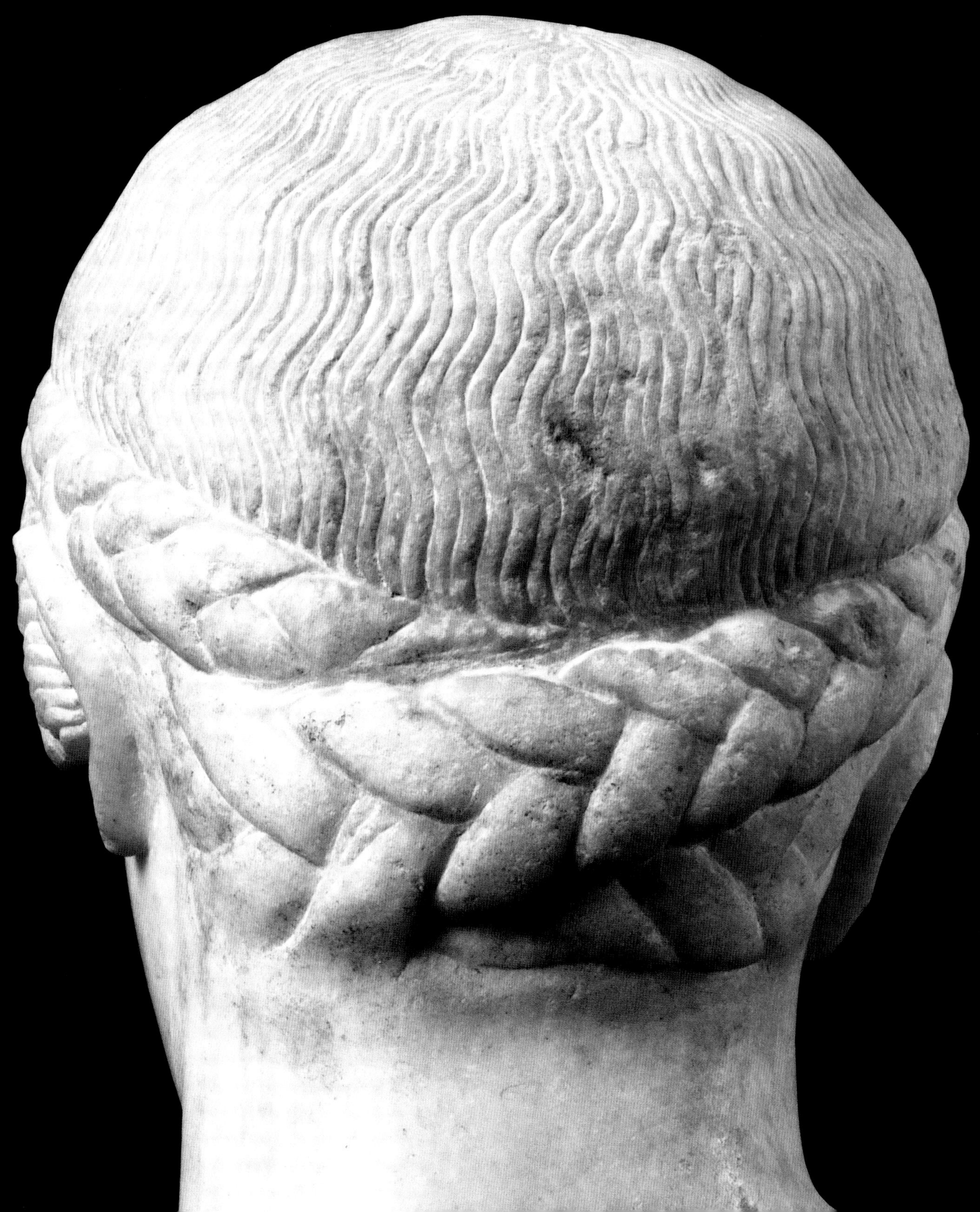

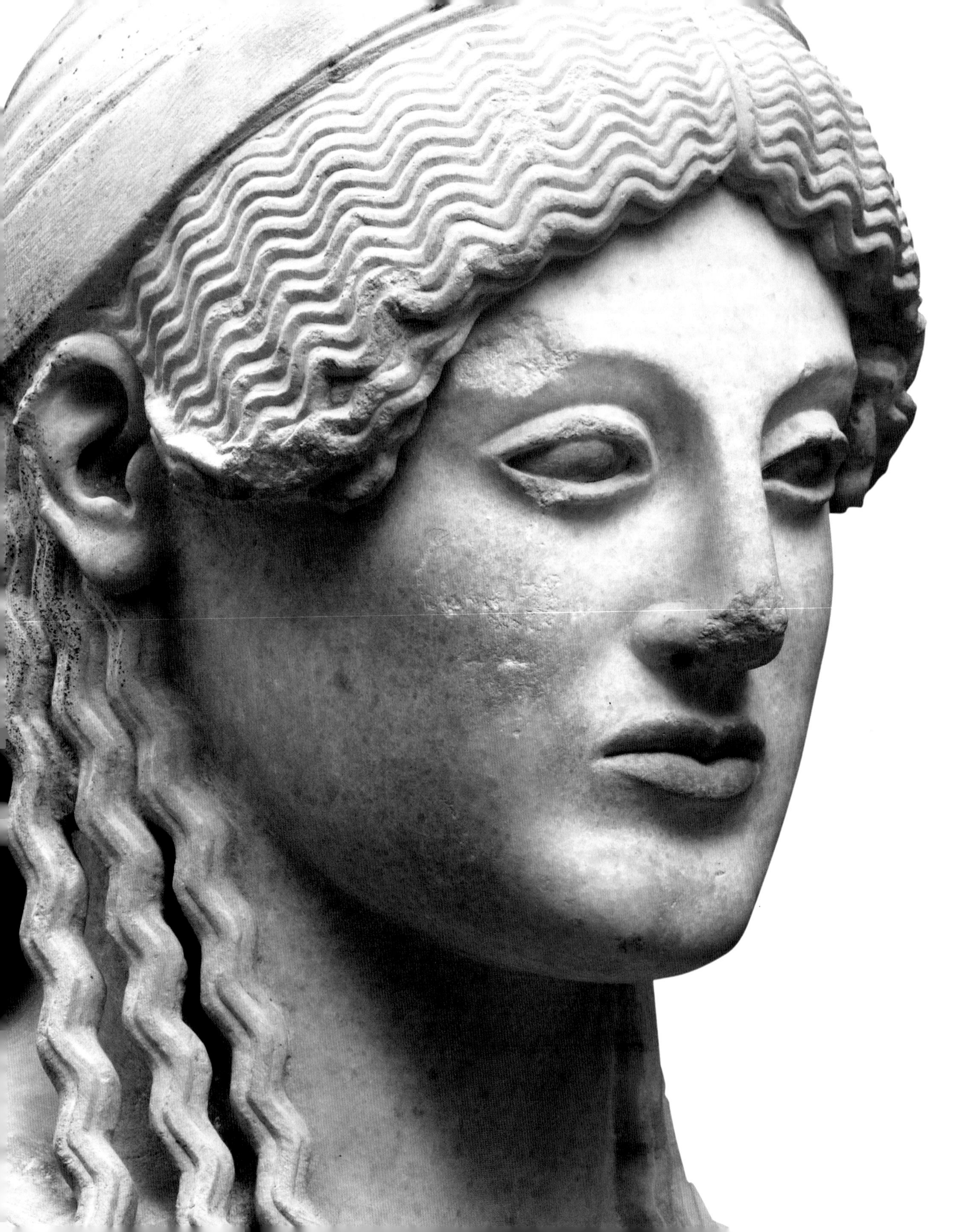

THE KORE OF EUTHYDIKOS

ATHENS, ACROPOLIS, EAST OF THE PARTHENON (THE UPPER PART) AND NEAR THE ERECHTHEION (THE LOWER PART)
C. 480 BCE
MARBLE. HEIGHT OF TORSO 1.93 FEET (0.589 M); HEIGHT OF LOWER BODY 1.35 FEET (0.41 M)
ATHENS, ACROPOLIS MUSEUM

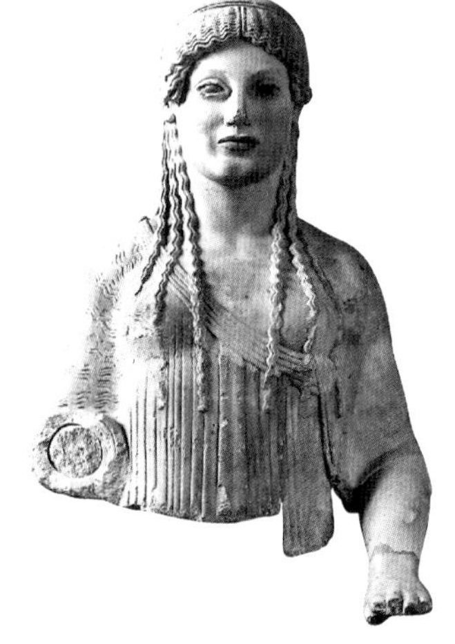

This kore, known as *la boudeuse* (the sulky one), represents a young girl with heavy features and a petulant expression. She wears a fine chiton, which she draws up at the sides with her left hand, and a diagonal himation pinned over her right shoulder. Her long hair is held in place by a broad fillet tied at the back, leaving its long ends to hang down. The hairstyle is elaborate, set in waves above the forehead and ending in the front in long tresses and in the back in a single mass with horizontal grooves. The lips and the pupils of the eyes were painted red. The statue was found in two pieces that cannot be mended together. Preserved from the lower part are the slim legs, from about the knees down, and the integral, round base, on which an inscription records that a certain Euthydikos dedicated the kore to the goddess Athena.

The morphological traits of this statue—the squarish face, the wide, heavy chin, the horizontally placed eyes, the simplicity of the garment in relation to earlier korai, and even the small feet—classify it as belonging to the new age. It is perhaps one of the first examples of the form the kore type would have taken had the Persian destruction not cut short its development.

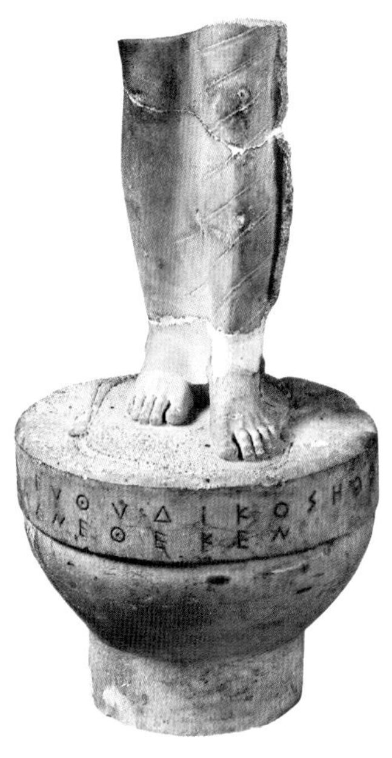

PART OF A MALE FIGURE

PAROS, PAROIKIA

C. 480 BCE

PARIAN MARBLE. PRESENT HEIGHT 2.43 FEET (0.74 M)

PAROS, ARCHAEOLOGICAL MUSEUM

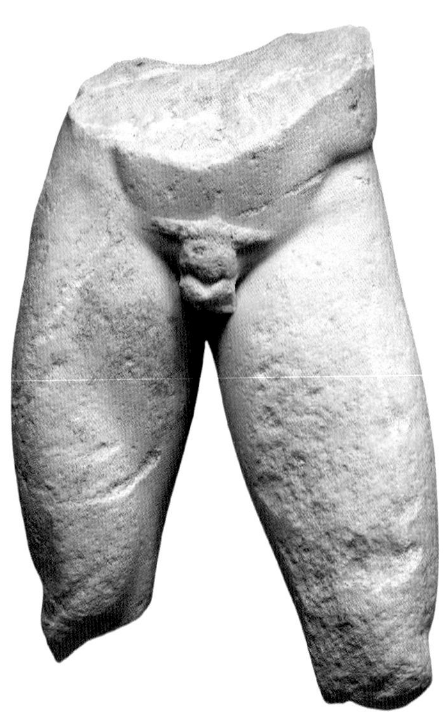

The surviving piece of this figure belongs to the lower body (from the pelvis to the knees) of a nude, young male, larger than life size, represented in rushing movement. Despite its fragmentary state, this is a particularly impressive work: The figure is rendered in three dimensions, in an ideal fusion of art and technique, and the modeling of the volumes and working of the marble are superb.

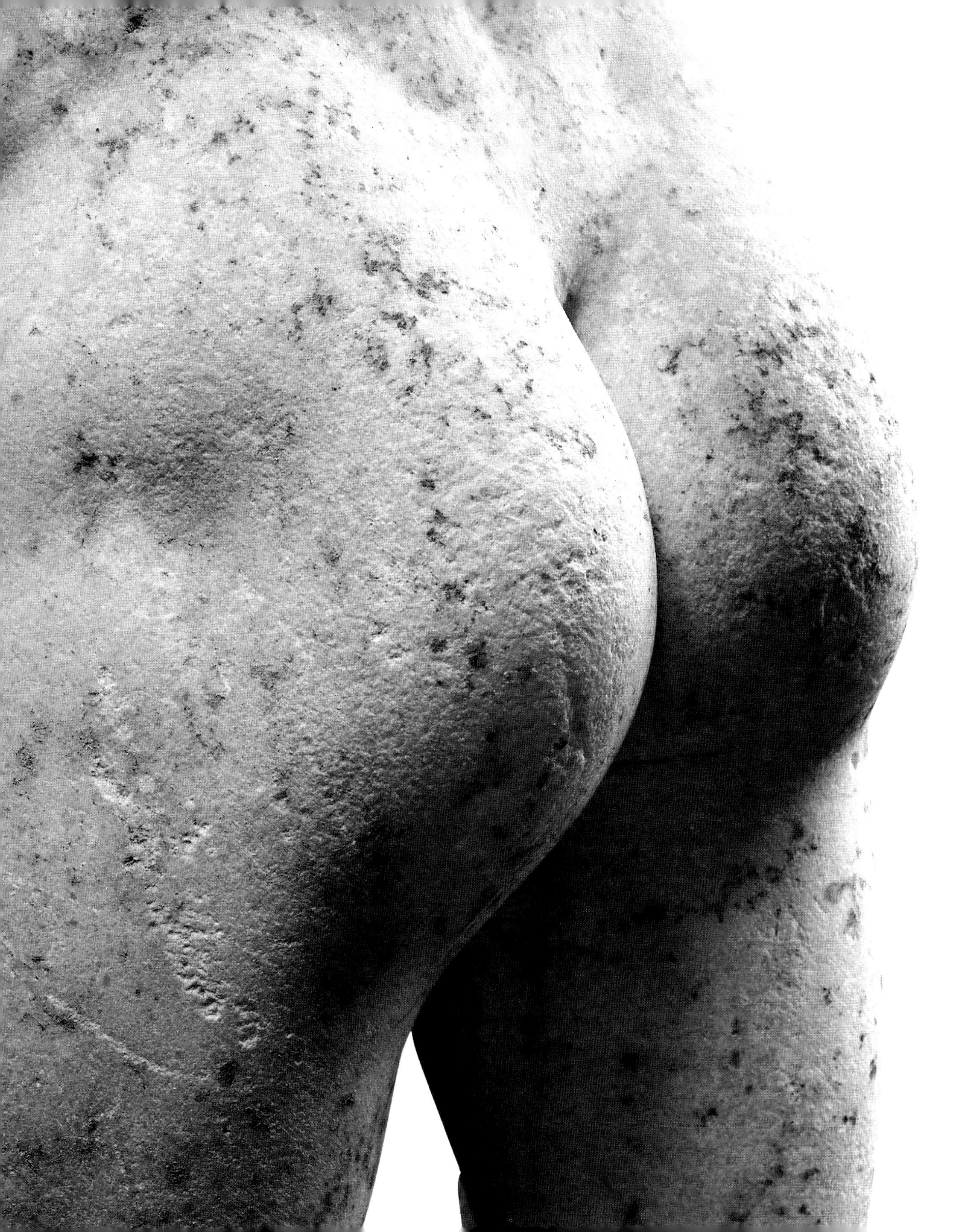

ZEUS AND GANYMEDE

OLYMPIA, CENTRAL ACROTERION OF A BUILDING IN THE SACRED ALTIS
489–470 BCE
TERRA-COTTA. HEIGHT INCLUDING BASE 3.58 FEET (1.09 M)
OLYMPIA, ARCHAEOLOGICAL MUSEUM

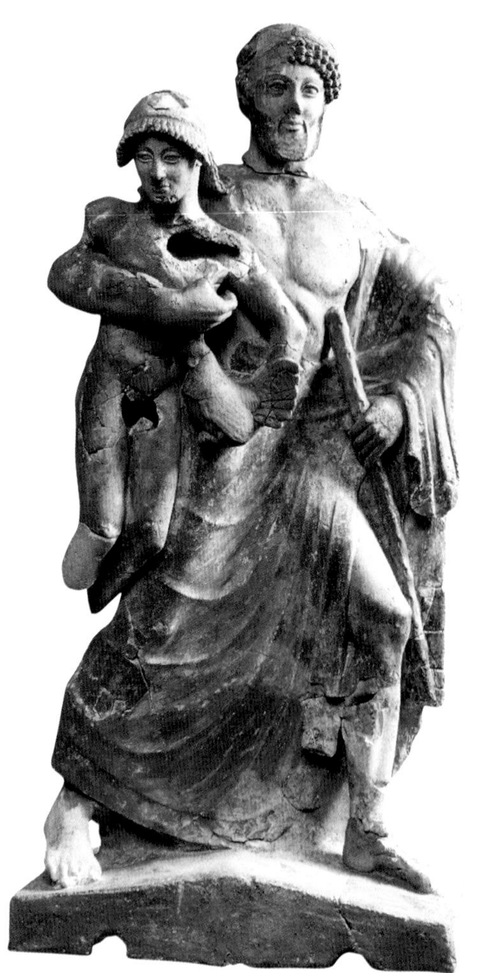

Zeus, who ordained the fortunes of gods and humans, had, like all members of the Olympian Pantheon, not only the hypostasis of a god but also mortal qualities, both good and bad (depending on the prevailing morality). Among his weaknesses was his love of beauty in any form, and since he was omnipotent he lost no opportunity to satisfy his appetites. We learn this from the ancient authors, whom the artists frequently followed faithfully (or vice versa).

This terra-cotta *acroterion* (ornamental finial from the pediment of a temple) bespeaks the coroplast's playfulness in rendering eloquently and explicitly one of

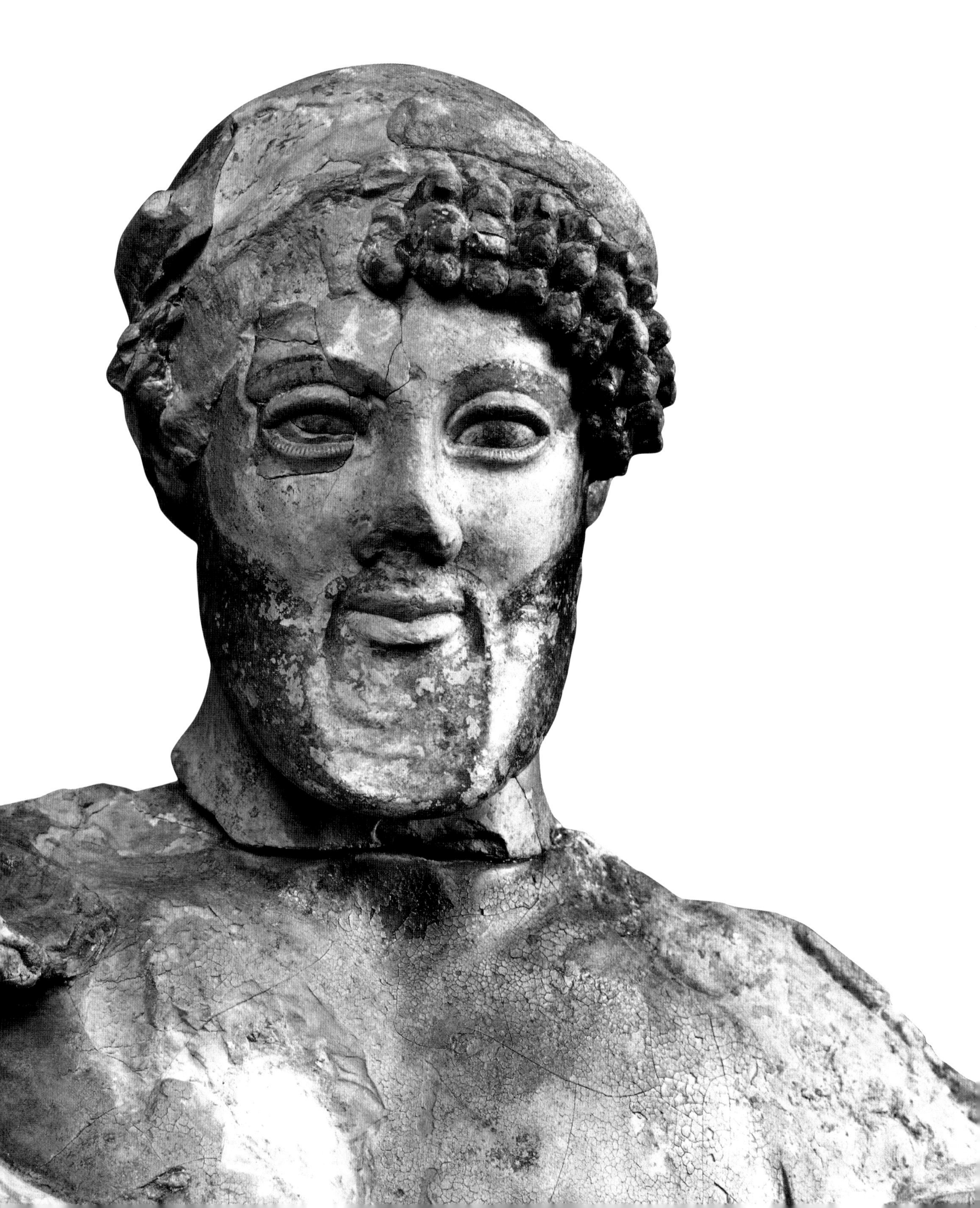

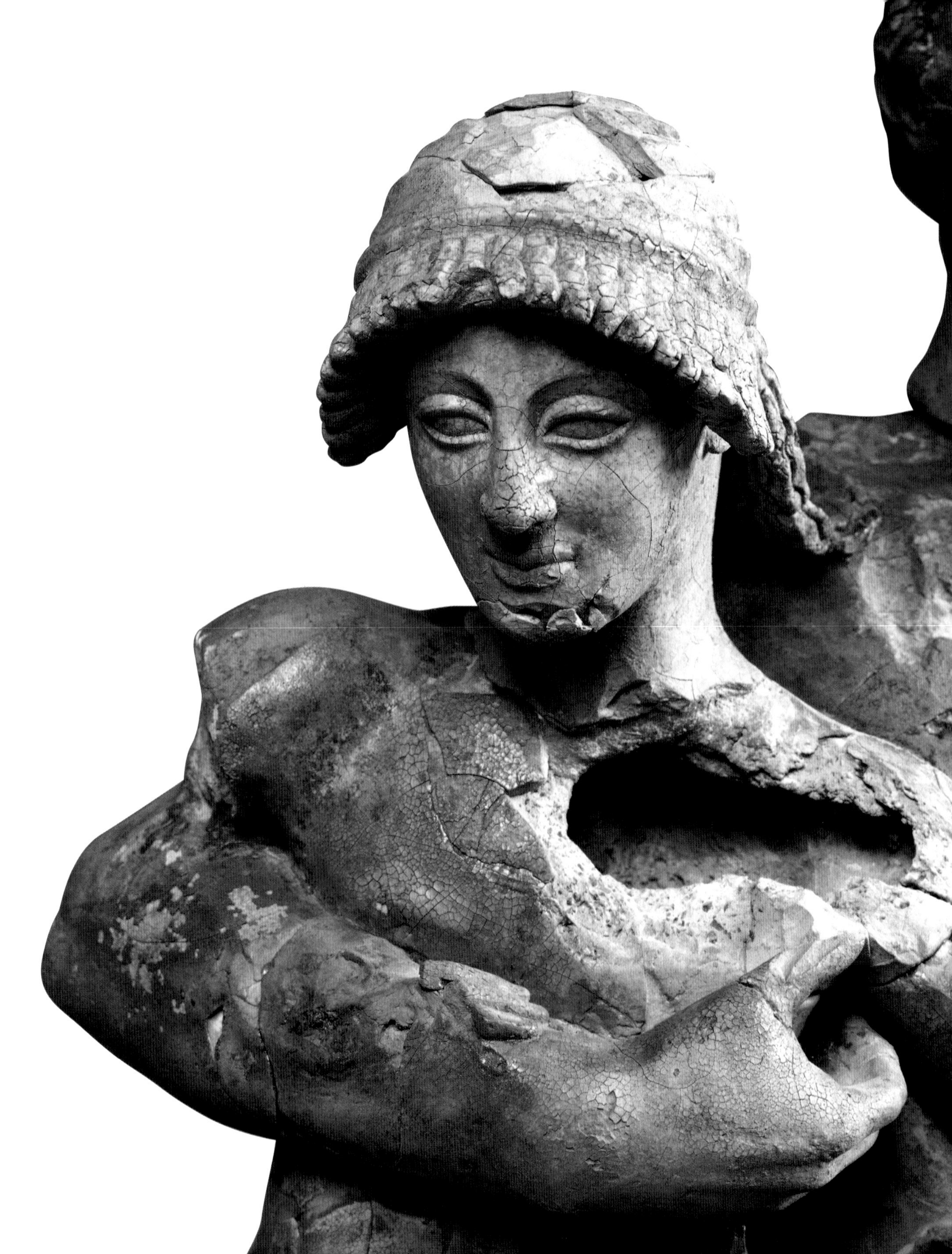

Zeus' amorous lapses, on a monument within his own sanctuary no less, referencing the very human side of the otherwise cloud-gathering father of the gods. Zeus, wearing only a himation that leaves his chest bare and opens downward at the sides, revealing his left leg from the thigh, is represented in wide stride, holding a staff in his left hand. In his right he has seized the young Ganymede, future wine-pourer of the gods. Grabbing him by the waist and clutching him tightly to his chest, Zeus heads toward Mount Olympos. Ganymede holds in his left hand a cockerel, an erotic symbol. The work preserves traces of the pigments with which it was embellished: blue on the hair and beard of Zeus, the hair of Ganymede, the pupils of the eyes, and a broad band around the hem of the god's himation; deep red on the rest of the garment; and a yellowish hue on the flesh. The artist has aimed to create a blissful expression on the god's face, to convey his mood at having acquired the precious "booty," while the youth appears without protest, resigned to his fate. The terra-cotta is from a Corinthian workshop.

NIKE

PAROS, PAROIKIA
475–450 BCE
PARIAN MARBLE. PRESENT HEIGHT 4.53 FEET (1.38 M)
PAROS, ARCHAEOLOGICAL MUSEUM

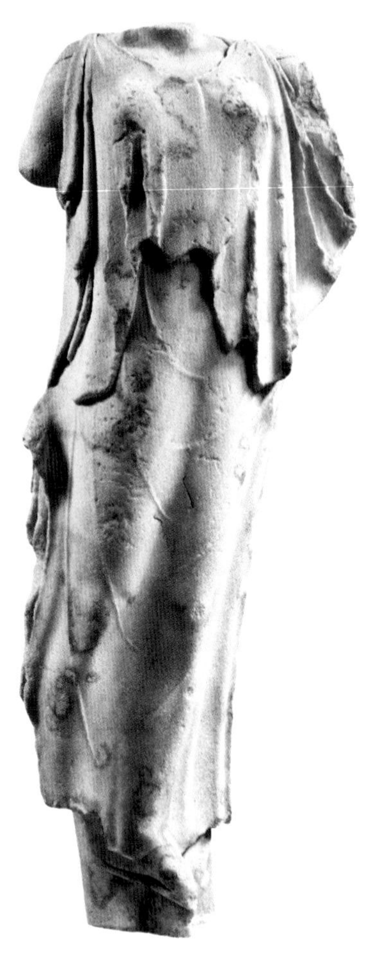

A pinnacle of Parian and ancient Greek art in general, this sculpture represents a young female figure wearing a peplos, open down the sides, and sandals on her feet. The head, the wings (the beginning of which are preserved on her back), and the arms are missing. The Nike's head was turned to the left and her left arm was raised. In her right hand she held the edge of the opening of the peplos in check. The right leg hovered, while the left barely touched the ground. The impetuous movement leaves the peplos to waft open at the side, revealing the supple outlines of the tender, youthful flesh. The flimsy textile clings to the front of the body, visible beneath and likely to shiver at the slightest touch.

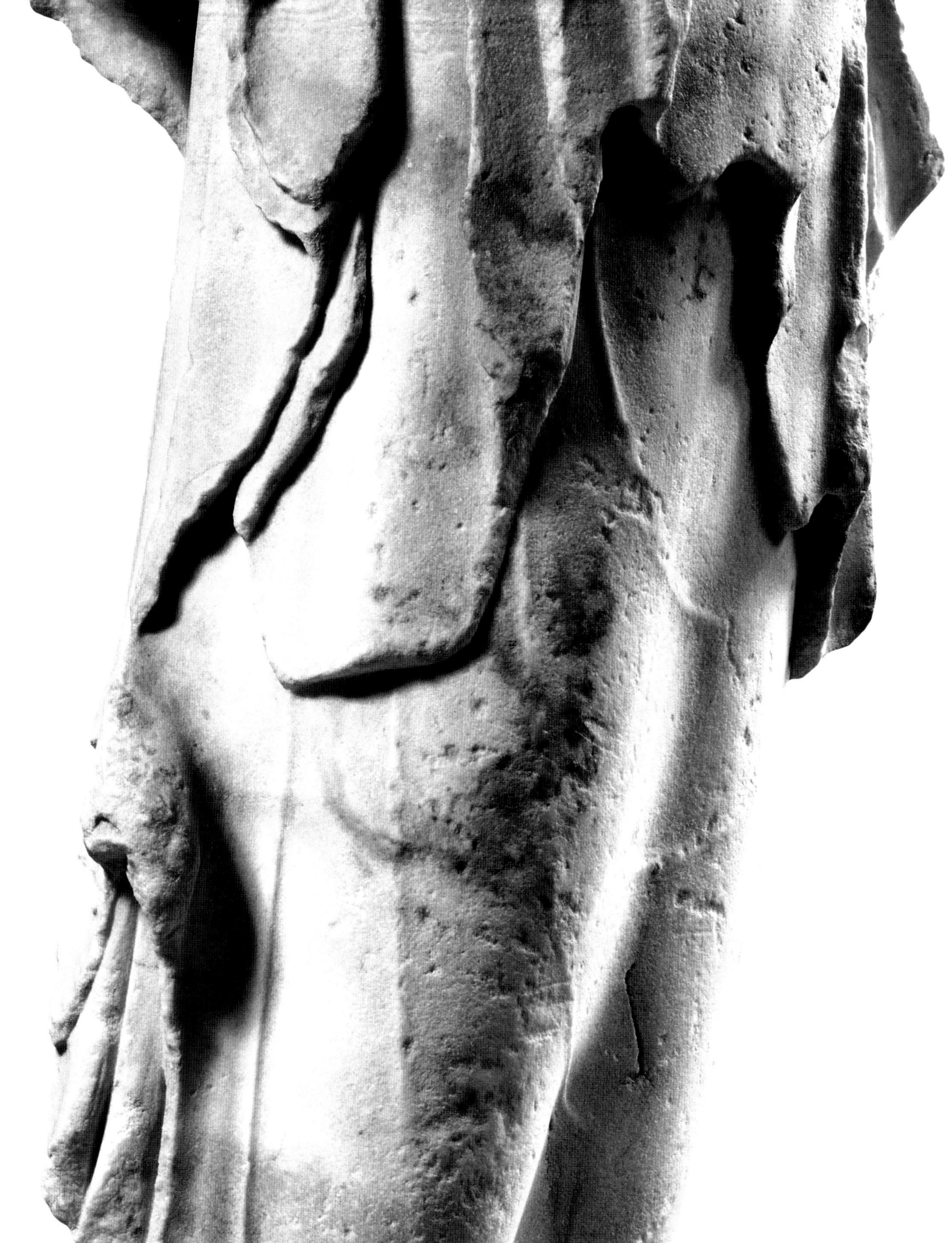

PART OF A RELIEF DISC

MELOS
460–450 BCE
ISLAND MARBLE. PRESENT HEIGHT 1.05 FEET (0.32 M)
ATHENS, NATIONAL ARCHAEOLOGICAL MUSEUM

This relief disc featured a female bust in profile, facing right. Her hair is drawn back into a *sakkos* (snood, kerchief) that falls heavily on the nape of the neck, forming a full curve. The hole in the temple was likely used for inserting appliquéd metal curls not covered by the snood.

Some suggest that a goddess is represented, perhaps Aphrodite. The delicacy of the profile and nobility of the figure suggest the work of a Parian artist.

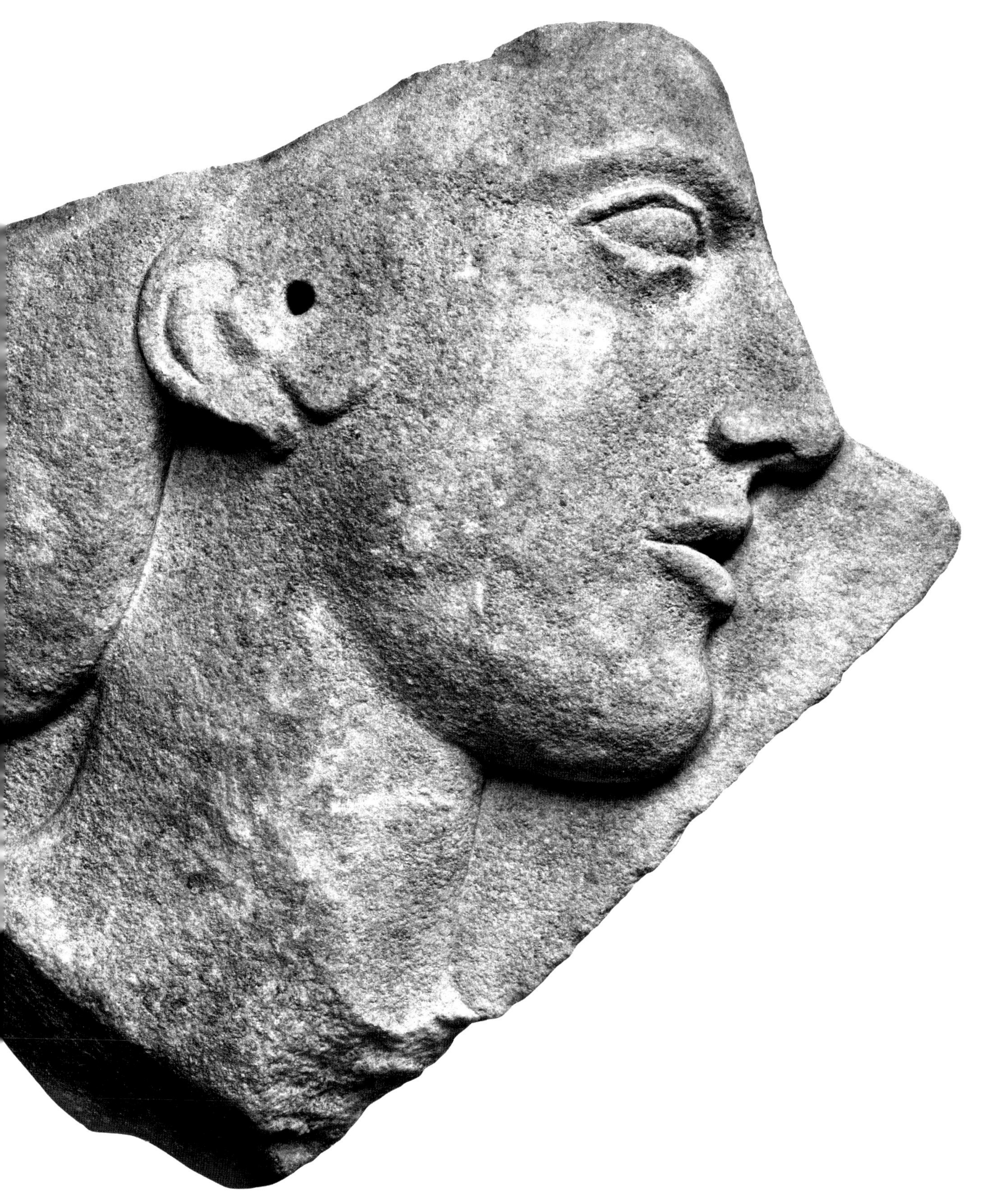

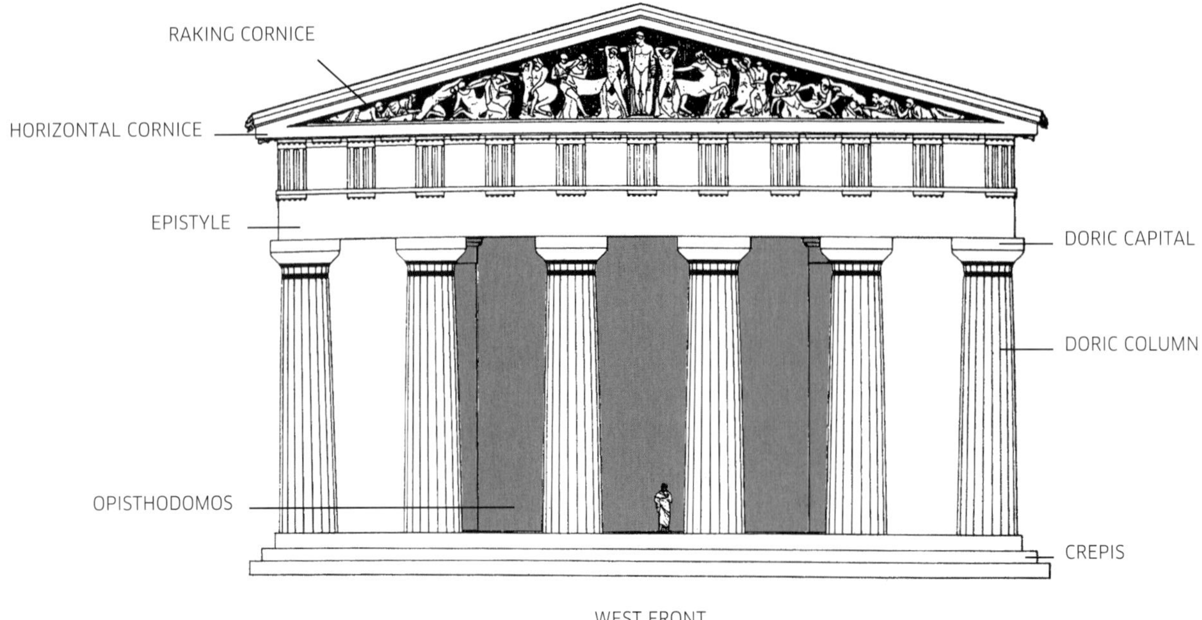

WEST FRONT

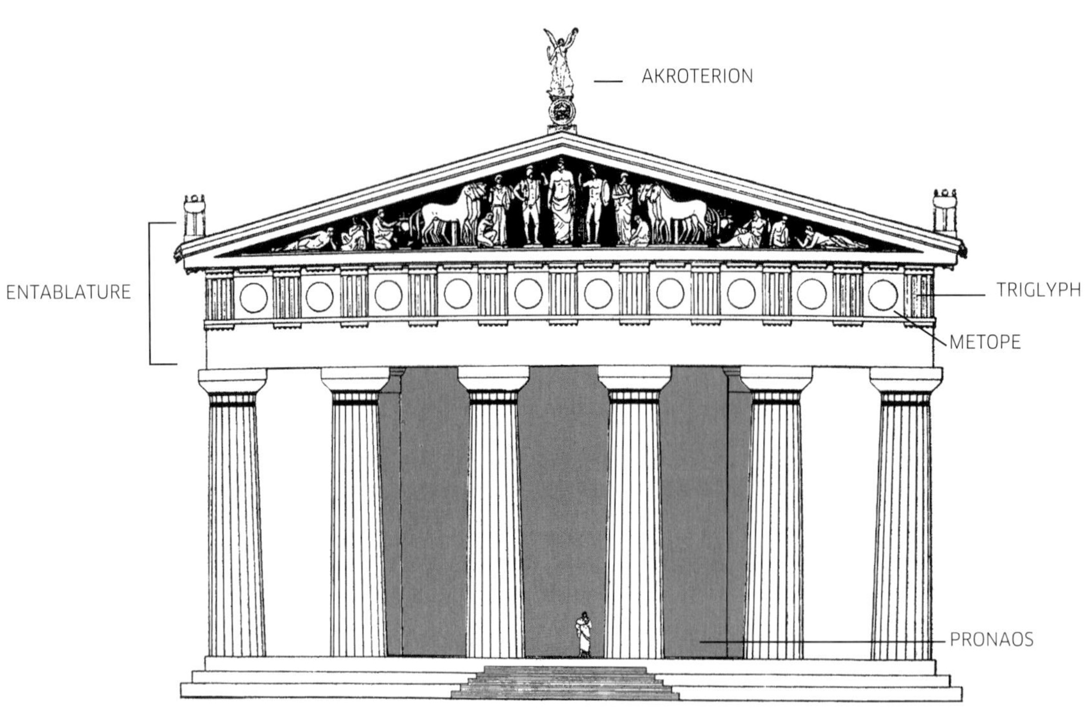

EAST FRONT

THE TEMPLE OF ZEUS AT OLYMPIA

470–460 BCE

The Temple of Zeus at Olympia was one of the largest Doric temples in Greece. The temple is peripteral, featuring six columns at the front and back, thirteen columns on the long sides, and ***prodomos*** (an open vastibule) and ***opisthodomos*** (the rear porch of a temple), on the ***cella*** (the inner chamber of a temple). Building must have commenced c. 470 BCE and was completed in 457 BCE. Its sculpted decoration, on the pediments and on the metopes of the prodomos and the opisthodomos, was executed between 465 and 457 BCE. The temple was constructed of local shelly limestone, but the sculptures on the pediments and metopes are in island (likely Parian) marble.

The subject on the east pediment, which crowned the front entrance, was taken from the mythological cycle of the founding of the sanctuary at Olympia. The subject on the west pediment drew on the corresponding Thessalian cycle, with the centaurs and Theseus. The decoration on the metopes was limited to the Labors of Herakles, the demigod son of the divine couple Zeus and Hera and the paramount Doric hero. The sculptures of the Temple of Zeus are significant not only as works of art but also because they number among the few original sculptures of this period to have survived. The pedimental figures, which are slightly larger than life-size and are in the round, were affixed to the ***tympanum*** (the recessed space enclosed by the cornices of a pediment) of the pediment by metal clamps. The two pedimental compositions were developed in the triangular frame, 10.83 feet (3.30 m) high at the apex and 86.61 feet (26.40 m) long at the base.

Scholars have not reached consensus about the workshop to which the temple's creators belonged; some suggest a Peloponnesian (Argeian) workshop, others a Parian workshop, and still others some combination of the two. Whatever the case, a team of artists must have

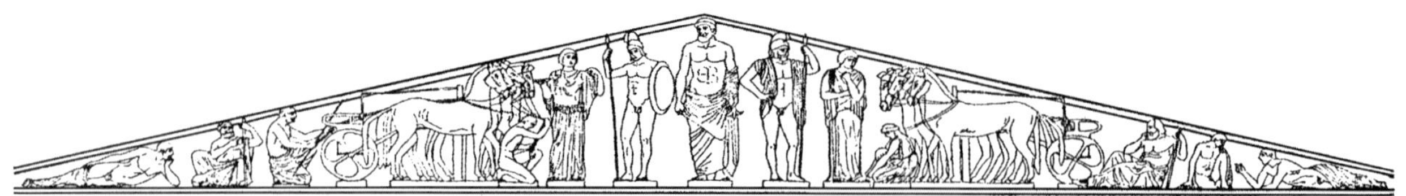

EAST PEDIMENT

collaborated for at least ten years on such an ambitious project. They had to convey through the sculpted decoration a single message worthy of a temple dedicated to Olympian Zeus: It should convey in the god's principal place of worship the bases for "fair play," that is, noble athletic competition, far from any rivalries and conflicts.

Represented on the east pediment is the mythological chariot race that took place between two kings who claimed their right to the sovereignty of the same region: the island (*nesos*) of Pelops, the subsequent Peloponnese. The king of neighboring Pisa, Oenomaos, wanting to marry off his daughter Hippodameia, announced that he would give her hand to whomever defeated him in a chariot race. Among the suitors were Pelops, son of King Tantalos, from far-off Phrygia. In the race that followed, Pelops triumphed, but by trickery. He had bribed Myrtilos, Oenomaos' charioteer, to replace the metal wedges of his master's chariot with wax ones. To prevent his bribery from coming to light, Pelops then slew Myrtilos, who with his dying breath cursed him and his descendants. These were none other than the Atreids, the tragic family of Agamemnon.

The subject of the west pediment is the Centauromachy, the battle between the Lapiths and the centaurs, which took place in Thessaly, their birthplace and home. At the marriage of Pirithous, the Lapith king and friend of the Athenian hero Theseus, who was a guest at the celebrations, the centaurs, also among the guests, became drunk and attacked the Lapith women and children. Mayhem ensued, and the Lapiths defeated the centaurs, with the help of Theseus.

The representation on the east pediment, the cen-

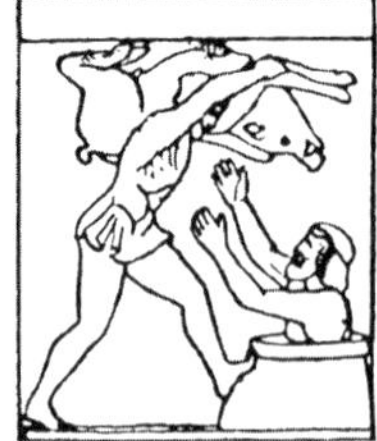 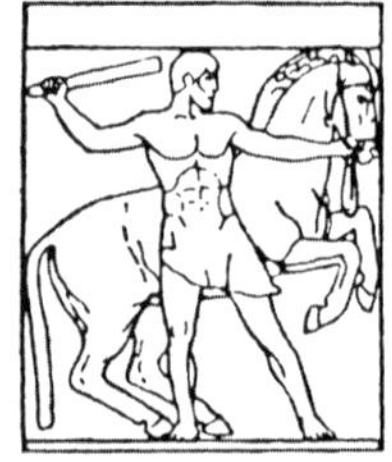 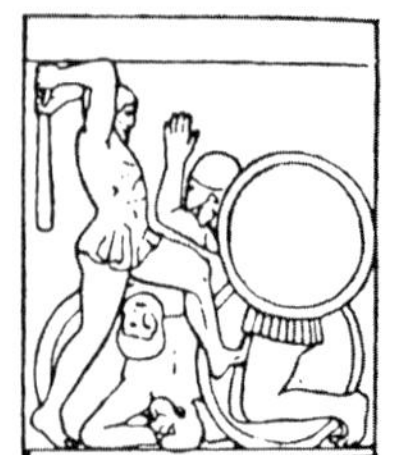 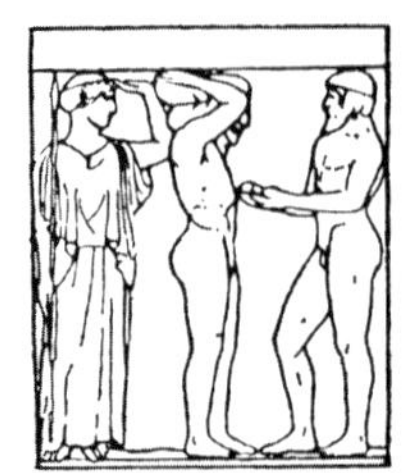 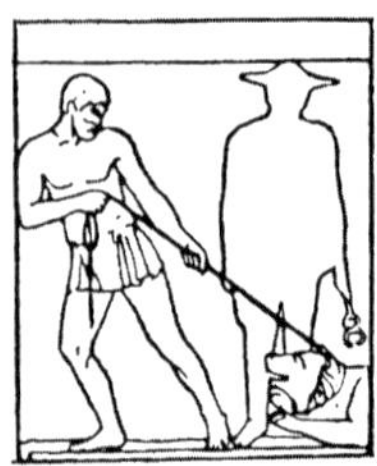 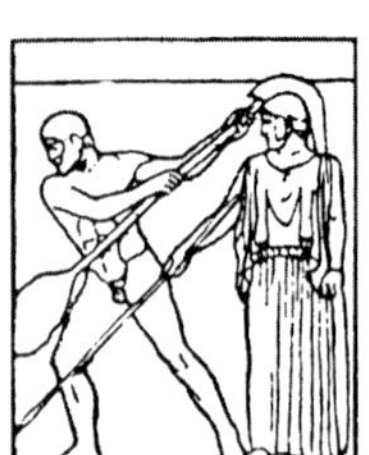

METOPES OF EAST FRONT

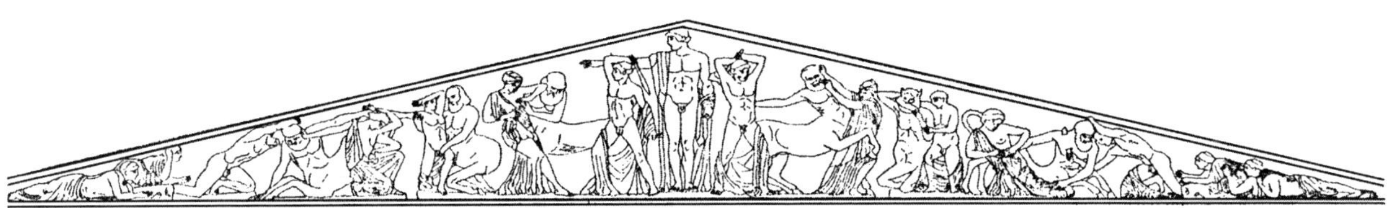

WEST PEDIMENT

tral axis of which includes the imposing figure of Zeus, adjudicator of the race, features two similar compositions. On either side of Zeus is a couple—Oenomaos and Sterope on his right, Pelops and Hippodameia on his left—followed by a half-kneeling young female figure, a nursemaid or charioteer, the four-horse chariot, a seated figure, and, in the cuneus of the pediment, a recumbent figure: on the viewer's left the personification of the Alpheios, and on the right, the Kladeos, the two rivers of the region.

In the middle of the west pediment stands Apollo. Represented on either side of him are violent clashes between figures wrestling in groups of two or three. In each cuneus of the pediment are two reclining Lapith women. The composition of the west pediment consists of figures in extreme movement, whereas that of the east pediment is comparatively calm. Both pediments are believed to symbolize two spectacular and popular contests: on the east the chariot race, and on the west wrestling.

The metopes on the Temple of Zeus comprise twelve rectangular plaques, 5.25 feet (1.60 m) high by about 4.92 feet (1.50 m) wide, set between the triglyphs and decorating the cornice of the pronaos and the opisthodomos with relief representations of the Twelve Labors of Herakles, six on each side. Herakles, credited by some with the founding of the Olympic Games, performed the Labors on the order of Eurystheus, King of Mycenae, Tiryns, and Argos, as ordained by a Delphic oracle, to expiate his murder of his wife and children in a fit of madness induced by Hera.

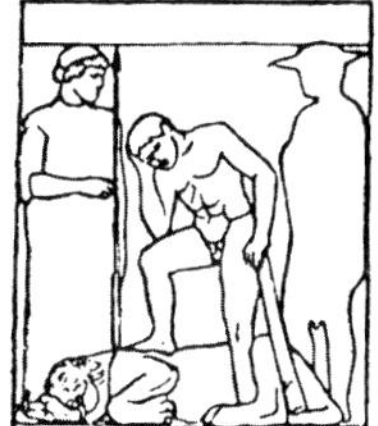
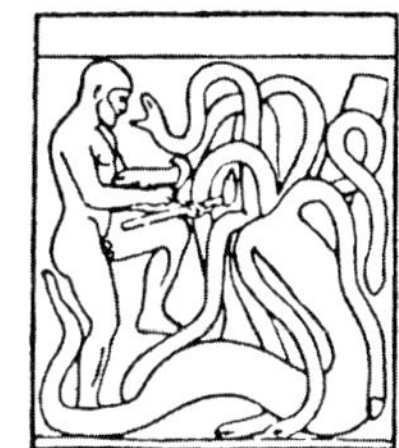
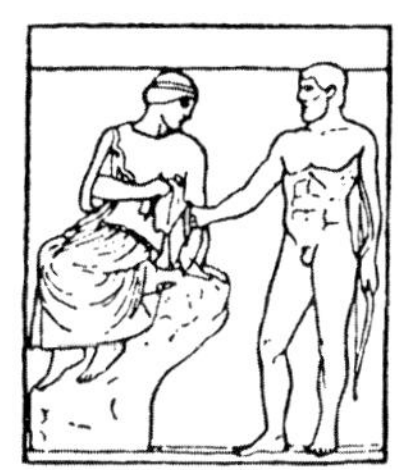
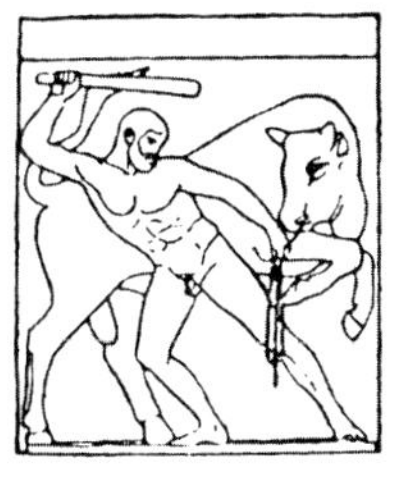
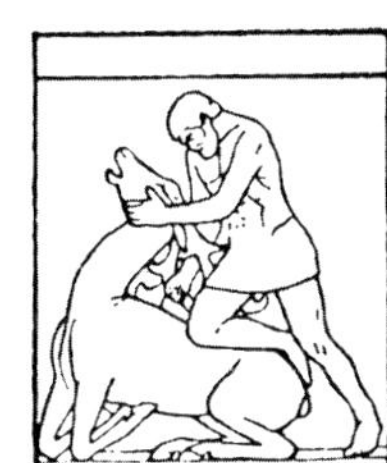
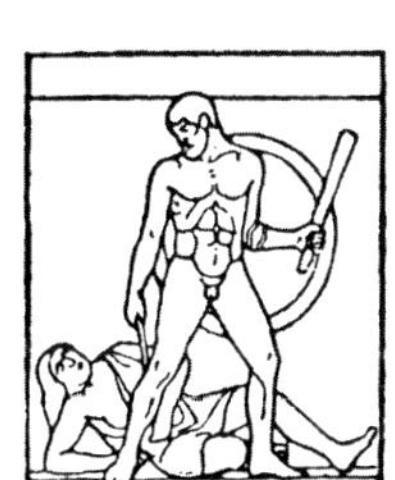

METOPES OF WEST FRONT

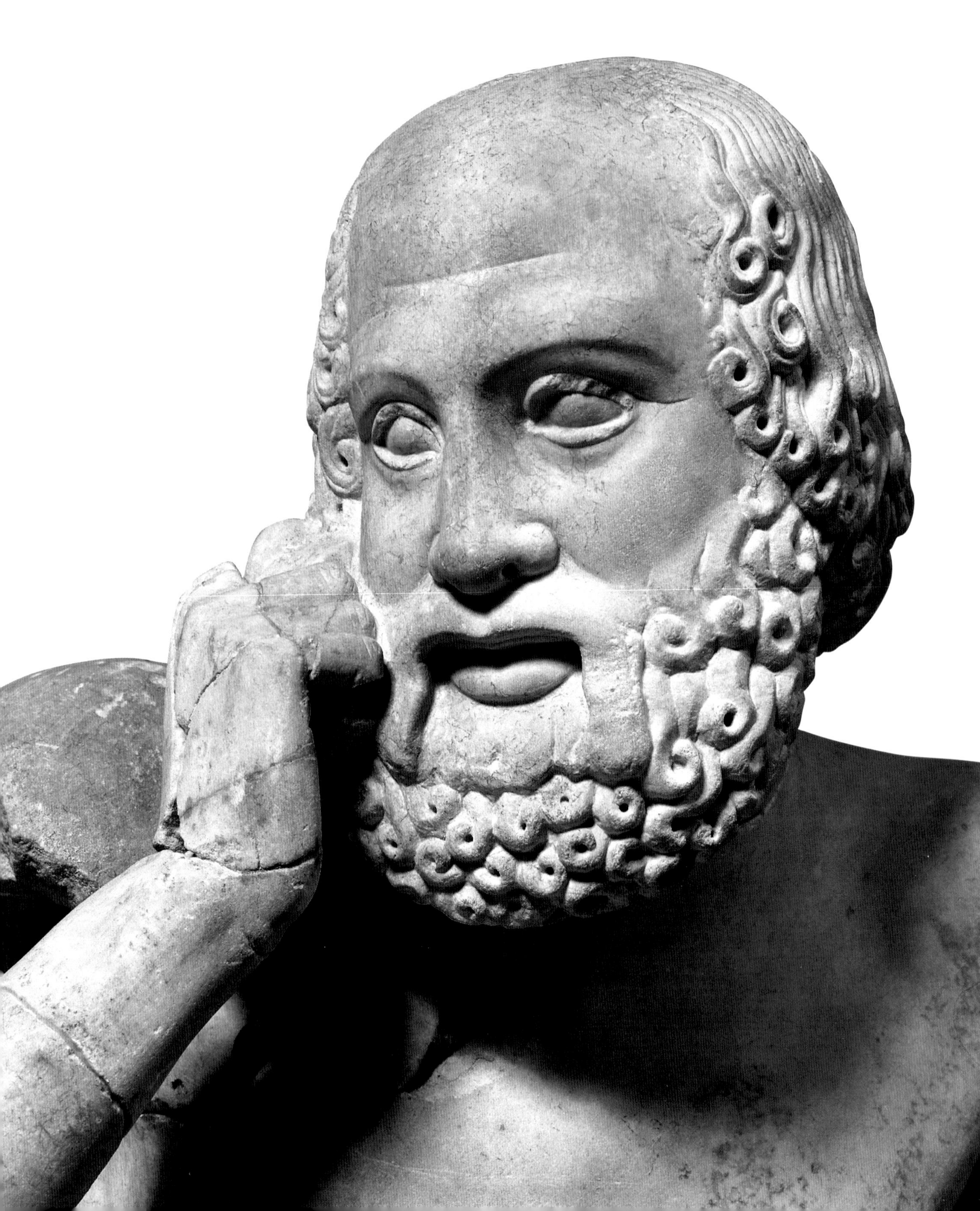

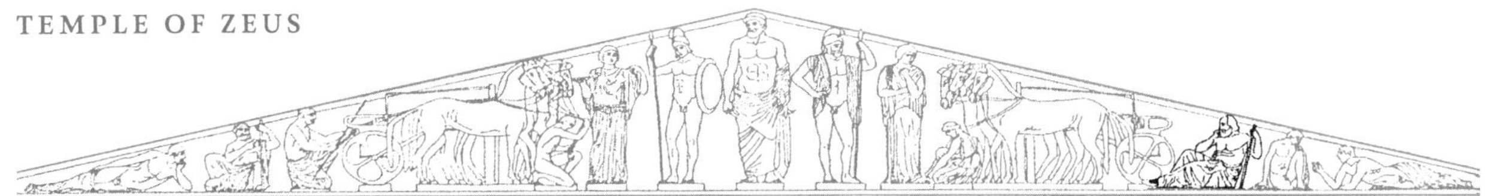

OLD MAN, SEER

OLYMPIA, TEMPLE OF ZEUS, EAST PEDIMENT
465–457 BCE
PARIAN MARBLE. HEIGHT 4.53 FEET (1.38 M)
OLYMPIA, ARCHAEOLOGICAL MUSEUM

A semireclining elderly male figure, turned three-quarters toward the center, brings his bent right arm to his face, touching his cheek in a gesture of fear and perhaps desperation. With his left hand he props himself on a stave. A himation covers the lower part of his body. This figure is in all probability Oenomaos' seer, one of the most expressive figures in the entire pedimental composition.

The artist has linked the figure's psychological state with the aspect of an old man, whose heavy body is in need of support. The seer is melancholic upon foreseeing the sad fate of Oenomaos.

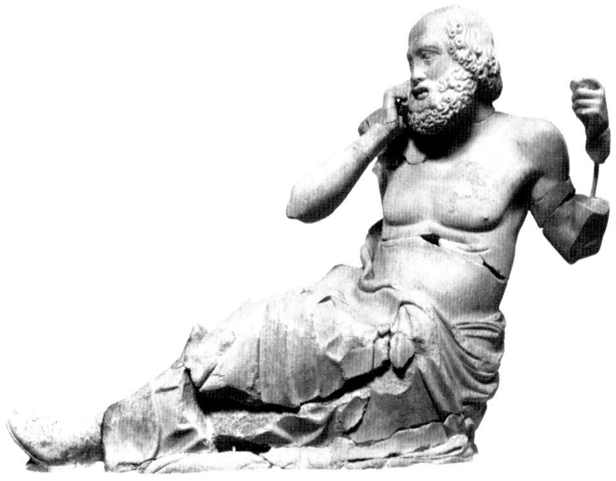

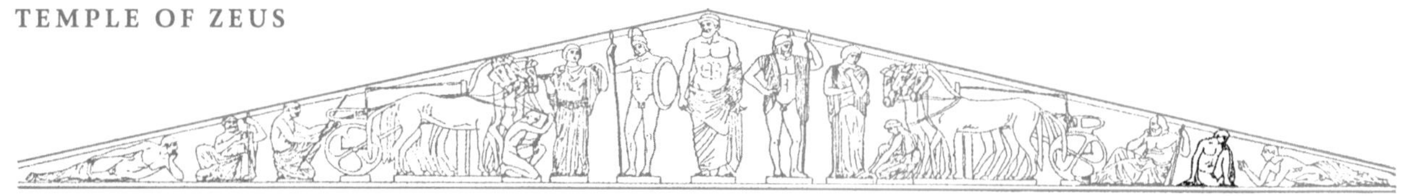

SITTING YOUTH

OLYMPIA, TEMPLE OF ZEUS, EAST PEDIMENT
465–457 BCE
PARIAN MARBLE. PRESENT HEIGHT 3.61 FEET (1.10 M)
OLYMPIA, ARCHAEOLOGICAL MUSEUM

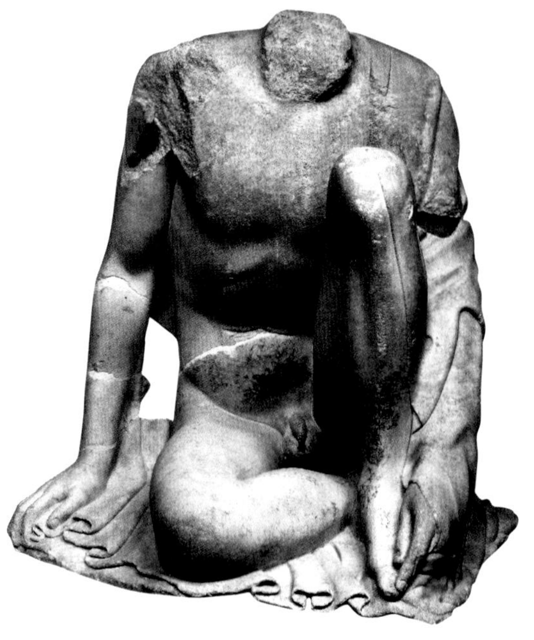

This headless statue depicts a young man in a frontal pose sitting on his right hip and leaning on his right hand. He sits on an overfolded, multipleated himation, part of which falls from his left shoulder and covers his left hand, with which he touches the toes of his left foot. His left calf is upright and the leg is bent at the knee.

This composition expresses the youthful vigor of the figure, which stands in marked contrast to the limp old seer semireclining beside him and emphasizes the insouciance of youth compared to the anxiety and fears of old age.

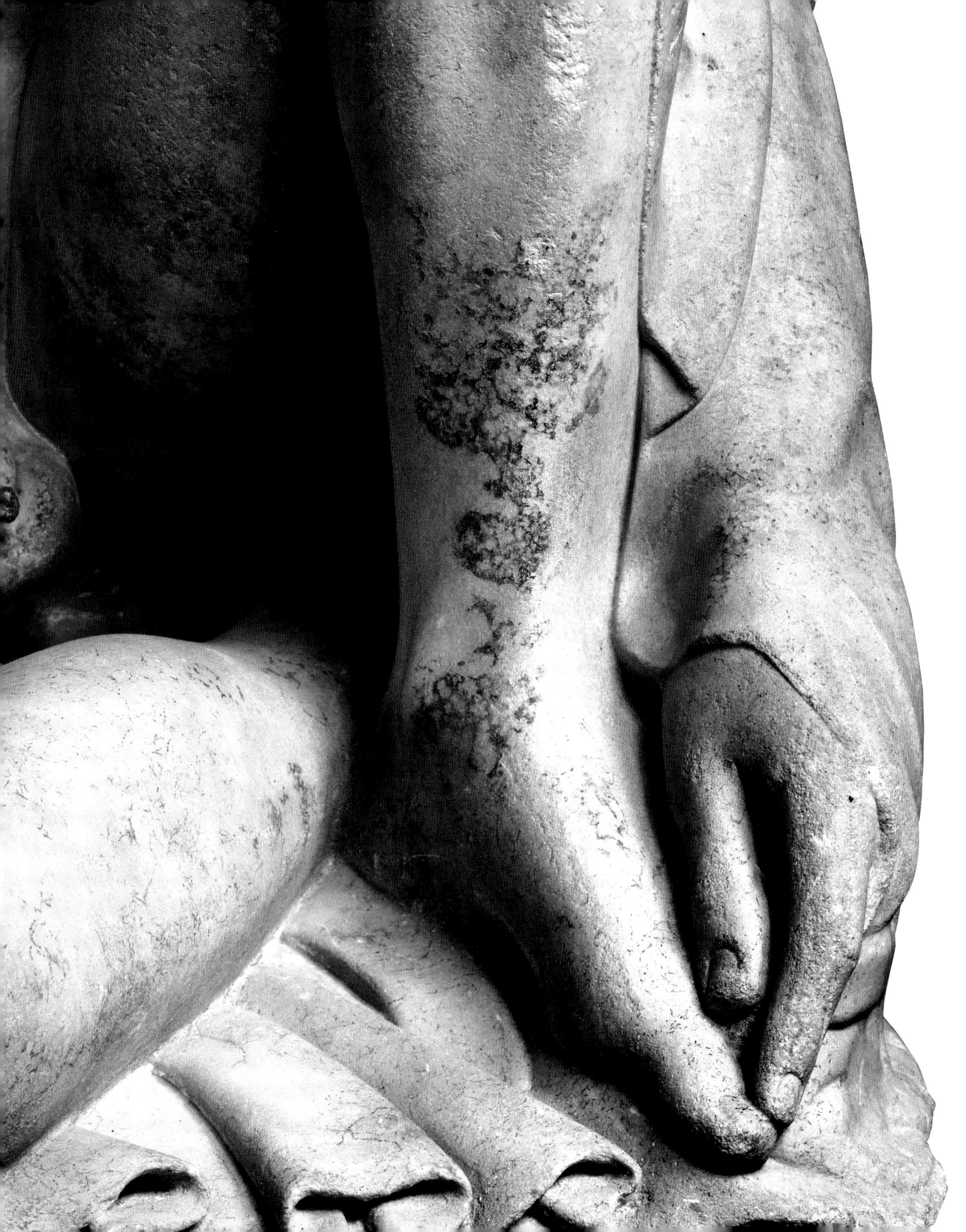

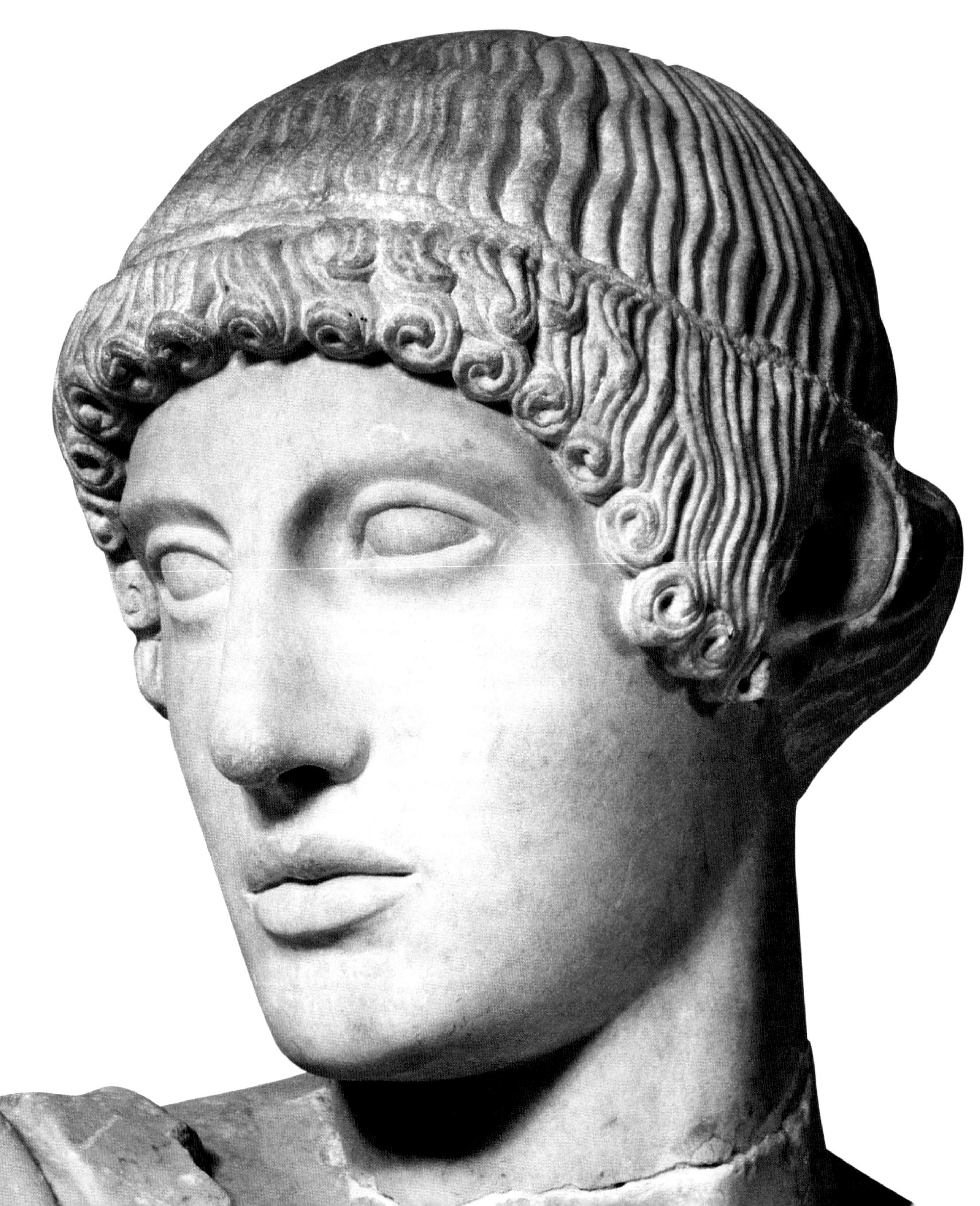

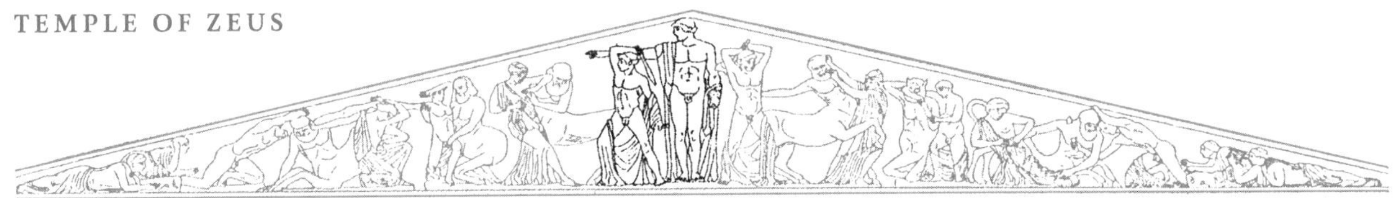

APOLLO

OLYMPIA, TEMPLE OF ZEUS, WEST PEDIMENT
C. 460 BCE
PARIAN MARBLE. PRESENT HEIGHT 9.02 FEET (2.75 M; ORIGINAL HEIGHT 10.17 FEET [3.10 M])
OLYMPIA, ARCHAEOLOGICAL MUSEUM

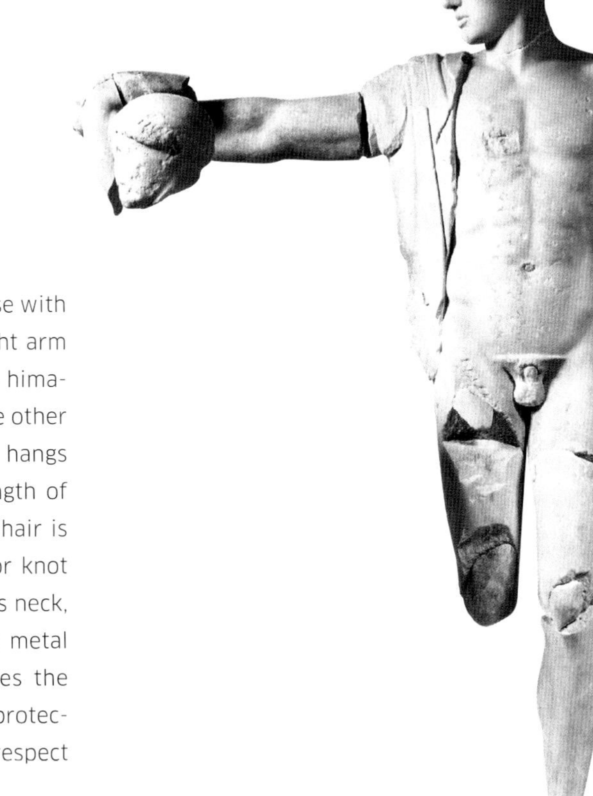

Apollo is represented here in a frontal pose with his head turned to the right and his right arm outstretched. He is naked save for the himation that falls vertically from his right shoulder; the other end of the garment covers his left forearm and hangs to the feet. His left arm is lowered down the length of his body and in his left hand he held a bow. The hair is drawn back and looped up in a *krobylos* (a roll or knot of hair behind the head) set low on the nape of his neck, while above the forehead it is held in place by a metal fillet. The austere, commanding figure dominates the pedimental composition, as is appropriate to the protector of humans whose presence imposes order and respect for the laws.

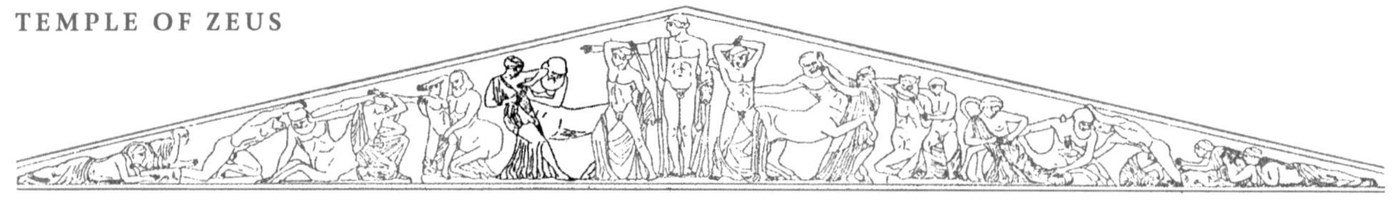

EURYTION AND DEIDAMEIA

OLYMPIA, TEMPLE OF ZEUS, WEST PEDIMENT
465–457 BCE
PARIAN MARBLE. HEIGHT 7.71 FEET (2.35 M)
OLYMPIA, ARCHAEOLOGICAL MUSEUM

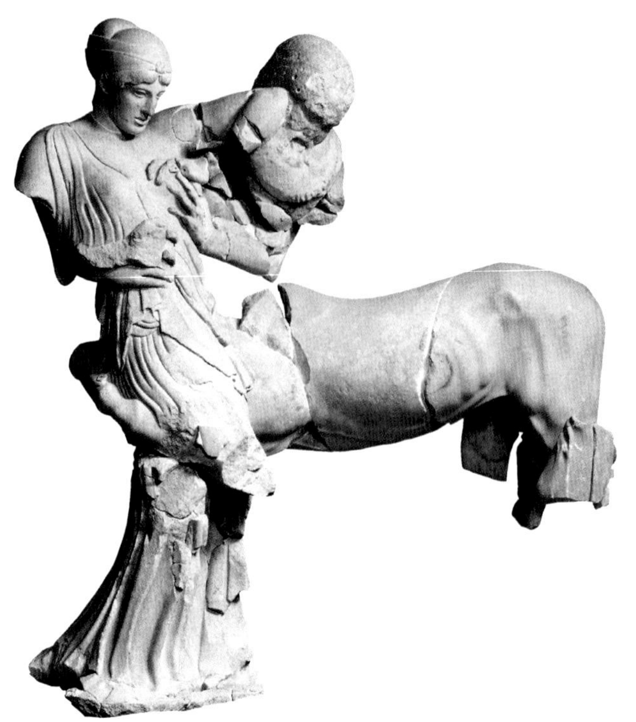

This group of three figures stands to Apollo's right: Peirithous, in a corresponding pose to that of Theseus, readies to strike the centaur Eurytion (according to Pausanias' description), who has grabbed by the breast the hero's betrothed, Deidameia. Deidameia struggles to free herself and, like the other Lapith women, wears a peplos. Her hair is drawn back into a *kekryphalos* (a female headdress consisting of a net, or a light cloth or kerchief) tied in a knot above the part in the middle of her forehead. The violence of the scene is conveyed not only by the rushing movements of both figures but also by the agitated folds of the female's garment. Each figure's facial expression captures the success of his or her effort.

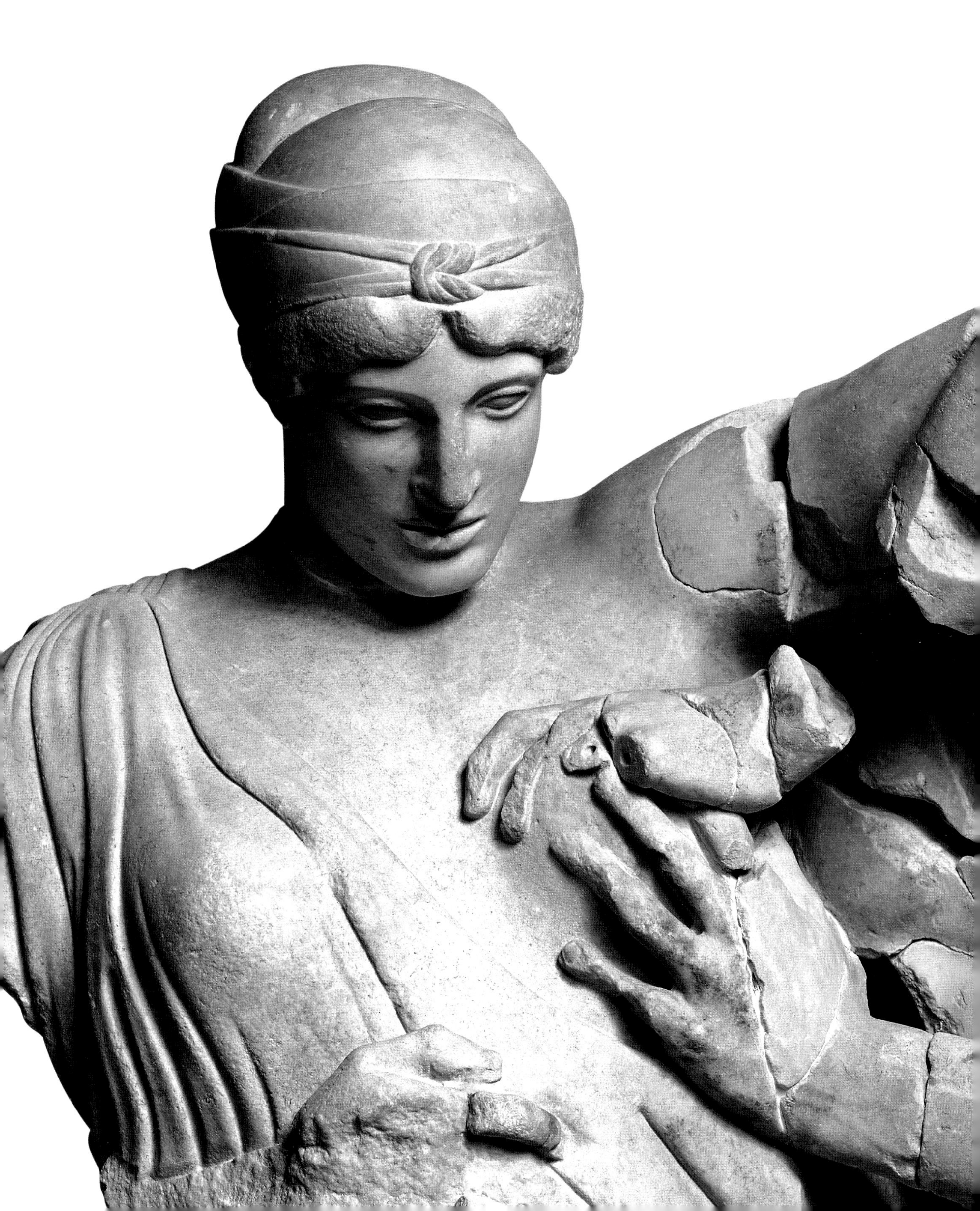

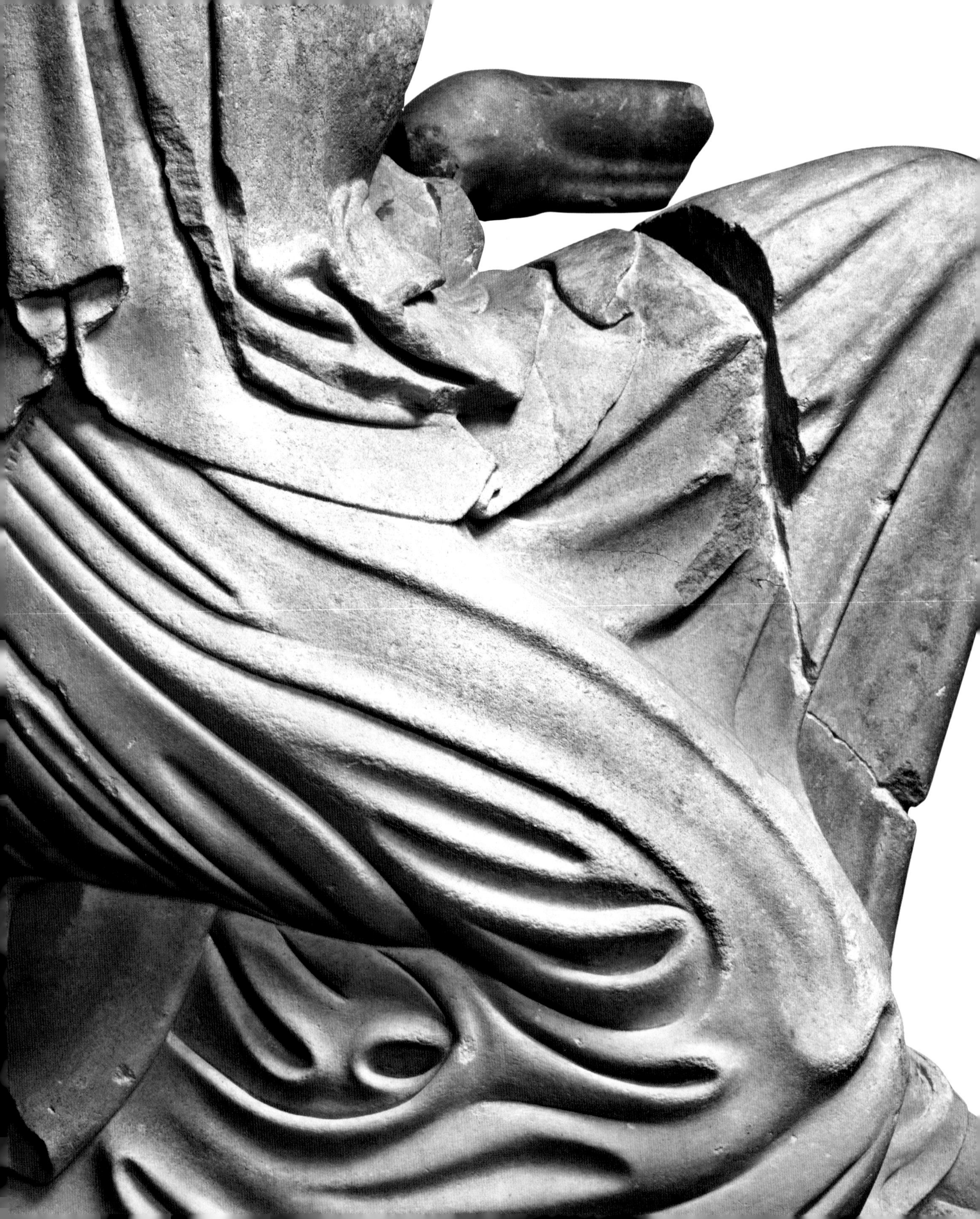

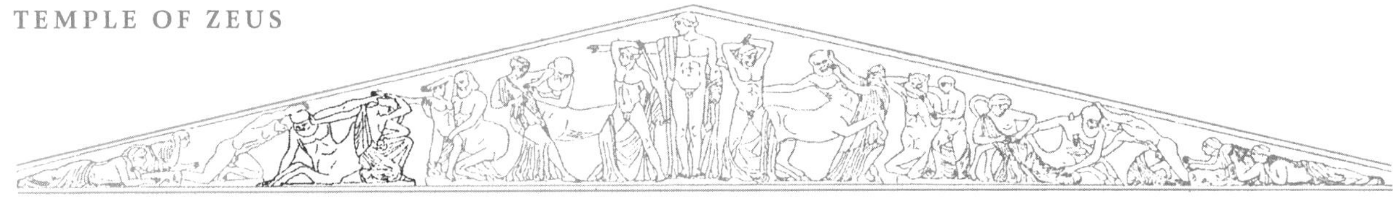

CENTAUR AND LAPITH WOMAN

OLYMPIA, TEMPLE OF ZEUS, WEST PEDIMENT
465–457 BCE
PARIAN MARBLE. HEIGHT 5.15 FEET (1.57 M)
OLYMPIA, ARCHAEOLOGICAL MUSEUM

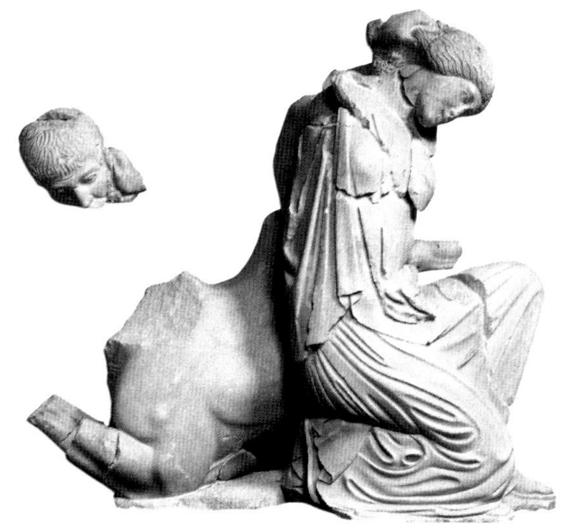

These two figures belong to a three-figure group situated near the left edge of the pediment. The Lapith woman, in her effort to escape, sinks halfway to her knees under the pressure of the centaur's outstretched left hand. Her attacker, turned in the opposite direction, has grabbed her by the hair and holds on to her, even as he collapses under the blow dealt by the Lapith man attacking from his right. The naturalistic rendering of the multiple folds of the woman's garment, which tumble down the outside of the kneeling leg under the weight of the body, heightens the dynamism of the composition.

Powerful too is the rendering of the centaur's head; its short, ruffled hair, which recalls boar's tusks, emphasizes the figure's bestial violence, as do the deep creases on the nostrils, flaring from the effort, and the wrinkles on the low forehead. Next to this monstrous head is the chubby hand of the Lapith woman, who tries to ward him off by digging her fingers into the left side of his face.

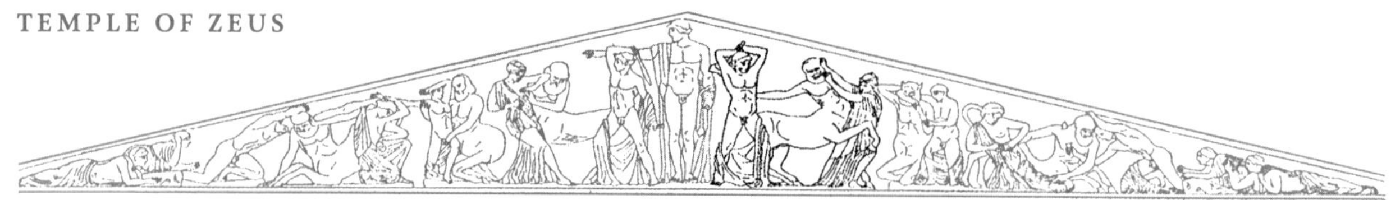

THESEUS AND CENTAUR

OLYMPIA, TEMPLE OF ZEUS, WEST PEDIMENT
465–457 BCE
PARIAN MARBLE. ORIGINAL HEIGHT 8.53 FEET (2.60 M)
OLYMPIA, ARCHAEOLOGICAL MUSEUM

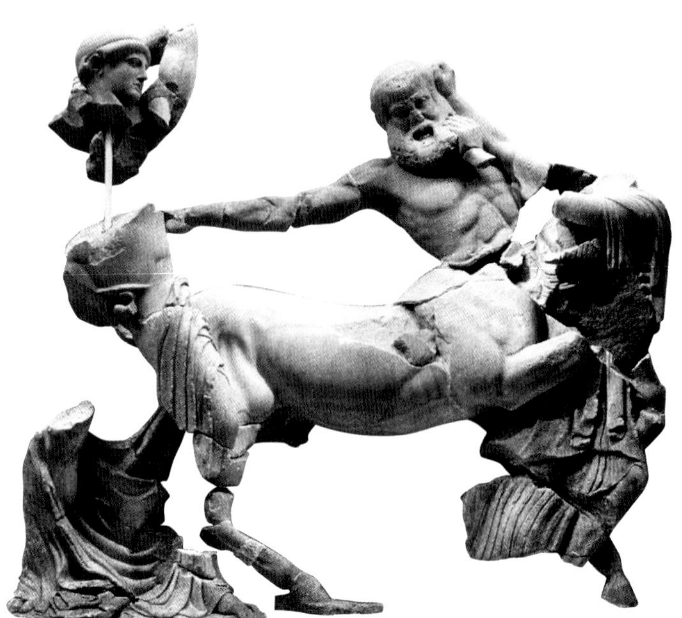

This figure of Theseus is preserved in fragments; illustrated opposite is the fragment from the neck upward. The Athenian hero is portrayed in profile, to Apollo's left, with his arms (only the left is preserved) raised above his head, poised to strike with an axe a centaur who has seized a Lapith woman between its equine legs. The lower part of the hero's body is covered by a heavy, multipleated himation. The nobility of the youthful figure contrasts with the violence of the scene and the brutish expression of the centaur.

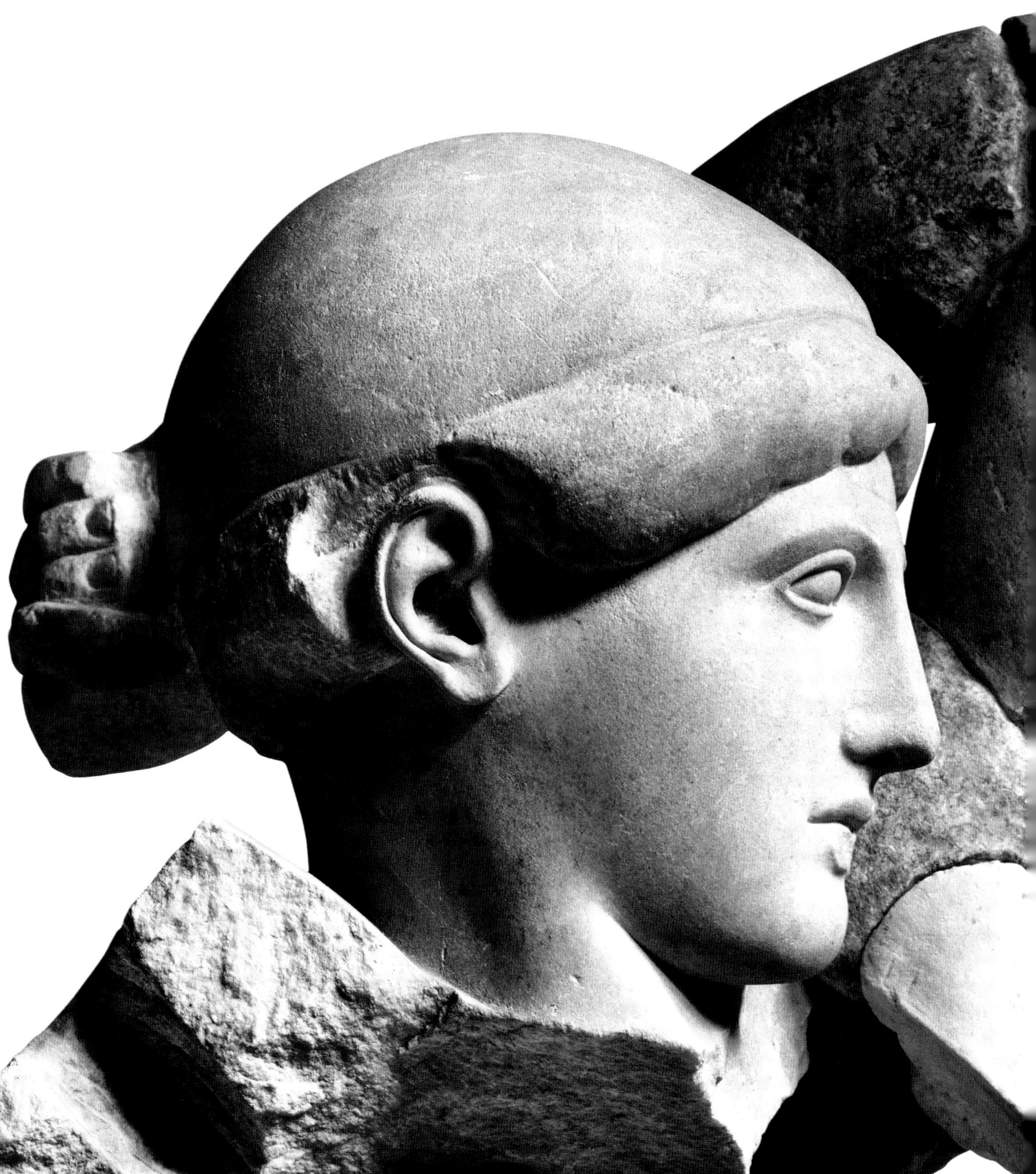

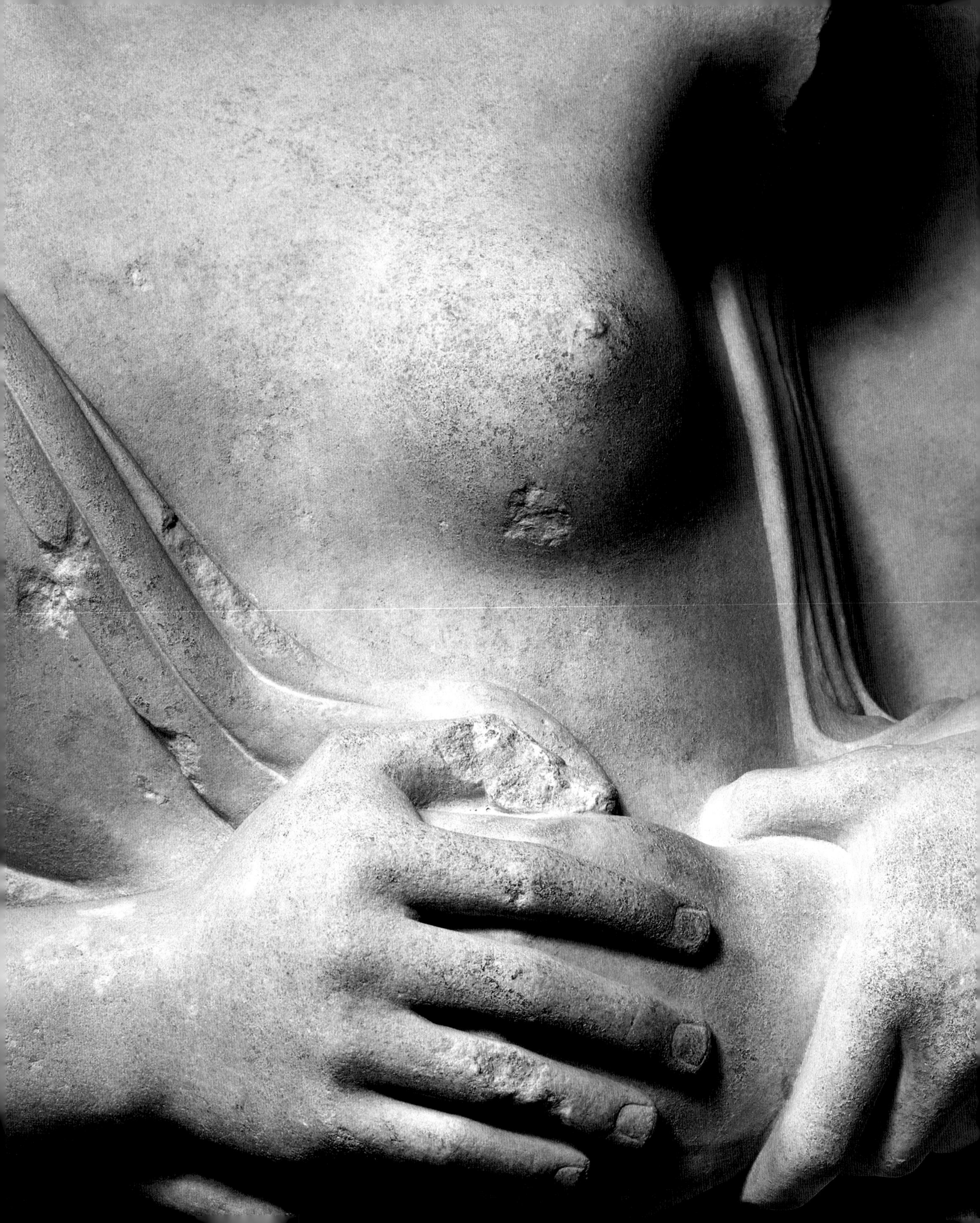

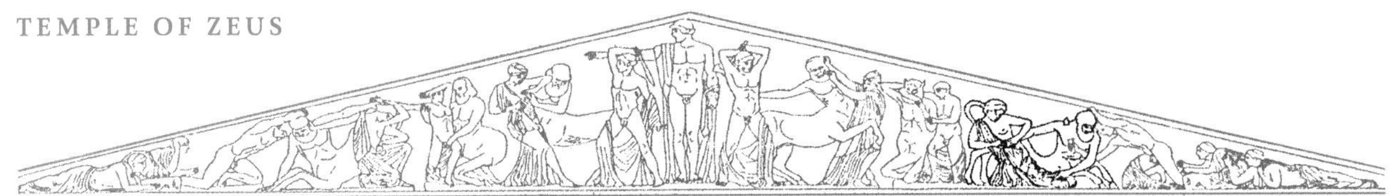

CENTAUR AND LAPITH WOMAN

OLYMPIA, TEMPLE OF ZEUS, WEST PEDIMENT
465–457 BCE
PARIAN MARBLE. HEIGHT 5.15 FEET (1.57 M)
OLYMPIA, ARCHAEOLOGICAL MUSEUM

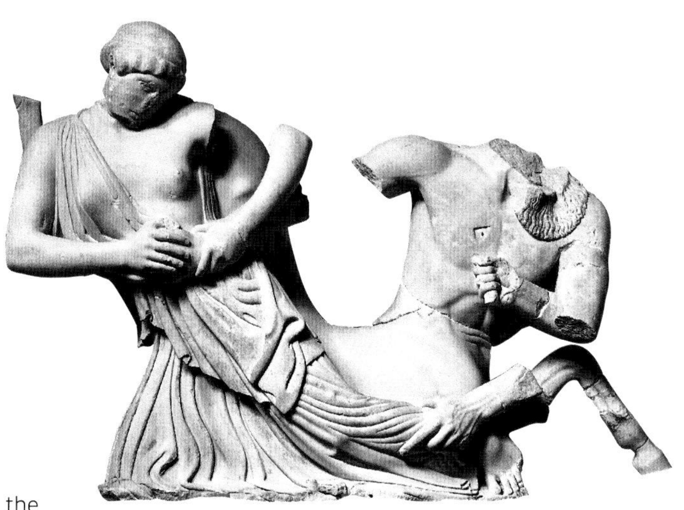

In this group of three figures, a centaur runs to the right, his human torso turned backward in three-quarter pose to seize by the waist and left leg a Lapith woman who flees in the opposite direction. A Lapith man, half-kneeling in front of the centaur, leans toward the creature and delivers a blow to its chest with his sword. The Lapith woman wears a peplos pinned over her shoulders, but in the violent attack by the centaur the left side has been torn, exposing her bare breast. In this highly realistic creation, the veins of the centaur's arms appear dilated by the strenuous effort, and the pronounced muscles of the Lapith woman's leg, the soft flesh of her bosom, and her tender hands contrast with the brawny male hand she tries to pry off of her waist.

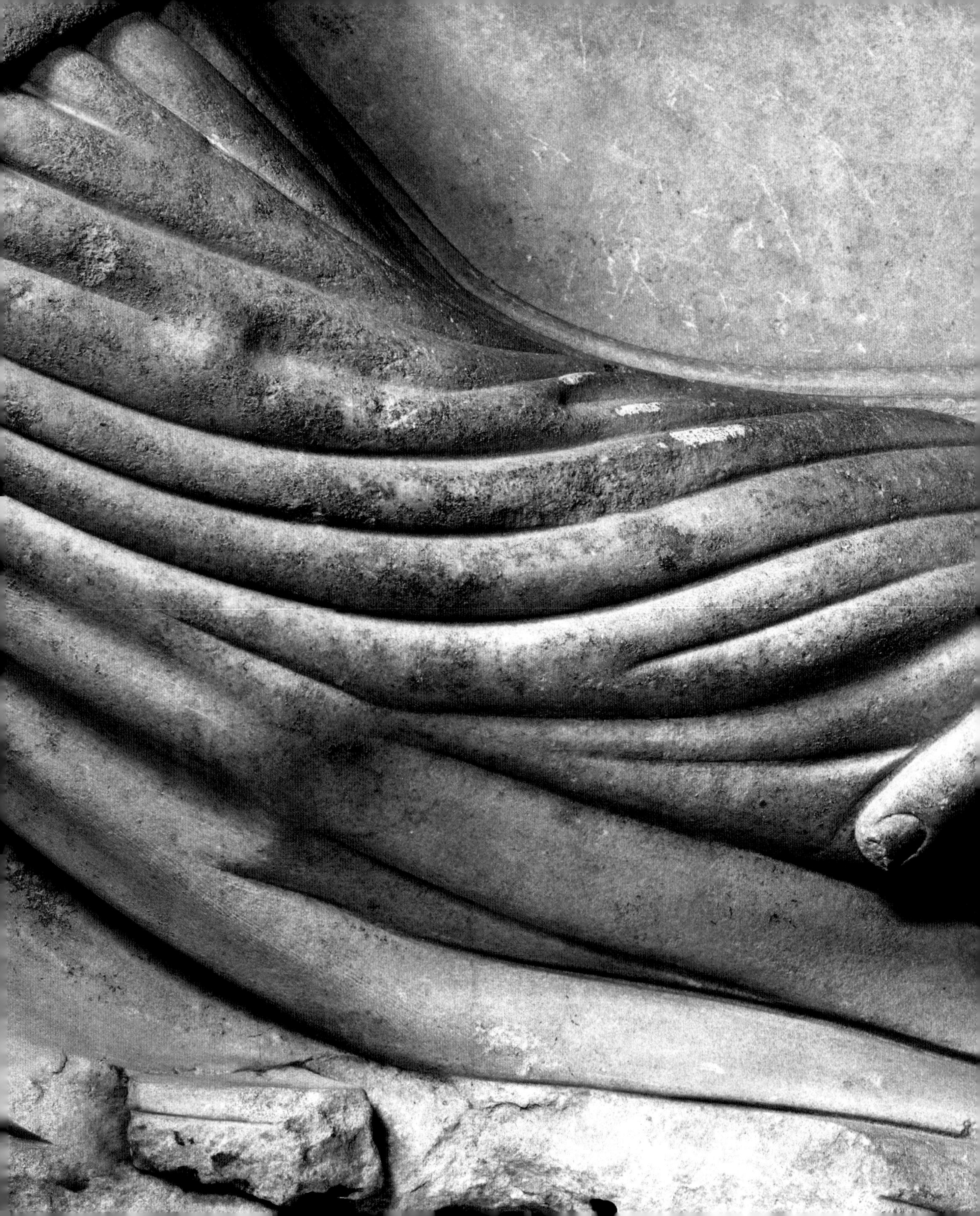

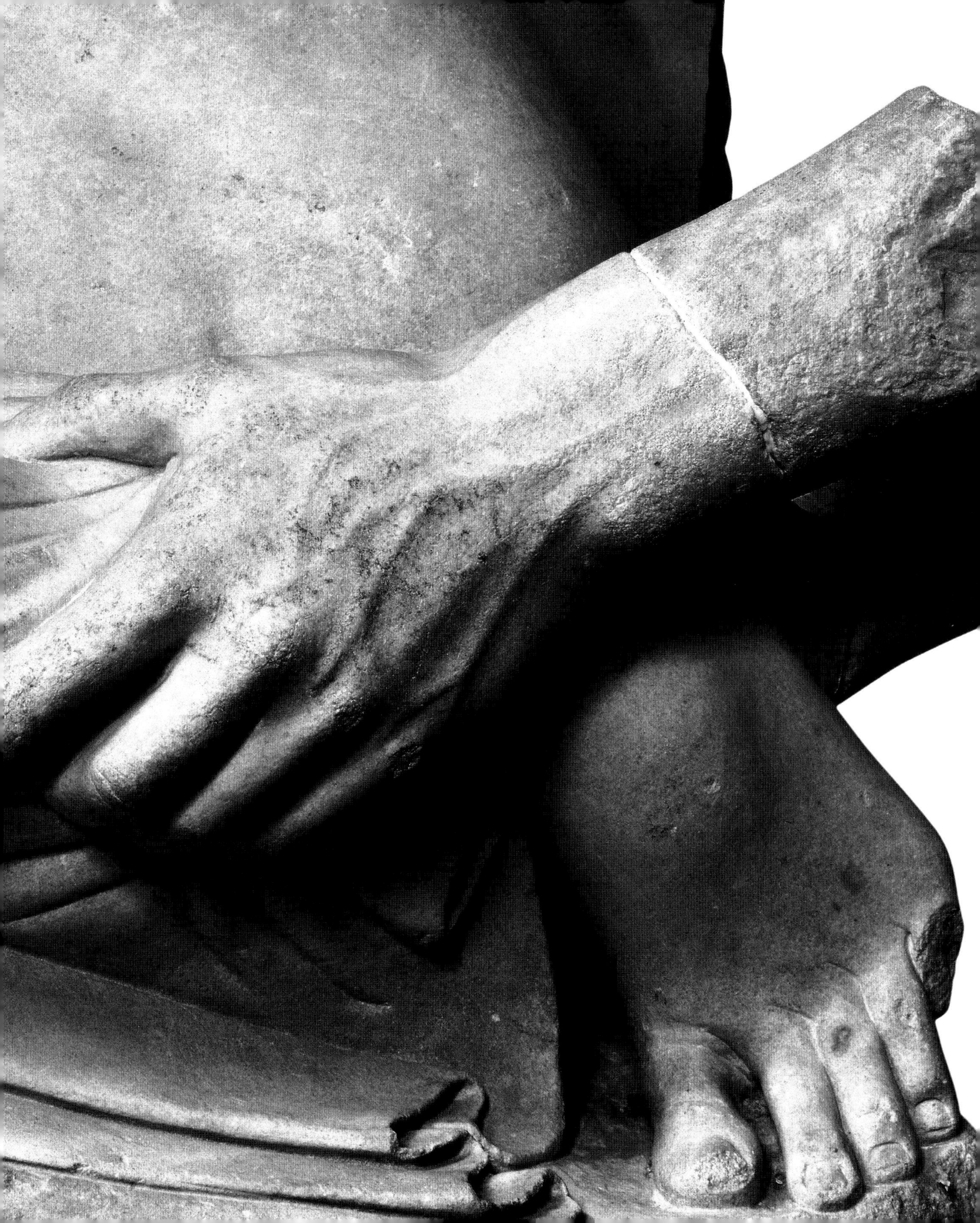

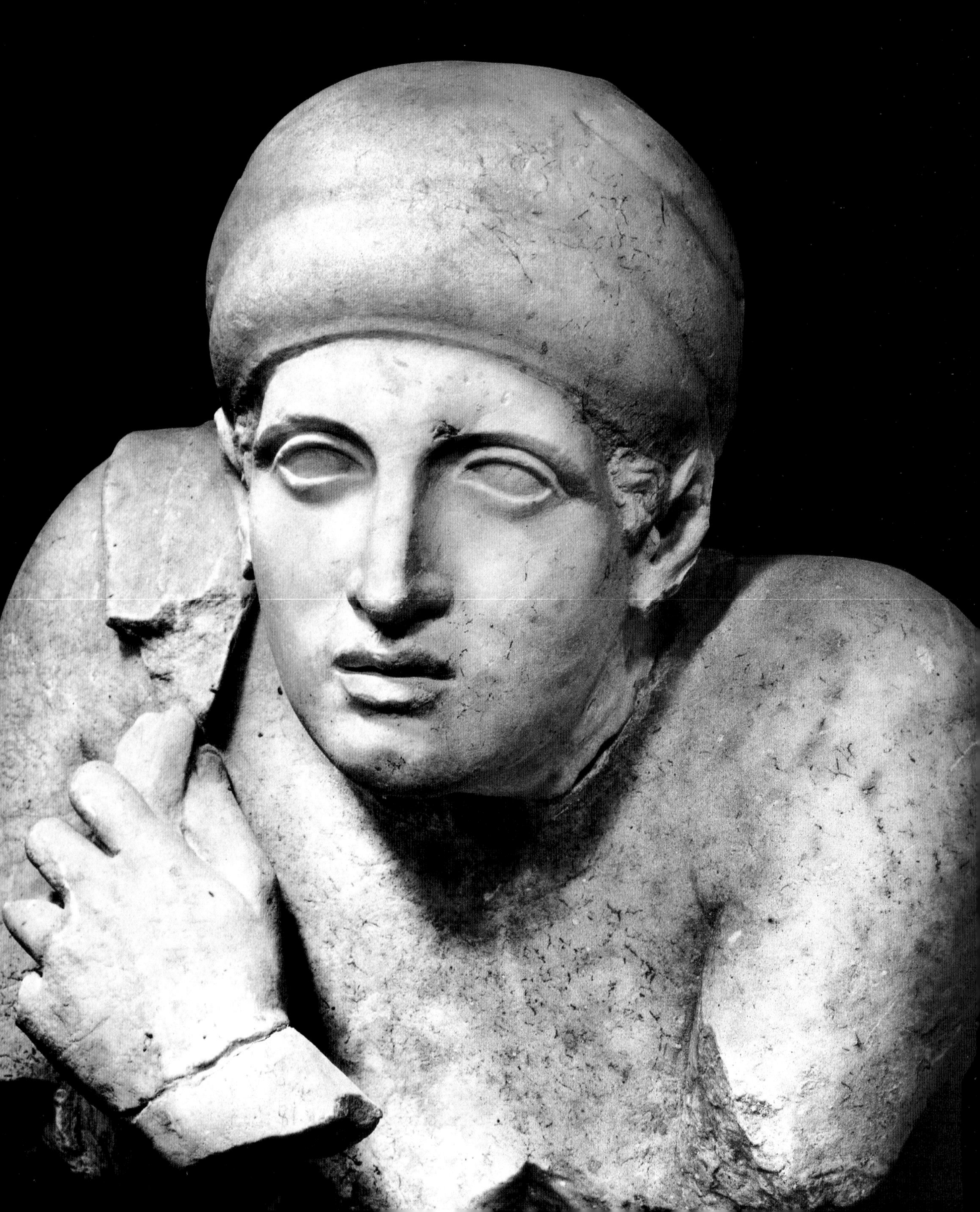

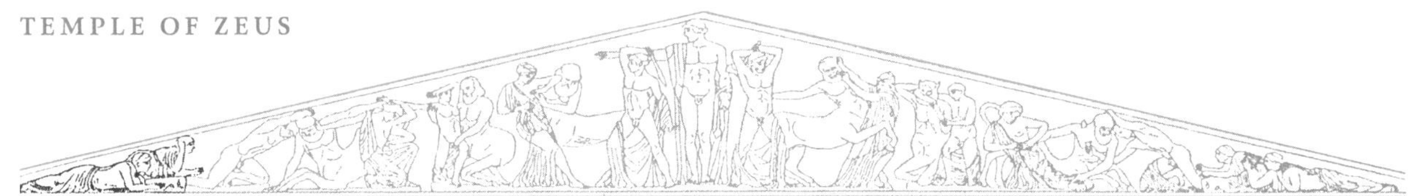

GROUP OF TWO LAPITH WOMEN

OLYMPIA, TEMPLE OF ZEUS, WEST PEDIMENT
465–457 BCE
PARIAN MARBLE. HEIGHT APPROX. 2.79 FEET (0.85 M)

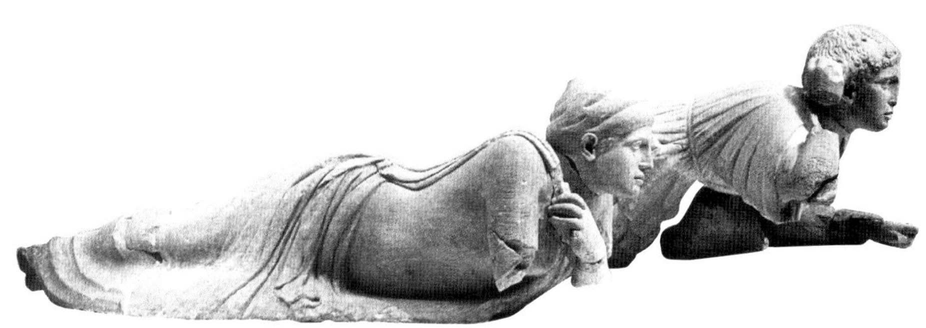

Occupying the left cuneus of the pediment are two Lapith women lying prone on the ground, the younger hiding behind the older. Illustrated opposite is the younger woman. What appears to be a peplos covers her lower body and perhaps her back but leaves her torso bare. Her hair is drawn into a kekryphalos. As she awaits the resolution of the fray, her anguish is vividly expressed in her gaze, her half-open lips, and her nostrils, which seem to flare with dread.

The plasticity of the volumes and the alternation of light and shadow endow the work with an unprecedented sense of living, breathing flesh, of a figure participating actively in the events taking place around her.

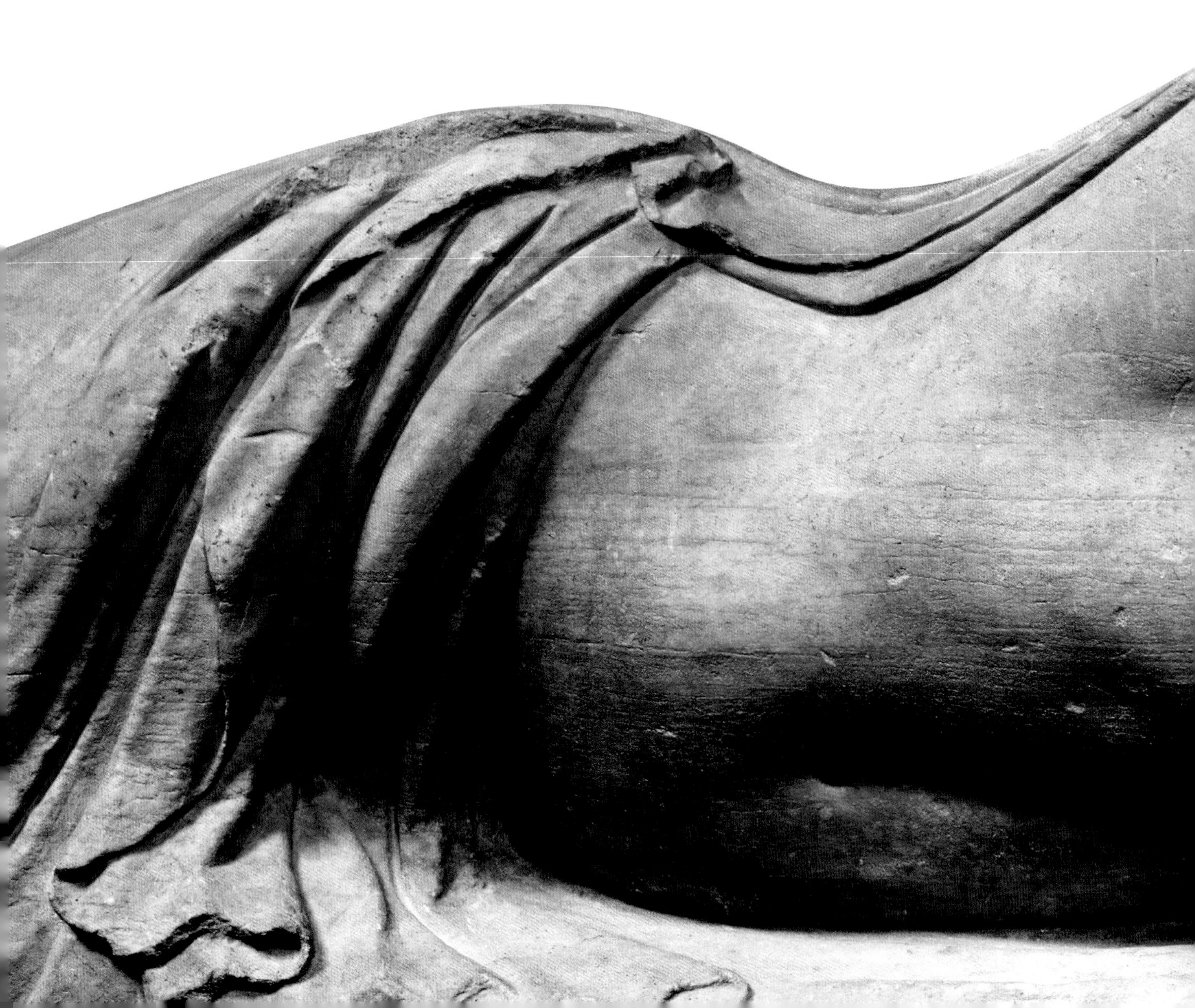

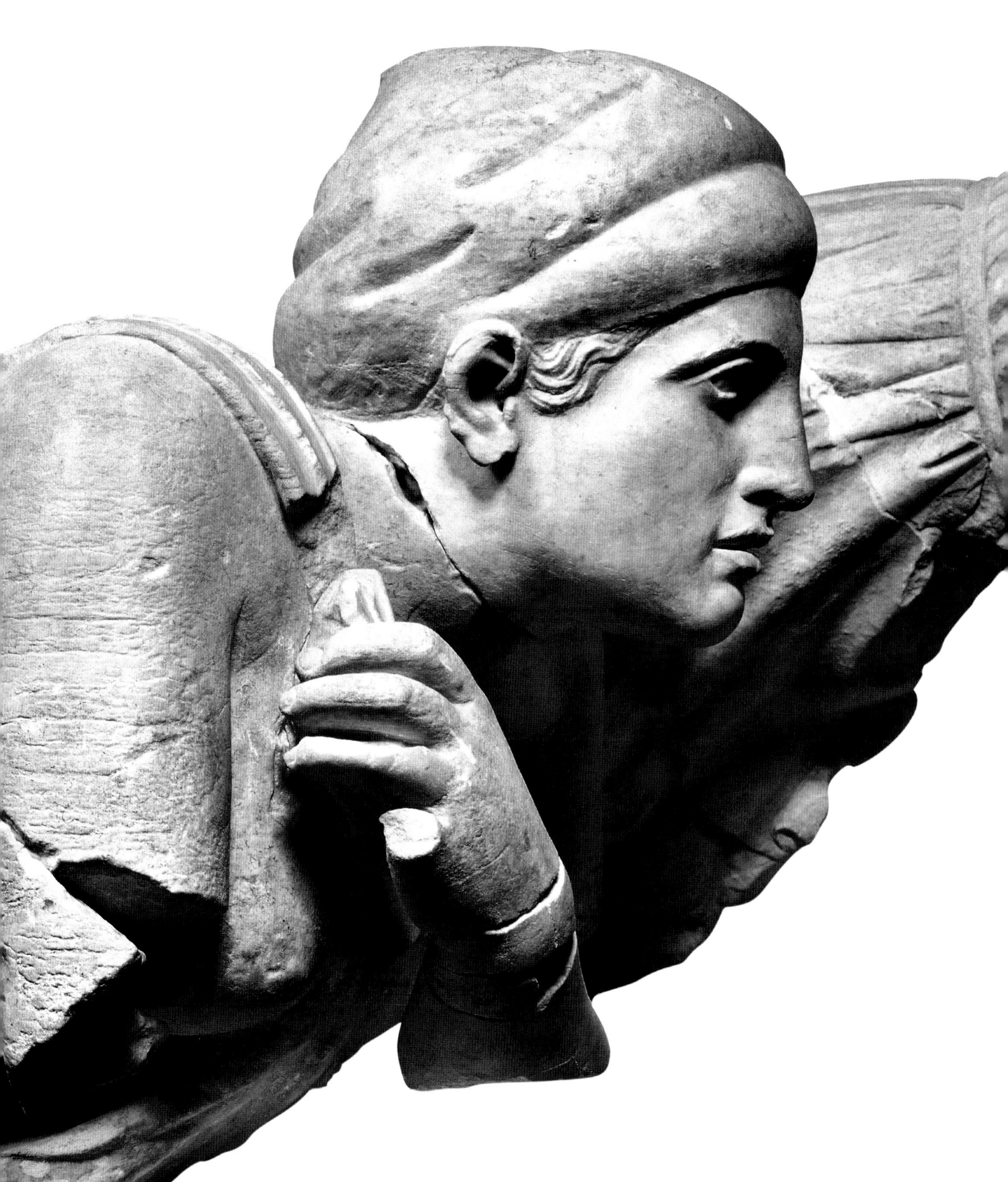

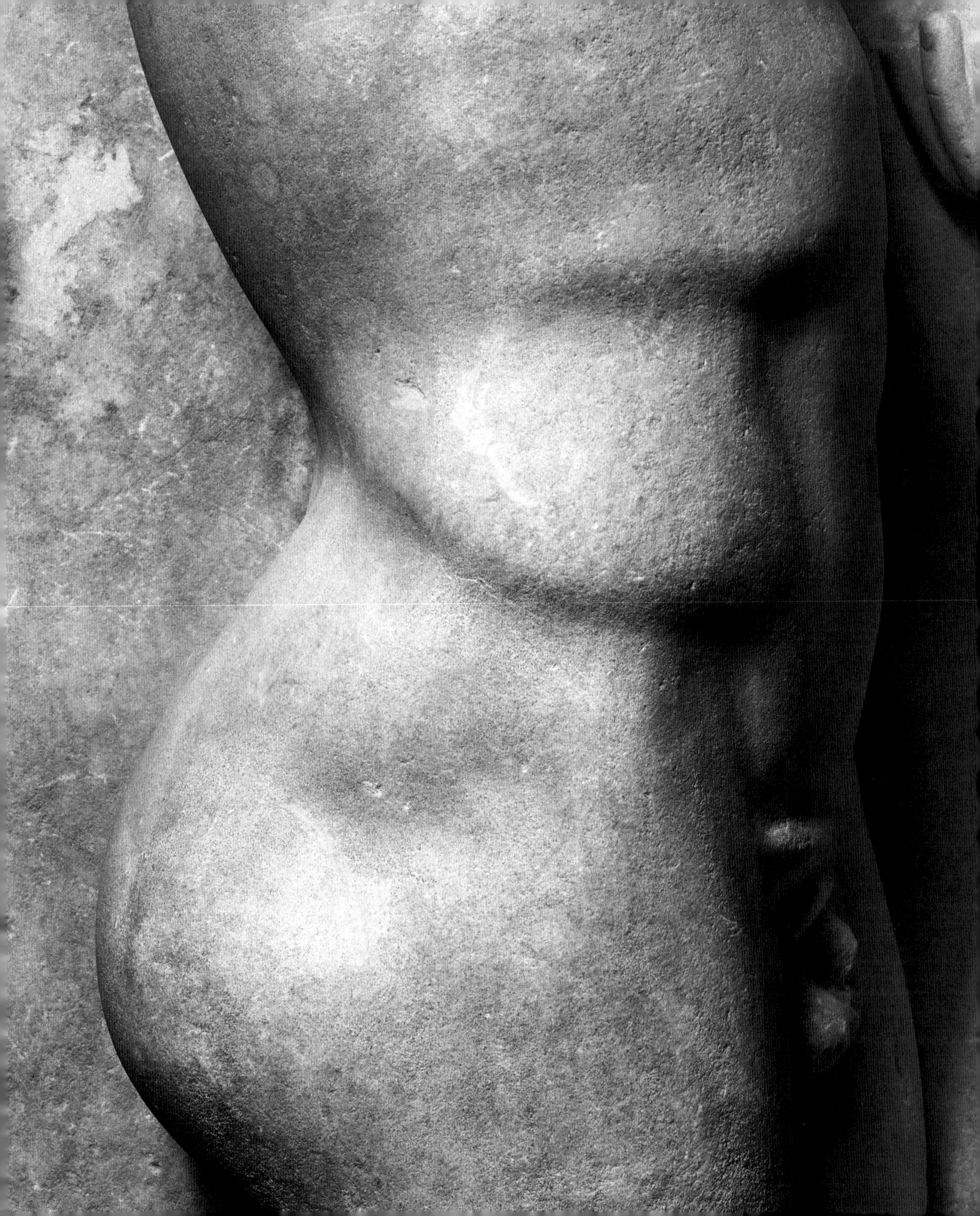

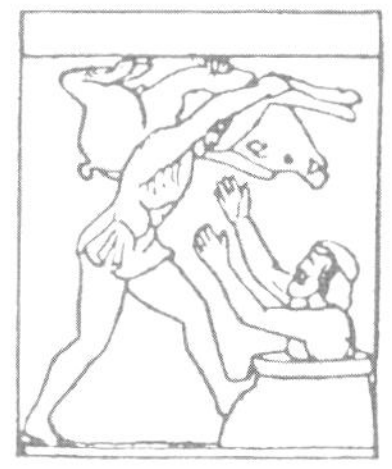
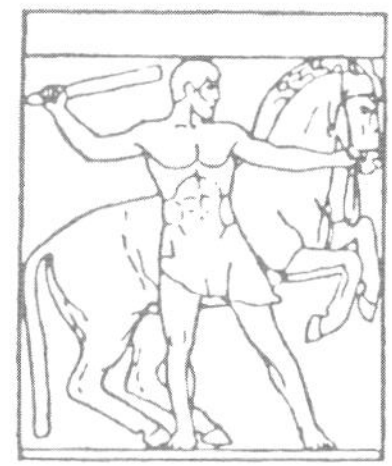
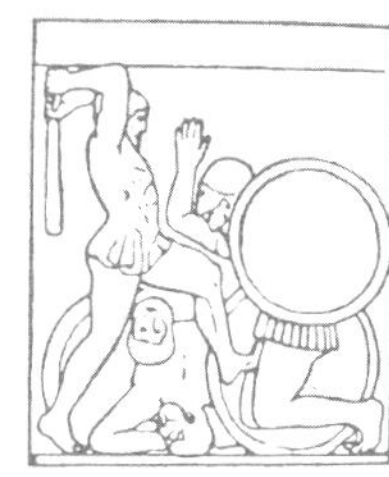
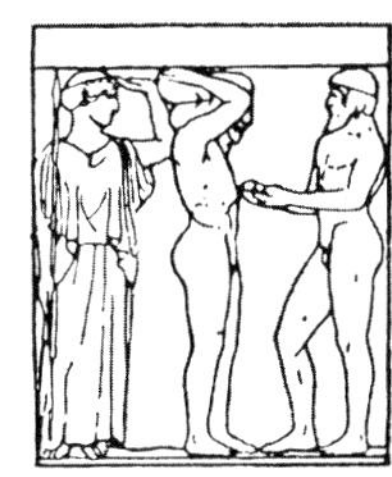
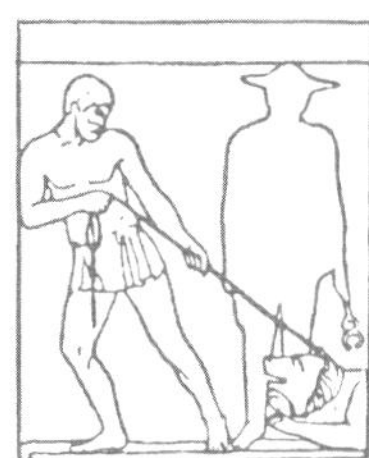
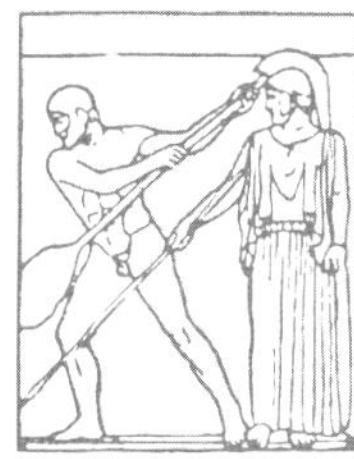

HERAKLES AND ATLAS

OLYMPIA, TEMPLE OF ZEUS, METOPE OF THE EAST SIDE
465–457 BCE
PARIAN MARBLE. HEIGHT 4.92 FEET (1.50 M); WIDTH 5.25 FEET (1.60 M)
OLYMPIA, ARCHAEOLOGICAL MUSEUM

This three-figure representation of Athena (left), Herakles (center), and Atlas (right) represents the myth of the Apples of the Hesperides, according to which one of the ten labors of Herakles involved bringing the golden apples to Eurystheus—but these were guarded by the Hesperides nymphs. In one version of the myth, the apples were brought to Herakles by Atlas, father of the Hesperides, who held up the Earth—or as others claim, the Sky—on his shoulders. Depicted here is the moment when Atlas delivers the apples to Herakles, who has taken over his post in his absence. Both men are nude and face each other, while the goddess, in a long peplos, stands with her body in a frontal pose and her head turned to her left as she assists Herakles with her raised left arm. The hero bears the burden with a folded cushion on his neck, to relieve the weight.

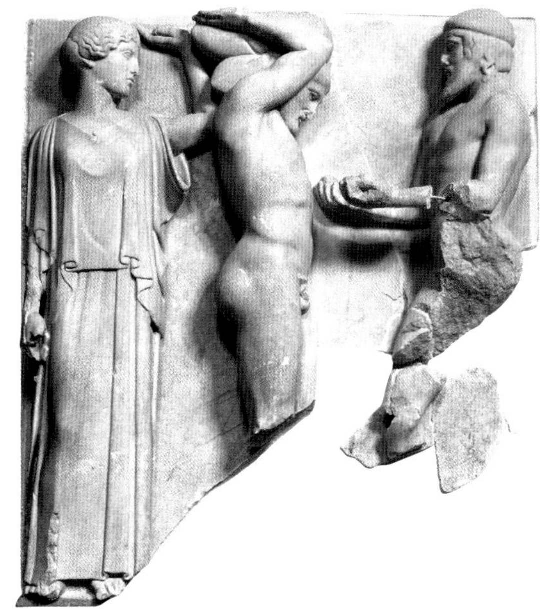

The three vertical axes, each one different, make this one of the loveliest compositions: Atlas is shown in three-quarter view, Herakles in profile, and Athena with body *en face* and head in profile. All three figures are in perfect harmony. Athena's divine serenity is offset by the tension in Herakles' muscular body and complemented by the motion in the robust figure of Atlas.

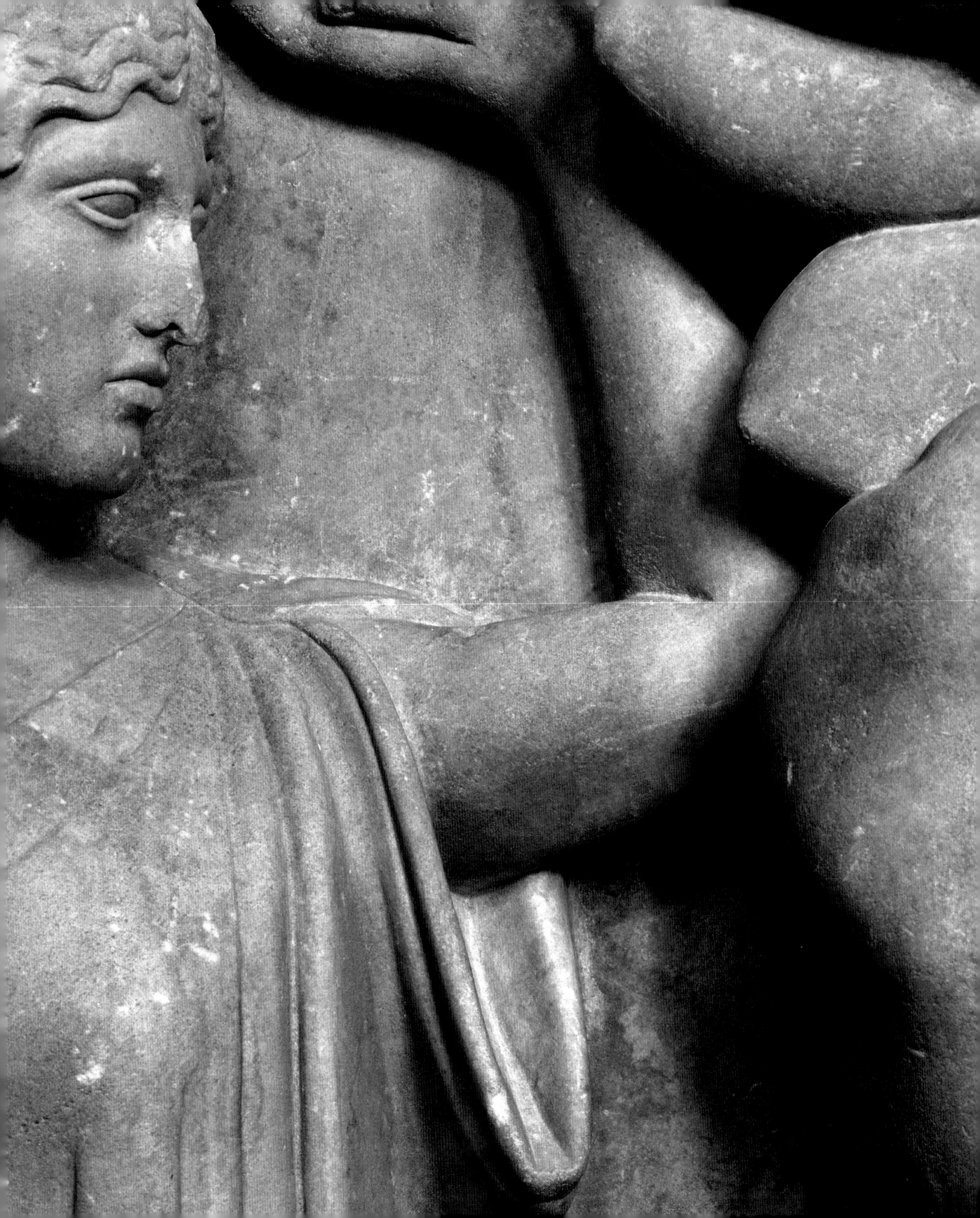

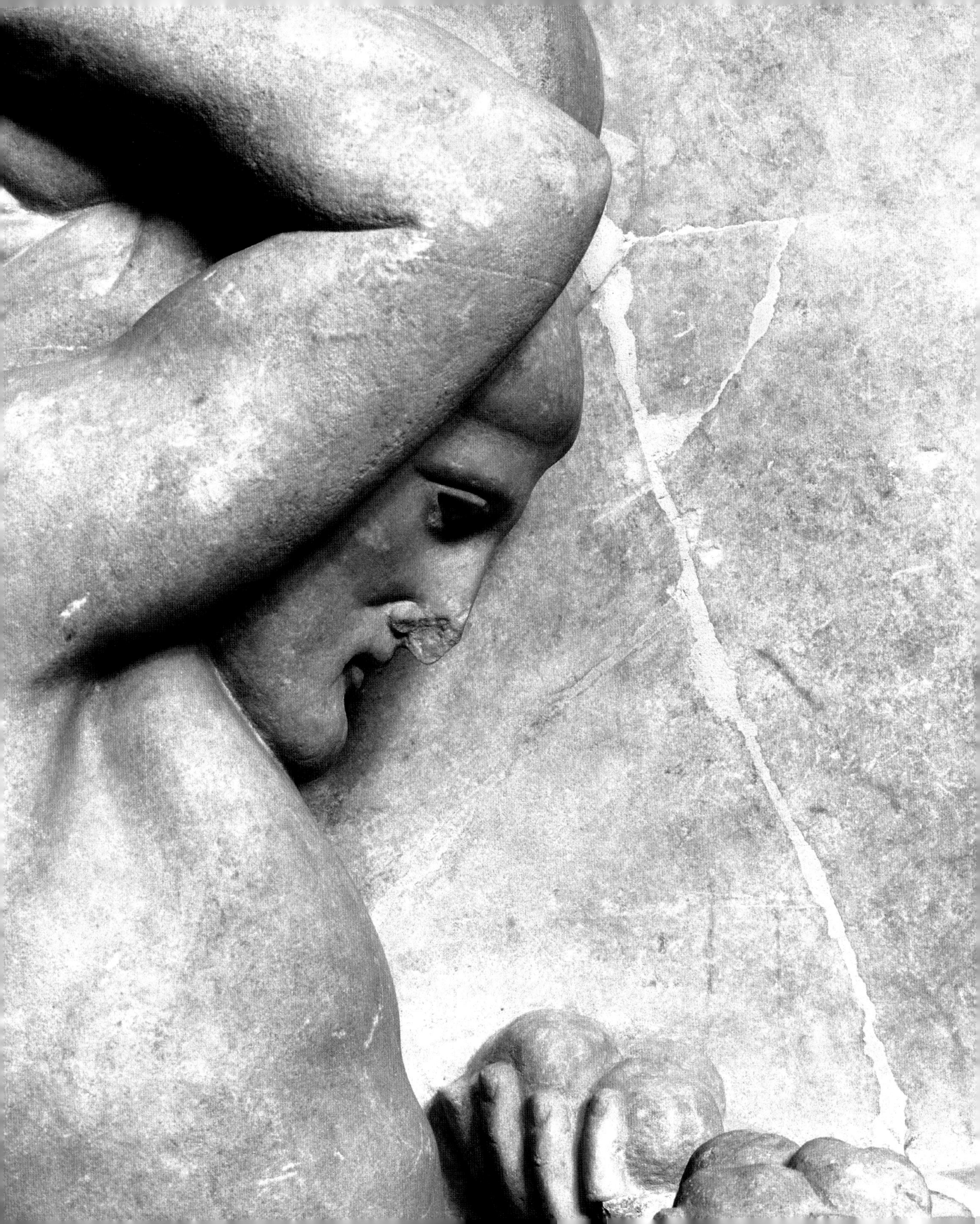

THE CHARIOTEER OF DELPHI

DELPHI, FROM THE SANCTUARY, BEHIND THE TEMPLE OF APOLLO
C. 470 BCE
BRONZE. HEIGHT 5.90 FEET (1.80 M)
DELPHI, ARCHAEOLOGICAL MUSEUM

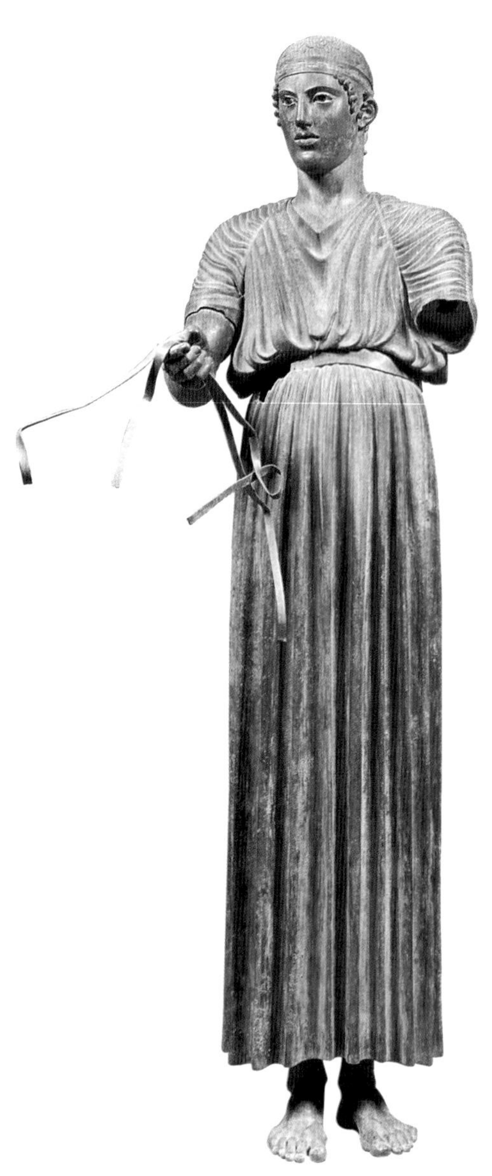

This statue was part of a large ex-voto that included a quadriga. The inscribed base confirms that the work was dedicated in the Delphic sanctuary by Polyzalos, a member of the eminent family of tyrants from Syracuse in Sicily, to commemorate his victory in a chariot race at the Pythian Games.

In the original composition, the young man stood on the chariot board, dressed in the long chiton typical of charioteers, the upper part of which was held in place by a belt to prevent it from blowing out and affecting the speed of the racing chariot. This part of the garment was also tied crosswise at the back with a strong cord, which passed in front, under the armpits, so as not to obstruct the charioteer's maneuvers. On the charioteer's head, holding his short hair in place, is the victor's fillet, tied in a knot at the back of the neck.

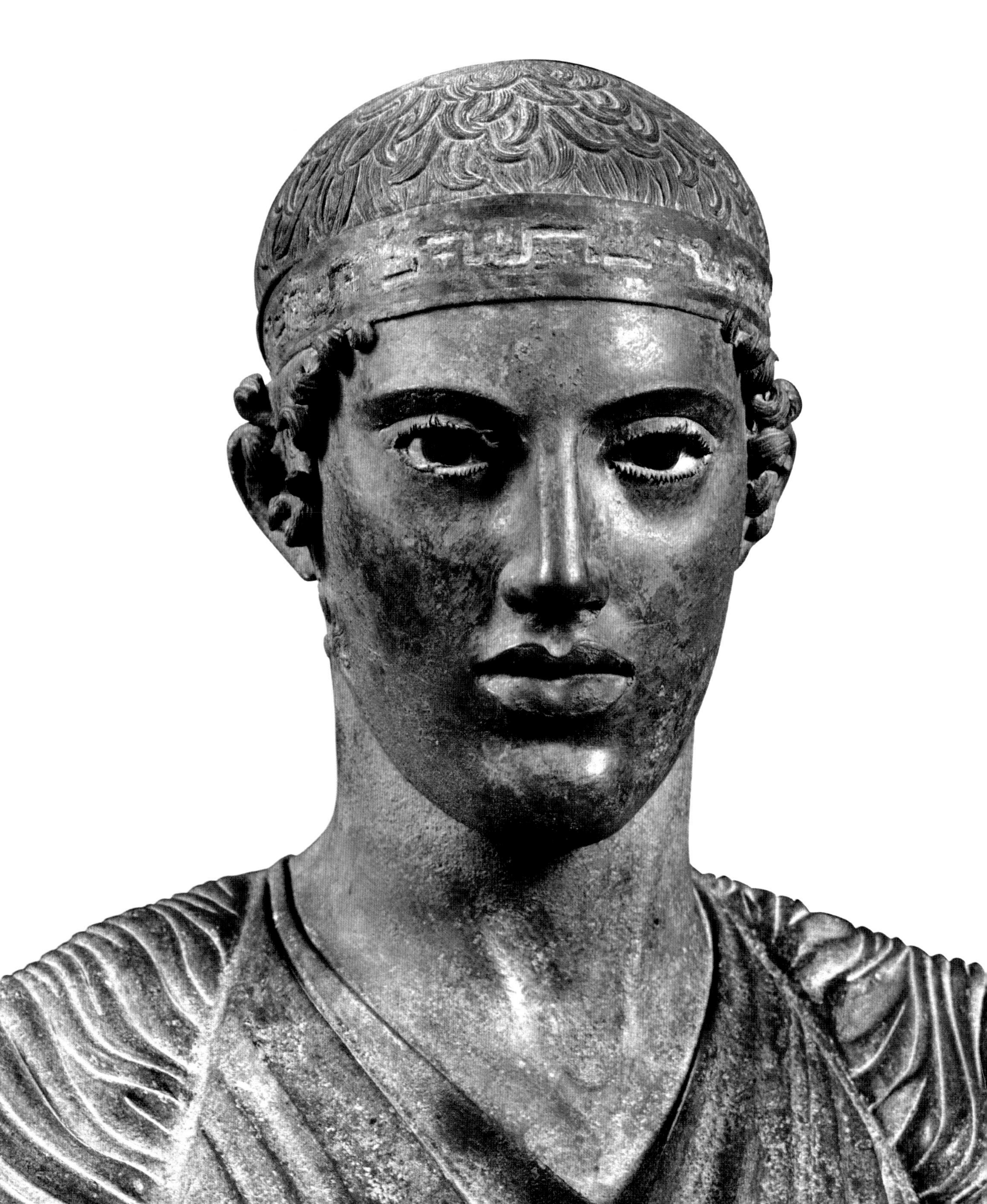

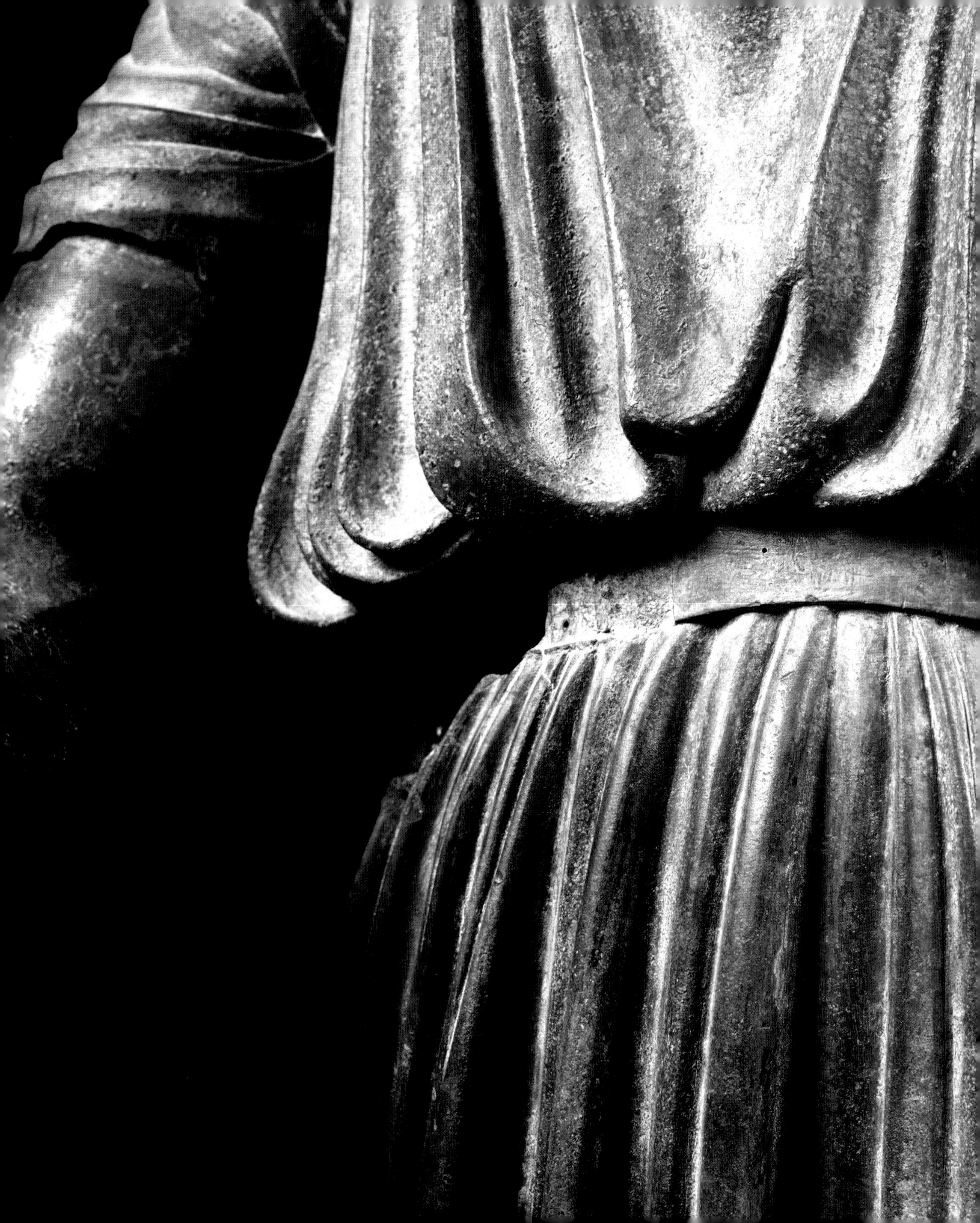

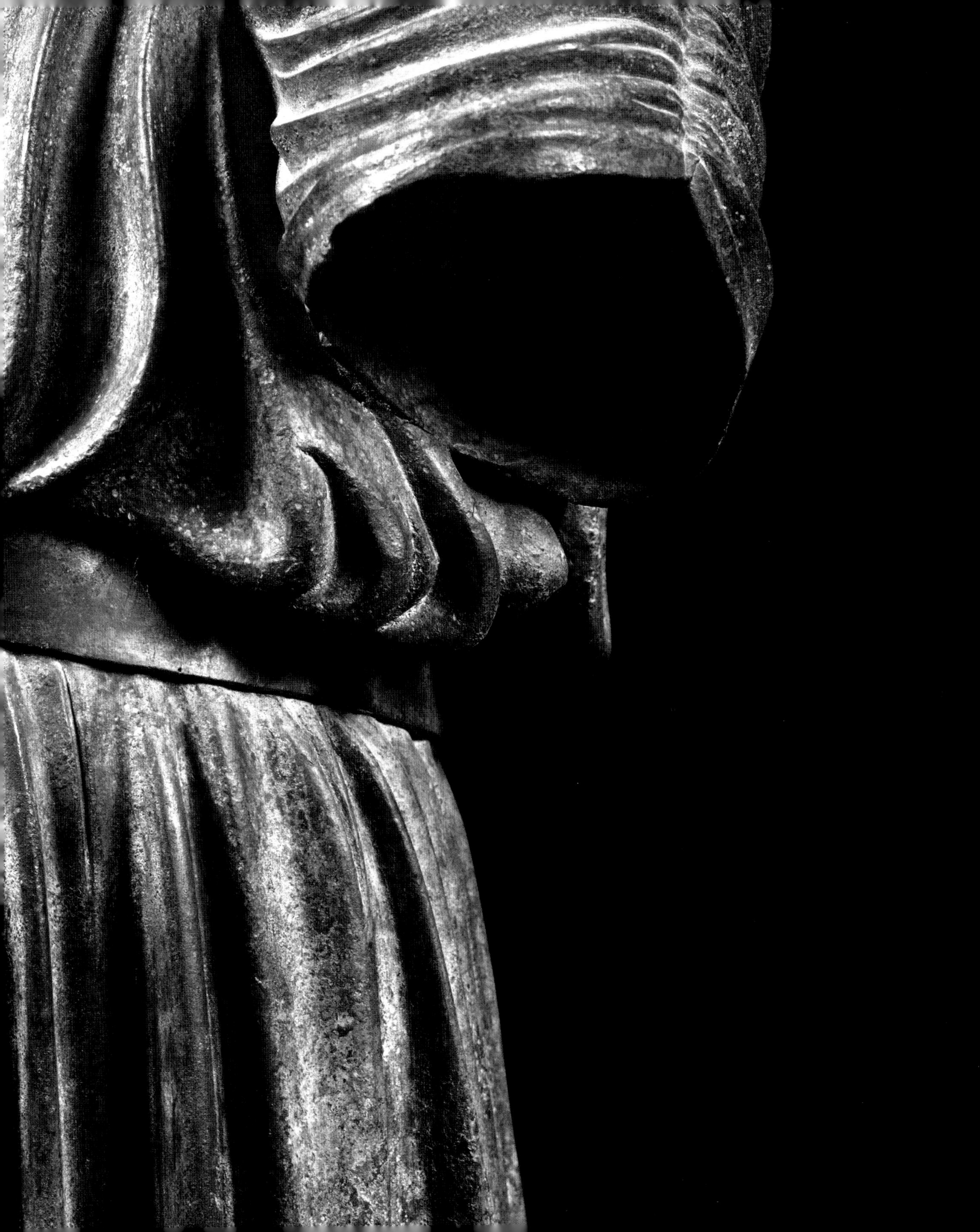

The statue was cast in a mold according to the *cire perdue* (lost-wax) technique. The eyes (preserved) are inlaid with white paste inset with a dark semiprecious stone for the iris and tiny bronze threads for the eyelashes. The inlaid meander pattern decorating the fillet on the head is made of silver and bronze, while wafer-thin leaves of copper, perhaps mixed with silver, cover the lips.

The Charioteer is an exceptional work and one of few to have survived from antiquity. The athlete is not represented in the moment of action, but his pose and expression combine the concentrated effort and focused attention demanded during the race with pride at the anticipated victory. The artist has sculpted the body with volume and depth, presenting it as a living organism; with its internal design, the torsion of the upper body in relation to the lower conveys not immobility but the momentary, and therefore motion. The eminent Greek archaeologist Christos Karouzos declares in his description of the work: "We feel a pure tectonic force that rises from below in steady motion, stretches out slightly in the torso and comes to a climax on the dome of the skull." Despite the fact that the statue is now alone, bereft of the composition—the chariot and horses—that developed horizontally over a considerable width, it stands wonderfully on its vertical axis, impressing and delighting those who behold it today, just as it did in antiquity. It is possibly an Attic work.

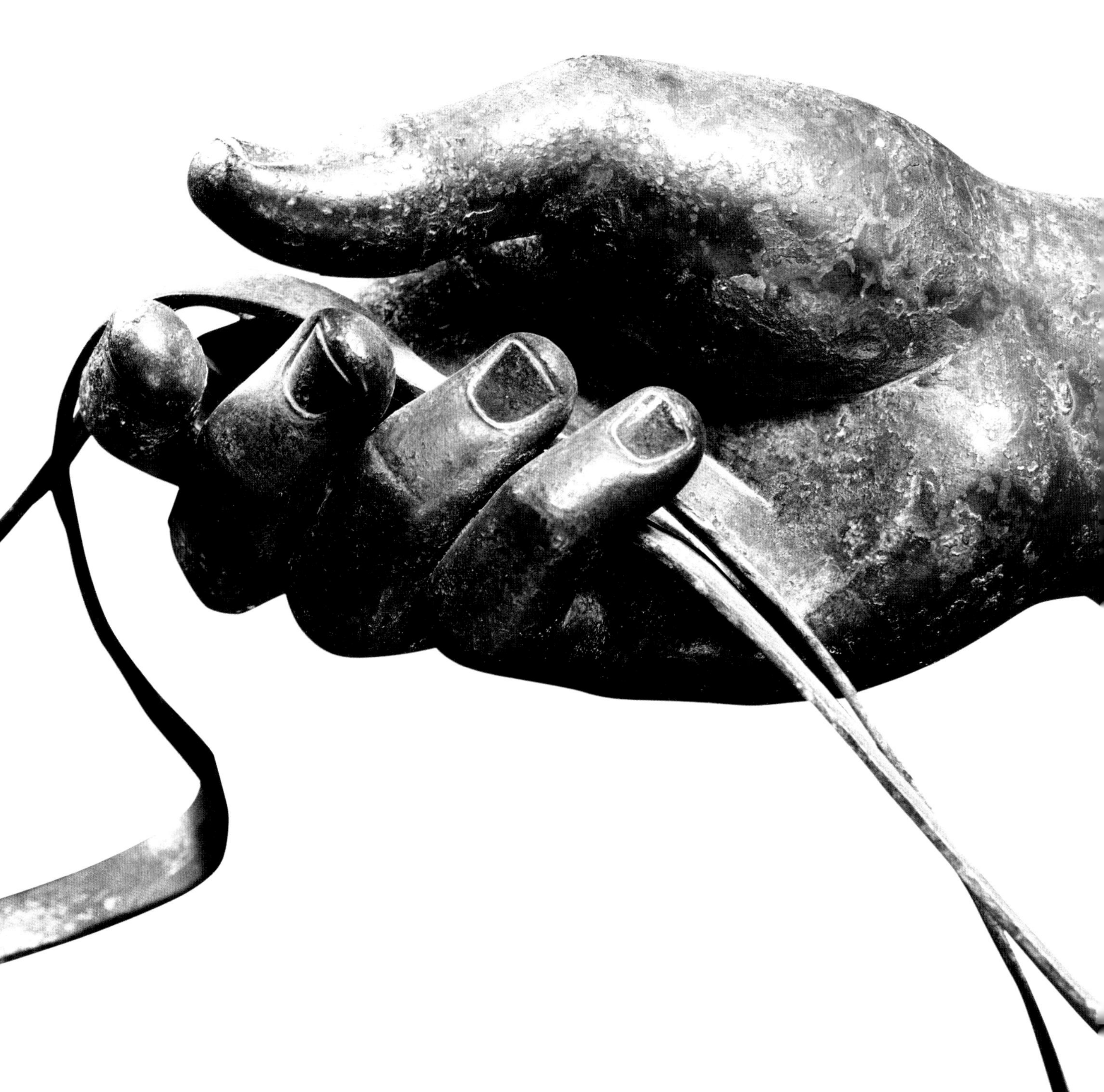

ZEUS OR POSEIDON OF ARTEMISION

ARTEMISION, FOUND IN A SHIPWRECK ON THE SEABED
C. 460 BCE
BRONZE. HEIGHT 6.86 FEET (2.09 M)
ATHENS, NATIONAL ARCHAEOLOGICAL MUSEUM

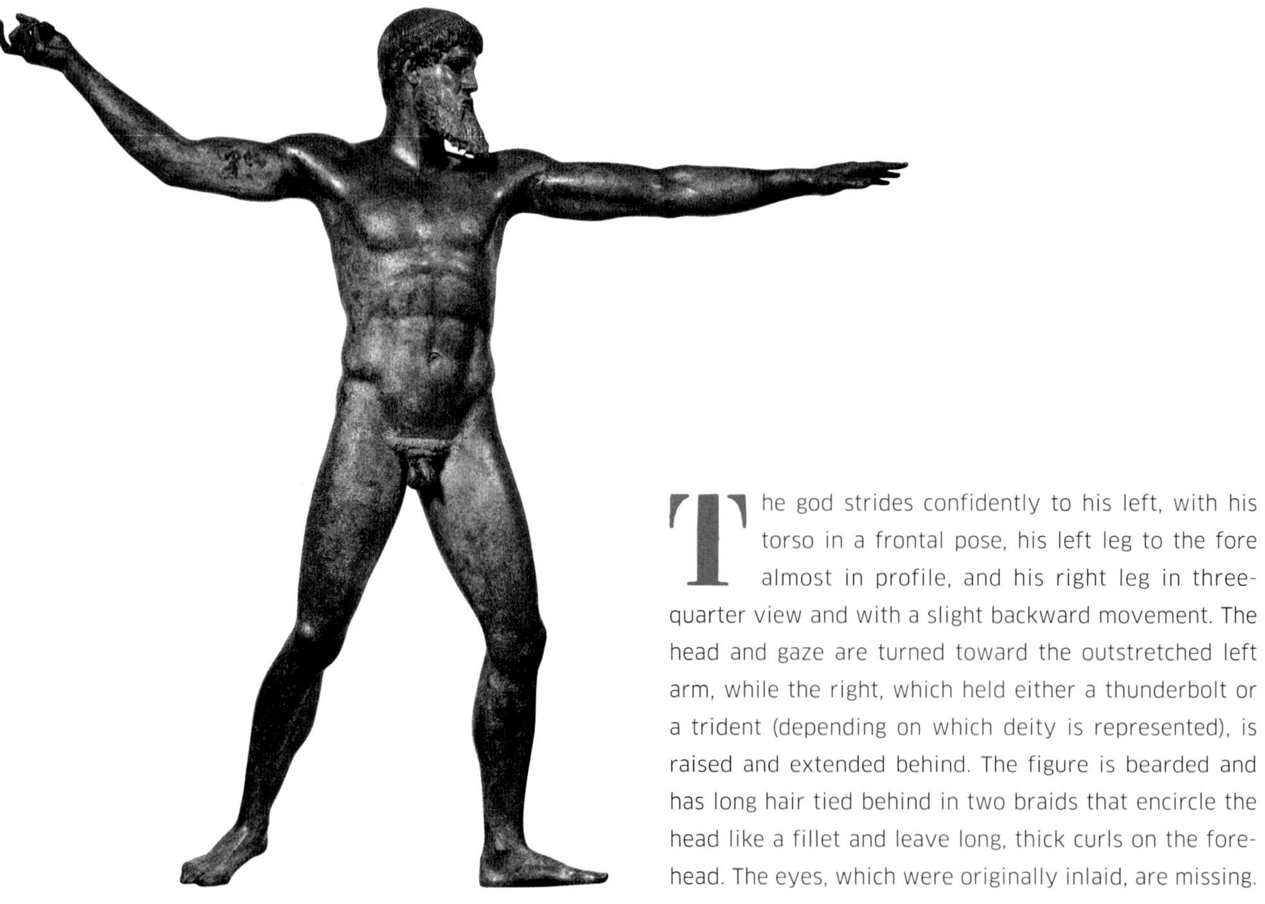

The god strides confidently to his left, with his torso in a frontal pose, his left leg to the fore almost in profile, and his right leg in three-quarter view and with a slight backward movement. The head and gaze are turned toward the outstretched left arm, while the right, which held either a thunderbolt or a trident (depending on which deity is represented), is raised and extended behind. The figure is bearded and has long hair tied behind in two braids that encircle the head like a fillet and leave long, thick curls on the forehead. The eyes, which were originally inlaid, are missing.

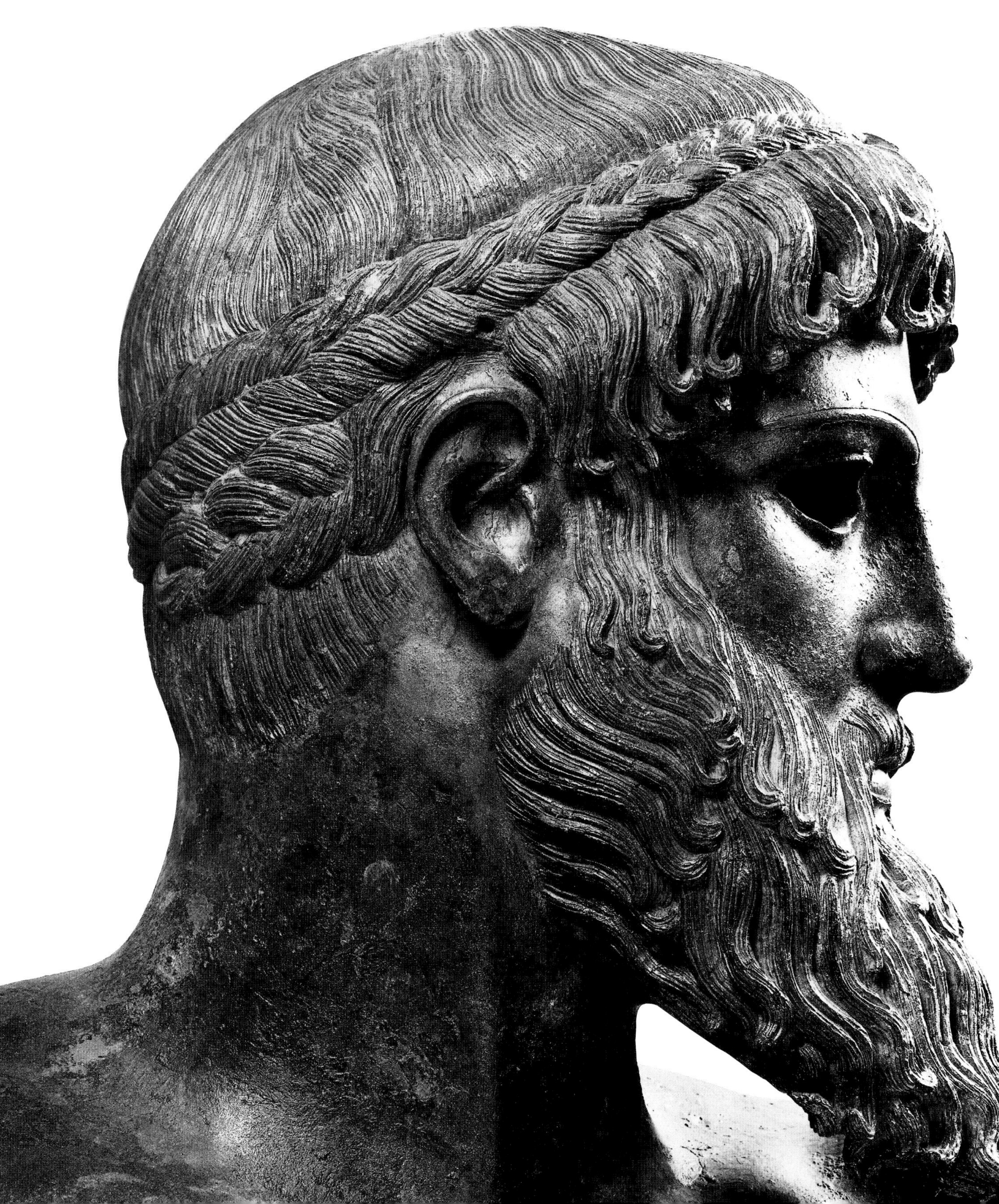

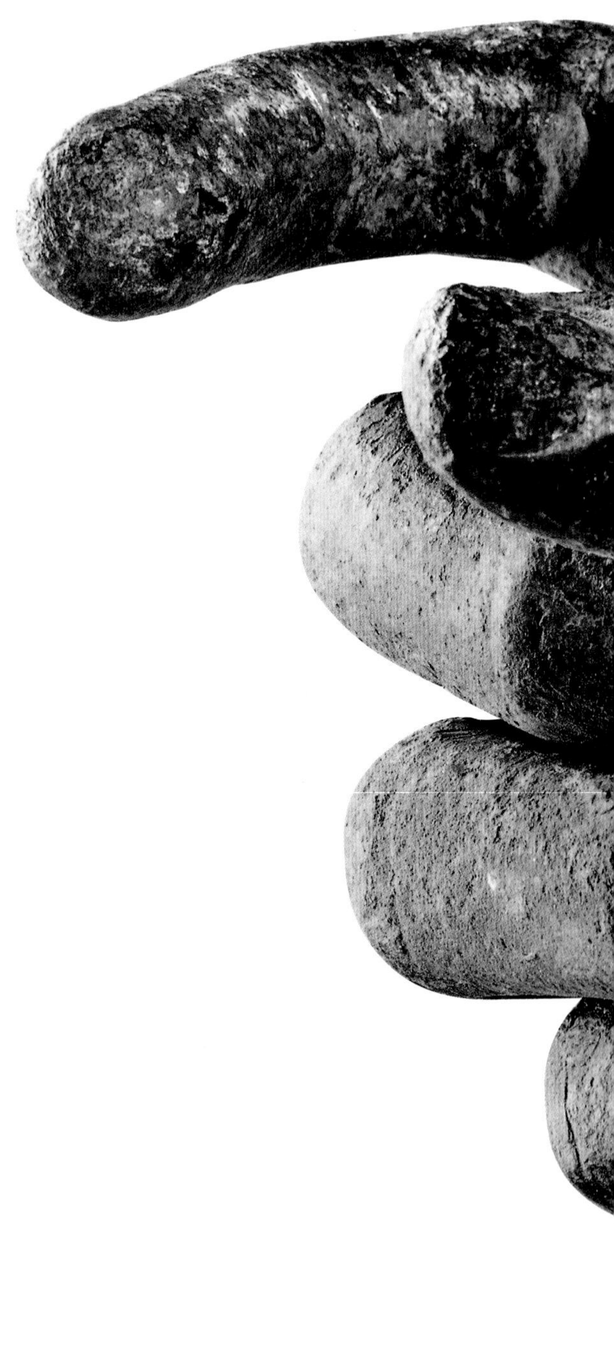

This ambitious work, likely an avant-garde creation of Kalamis, a famed sculptor in bronze who was at the peak of his career in the second quarter of the fifth century BCE, is one of the most important sculptural works in bronze to have survived from ancient Greece. The god is portrayed in a moment of impetuous movement (poised to hurl either the thunderbolt or the trident at an adversary) in which the entire body participates: From the tips of the toes of the right foot and the heel of the left, which support the statue, to the various muscles, the rendering conveys the effort expended. Perhaps the determined pursing of the lips and the austere expression on the face manifest the figure's disciplined concentration on hitting the target.

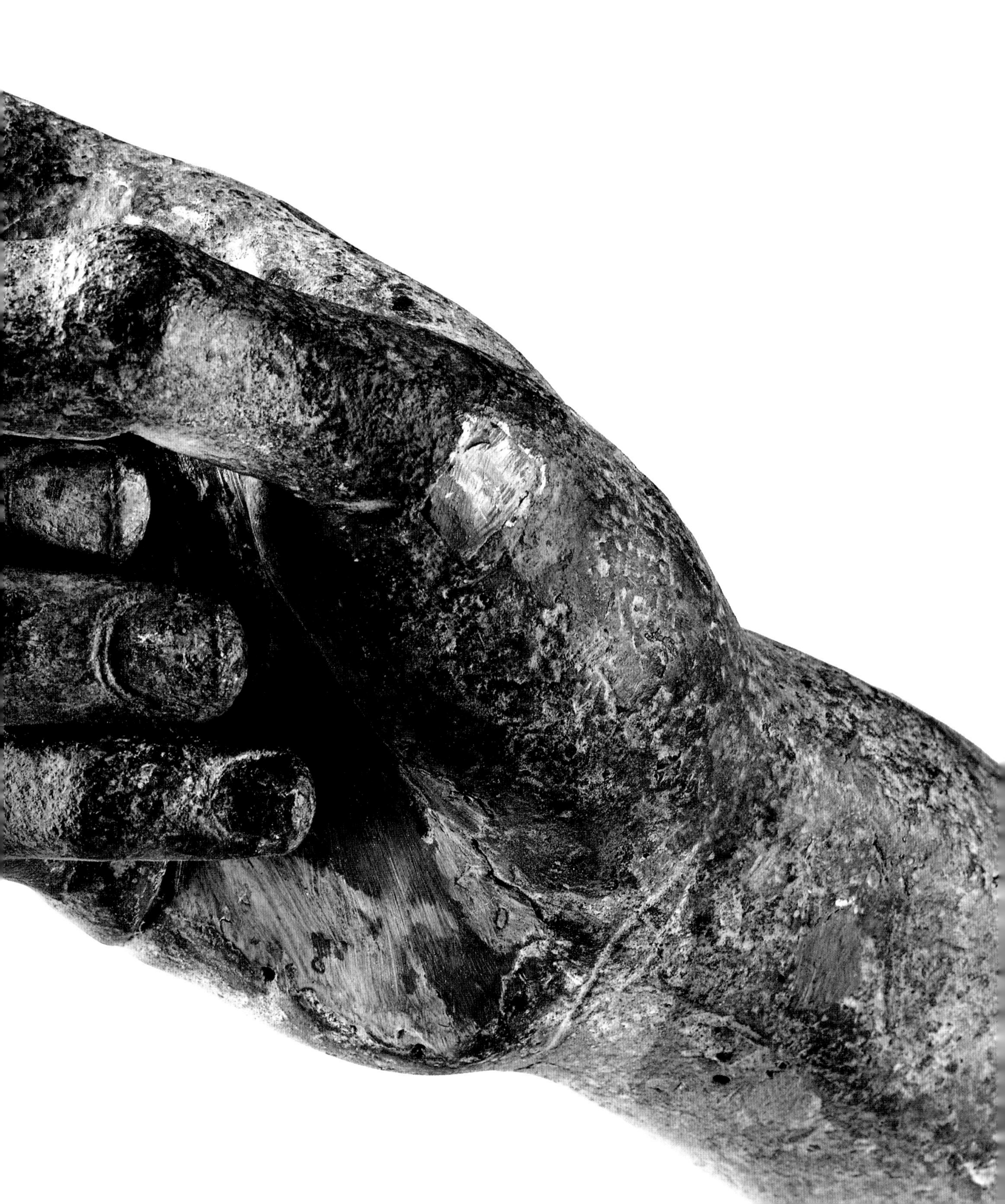

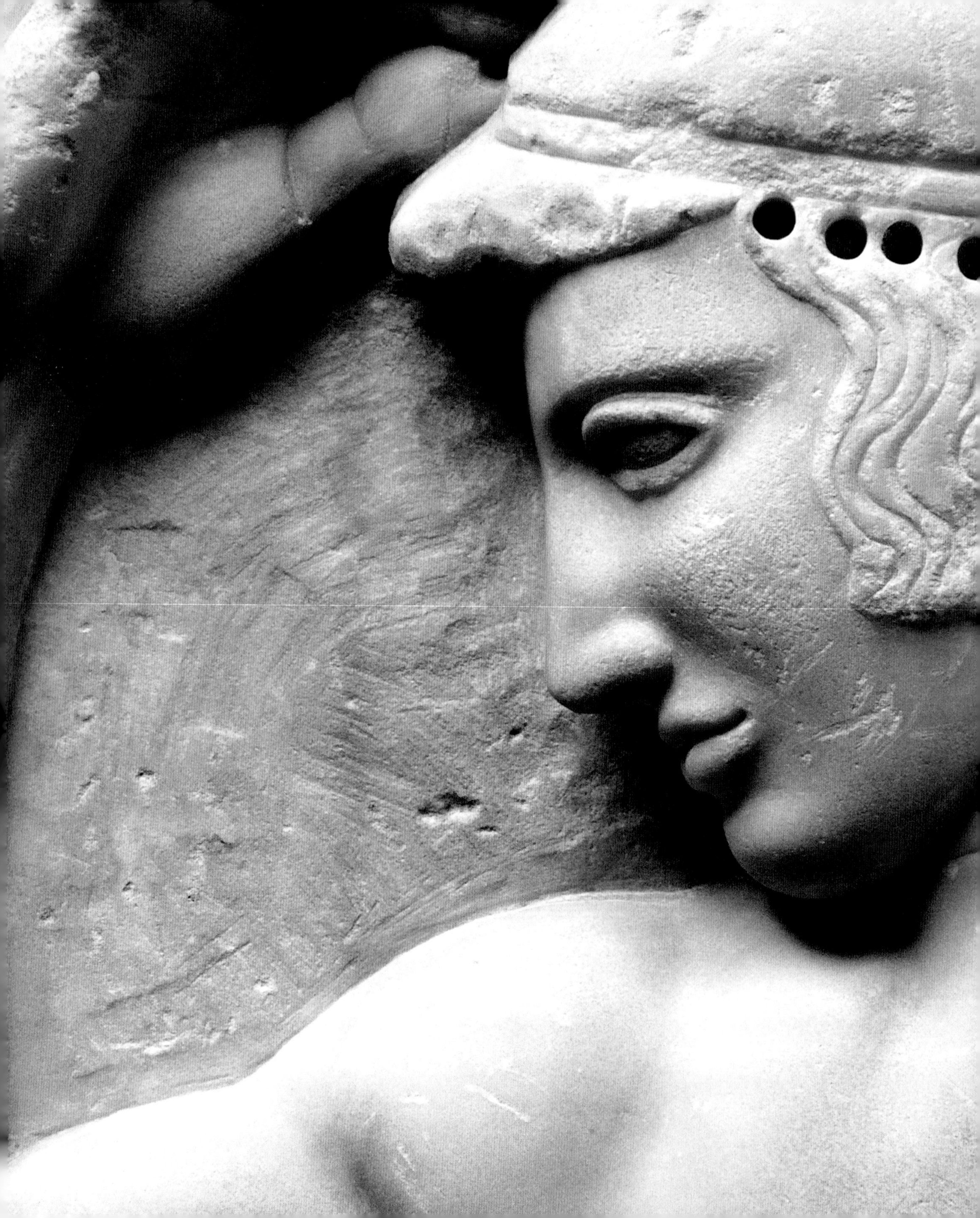

VOTIVE STELE OF THE AUTOSTEPHANOUMENOS

SOUNION, CLOSE TO THE TEMPLE OF ATHENA
C. 470–460 BCE
PENTELIC MARBLE. PRESENT HEIGHT 1.57 FEET(0.48 M); WIDTH 1.61 FEET (0.49 M)
ATHENS, NATIONAL ARCHAEOLOGICAL MUSEUM

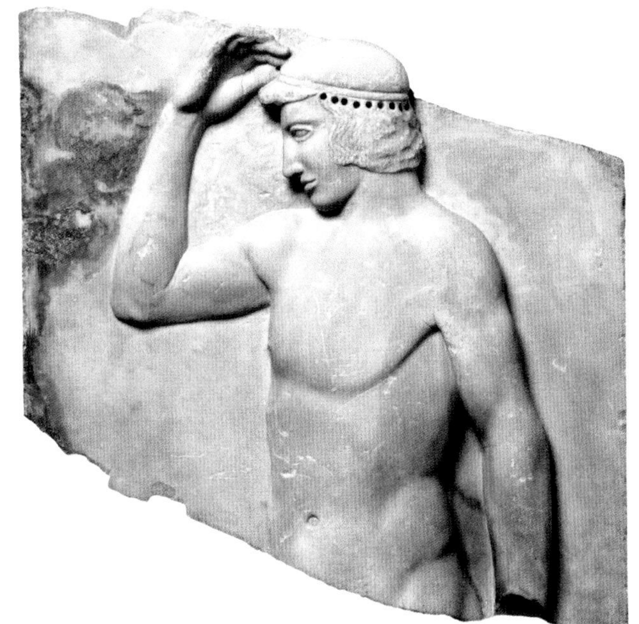

Represented is a standing, nude youth, facing left, with his body in three-quarter pose and his head in profile. With his right hand he either puts on or removes from his head a wreath—hence the sobriquet "autostephanoumenos," or "he who crowns himself." The holes for affixing the wreath to the head indicate that the wreath was made of metal. A fillet encircling the wreath holds in place the youth's short hair, which falls in waves to the neck. The figure was projected against a blue background.

The young man is perhaps an athlete, possibly a citizen of the demos of Sounion, who was victorious in a contest and prepares to offer his wreath to Athena Sounias. Charming is the tender innocence with which the almost adolescent youth carries out a sacred duty.

THE MOURNING ATHENA

ATHENS, ACROPOLIS, SOUTH OF THE PARTHENON
C. 460 BCE
PARIAN MARBLE. HEIGHT 1.77 FEET (0.54 M); WIDTH 1.02–1.03 FEET (0.31–0.315 M)
ATHENS, ACROPOLIS MUSEUM

Athena, turned to her left, is barefoot and wears a Doric peplos and a Corinthian helmet. She plants her weight on her left leg and leans on a spear, which she holds obliquely with her left arm, bent at the elbow, with the tip on the ground. Her right hand rests on her waist. Her head turns to the front and her forehead is pressed lightly against the butt of the inverted spear shaft. Her expression is pensive, and she contemplates a small stele, or *cippus*, in front of her.

The harmony of the composition, with its two diagonals, of the body and of the spear, is complemented by the plain but elegant stele. A serious calm, appropriate to the spirituality suffusing the tender face of the patron goddess of Athens, characterizes the work. Diverse interpretations of the representation have been proposed but none has been accepted. Perhaps it was a votive offering of the masons who built the Kimoneian Wall, as some scholars have proposed.

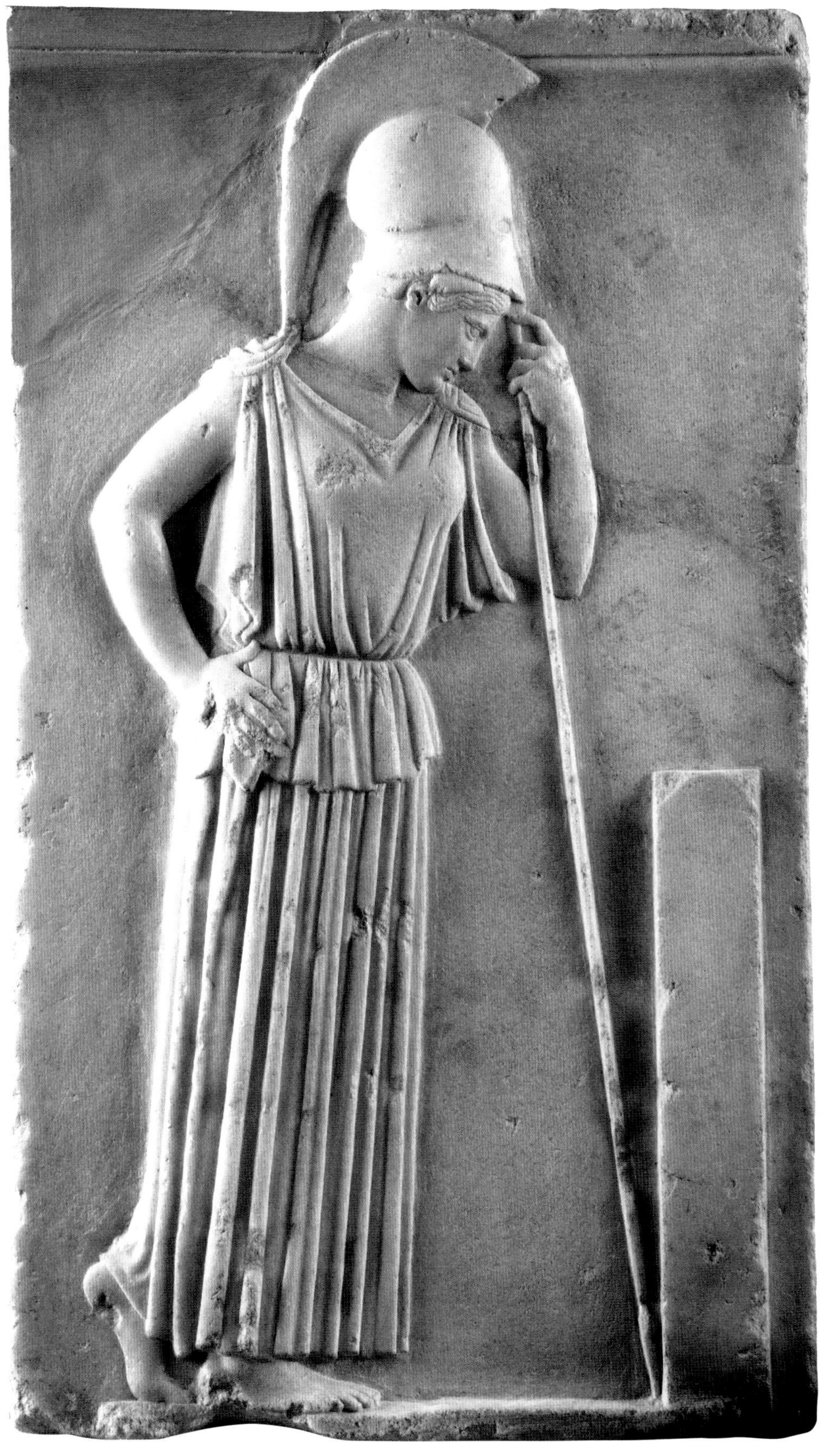

GRAVE STELE

PAROS
440–430 BCE
PARIAN MARBLE. HEIGHT 2.62 FEET (0.80 M);
WIDTH BELOW 1.31 FEET (0.40 M)
AND ABOVE 1.19–1.25 FEET (0.36–0.38 M)
NEW YORK, METROPOLITAN MUSEUM OF ART

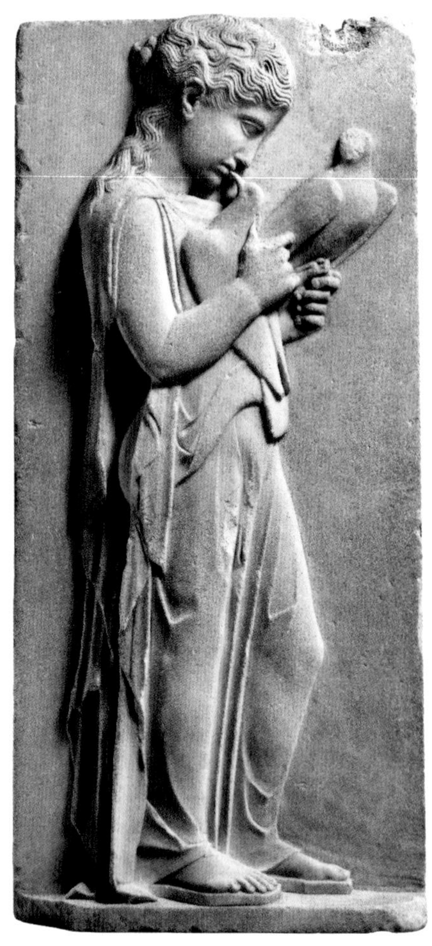

Depicted in this stele is a girl facing right and holding two doves. Her hair is long and wavy, and she wears an open peplos pinned over the right shoulder and a long apoptygma that falls below the waist. In her closed right hand she clasps tightly to her chest one of the doves, whose beak she kisses, while in the left hand she clutches a second dove by the legs.

The delicate treatment of the figure in combination with the inventive dramatic elements in the girl's personal space—which serve to isolate her from the earthly milieu and thus convey the tragedy of death—are consistent with the artistic spirit of the classical age. This relief is characteristic of Parian sculptors, who, together with their Attic colleagues, have bequeathed us works of art nonpareil.

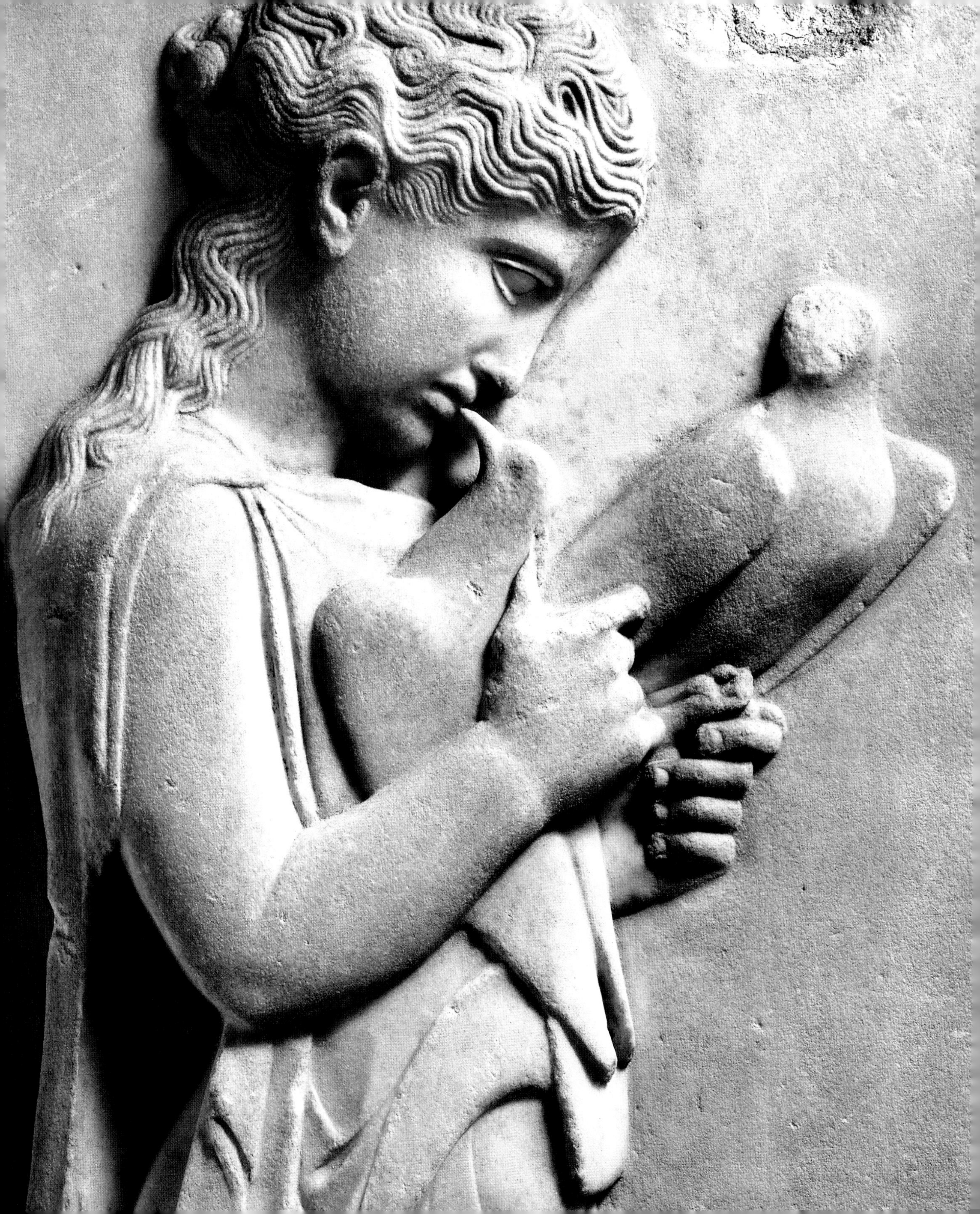

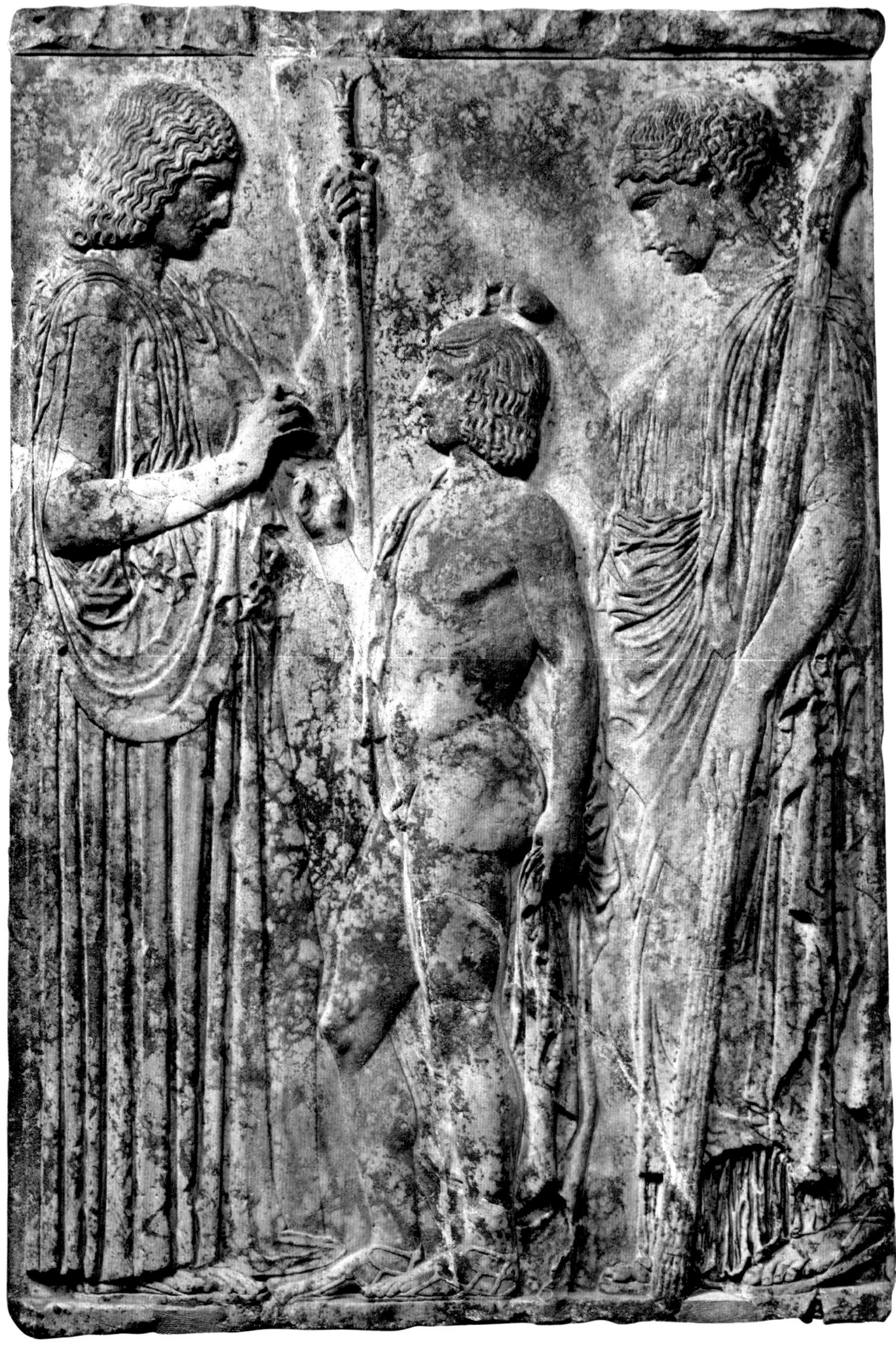

DEMETER, PERSEPHONE AND TRIPTOLEMOS

ELEUSIS
C. 440–430 BCE
PENTELIC MARBLE. HEIGHT 7.22 FEET (2.20 M); WIDTH 4.99 FEET (1.52 M)
ATHENS, NATIONAL ARCHAEOLOGICAL MUSEUM

The three figures represented on this large relief stele are Demeter (left) in peplos, turned to her left; Persephone, her daughter (also known as Kore; right) in chiton and himation; and between them the young Triptolemos, son of King Keleus of Eleusis, naked and turned toward Demeter, who offers him ears of wheat—possibly made of gold—in her right hand. Flung over Triptolemos' shoulder is a himation, which he holds in check low down on the buttocks with his left hand. Demeter holds a scepter in her left hand, while Persephone in hers clutches a large torch and appears with her right hand to be blessing the boy, or perhaps placing a metal wreath on his head.

The two female deities emanate divine grandeur: Demeter, austerely majestic, and Kore, tenderly dignified, frame the young hero, who reverently takes on the task entrusted to him by the goddess—namely, to teach humans to cultivate wheat, the virtues of a peaceful existence, and a love for life. This ambitious work, in which some scholars detect Pheidias' genius, seems to have been well-known in antiquity, since two Roman reliefs have survived, one an exact copy and the other a related variation.

GRAVE STELE OF A YOUTH

SALAMIS OR AEGINA
430–420 BCE
PENTELIC MARBLE. PRESENT HEIGHT 3.44 FEET (1.05 M); WIDTH 2.79 FEET (0.85 M)
ATHENS, NATIONAL ARCHAEOLOGICAL MUSEUM

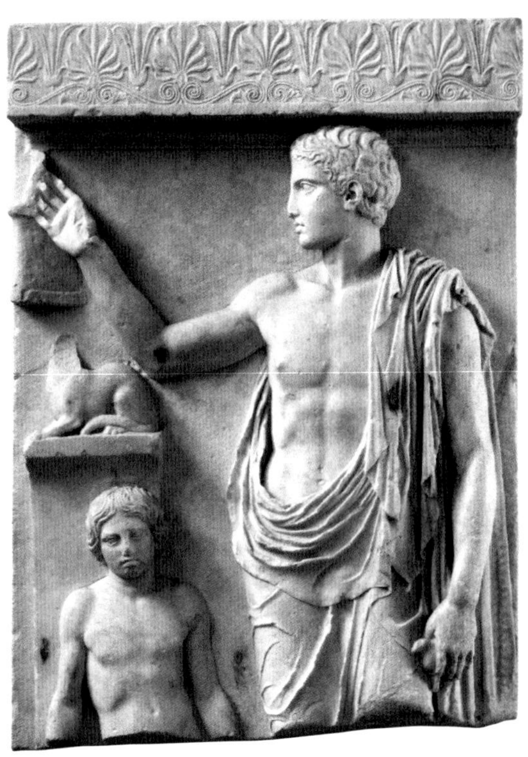

The lower part of this stele is missing, while the upper part is crowned by a wide cornice with wonderful decorations of palmettes and lotus blossoms. Represented is a young man facing to his right with his body in a frontal pose and his head in profile. He wears a lavishly draped himation that leaves the right side of his torso bare, extends his right hand toward a cage, and holds a bird in his lowered left hand. Below the cage a cat crouches on a pillar, in front of which, on a smaller scale, stands a slave boy, *en face*, nude and clearly grieving.

The modeling of both figures' bodies and their expressive countenances—the noble, otherworldly gaze of the youth, the sadness of the humble slave boy—the fluidity and movement of the drapery, and other elements, have led many scholars to ascribe the work to the gifted sculptor Agorakritos, the Parian pupil of Pheidias, who collaborated with his teacher on the sculpted decoration of the Parthenon.

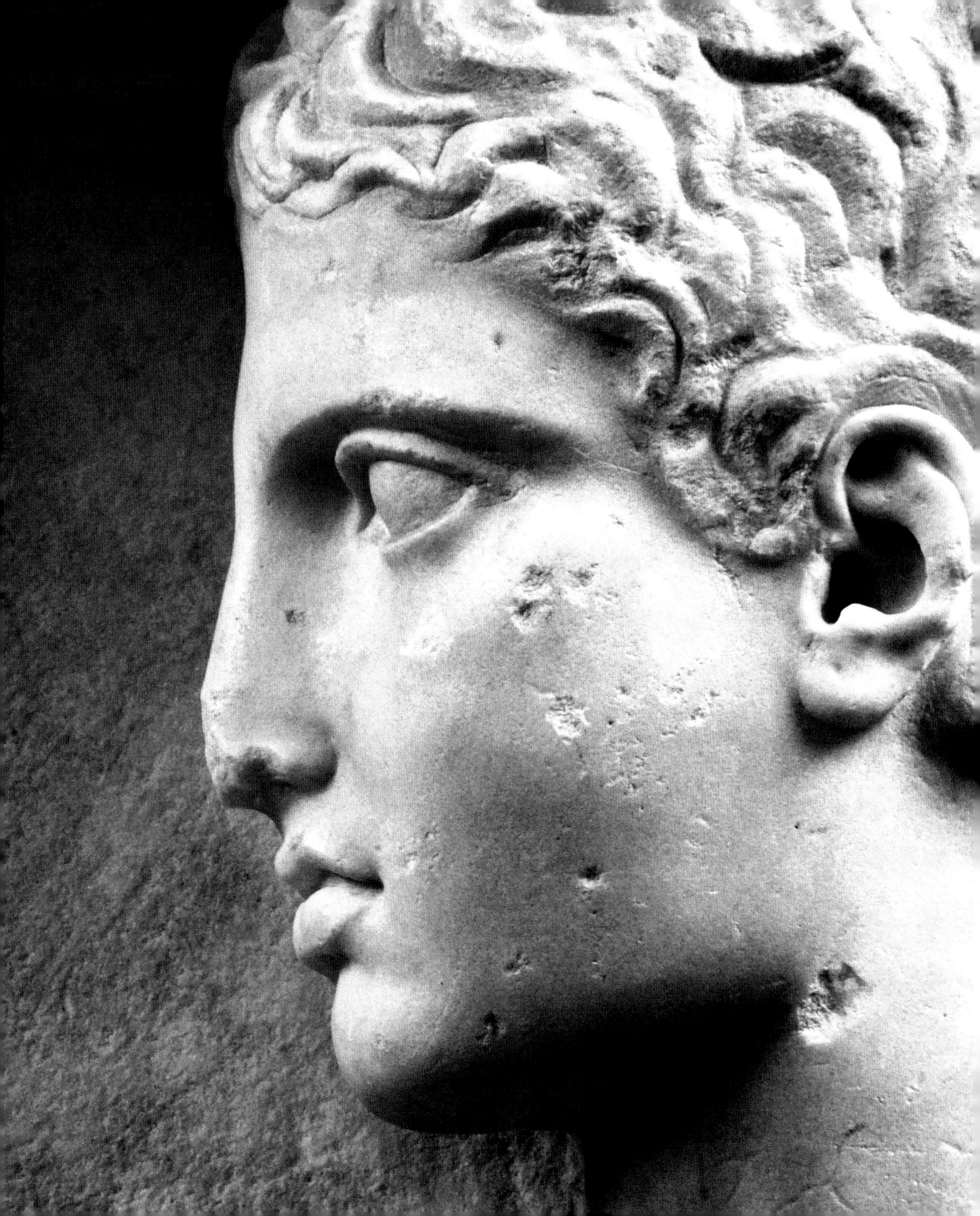

THE ACROPOLIS OF ATHENS

At the center of the city of Athens stands a rock on which, from the Mycenaean period (c.1600–1100 BCE) on, there stood the *megaron* (palace) of the ruler and perhaps the residences of nobles. This rock was fortified c. 1340–1230 BCE. With the advent of the Ionian tribes, at the beginning of the first millennium BCE, this rock remained uninhabited and revered among the sacred precincts of the gods, as it by then hosted altars and sanctuaries of deities and heroes. In Mycenaean times, kings, tradition has it, dwelt on the Acropolis. The institution of kingship continued until 682 BCE, when it was abolished officially and the Acropolis was dedicated exclusively to the gods.

The Sacred Rock, now dedicated to Athena Parthenos, patroness and protectress of the city of Athens, enjoyed its heyday during the fifth century BCE. In this golden age of creativity, outstanding works of art, architecture, and sculpture were produced, among which are admirable achievements of human genius, many of them unsurpassed. This bout of creation commenced after the victories of the Greeks over the Persian invaders, who beat an ignominious retreat, but only after they had set fire to the Archaic sanctuary of Athena on the Acropolis, in 480 BCE, and razed it to the ground. The Athenians, who had led the resistance against the Persian foe in the Hellenic world generally, assumed a hegemonic role among their Ionian allies and decided to make Athens the cultural and artistic center of the Greeks. Under the inspired leadership of Pericles they set to work implementing the plans of talented architects (such as Iktinos), sculptors (headed by Pheidias), and many others, building larger and more magnificent monuments in the sanctuary of their patron goddess to replace the destroyed Archaic ones. They preserved, however, the sculpted decorations from the old sanctuary, reverently burying them as holy heirlooms, along with the sculptural ex-votos that had adorned the Archaic Acropolis. The main temple on the Acropolis in this period was the famed Parthenon, designed by Iktinos and dedicated to Athena Parthenos, which occupied more or less the highest and flattest point of the long, narrow,

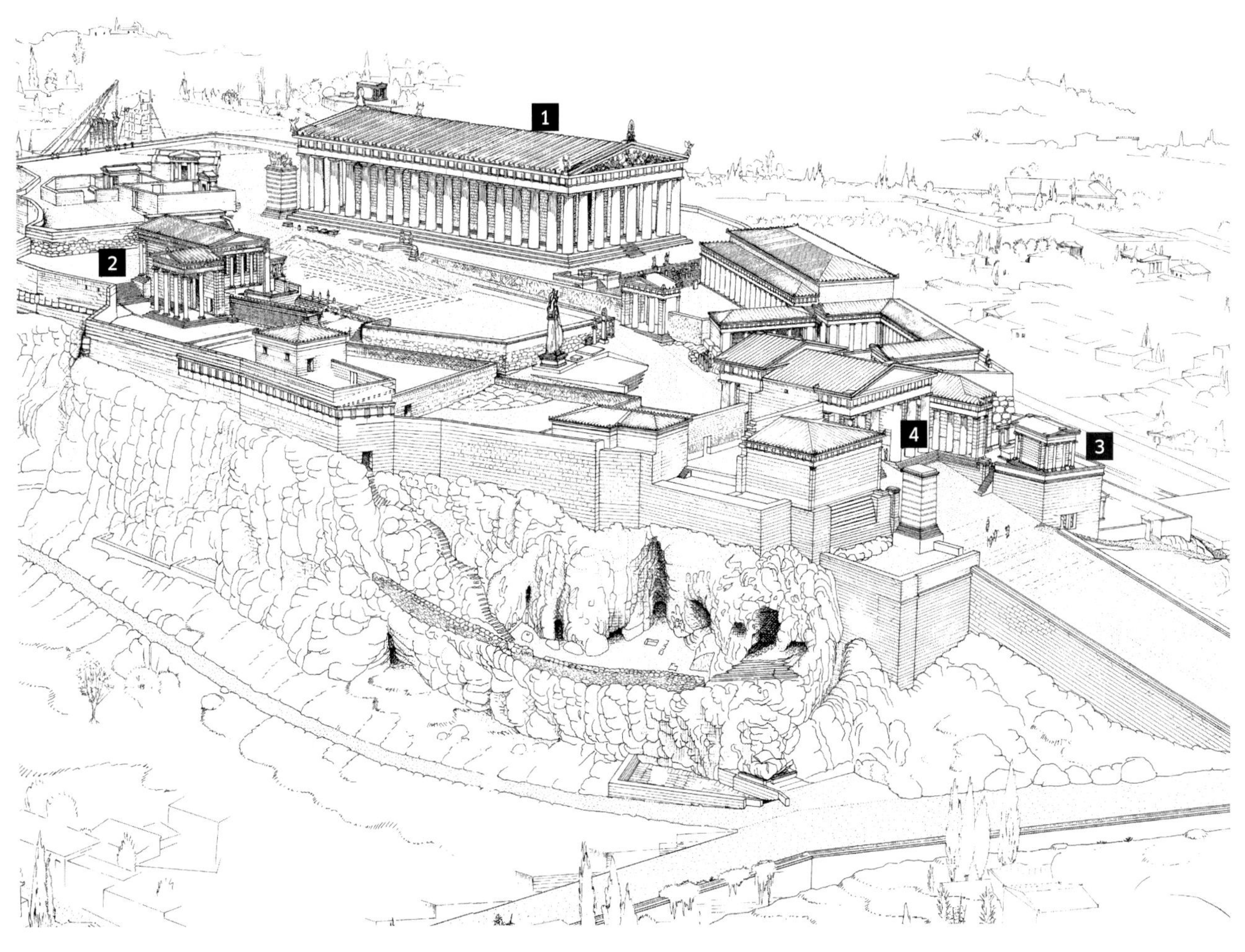

1. PARTHENON 2.ERECHTHEION 3. TEMPLE OF ATHENA NIKE 4. PROPYLAIA

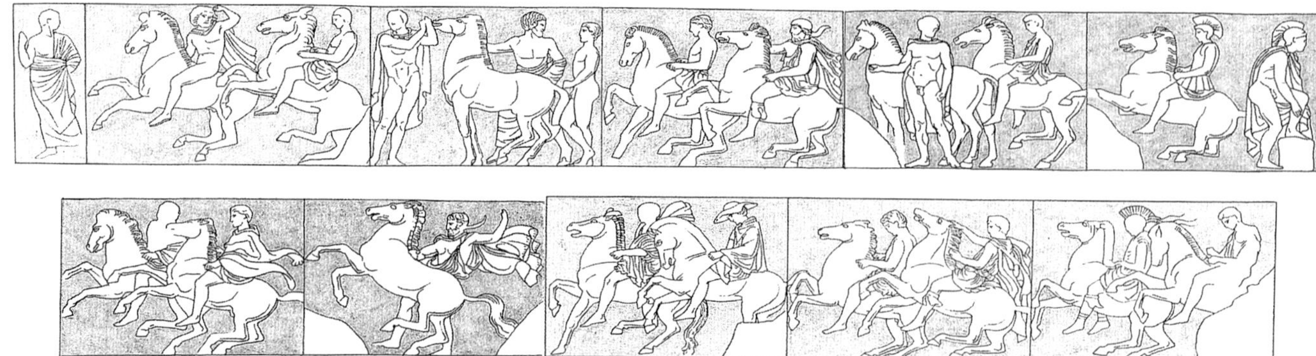

WEST FRIEZE

rocky eminence. Peripteral, with Doric columns of 26 x 55 feet (8 x 17 m), and made entirely of Pentelic marble, it measured 228.05 x 101.25 feet (69.51 x 30.86 m) and was richly decorated, with superb sculptures by Pheidias and his excellent collaborators on the pediments, metopes, and frieze.

The frieze, which crowned the outside of the walls of the pronaos, the cella, and the opisthodomos, was approximately 3 feet (1 m) high and 525 feet (160 m) long. The blocks bearing the reliefs were 1.97 feet (0.60 m) thick and very heavy, which is why when Lord Elgin removed them from the monument he cut away the back part to create slabs or plaques that were easier to handle and transport; the Parthenon marbles in the British Museum and the one in the Louvre Museum are consequently described as plaques. The sawn-off parts of the blocks were left on the Acropolis and during recent renovation have been gathered close to the southwest corner of the temple, awaiting their return to their original positions on the monument. The figures on the narrow sides of the monument were rendered on each stone separately, while those on the long sides are in continuum.

Represented on the frieze was the largest and most sacred festival of Athens, held in honor of the patron goddess Athena: the procession of the Panathenaia. This representation begins in the southwest corner and proceeds eastward in two branches, one along each long side, to terminate on the east side, which is the front of the temple. There were a wide range of participants in this celebration: priests, archons, musicians, *theoroi* (ambassadors) from the colonies, young horsemen and others driving animals for the sacrifices, maidens with *hydriaphoroi* (maidens bearing water pitchers) and *kanephoroi* (maidens with baskets), *thallophoroi* (old men carrying branches), and men and women with offerings. *Teletarchai* (masters of ceremonies) and servants are dispersed along the entire course. On the west side is

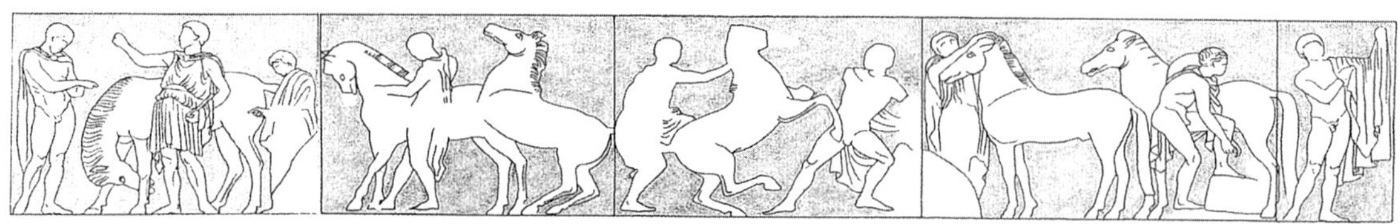

WEST FRIEZE

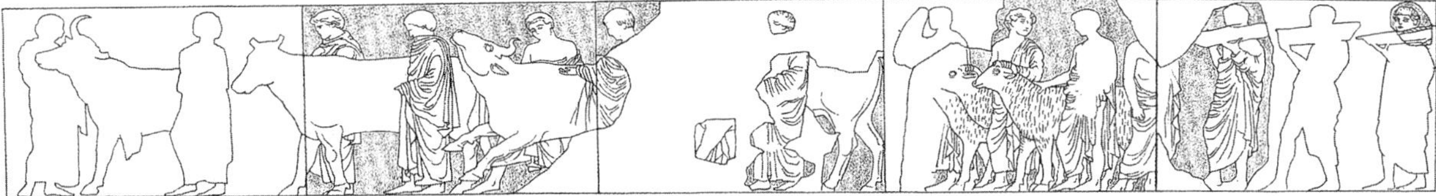

PART OF NORTH FRIEZE

depicted the preparation of the horsemen, who appear on the other sides in trot, canter, or gallop, while in the middle of the cavalcade is the contest for *apobatai*, armed men, or hoplites, who jumped on and off racing chariots.

The procession terminates in the middle of the east side, where the gods are represented seated and where Athena received her new peplos, the transport of which was the main purpose of the ascent from the Pompeion in the lower city up to the Acropolis. The Pompeion was a large public building outside the Kerameikos cemetery between the Sacred Gate and the Dipylon, the two official western entrances to the city of Athens. It was built where preparations for the Great Panathenaia, a quinquennial festival, initially took place in the open air. It seems that in the third year of the 53rd Olympiad (566 BCE) the Great Panathenaia was celebrated officially for the first time and henceforth was repeated in the third year of each Olympiad, that is, every four years. The regular Panathenaia, on the other hand, was held annually and included horse races and music contests, as well as processions, the highpoint of which was the delivery of the peplos to the *xoanon* (the wooden cult effigy of the goddess). The first building of the Pompeion is believed to have been constructed some time in the second half of the fifth century BCE. Kept inside its rooms were the sacred paraphernalia—the "pompeia"—used in the civic festivals. During the Great Panathenaia, which lasted at least four days, the offerings for the goddess were gathered in the Pompeion, on the twenty-seventh day of the month Hekatombaion (shortly before mid-August), to be processed the next day to the Acropolis. The offerings were the sacred peplos, woven by selected Athenian maidens known as the ergastines; baskets of gifts carried by the *kanephoroi*; and honeycombs and other sweetmeats brought in silver or bronze vessels and trays by the *skaphephoroi* and *hydriaphoroi*. The next day those girls who had been chosen took the offerings from the

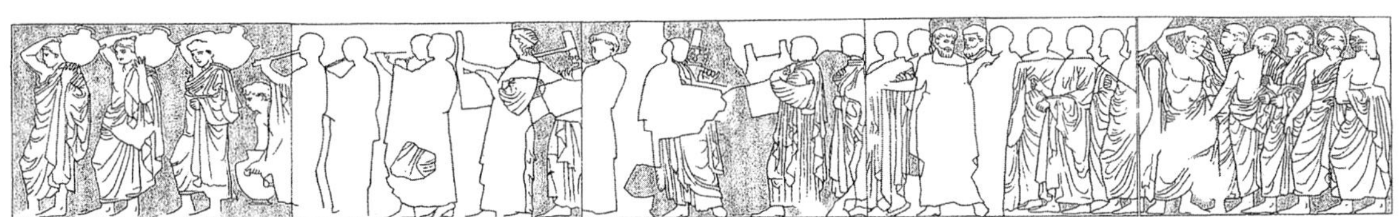

PART OF NORTH FRIEZE

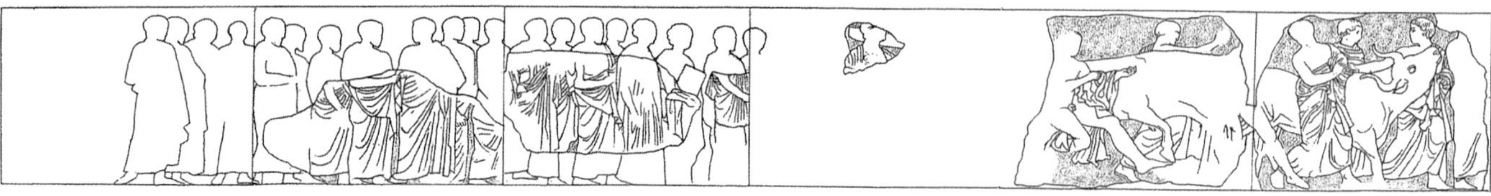

PART OF SOUTH FRIEZE

priests and set off with the procession from the propylon of the Pompeion (when the edifice existed in this place of preparation). The procession made its way with a ship on wheels (the *hypotrochos naus* of the ancient sources) on whose masts the peplos of the goddess had been hung. Young men on horseback preceded or ushered the procession and after them came the animals—cattle and sheep—for sacrifice. All citizens would take some meat from the sacrificed animals, for the "good new year."

The city of Athens invited the banquet members of the *theoriai* (embassies) from allied cities, since many of the sacrificial animals were offered by the cities of the Athenian League. The procession from the Pompeion continued along the Sacred Way, through the Agora, and reached the Areios Pagos, a rocky hill to the south of the Acropolis, where the peplos was removed from the masts of the ship and carried by hand to the *xoanon* of Athena, before which it was delivered to the priests.

The Parthenon frieze contains around 360 human and divine figures and more than 220 animal likenesses. The greater part of the frieze was probably created between 442 and 438 BCE, when the temple was inaugurated on the occasion of the festival of the Panathenaia, which coincided with the third year of the 85th Olympiad. The rest of the sculptural decoration was completed in 432 BCE. The sculptural ensemble on the Parthenon frieze constitutes the climax of ancient Greek artistic creation, expressing the magnificence of the Athenian Democracy.

In addition to the Parthenon, other important edifices were founded on the Acropolis, among them the Propylaia, or the monumental gateway; the Erechtheion, a small temple in the Ionic order with the famous porch of the Karyatides, inside which the local hero Erechtheus was worshipped along with Athena; and the Ionic Temple of Athena Nike, which topped a tower to the south of the Propylaia and the entrance to the Sacred Rock. The small Nike temple, built after the Peace of Nikias in 421 BCE,

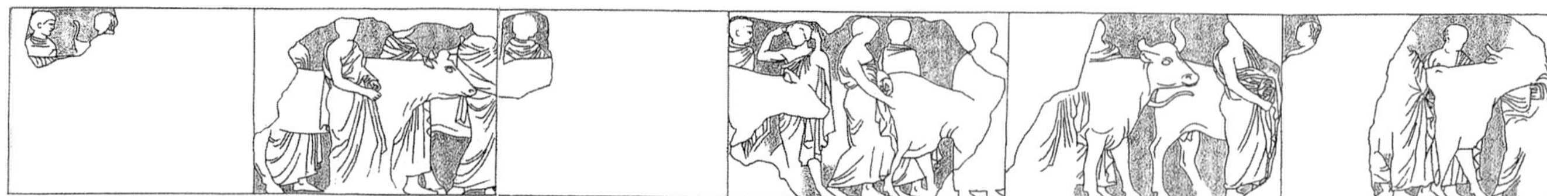

PART OF SOUTH FRIEZE

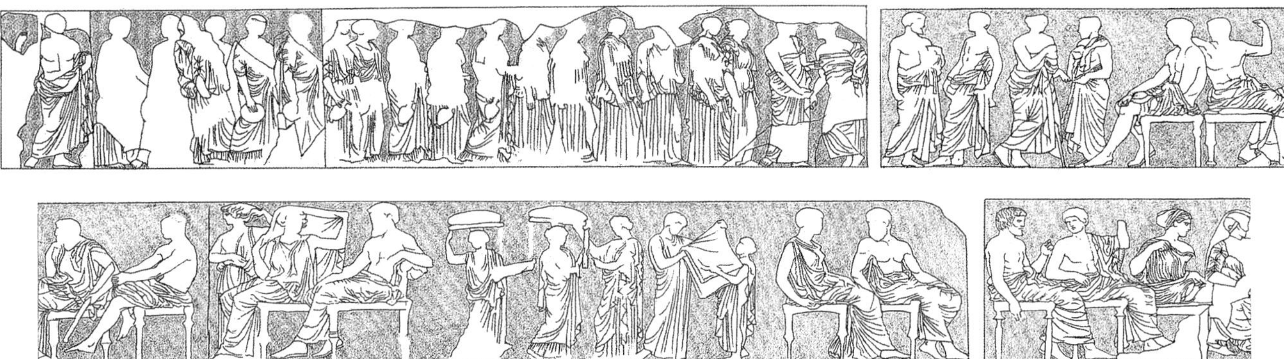

EAST FRIEZE

during a lull in the Peloponnesian War, is amphiprostyle (four Ionic columns on the east and the west fronts) and was surrounded on all four sides by a relief frieze 1.5 feet (0.45 m) high, the subject of which was battles between Greeks and Persians. The pediments of the temple would also have carried relief representations. To better protect this charming edifice, a balustrade was constructed on top of the cymatium crowning the final course of stone blocks of the north, west, and south sides of the tower. The plaques of this balustrade were decorated on the exterior with about fifty relief figures, usually two on each plaque, which pilgrims beheld as they ascended the Acropolis.

The principal figure on each of the three sides is Athena, sitting on a rock with her shield beside her and receiving trophies and sacrificial animals from the Nikai. The Nikai—some with their peplos freely flowing, others with it tightly girdled or held in place with straps crossed on the bosom—are represented in various unusual poses, for example, fastening or loosening a *sandalizousa* (sandal); with hands raised in front and the himation enveloping the lower body symmetrically and bunched between the legs; rushing to the right poised to slay the sacrificial bull; and running to the right with wings wide open. Even though Athena was wingless, most of the Nikai, her worshippers, were winged. Six sculptors are believed to have worked on the decoration of the temple, among them Paionios and Kallimachos, who clearly drew inspiration from the Parthenon frieze. Nonetheless, the dedication of the temple to Athena Nike and the symbolism of the representations served a different purpose from that of the Parthenonian creations. Athens was at the time struggling to survive in the midst of a catastrophic civil war and was petitioning the patron deity for protection.

In addition to the architectural monuments on the Acropolis, there were a host of ex-votos, primarily sculptural, such as statues of korai, horsemen, animals, and more.

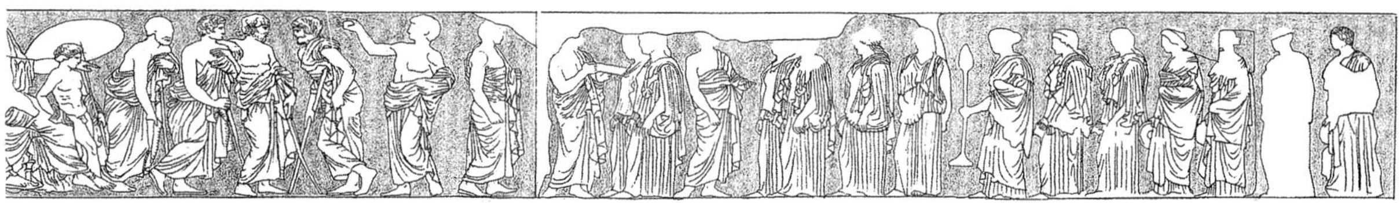

EAST FRIEZE

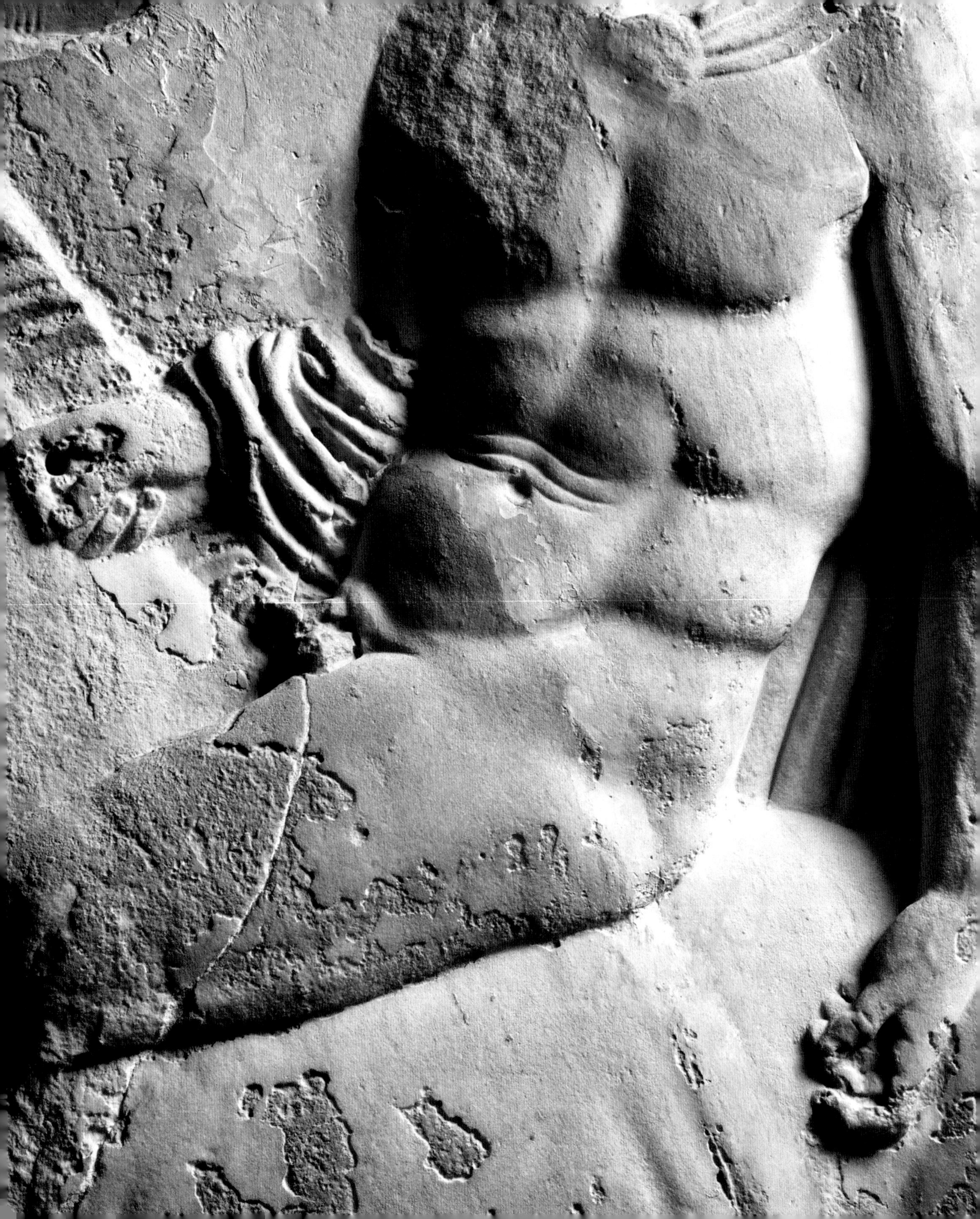

PARTHENON FRIEZE

HORSEMEN

ATHENS, ACROPOLIS, PARTHENON, NORTH FRIEZE, BLOCK XXXIV
442–438 OR 432 BCE
PENTELIC MARBLE. HEIGHT 3.35 FEET (1.02 M); PRESENT WIDTH 4.02 FEET (1.23 M)
ATHENS, ACROPOLIS MUSEUM

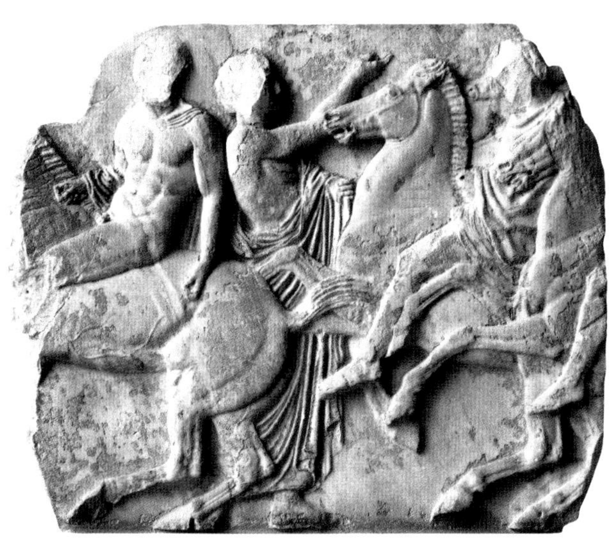

A single rider, sitting comfortably on his horse, turns his entire upper body backward. He wears a himation pinned below the neck that hangs back, revealing his naked body. One edge is folded over his right forearm, which rests on the neck of his mount. Behind him is a *teletarches* (young master of ceremonies), whose himation also leaves his torso bare. With his back turned on the horseman, he makes a calm gesture, regulating the movement of the two horsemen advancing toward him.

The composition, considered one of the loveliest from the north side of the frieze, is unique in its back-to-back placement of the two figures and in the dynamic arrival of the two steeds, in brisk canter. This contrasts with the relaxed pose of the horseman (emphasized by his freely hanging left hand) and the composure of the *teletarches*. The block is attributed to one of the important artists who worked on the frieze, possibly Alkamenes.

PARTHENON FRIEZE

HORSEMEN

ATHENS, ACROPOLIS, PARTHENON, WEST FRIEZE, BLOCK II
442–438 BCE
PENTELIC MARBLE. HEIGHT 3.34 FEET (1.017 M); WIDTH 5.25 FEET (1.60 M)
LONDON, BRITISH MUSEUM

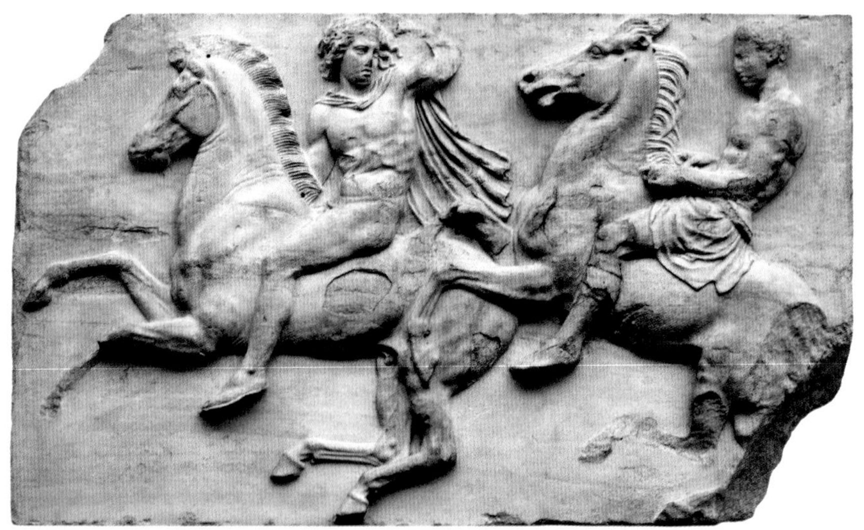

Represented here are two young horsemen on galloping steeds. The first, whose *chlamys* (short, oblong mantle) billows behind him, leaving his torso bare, is the only horseman with long hair. The second, wearing a short chiton around his pelvis and high boots, is likely the servant of the first. The naked youth had in his hair a fillet, or some other metal ornament. He is seated firmly on the back of his horse, which gallops to the left, with his torso in an almost frontal pose and displaying a superb torsion of his waist and his head. His gaze is fixed behind him toward the other rider. Full of youthful vigor, the figure immortalizes the vitality of a fleeting moment from the splendid cavalcade in which he participated.

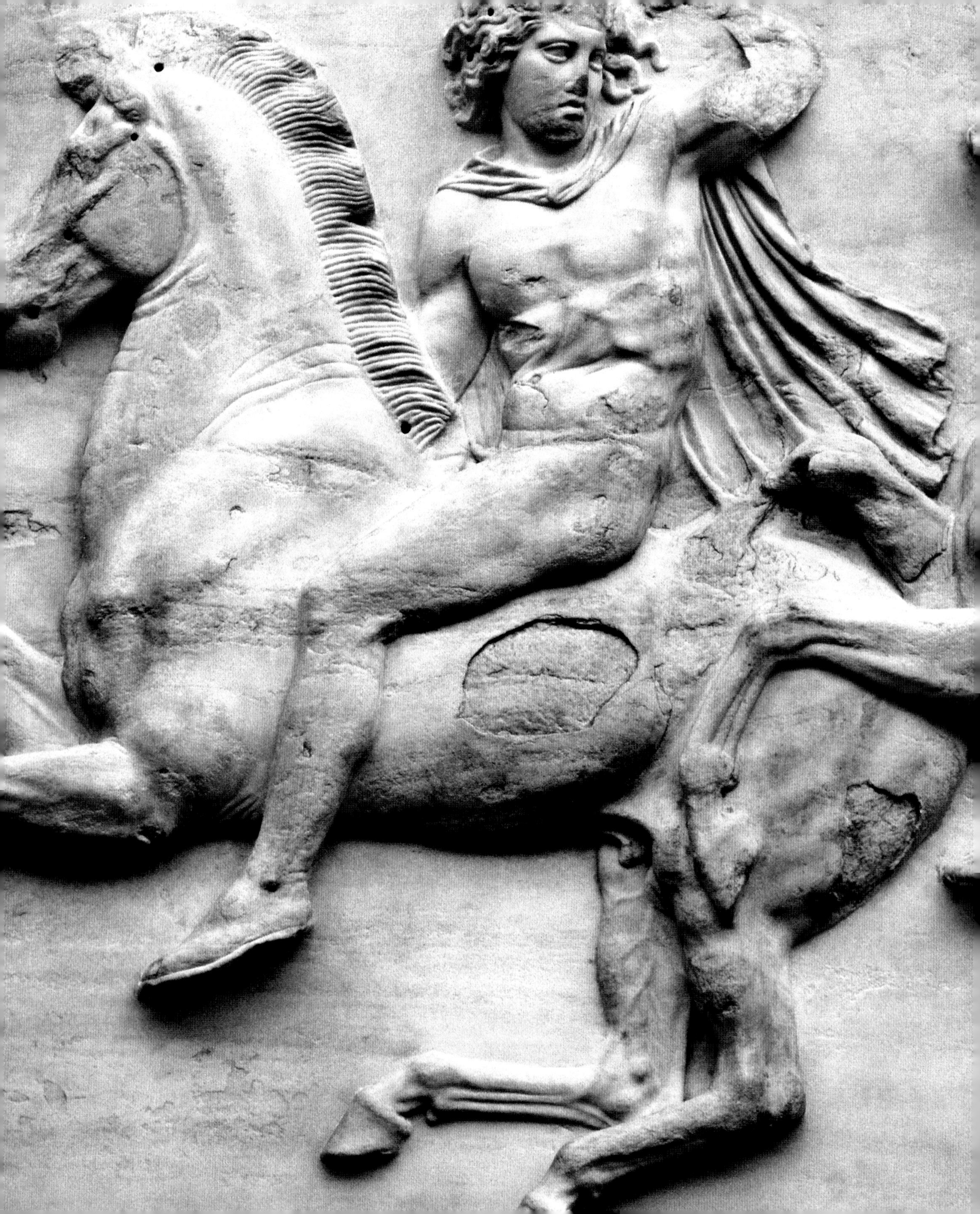

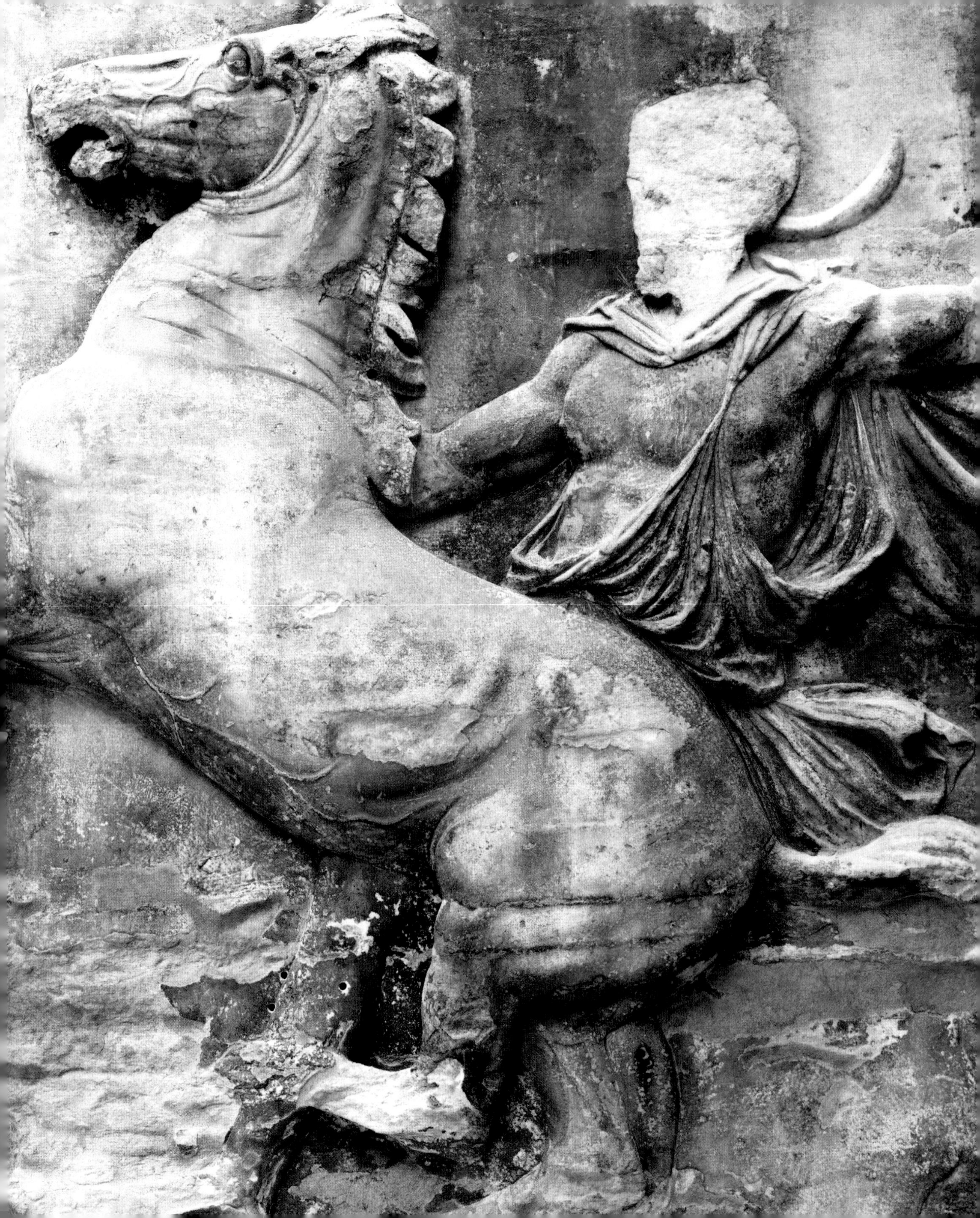

PARTHENON FRIEZE

HIPPARCHUS AND HORSE

ATHENS, ACROPOLIS, PARTHENON, WEST FRIEZE, BLOCK VIII
442–438 BCE
PENTELIC MARBLE. HEIGHT 3.34 FEET (1.017 M); WIDTH 4.56 FEET (1.39 M)
ATHENS, ACROPOLIS MUSEUM

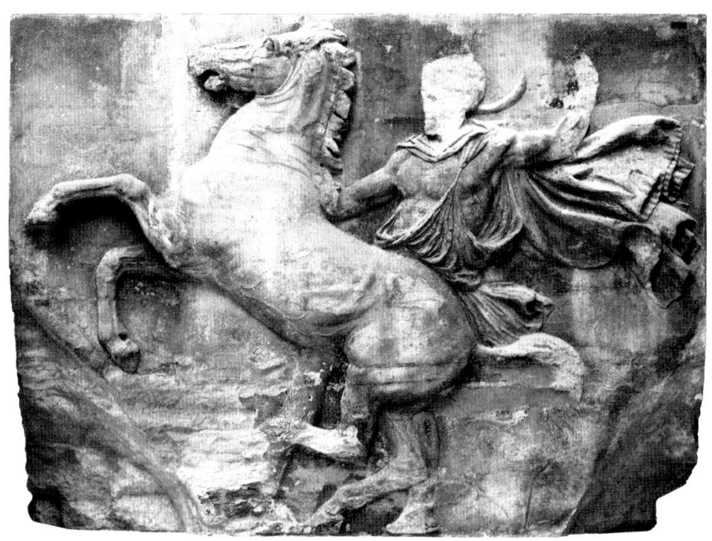

Here, a bearded *hipparchus* (cavalry officer), in a short chiton and a heavy, multipleated chlamys that blows out behind him, struggles to keep a rearing horse in check. The conception and execution of this work is remarkable: Man and animal are represented as if soaring in the Attic sunlight. It is the only representation of a single man and animal on the entire frieze and is ascribed to Pheidias himself.

PARTHENON FRIEZE

HORSEMEN

ATHENS, ACROPOLIS, PARTHENON, WEST FRIEZE, BLOCK IX
442–438 BCE
PENTELIC MARBLE. HEIGHT 3.34 FEET (1.017 M); WIDTH 4.56 FEET (1.39 M)
ATHENS, ACROPOLIS MUSEUM

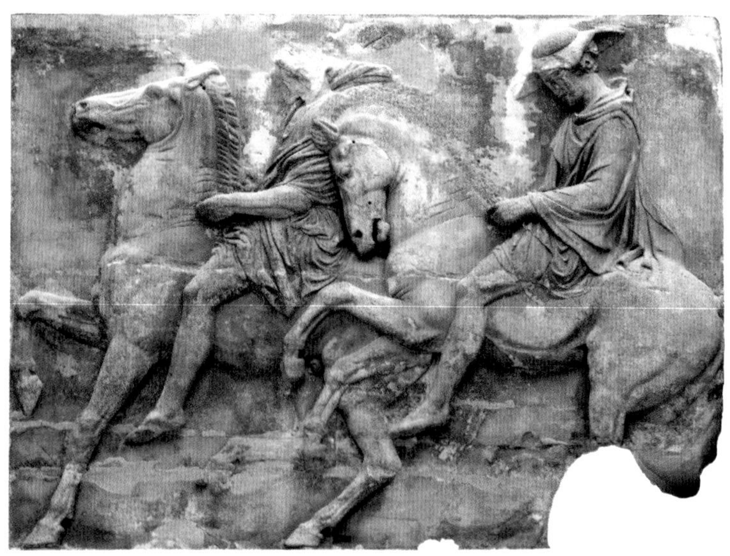

Two youths on horseback, both dressed in short chitons and short himations, take part in the procession at a brisk canter. The second figure, whose head survives, wears a *petasos* (a wide-brimmed hat), which shades his serious, youthful face and its expression of pious meditation on his mission: to honor the patron goddess and protectress of his city.

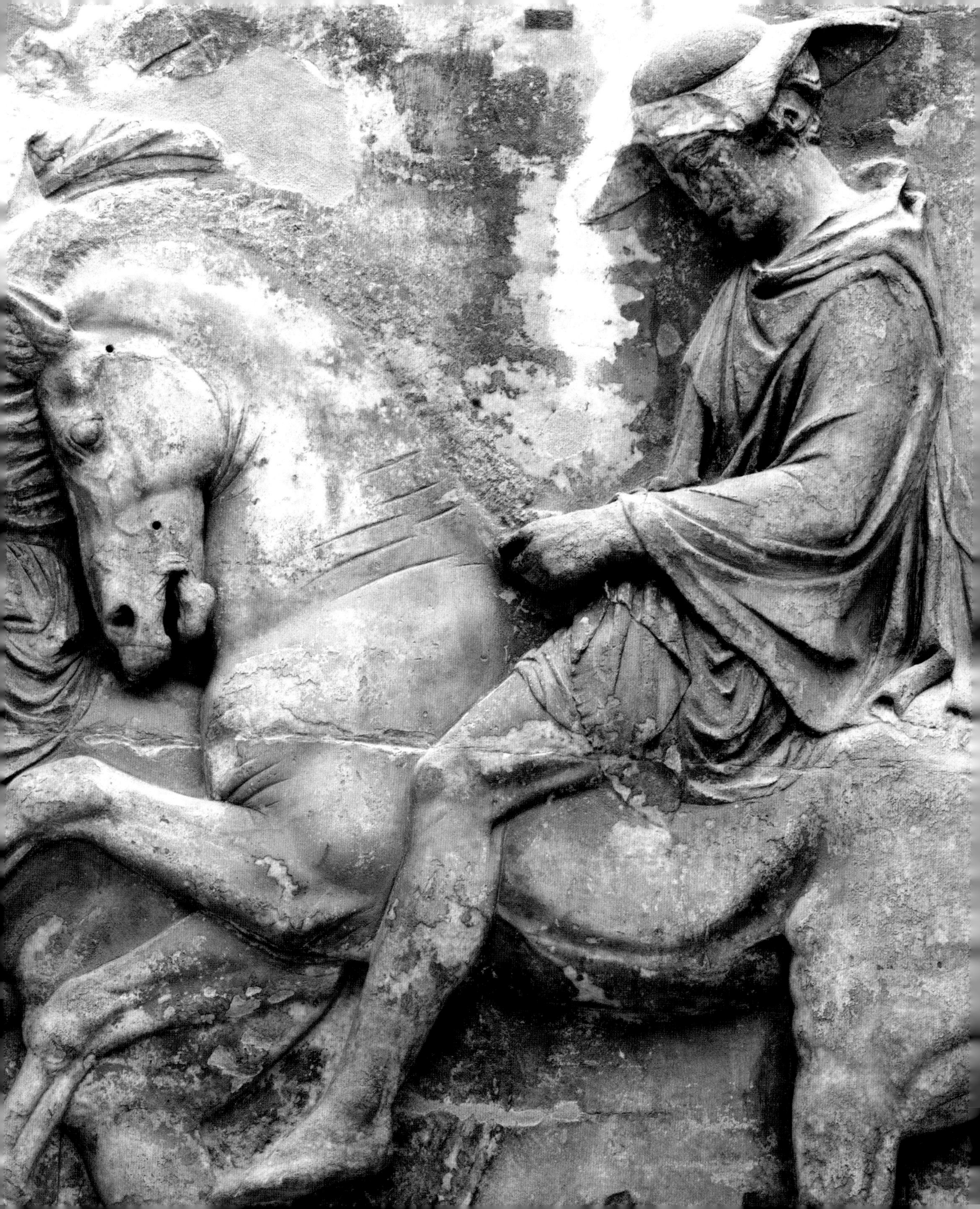

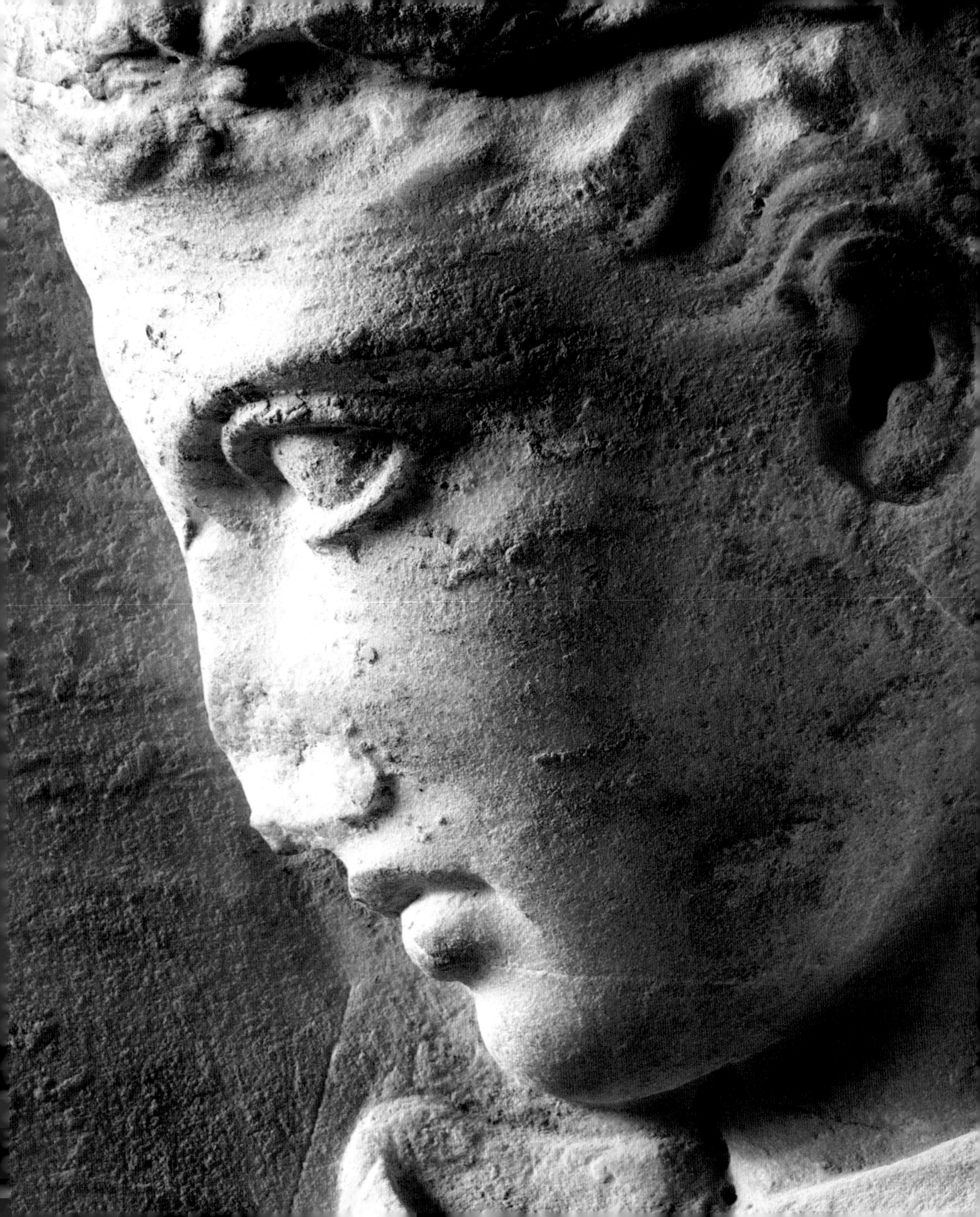

PARTHENON FRIEZE

CATTLE DRIVERS

ATHENS, ACROPOLIS, PARTHENON, NORTH FRIEZE, BLOCK II
442–438 BCE OR 432 BCE
PENTELIC MARBLE. HEIGHT 0.40 FEET (1.02 M); WIDTH 3.44 FEET (1.407 M)
ATHENS, ACROPOLIS MUSEUM

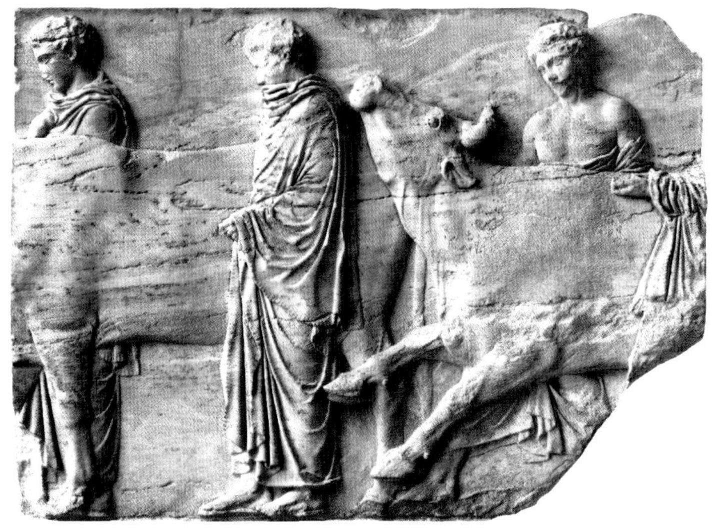

Three youths clad in himations drive two oxen to sacrifice. The first ox proceeds sedately, while the second resists. The first two *boidolatai* (cattle drivers) advance ceremonially, their heads slightly bowed and bearing contemplative gazes, conveying to the viewer the sanctity of the act in which they participate. There follows a troubled scene of the third youth trying to control the second ox, but this does not detract from the sober aesthetic of the representation. On the contrary, the composition gains in vitality and acquires a realistic character. To these elements is added the virtually flawless chiseling of the figures; the figure of the first young man undoubtedly belongs in the sphere of works that surpass normal human abilities.

The block was found at the east edge of the north side, exactly below the position it had occupied on the temple.

PARTHENON FRIEZE

HORSEMEN

ATHENS, ACROPOLIS, PARTHENON, NORTH FRIEZE, BLOCK XLVII
442–438 BCE
PENTELIC MARBLE. HEIGHT 3.34 FEET (1.017 M); WIDTH 5.25 FEET (1.60 M)
LONDON, BRITISH MUSEUM

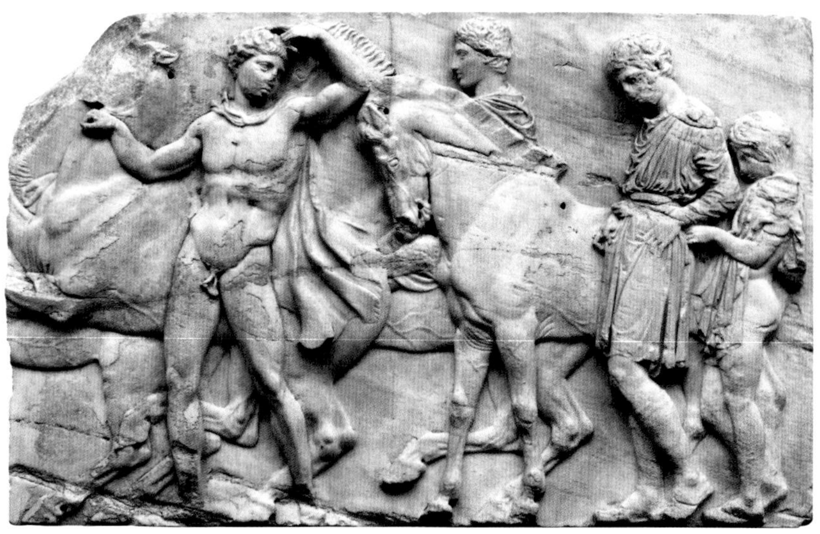

This block shows four youths walking alongside their horses, following the eastward flow of the procession. The movement of the second figure from the left, who is represented almost *en face*, links the figures in front with those behind. He turns his head backward and, with his left hand, places a fillet on his short curly hair, while his right arm stretches along the neck of his galloping steed. He wears a short chiton fastened at the neck and blowing behind him, which leaves his body bare and enhances the sense of his movement against the horses' bodies. The result is an exciting composition of considerable complexity.

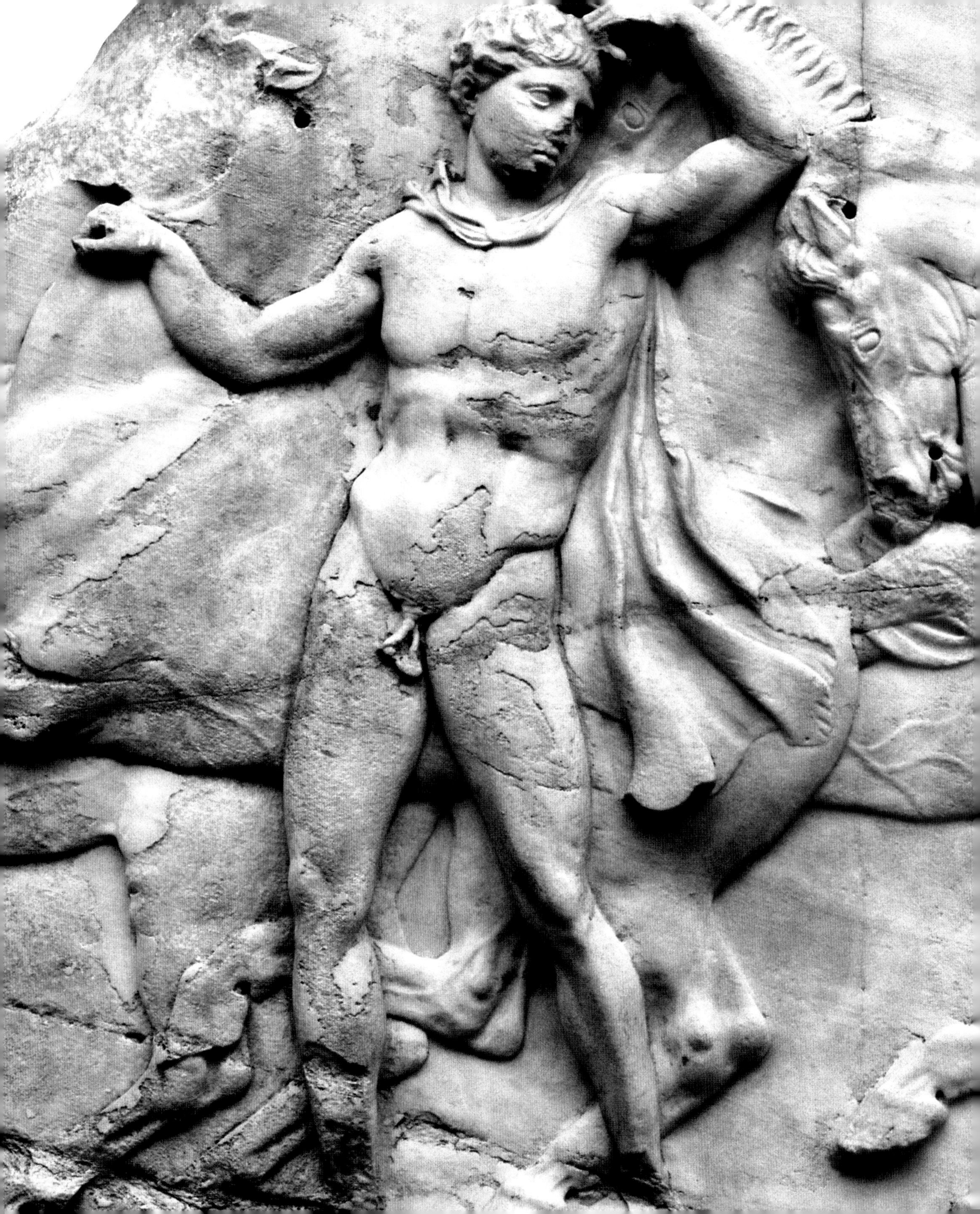

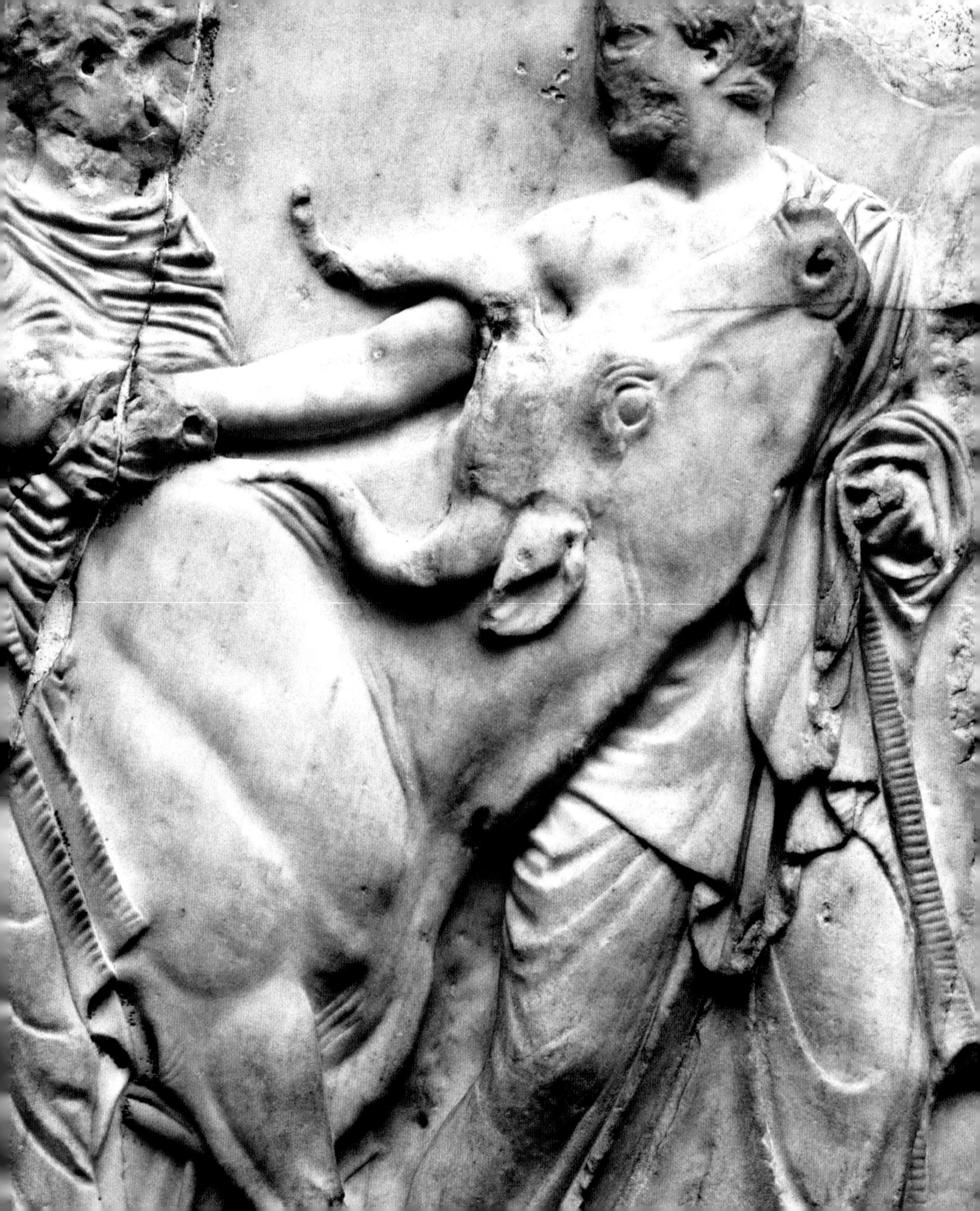

PARTHENON FRIEZE

CATTLE DRIVERS

ATHENS, ACROPOLIS, PARTHENON, SOUTH FRIEZE, BLOCK XLIV
442–438 BCE
PENTELIC MARBLE. HEIGHT 3.34 FEET (1.017 M); PRESENT WIDTH 4.00 FEET (1.22 M)
LONDON, BRITISH MUSEUM

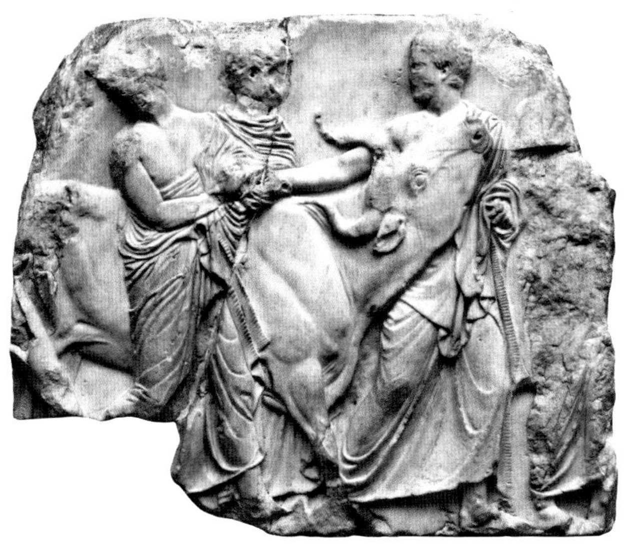

Three youths clad in himations lead a protesting calf. The calf rears its head forcibly in front of the torso of the first young man, who, although walking to the right, turns his head backward and stretches his right hand toward the third of his companions, perhaps in an effort to restrain the animal. The smooth surface of the bovine's body, which is the dominant feature of the composition, is interrupted by the vertical axes of the cattle drivers wrapped in their amply draped garments—an inventive and lively representation.

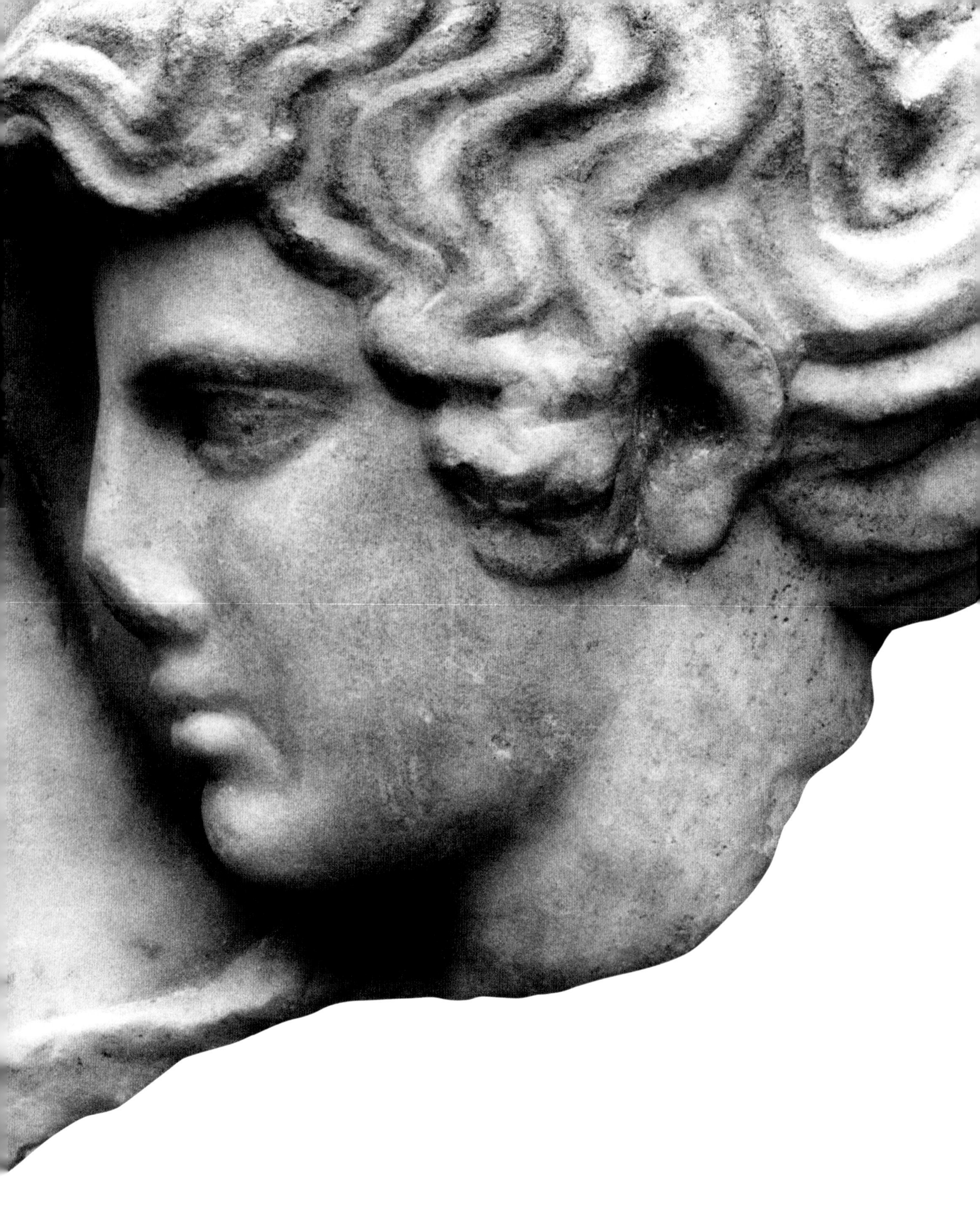

PARTHENON FRIEZE

IRIS

ATHENS, ACROPOLIS, PARTHENON, EAST FRIEZE
442–438 BCE OR 432 BCE
PENTELIC MARBLE. PRESENT HEIGHT 0.72 FEET (0.22 M); PRESENT WIDTH 0.90 FEET (0.275 M)
ATHENS, ACROPOLIS MUSEUM

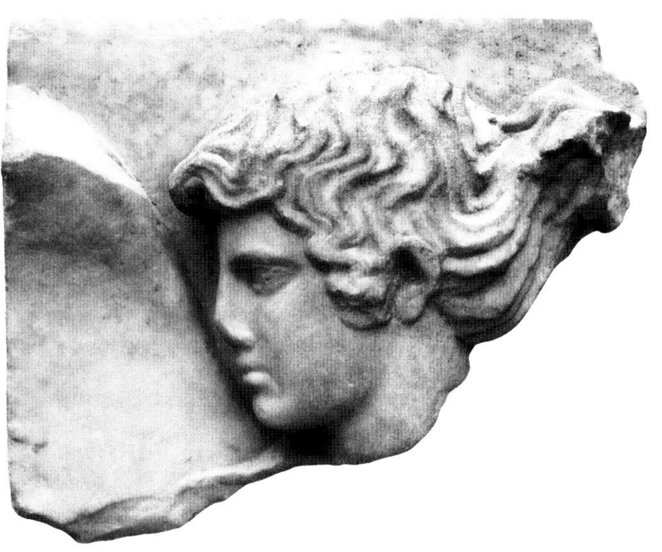

The messenger goddess of the Olympian deities, golden-winged Iris, turns to the left and with her left hand smoothes her hair, which flows out behind her in ruffled waves. Her countenance is proud and radiant, as befits her status, with perhaps a hint of youthful impatience. Along with the other gods she awaits the arrival of the procession and the offerings of the pilgrims. This breathtaking figure sculpted by the chisel of a great artist was found built into a Byzantine wall southwest of the Acropolis in 1889.

NIKE "SANDALIZOUSA"

ATHENS, ACROPOLIS, TEMPLE OF ATHENA NIKE, BALUSTRADE
421–415 BCE OR 410 BCE
PENTELIC MARBLE. HEIGHT 3.48 FEET (1.06 M);
PRESENT WIDTH 4.99 FEET (0.52 M)
ATHENS, ACROPOLIS MUSEUM

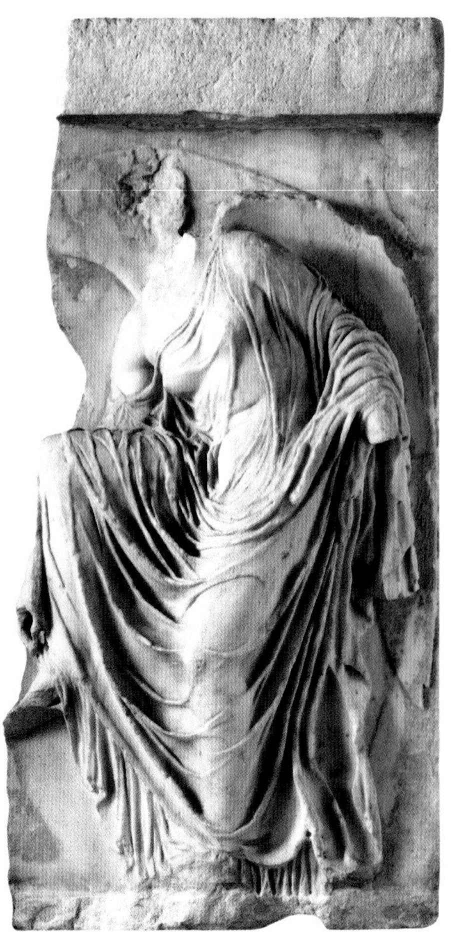

Nike (Victory), turned to her right, tries to adjust the sandal (hence the epithet "sandalizousa") on her right foot, which she has half lifted, her knee bent and body bowed. She wears a chiton and a flimsy himation, which leave her right shoulder bare and enhance the plasticity of her supple young body.

Characteristic of the figures on the parapet panels is the lavish drapery of their garments and the variety in its treatment: The folds flutter, wrap, curve, and undulate. Here the folds of the diaphanous himation fall calmly from the left shoulder, are gathered impetuously on the raised right thigh, and from there tumble between the legs to end at the ankles, exposing the fine vertical pleats of the chiton under the left, supporting leg. This composition emphasizes the vertical axis of the work, giving a stable base to the figure, which would otherwise appear to be hovering without support.

A work of special sensitivity and refinement in the execution of its details, Nike exudes a unique charm. Some scholars believe the artist is Kallimachos, one of the important sculptors active in the late fifth century BCE and known in antiquity as "catatexitechnus" (he who wastes his art), because of his love for working the minutest detail to perfection.

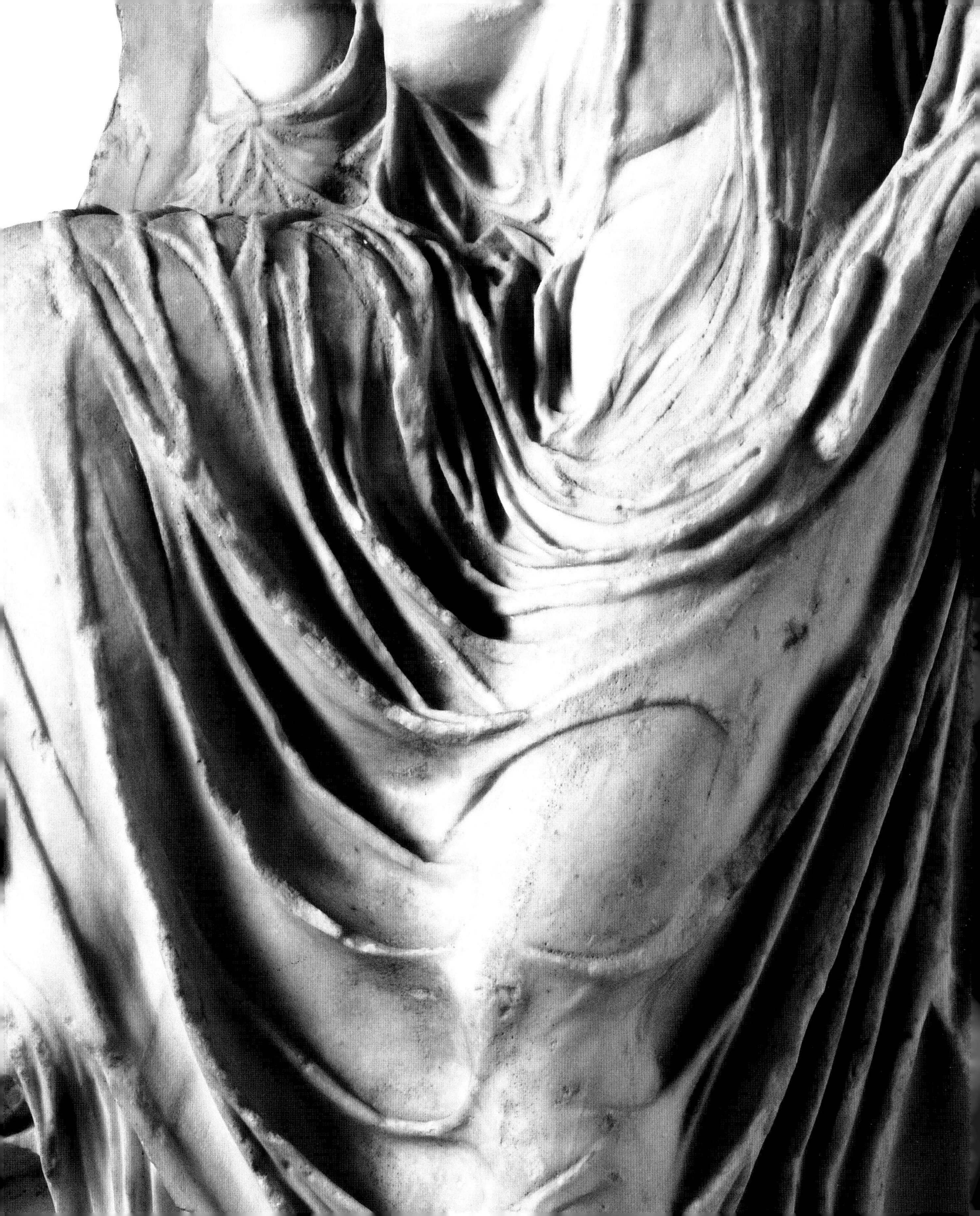

THE NIKE OF PAIONIOS

OLYMPIA, SACRED ALTIS
LAST QUARTER OF FIFTH CENTURY BCE
MARBLE. PRESENT HEIGHT 7.09 FEET (2.16 M; ORIGINAL HEIGHT 10 FEET [3 M])
OLYMPIA, ARCHAEOLOGICAL MUSEUM

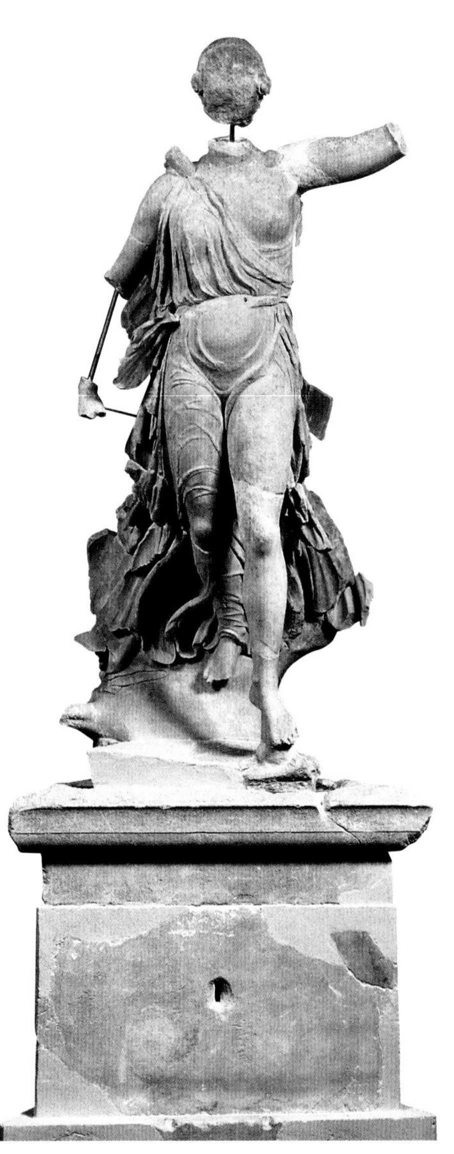

This work, by the sculptor Paionios, from Mende in the Chalkidike, is an ex-voto of the Messenians and Naupaktians to commemorate their victory over the Lacedaemonians at Sphakteria in 424 BCE. It stood close to the east side of the Temple of Zeus, upon a triangular pedestal 30 feet (9 m) high. Represented is a Nike (Victory) descending from the skies and alighting on the back of an eagle (an animal associated with Zeus) lying at her feet. She wears a gossamer chiton pinned over the right shoulder that clings to her body and blows back, with the rush of her rapid descent, revealing her left breast and left leg. In her raised left hand she held high the edge of her himation, which flutters freely behind her, while with the lowered right she held a ribbon or a branch. Her chiton was painted red with a gold girdle, and there was a gold fillet on her head. Some parts of the eagle must also have been made of metal. The stele is thought to have been painted blue, to blend in with the sky, thus creating the illusion that the Nike was hovering in space.

The perfect modeling of the sculpture's volumes, particularly on the windblown drapery of the garments and their exquisite interplay of light and shadow, and its bold composition (the figure essentially stands on one leg) establish its creator as one of the most important ancient Greek sculptors.

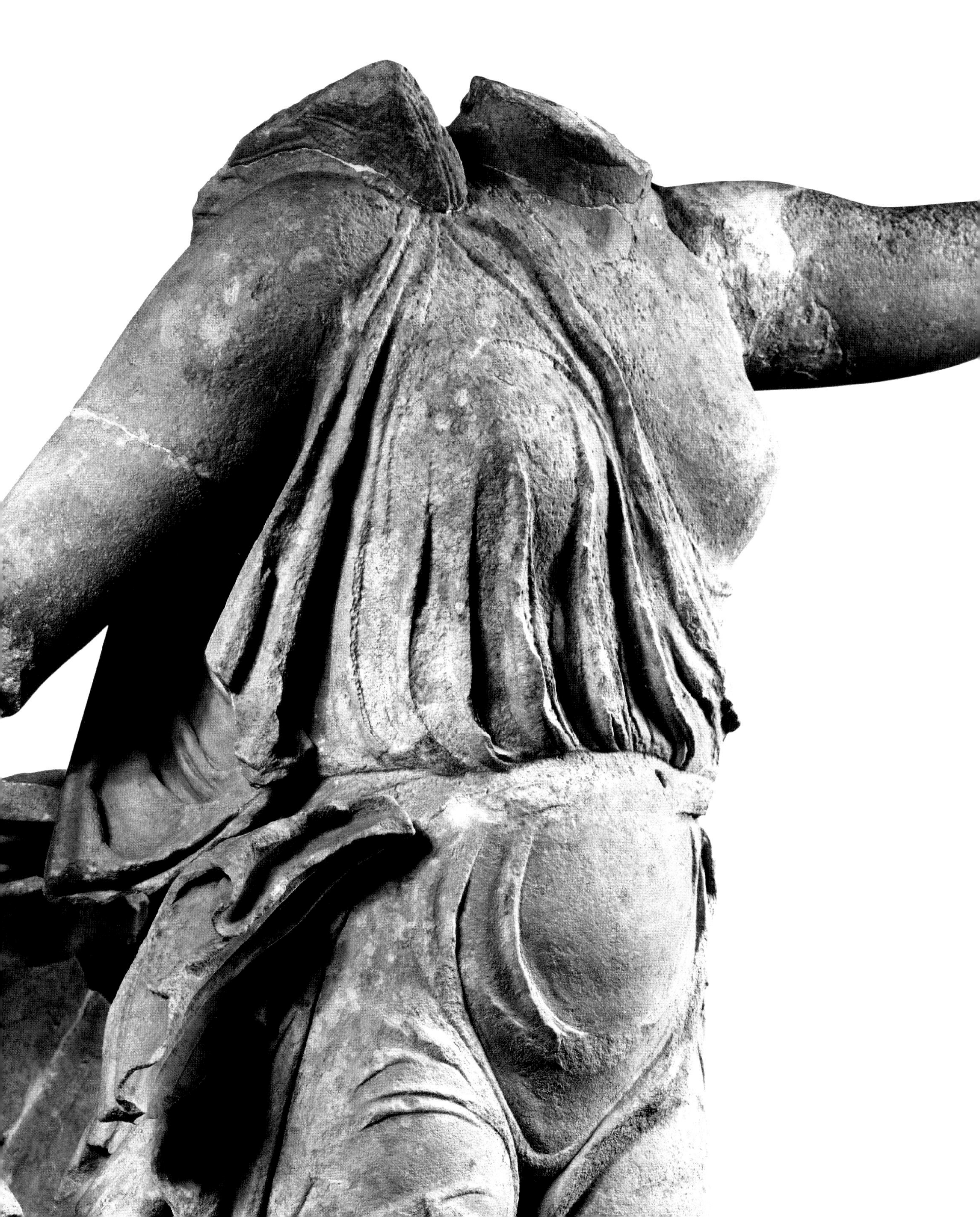

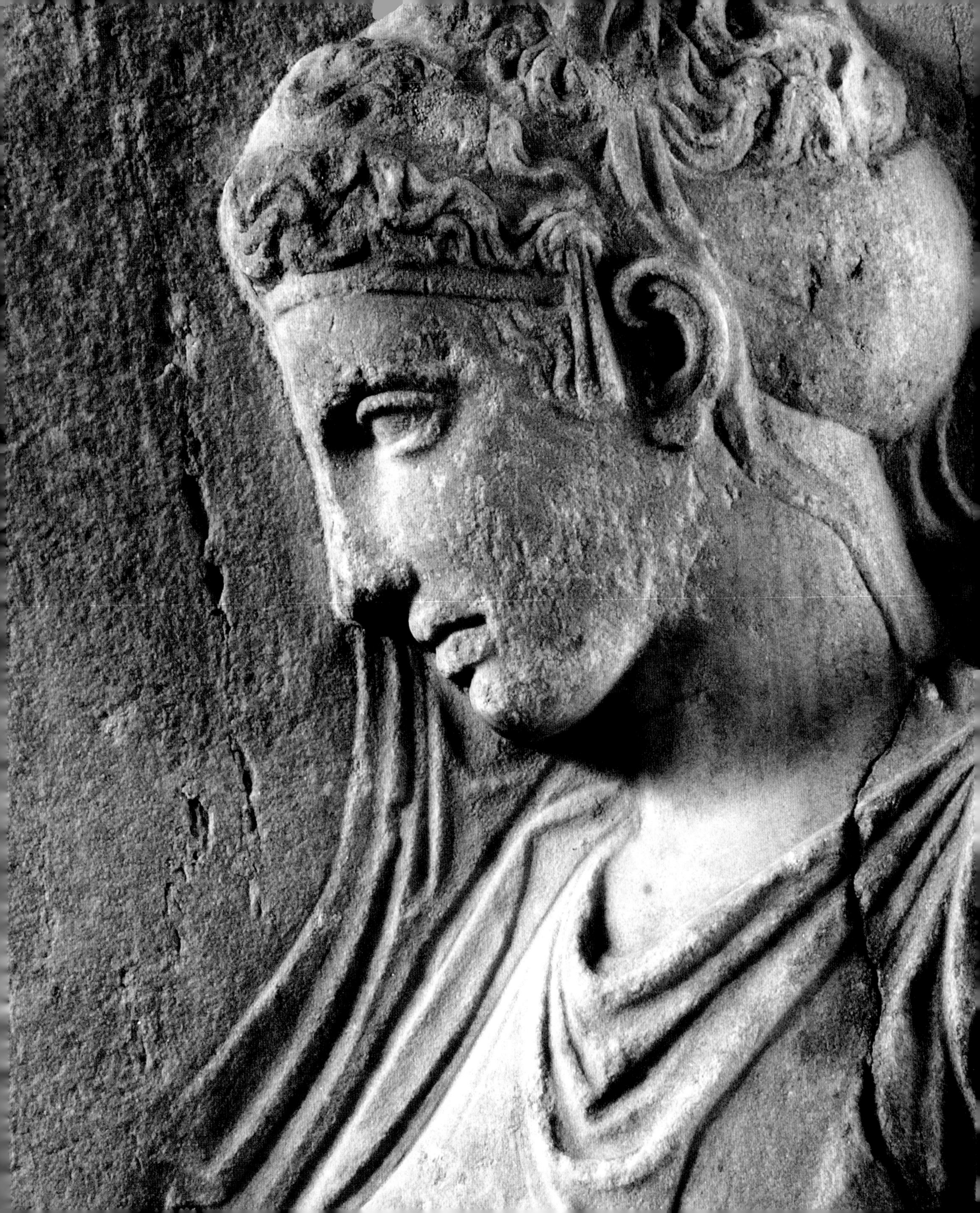

THE STELE OF HEGESO

ATHENS, KERAMEIKOS CEMETERY
410–400 BCE
PENTELIC MARBLE. HEIGHT 5.12 FEET (1.56 M); WIDTH 3.18 FEET (0.97 M)
ATHENS, NATIONAL ARCHAEOLOGICAL MUSEUM

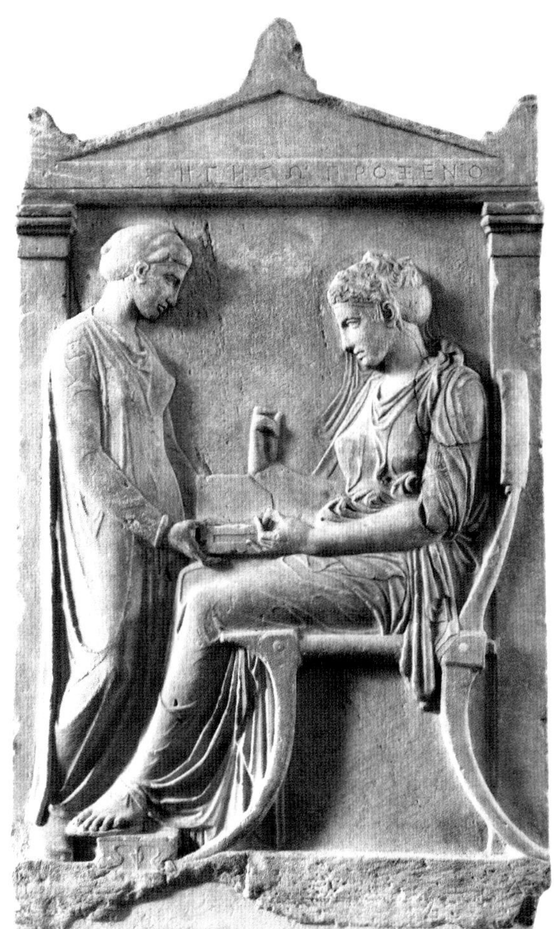

This grave stele is in the form of a *naiskos* (small temple), with *antae*, pediment, and palmette acroteria. On the horizontal cornice of the pediment is the inscription *Ηγησώ Προξένο* (Hegeso, daughter of Proxenos), the name of the deceased female who is represented seated on an elegant chair with curving legs and back. Hegeso wears a chiton, a draped himation, and a flimsy veil on her head. Her wavy hair is gathered in a kekryphalos at the nape of the neck. Her feet rest on a low footstool decorated with sculpted ivy leaves. In front of and turned toward her, a slave girl stands with her body in three-quarter pose and her head in profile. She is dressed in a closed barbarian garment with long sleeves and a sakkos on her head, covering her hair. Before her deceased mistress, she holds open a jewelry box, from which Hegeso has already removed, with her right hand, a trinket that was not shown in relief but was painted.

This stele is one of the loveliest of its kind. The spirituality of the figures, the perfect harmony of the composition, and the sensitivity and precision with which individual details were executed indicate the stele as the work of a great artist of the age, perhaps the "catatexi-technus" Kallimachos.

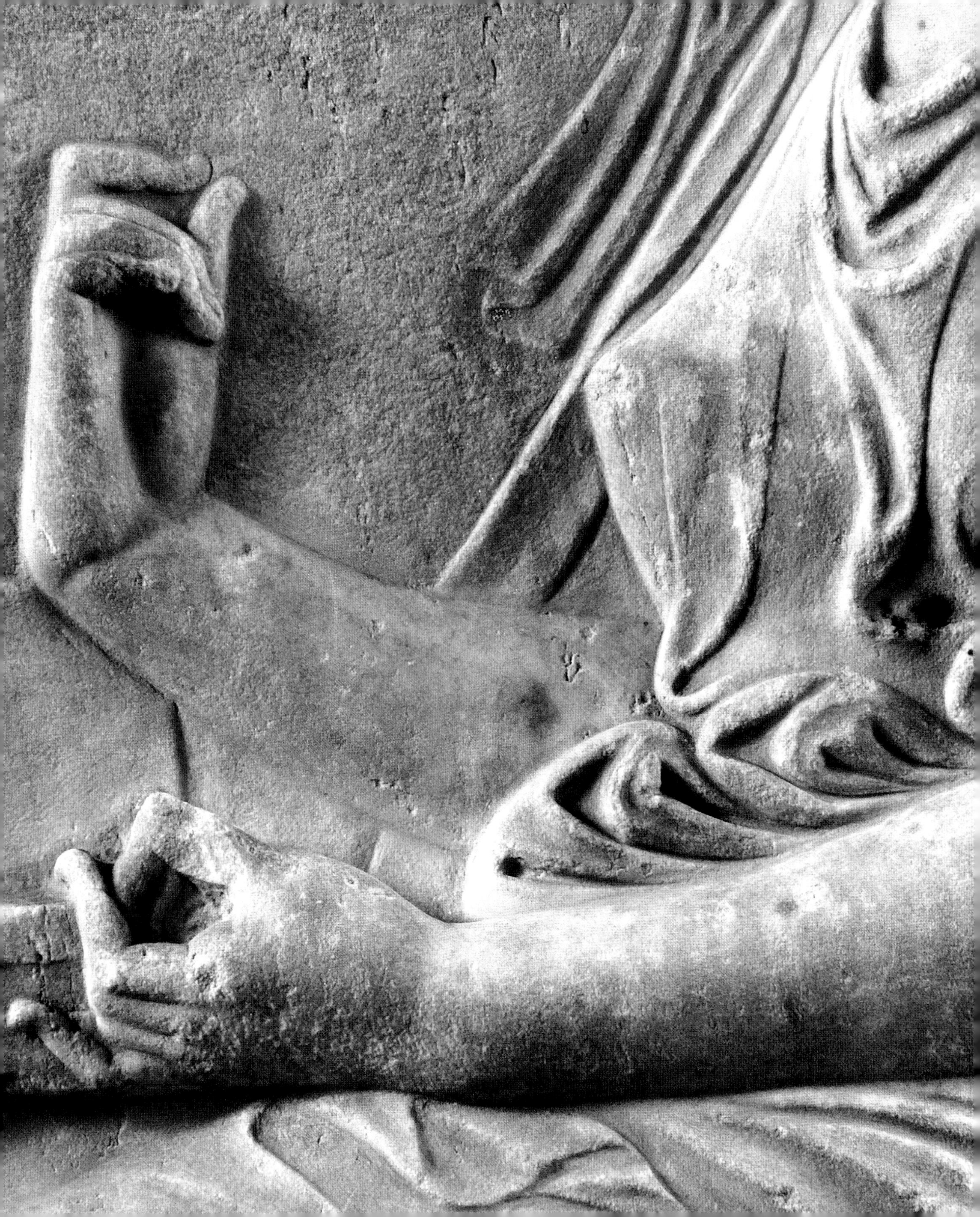

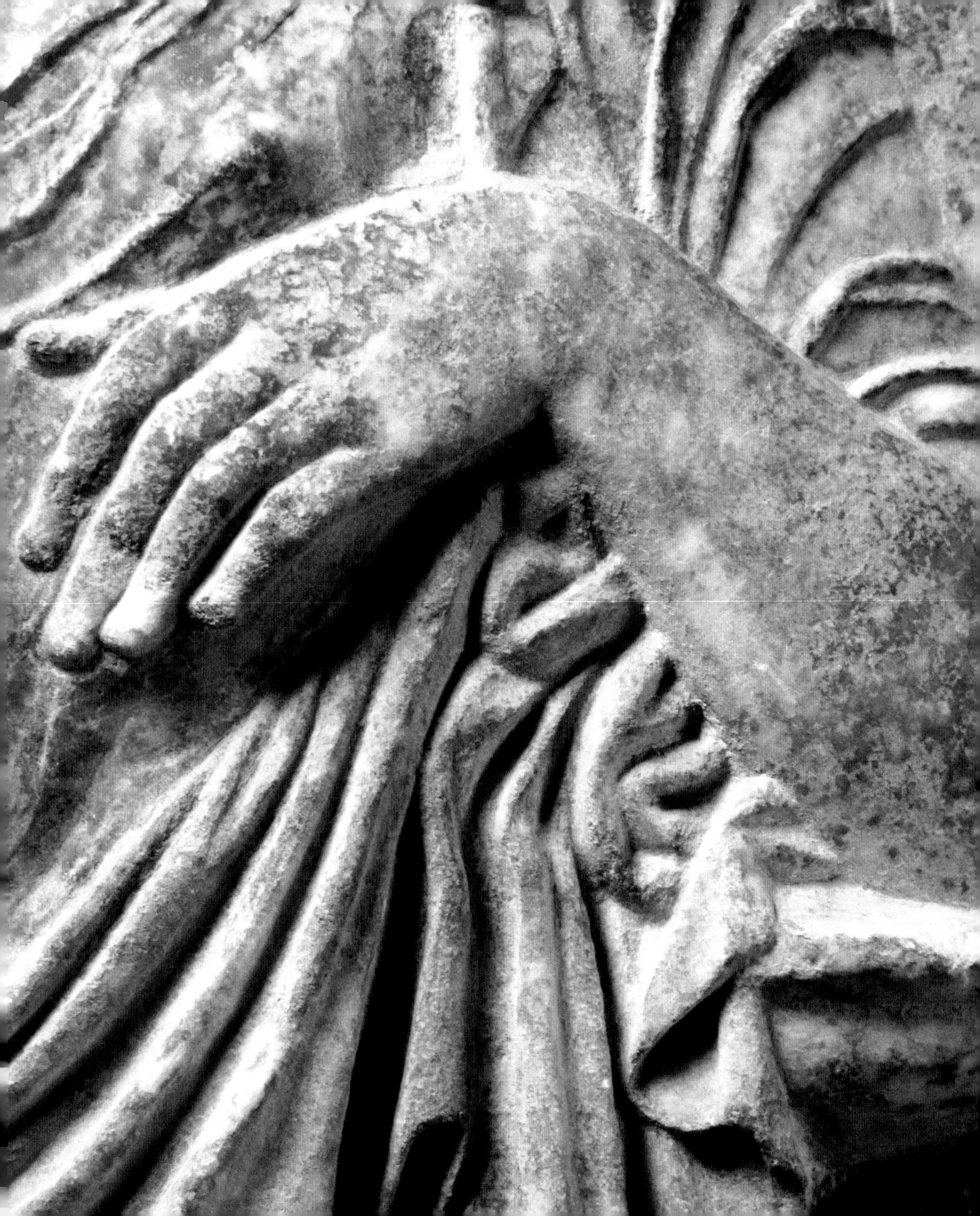

GRAVE STELE OF A YOUNG WOMAN

PROVENANCE UNKNOWN, PERHAPS ATHENS

C. 410 BCE

PENTELIC MARBLE. PRESENT HEIGHT 2.21 FEET (0.675 M); WIDTH 1.43 FEET (0.435 M)

ATHENS, NATIONAL ARCHAEOLOGICAL MUSEUM

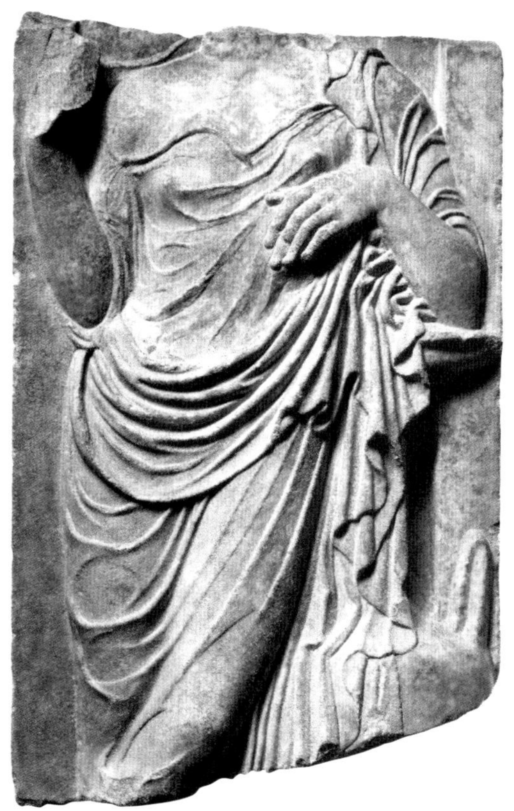

The entire surface of this long, narrow stele in the form of a naiskos is occupied with a young female figure in a frontal pose. The woman wears a sleeved chiton that leaves the right shoulder and the sternum bare and a himation that she draws up with her right hand. Her legs are crossed and her left elbow leans on the disc of the mouth of the large *loutrophoros* (ceremonial vase for water) next to her, placed upright. It's likely the sculptor of this work was inspired by the *Aphrodite en Kepois* (in the Gardens), a well-known statue of the period, by the Athenian artist Alkamenes.

GRAVE STELE OF DEXILEOS

ATHENS, KERAMEIKOS CEMETERY
394–393 BCE
MARBLE. HEIGHT 5.74 FEET (1.75 M)
ATHENS, KERAMEIKOS MUSEUM

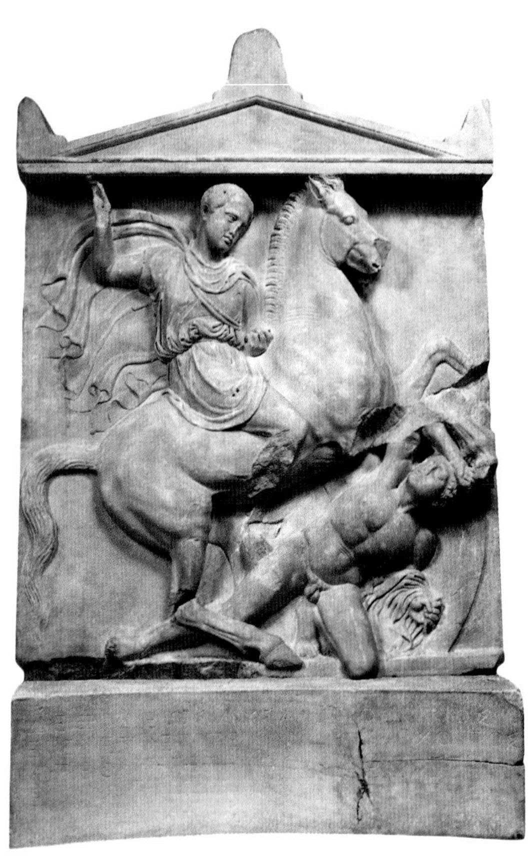

The representation on this pedimented and inscribed grave stele is in high relief. The deceased is portrayed as a young man riding a horse that rears and turns to his left. He is poised to plunge his spear into his adversary, who collapses supine upon his huge shield. He tries to protect himself from the forelegs of the steed above him, shielding himself with his bent and raised right hand, in which he held a sword. The rider wears a short chiton and a chlamys tied on his right shoulder; the chlamys billows backward, emphasizing the force of the assault. The fallen combatant is naked, his chlamys having slipped down behind him, between his body and the inside of the shield, and wound round his bent left arm, on which, together with his left knee, the figure supports himself. The composition is bold and yet expresses the spirit of late classical times in Attica.

The inscription on the base of the monument records that the young horseman is Dexileos from Thorikos, who fell in the battle at Corinth in 394–393 BCE, where the Athenians and their allies were defeated. The fatalities from this battle, as well as from another at Koroneia in the same year, were honored by the city of Athens, which erected a special state tomb, the Demosio Sema, where they were buried according to rank (e.g., the infantry separate from the cavalry). The names of the dead laid to rest in the Demosio Sema, Dexileos among them, are known from the inscription on its palmette finial, which was found in the excavation.

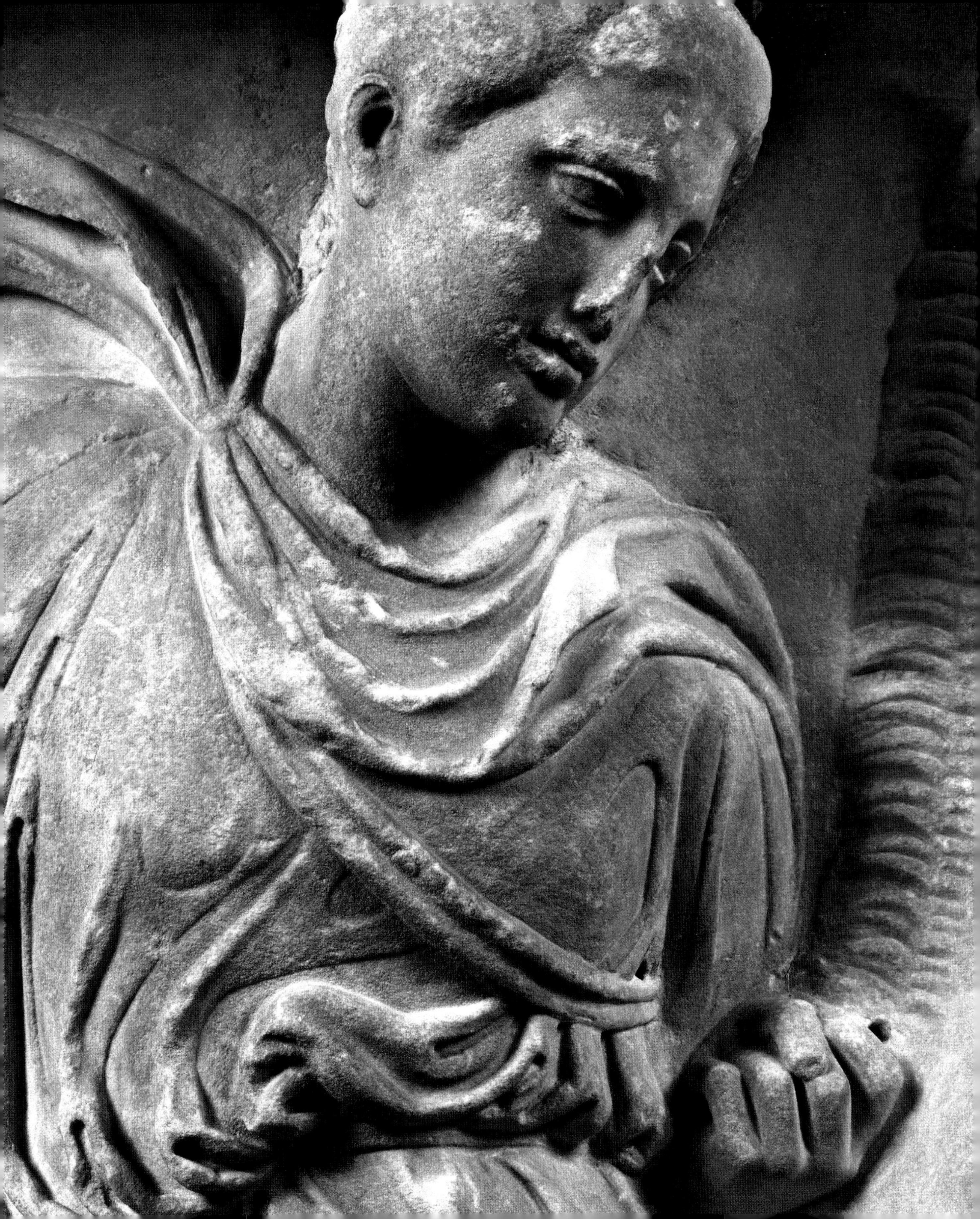

THE NEREID MONUMENT

ASIA MINOR, LYCIA, XANTHOS
390–380 BCE
LONDON, THE BRITISH MUSEUM

This tomb monument, constructed c. 390–380 BCE by Greek architects and sculptors for a king of Lycia, stands on a massive podium and is in the form of an Ionic temple. The rich sculptural decoration includes, between the columns surrounding the burial chamber, statues of female figures in lively movement. These have been interpreted as Nereids, that is, daughters of the sea god Nereus, after which this Lycian monument took its conventional name. In ancient Greek literature the Nereids, deities considered to be particularly friendly toward humans, numbered between fifty and one hundred and were seen as personifications of the waves. The best known Nereids were Amphitrite, wife of Poseidon (god-king of the seas and of earthquakes), and Thetis, wife of Peleas, King of the Myrmidonians, and mother of the Homeric hero Achilles.

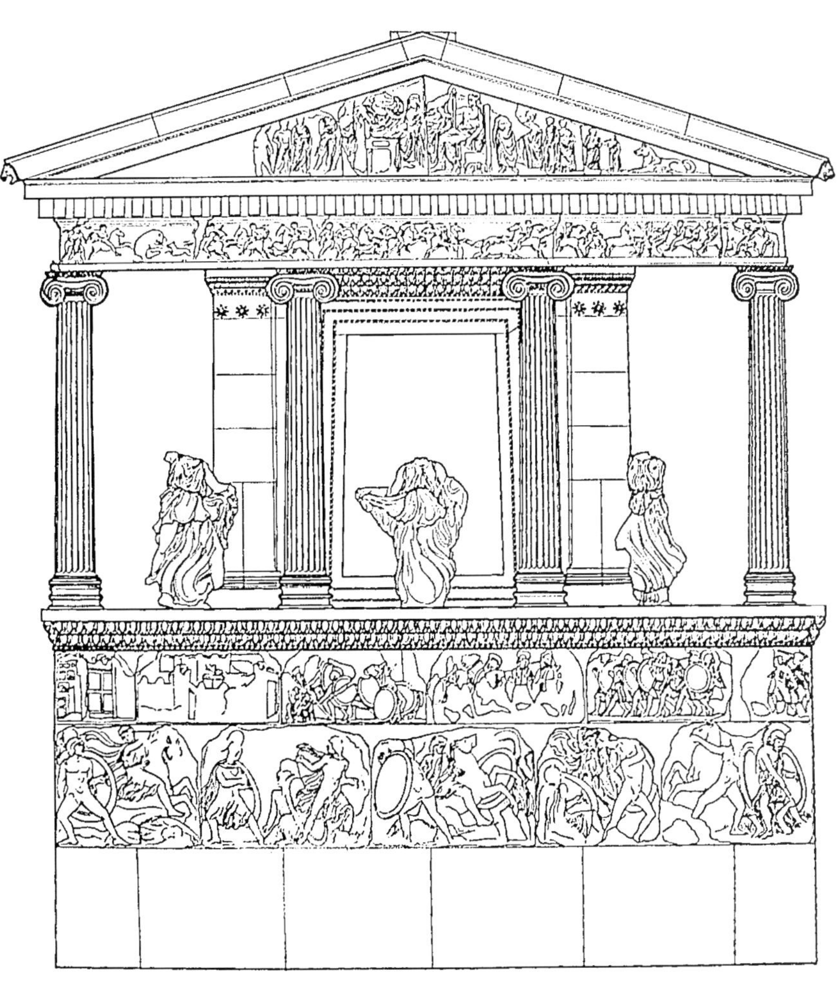

NEREID MONUMENT

NEREID

LYCIA, XANTHOS, NEREID MONUMENT
390–380 BCE
MARBLE. PRESENT HEIGHT 4.92 FEET (1.50 M)
LONDON, THE BRITISH MUSEUM

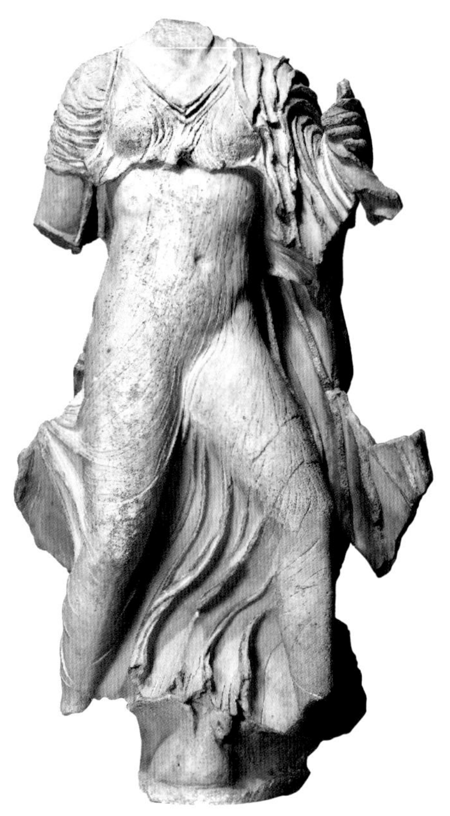

The figure is represented in vigorous movement to her left, her flimsy, diaphanous chiton clinging to her body and fluttering behind her, blown by the violent wind. The chiton's folds, indicated by fine, sheer ribbing close to the body, nonetheless acquire depth and volume and possess pronounced chiaroscuro between the legs. From the left shoulder hangs a heavy woolen himation that the Nereid holds in check, wound round her bent left arm. The Nereid appears to have been carrying a seabird, discernible beneath her chiton as a highly agitated mass between her arms.

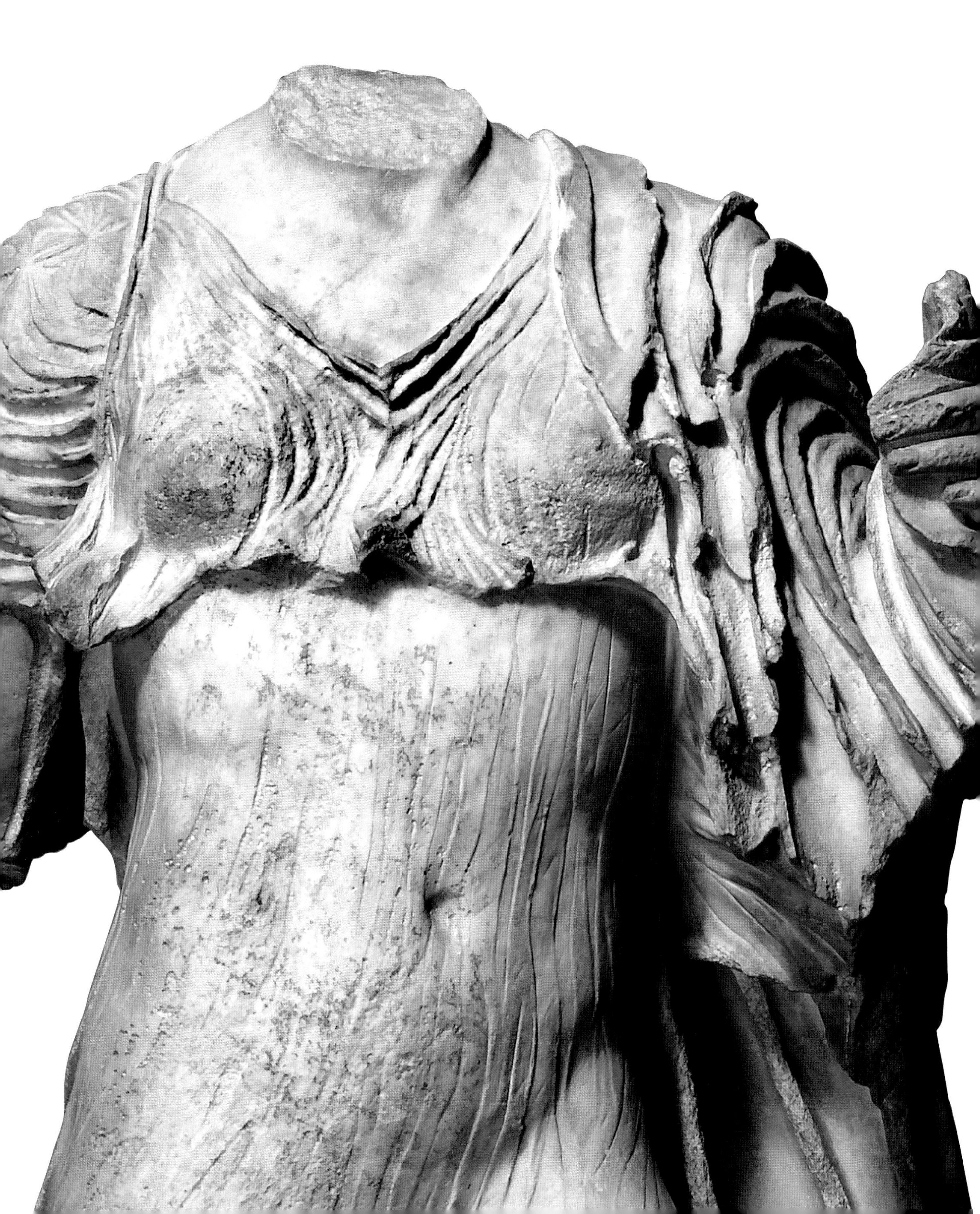

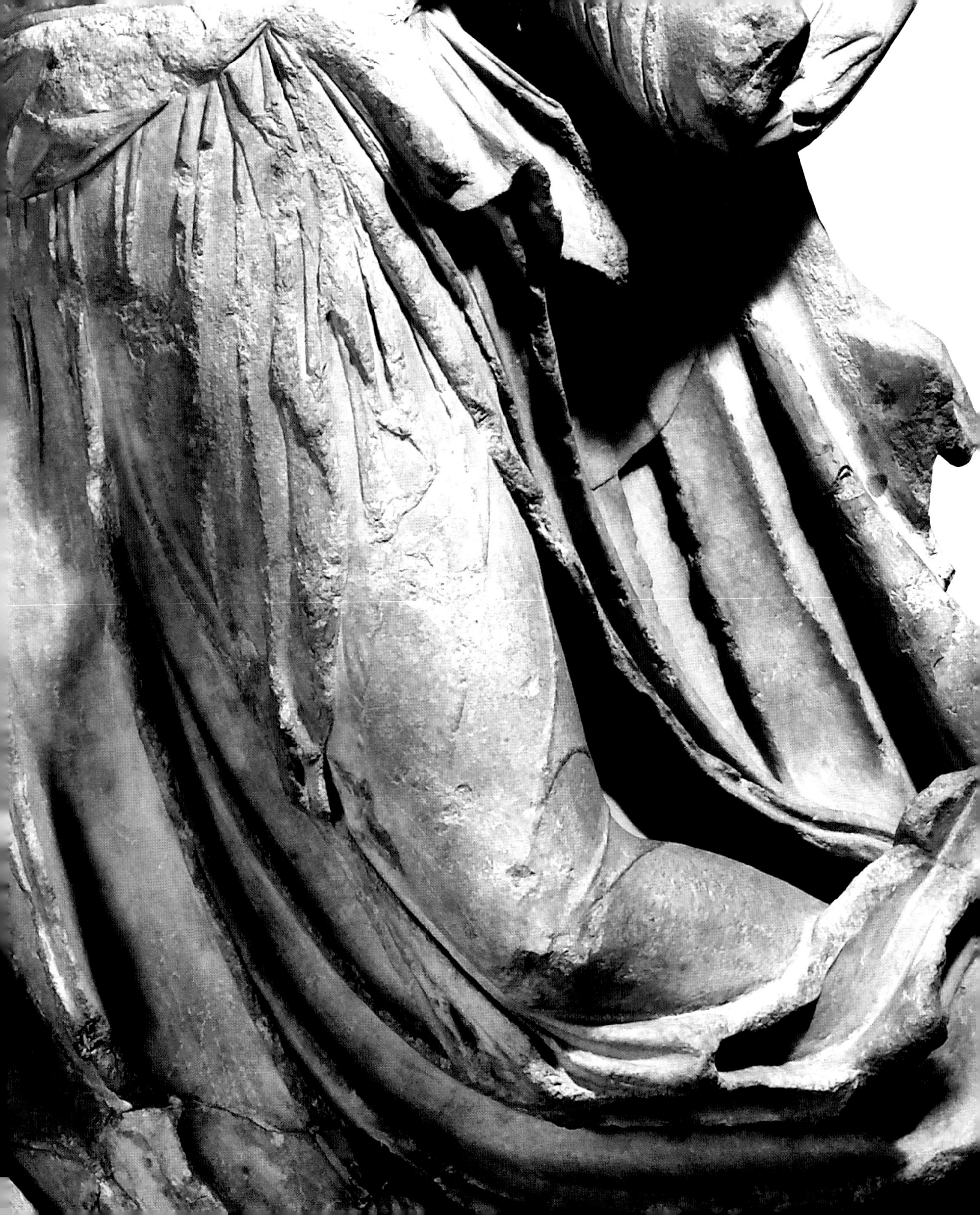

NEREID

LYCIA, XANTHOS, NEREID MONUMENT
390–380 BCE
MARBLE. PRESENT HEIGHT 4.92 FEET (1.50 M)
LONDON, THE BRITISH MUSEUM

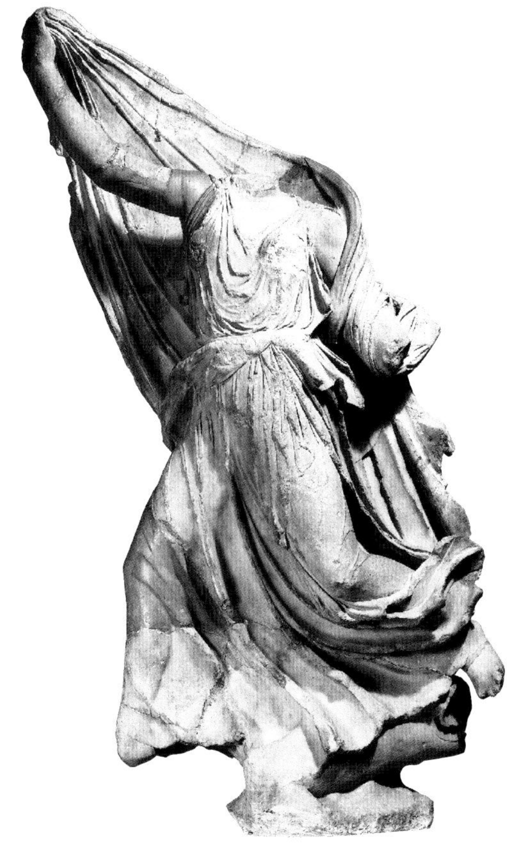

The Nereid is represented almost in flight, skimming to her right across the waves. She wears a gossamer chiton girdled at the waist and pinned over her shoulders, forming an apoptygma. Over this is a himation, one edge of which she holds behind her head with her raised right hand, like a wing. The other edge is swathed around her lowered left arm and hangs in deep folds at the back.

NEREID

LYCIA, XANTHOS, NEREID MONUMENT
390–380 BCE
MARBLE. PRESENT HEIGHT 4.92 FEET (1.50 M)
LONDON, THE BRITISH MUSEUM

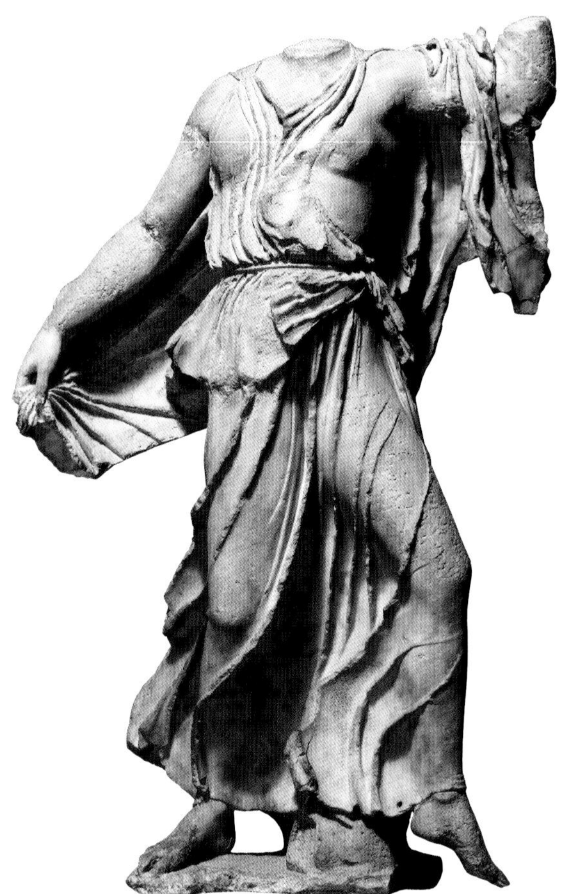

This Nereid corresponds to the previous one but moves in the opposite direction: She runs or flies to her left, clad in the same attire and with her arms in the same pose, extended diagonally so as to enhance the upper body in relation to the stride of her legs. Here, however, the himation is not raised above the head but held in check obliquely by both hands, low down and behind the back.

The rushing motion, the rippling drapery, and the interplay of light and shadow endow these sculptures of the Nereids with the airiness appropriate to them as deities of the water, the incessant tides of which sustain life on earth.

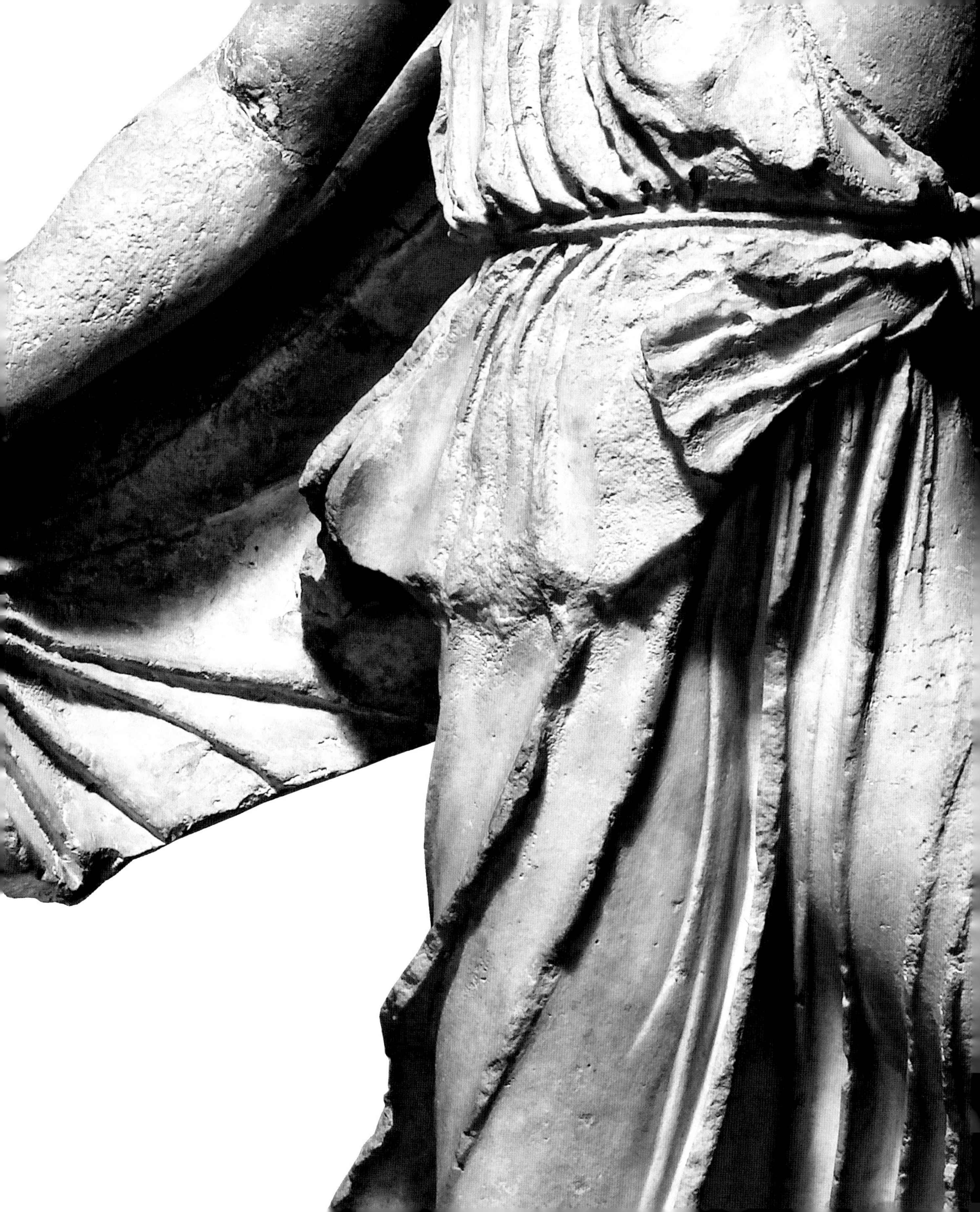

THE YOUTH OF ANTIKYTHERA

ANTIKYTHERA, FOUND IN AN ANCIENT SHIPWRECK ON THE SEABED
340–330 BCE
BRONZE. HEIGHT 6.36 FEET (1.94 M)
ATHENS, NATIONAL ARCHAEOLOGICAL MUSEUM

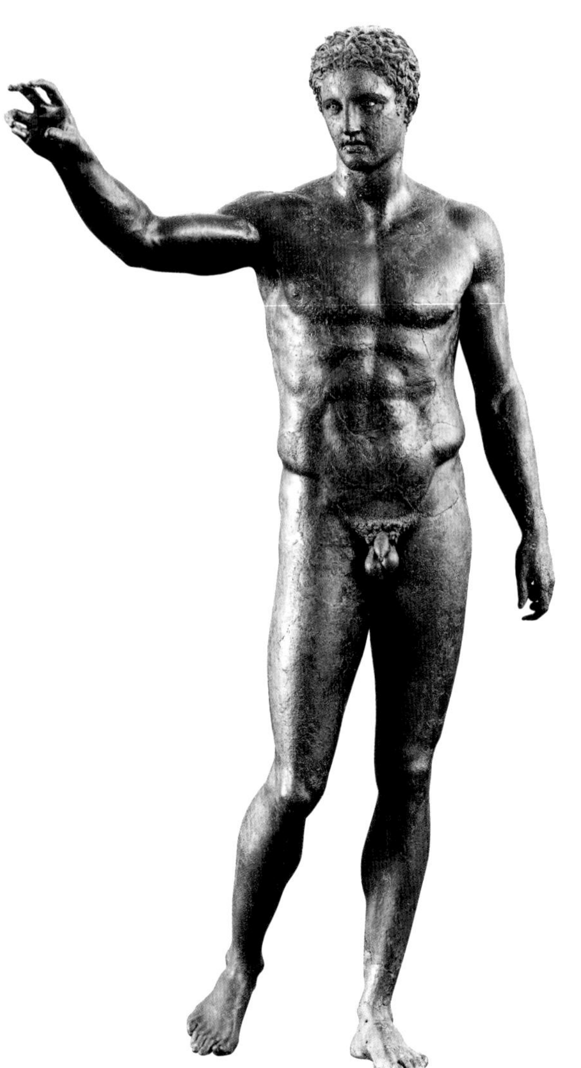

Represented is a standing figure of a nude young male with his weight placed on his left leg. His right leg is relaxed and slightly flexed, drawn back on tiptoe. His left arm is lowered in a free pose, while his right is raised and extended outward, holding an object that no longer exists. His hair is short and curly, and his eyes are inlaid in glass paste.

Some believe the young male is Perseus, in which case his extended right hand would have held the head of Medusa. Others believe he is Paris, presenting in his right hand the golden apple to the most beautiful of the three goddesses Hera, Athena, and Aphrodite, according to the myth.

A work in the tradition of Polykleitos, the bronze statue is attributed to the Sikyonian sculptor Euphranor.

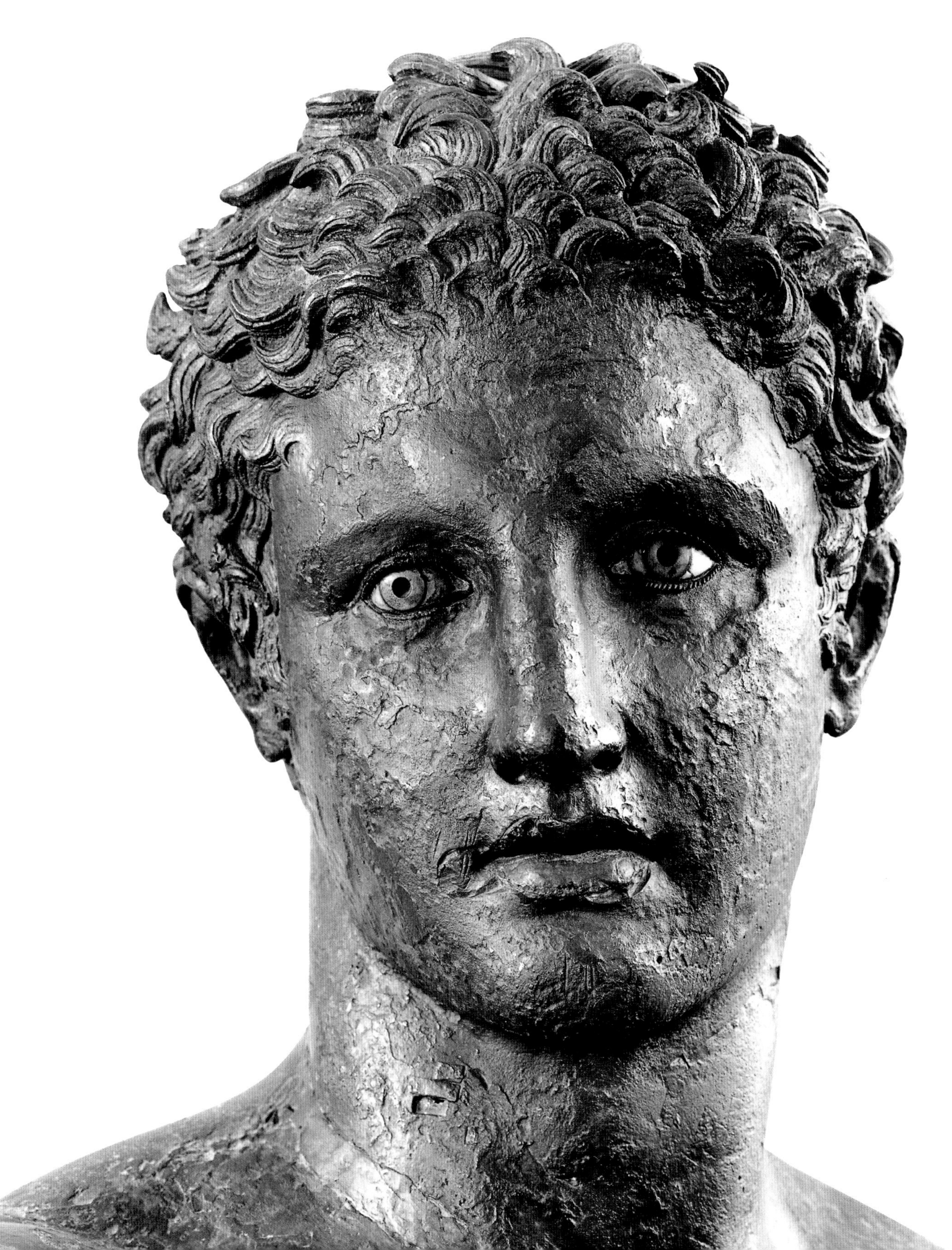

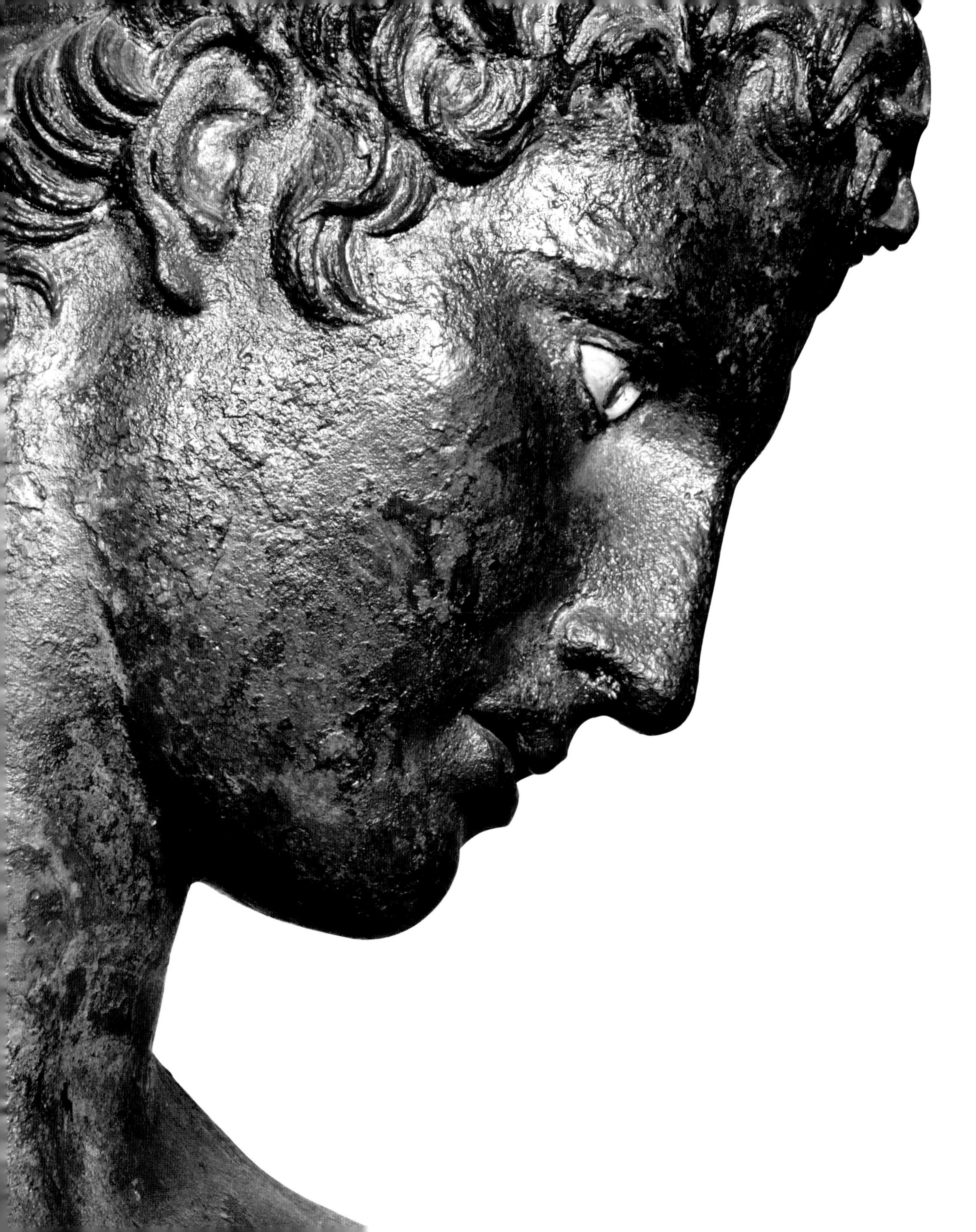

THE MARATHON BOY

FOUND IN THE SEA IN THE BAY OF MARATHON
340–330 BCE
BRONZE. HEIGHT 4.27 FEET (1.30 METERS)
ATHENS, NATIONAL ARCHAEOLOGICAL MUSEUM

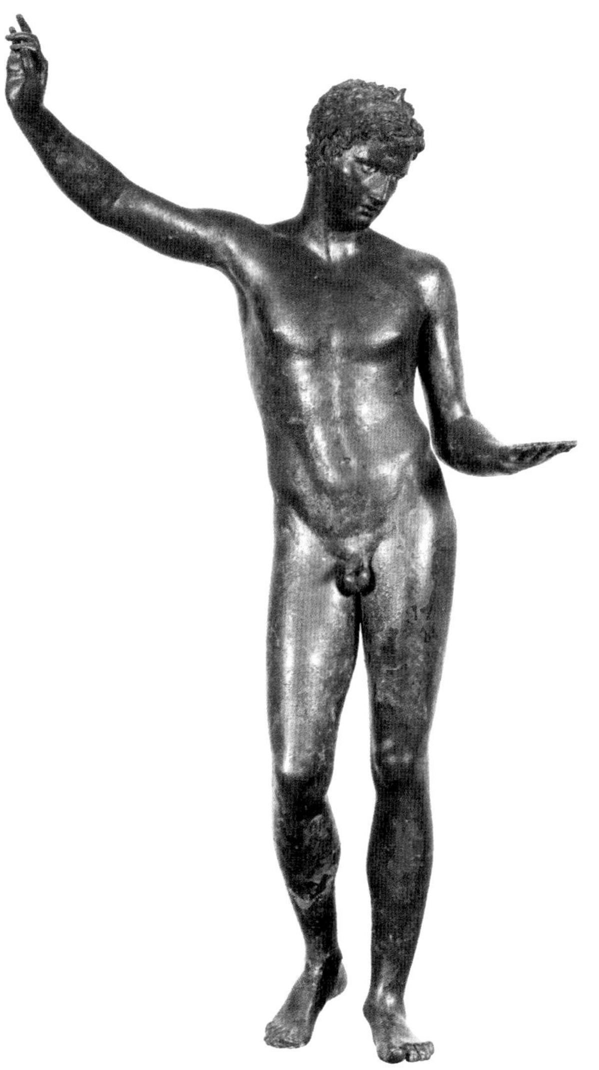

The naked boy is likely a victor in a contest, judging by the fillet on his head, which terminates above his forehead in a small leaf characteristic of victors. The youth rests on his left leg, while his right leg is relaxed, slightly flexed, and drawn back on tiptoe. He raises his right arm and extends it to the side, while in his left, bent and stretched in front, he held a lamp, a later addition. His head is turned to the left, his gaze fixed on the outstretched hand, at an object whose identity now eludes us, as is true also of the now lost object in the raised right hand. The short, curly hair crowns a face with a perfect profile—a fine nose, well-drawn lips—and expressive eyes inlaid with white glass paste, granting the figure the immediacy of a living young man.

The slim body's *contrapposto* (a pose in which the figure twists) and fluid outlines, in addition to the volumes' fine-tuned transitions and the harmonious proportions, are all characteristic of works of the Praxiteleian School. This is a masterpiece of ancient Greek statuary in the fourth century BCE.

AGIAS

DELPHI, FROM THE SANCTUARY, TO THE NORTHEAST OF THE TEMPLE OF APOLLO
C. 338–334 BCE
PENTELIC MARBLE. HEIGHT 6.46 FEET (1.97 M)
DELPHI, ARCHAEOLOGICAL MUSEUM

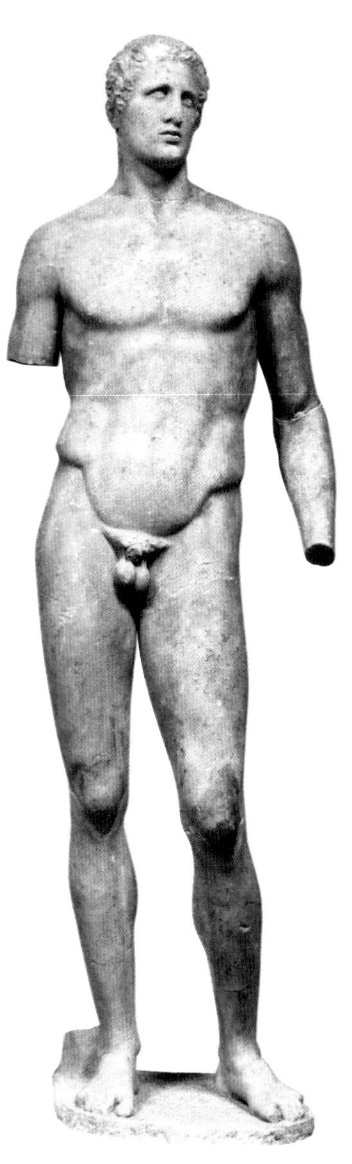

The young athlete who is the idealized subject of this portrait statue is ready to face his opponent. He is nude, has a narrow fillet in his short hair, and stands on both feet, turned in the direction of his slightly flexed left leg.

The work comes from the ex-voto of Daochos, a Thessalian magnate from Pharsala who was politically powerful and a *hieromnemon* (representative) of Thessaly to the Amphictyony in 338–334 BCE. Wishing to promote his noble family origin and the glory of his ancestors, he set up in the sanctuary of Apollo, close to the temple of the god, a large monument comprising nine statues: one of Apollo, one of himself, one of his son, and six of his forebears. The name and status of each figure were inscribed on the base of the monument.

The best figure, and the most important for art history, is that of Agias, great-grandfather of Daochos and a fierce competitor in *pankration* (a sporting event that combines wrestling and boxing) in the fifth century BCE. Agias was also a victor in the Olympic, Nemean, Pythian, and Isthmian Games.

Based on an inscription on a statue base found at Pharsala, some speculate that the great sculptor, and primarily bronze caster, of the period (i.e., the reign of Alexander the Great, 336–323 BCE), Lysippos from Sikyon, made a bronze statue of Agias in his home city. This statue has not survived and we can only hypothesize that the marble statue at Delphi mirrors it. Whatever the case, the sculpture of Agias has pronounced traits of Peloponnesian "eclecticism" in the tradition of Lysippos and was likely made by his collaborators in an Argeian-Sikyonian workshop.

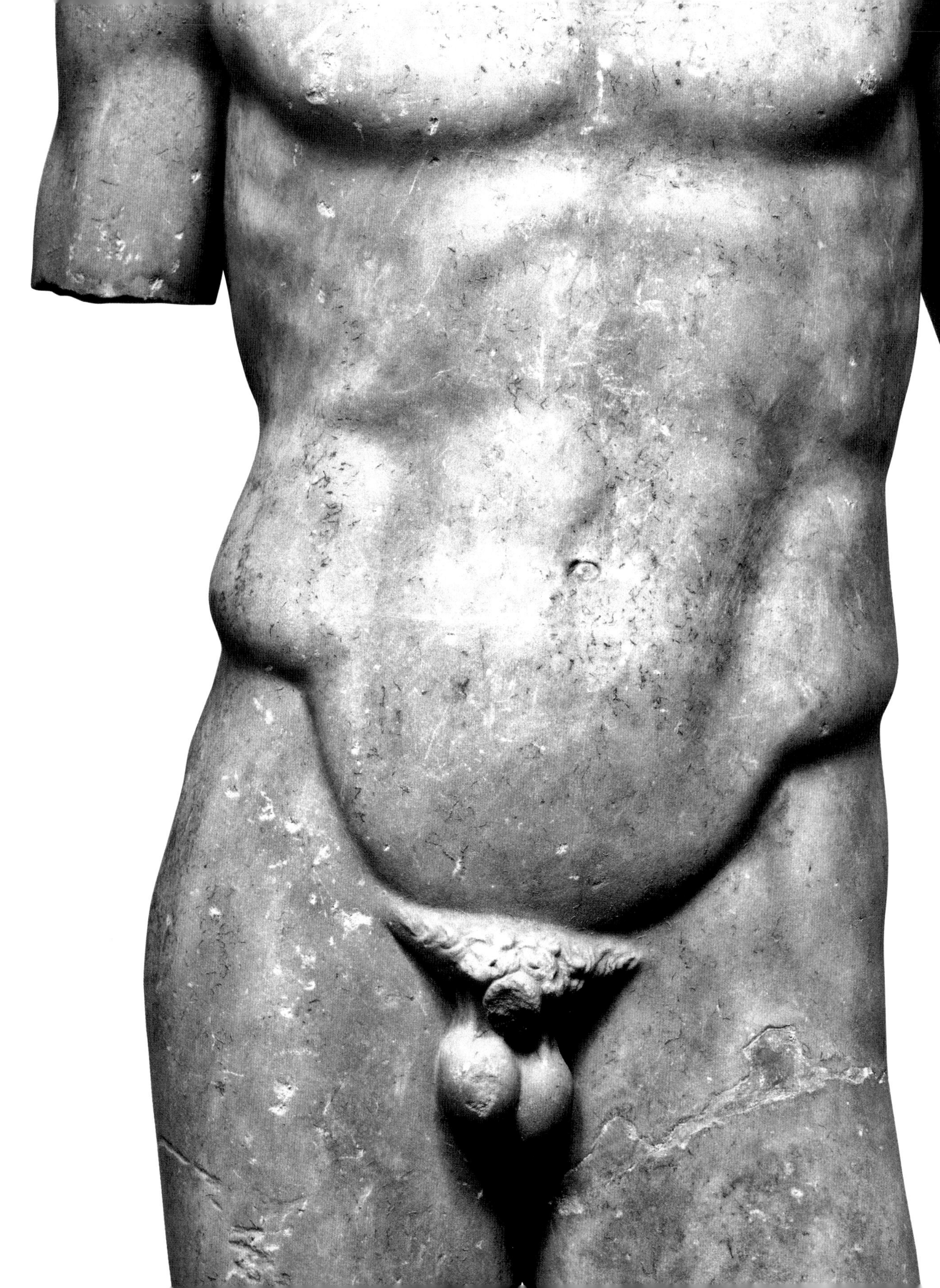

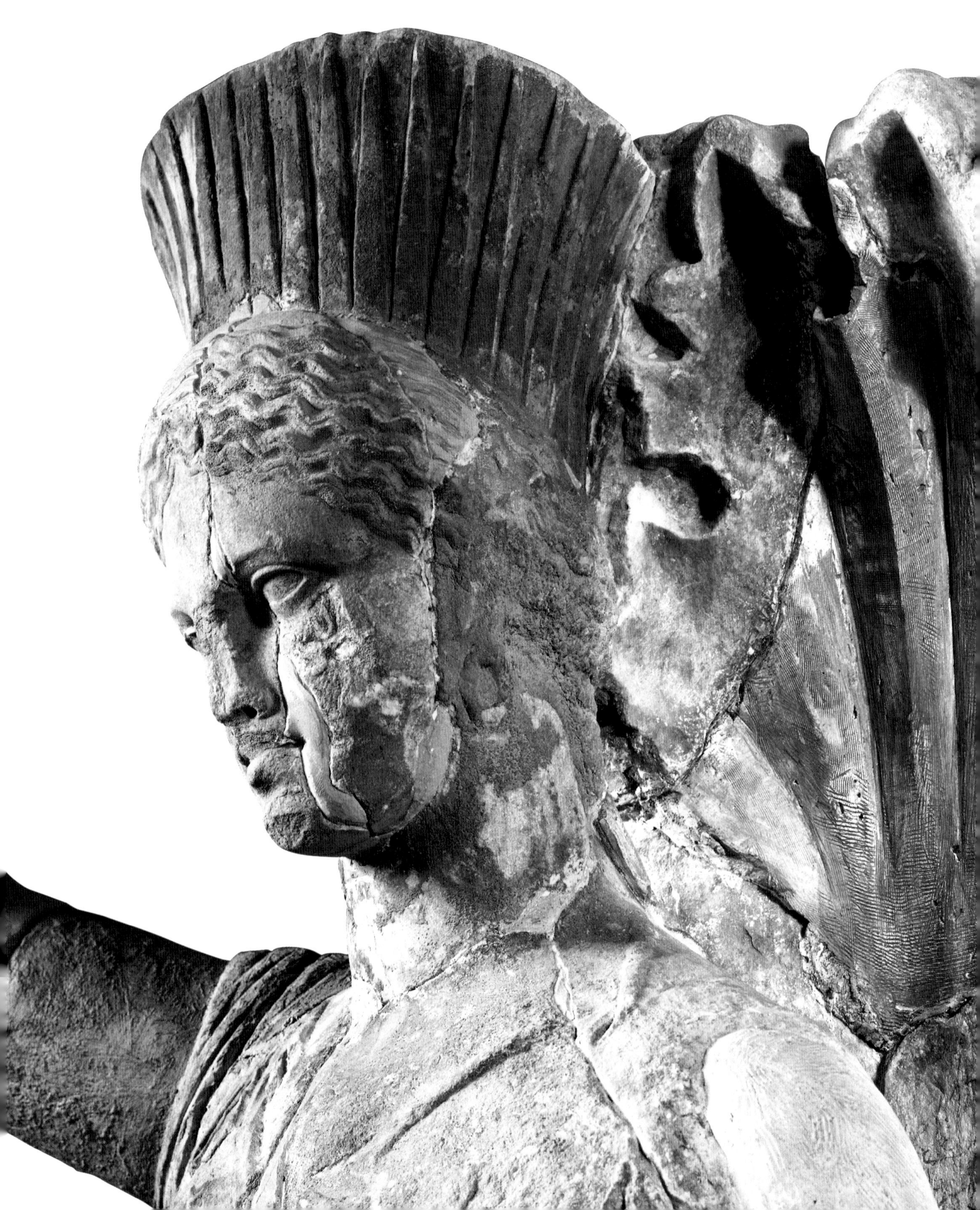

COLUMN WITH FEMALE DANCERS

DELPHI, FROM THE SANCTUARY, TO THE NORTHEAST OF THE TEMPLE OF APOLLO
C. 335–325 BCE
PENTELIC MARBLE, POROS BASE. HEIGHT OF DANCERS APPROX. 6.5 FEET (2 M); OVERALL HEIGHT OF THE COLUMN EXCEEDED 46 FEET (14 M)
DELPHI, ARCHAEOLOGICAL MUSEUM

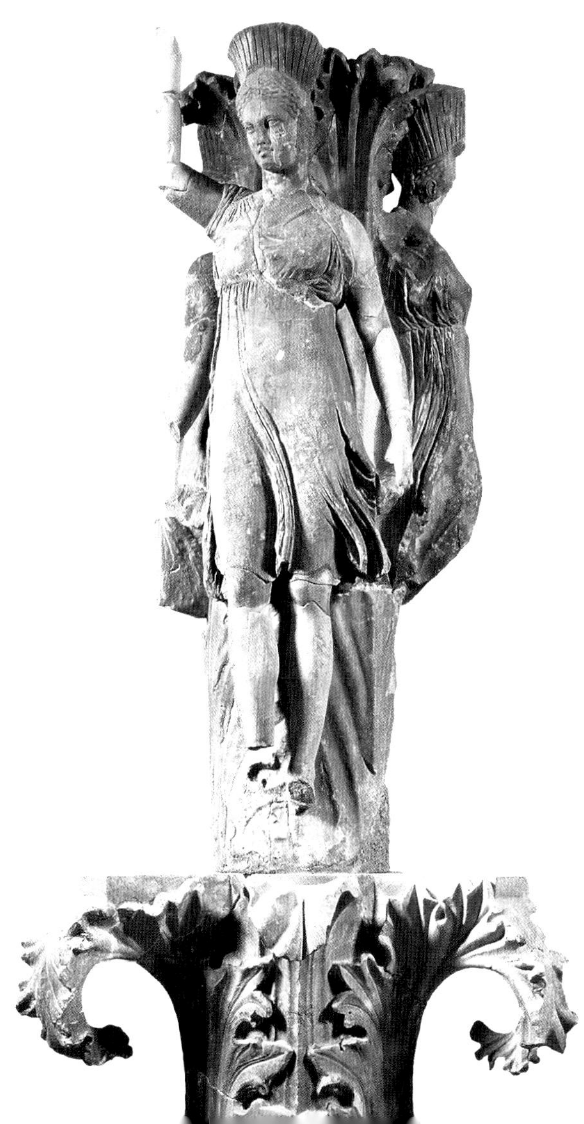

This column resembling the stem of a plant is wrapped at regular intervals by acanthus leaves. At the top, the leaves of a large acanthus grow out and downward, forming a base on which step three lissome, youthful female figures. The figures are developed in front of the central pillar with their backs in relief and each is dressed in a flimsy short chiton girdled high under the bosom. Each wears a *kalathiskos* (small basket) on her head and they give the impression that they are twirling around the pillar.

In fact, this group of dancers served as supports for an enormous tripod cauldron, probably bronze, that has not survived. In all likelihood the cauldron was set upon the heads of the figures and one of its three legs stood in each intervening space. At the base of the column, two large acanthus leaves, like those at the top, spread outward, consolidating it on its poros pedestal, part of

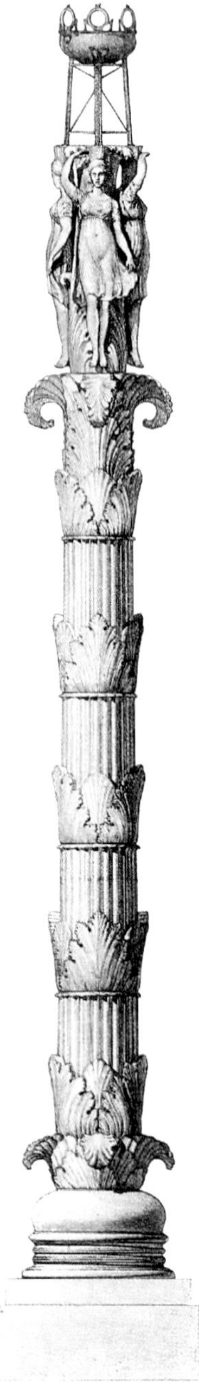

whose dedicatory inscription is preserved. The inscription records the pillar as an ex-voto of the demos of Athens constructed by a certain Pankrates from Argos, a contractor for projects in various sanctuaries. In light of this information and the fact that the *polos* (a headdress of female deities) takes the form of the religious kalathiskos, some suggest that a cult dance of the Aglaurides is represented. These three daughters of Kekrops, the mythical King of Athens, had already brought a bronze tripod cauldron as a gift to Apollo. Some scholars believe the column to be the work of the Athenian sculptor Leochares, who came to work with Lysippos at Delphi c. 320 BCE.

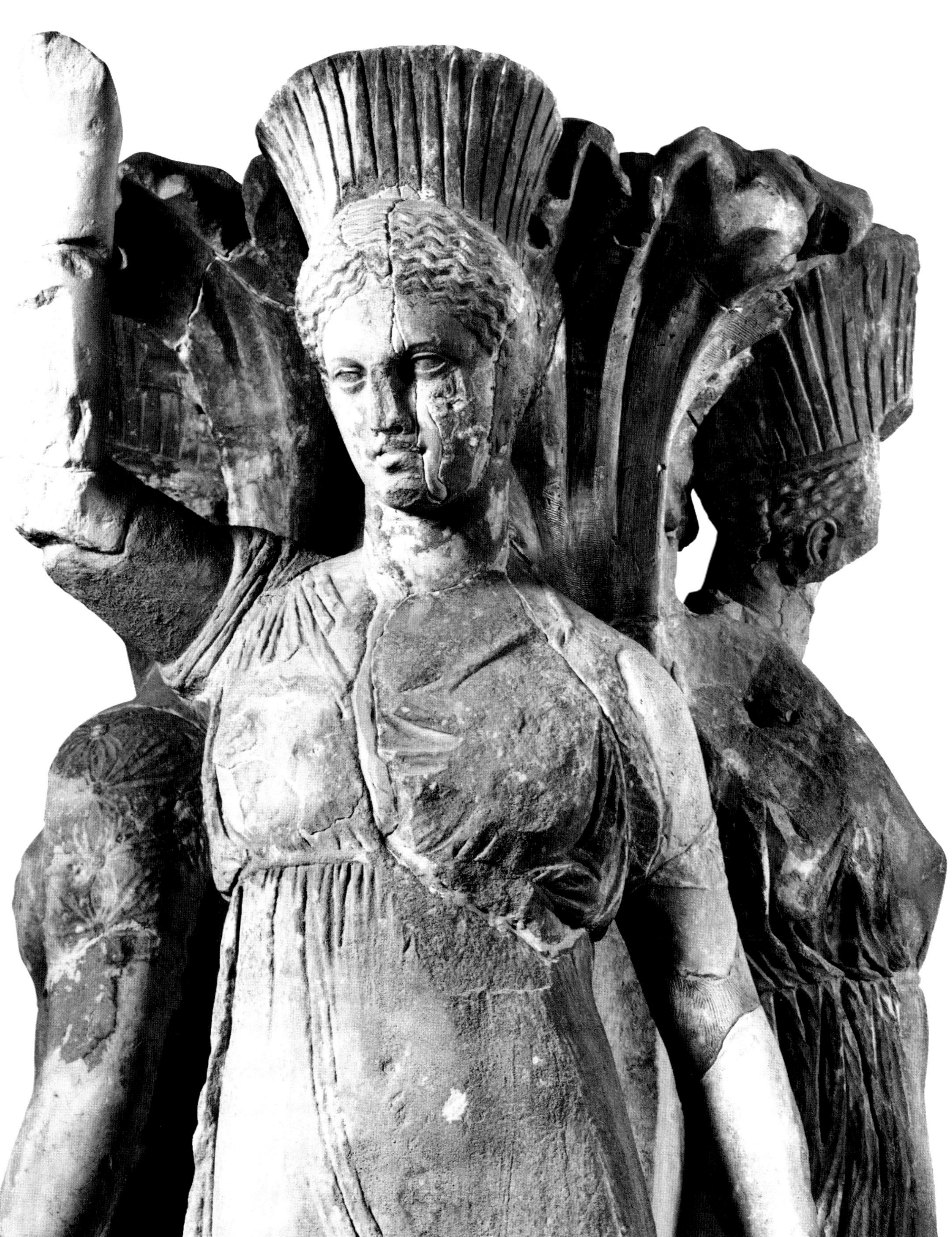

HERMES BY PRAXITELES

OLYMPIA, SACRED ALTIS
C. 330 BCE
PARIAN MARBLE. PRESENT HEIGHT 6.99 FEET (2.13 M)
OLYMPIA, ARCHAEOLOGICAL MUSEUM

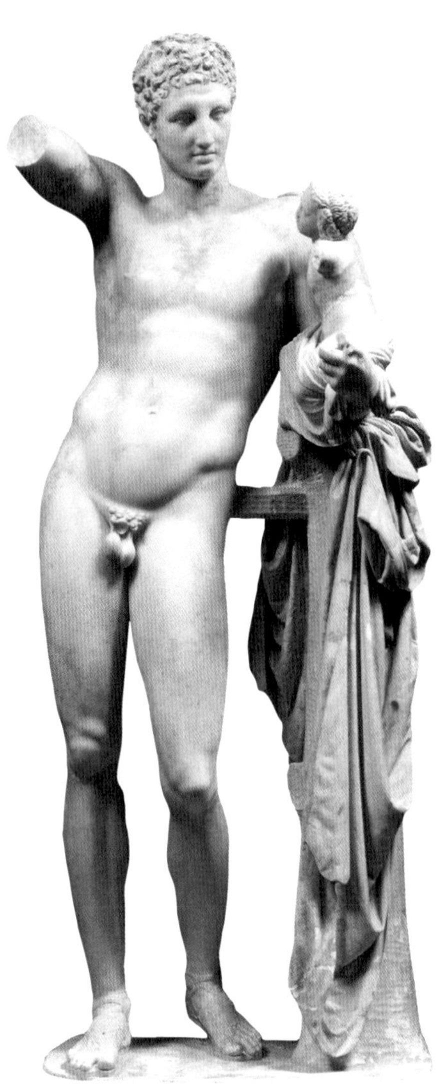

Found in the temple of Hera, this statue was identified as the work of Praxiteles, a great Greek sculptor of the fourth century BCE, based on Pausanias' precise description of the work. The god is represented as a youth, naked save for his sandals, and holds the infant Dionysus on his left forearm, which rests on a tree trunk. Over his left arm hangs a himation, and his right arm is raised, incompletely preserved—a bunch of grapes likely dangled from his hand. Dionysus touches Hermes' shoulder with his right hand and reaches his left one toward the object Hermes held. Hermes' tousled hair is worked in small curls and bears traces of red pigment and holes for affixing a metal fillet. Myth has it that the god was ordered by Zeus to take the infant Dionysus, upon his miraculous birth from the thigh of the father

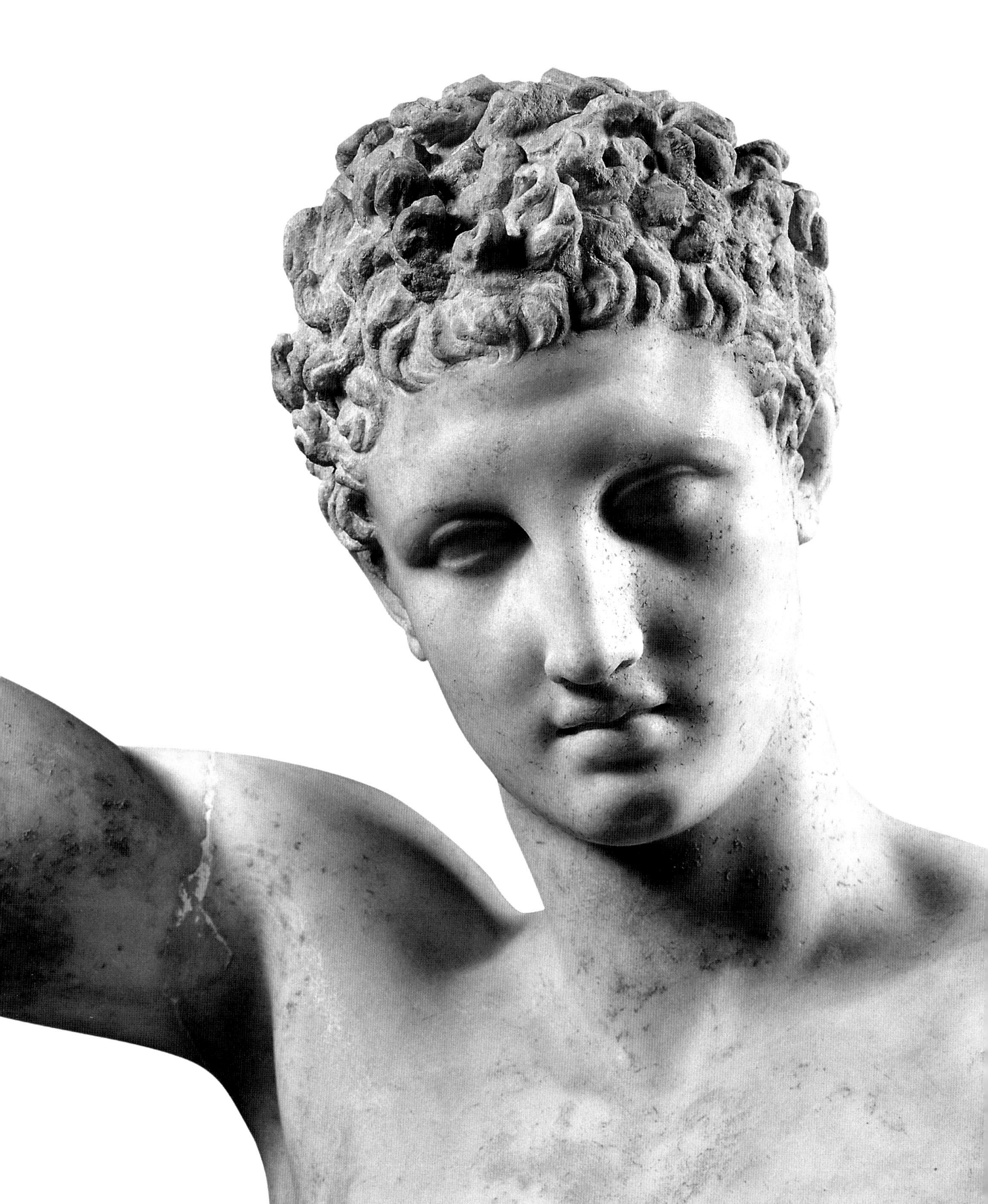

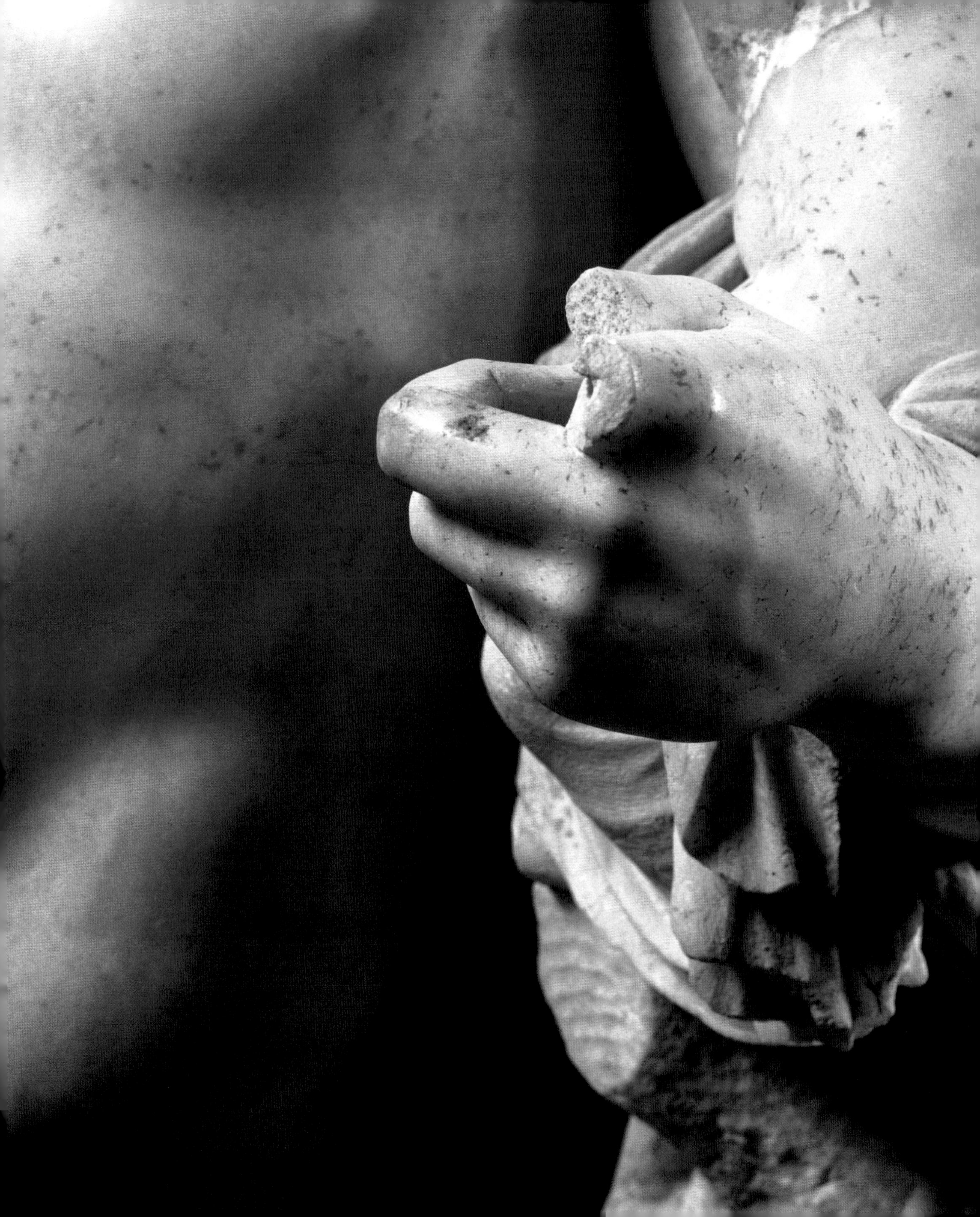

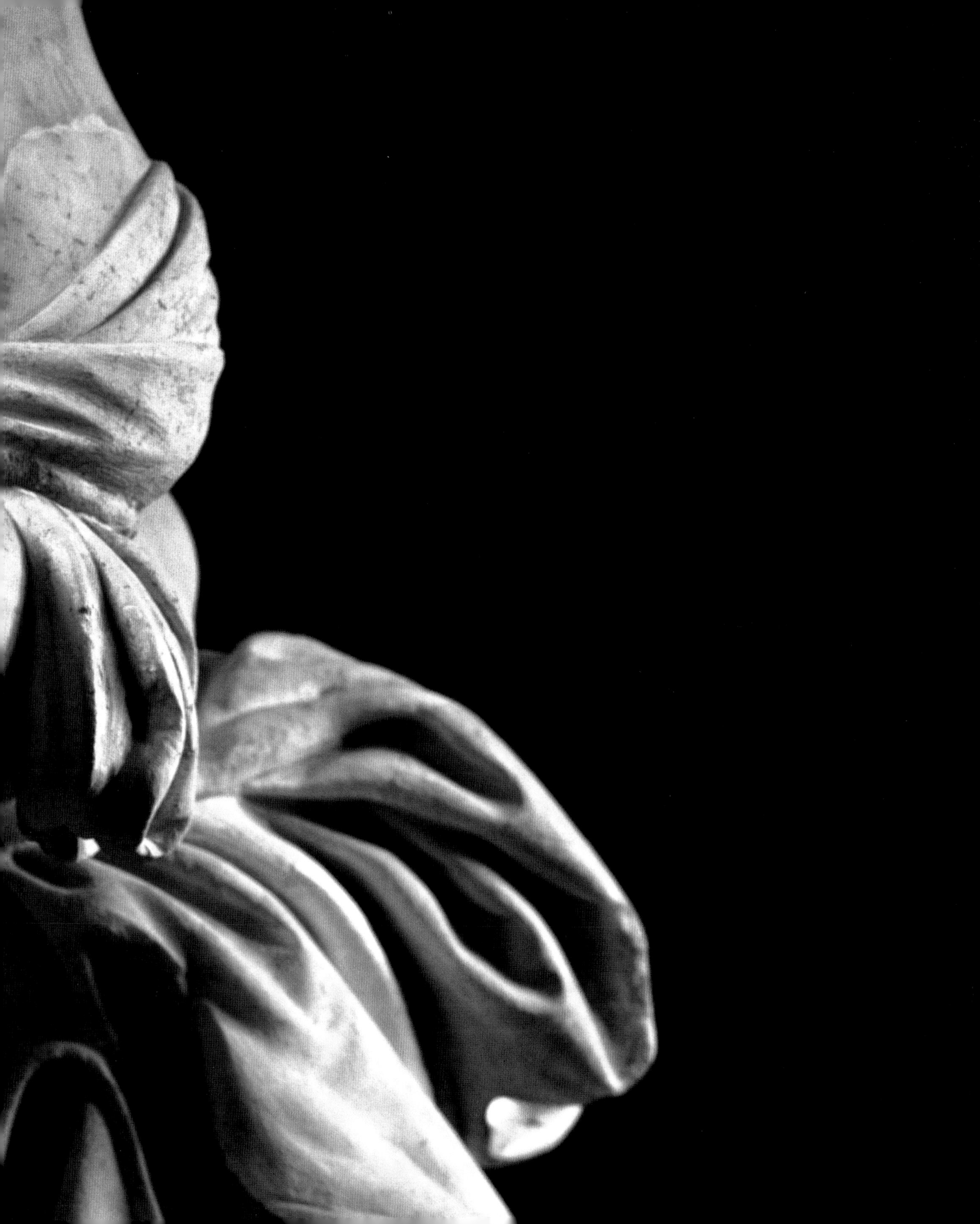

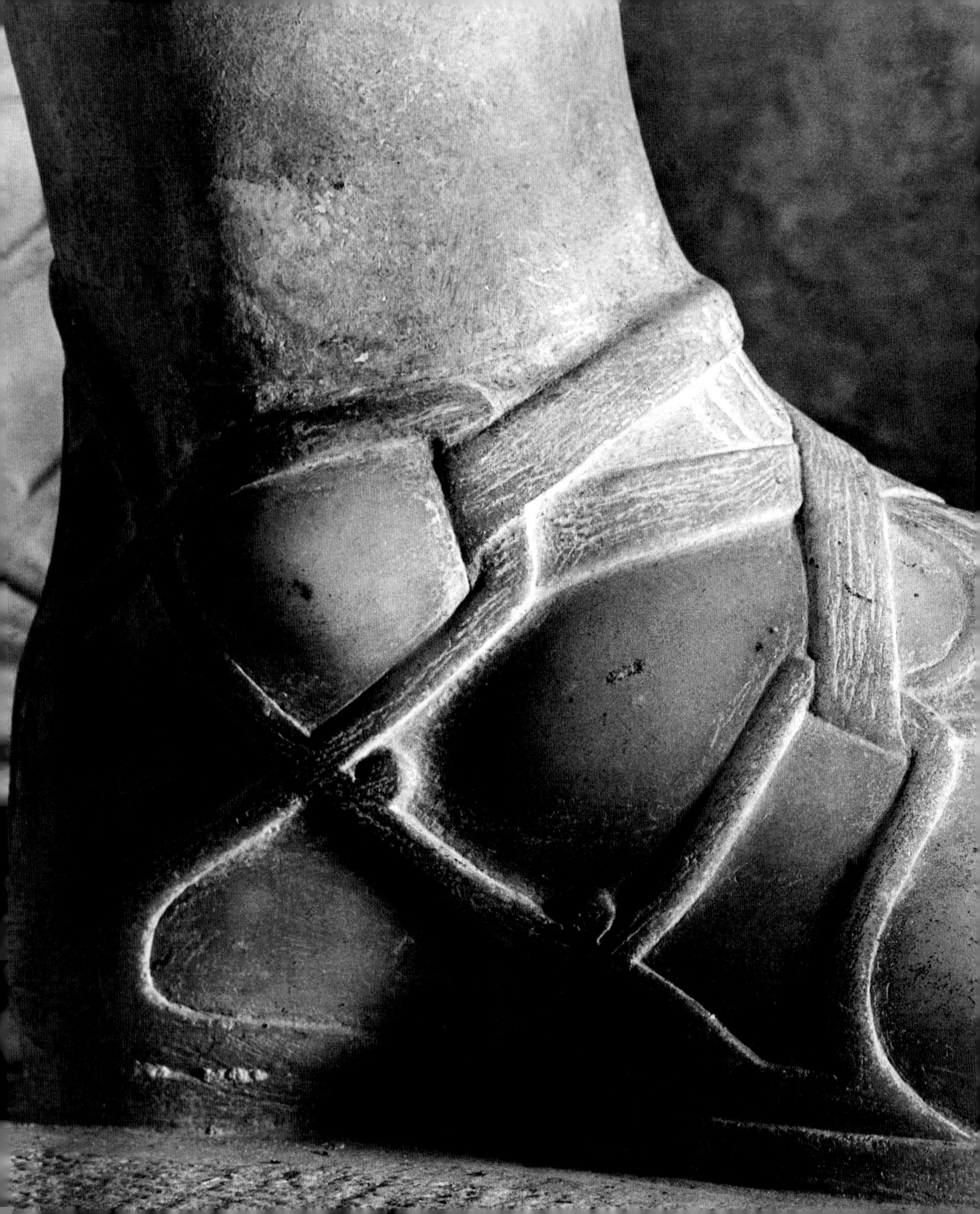

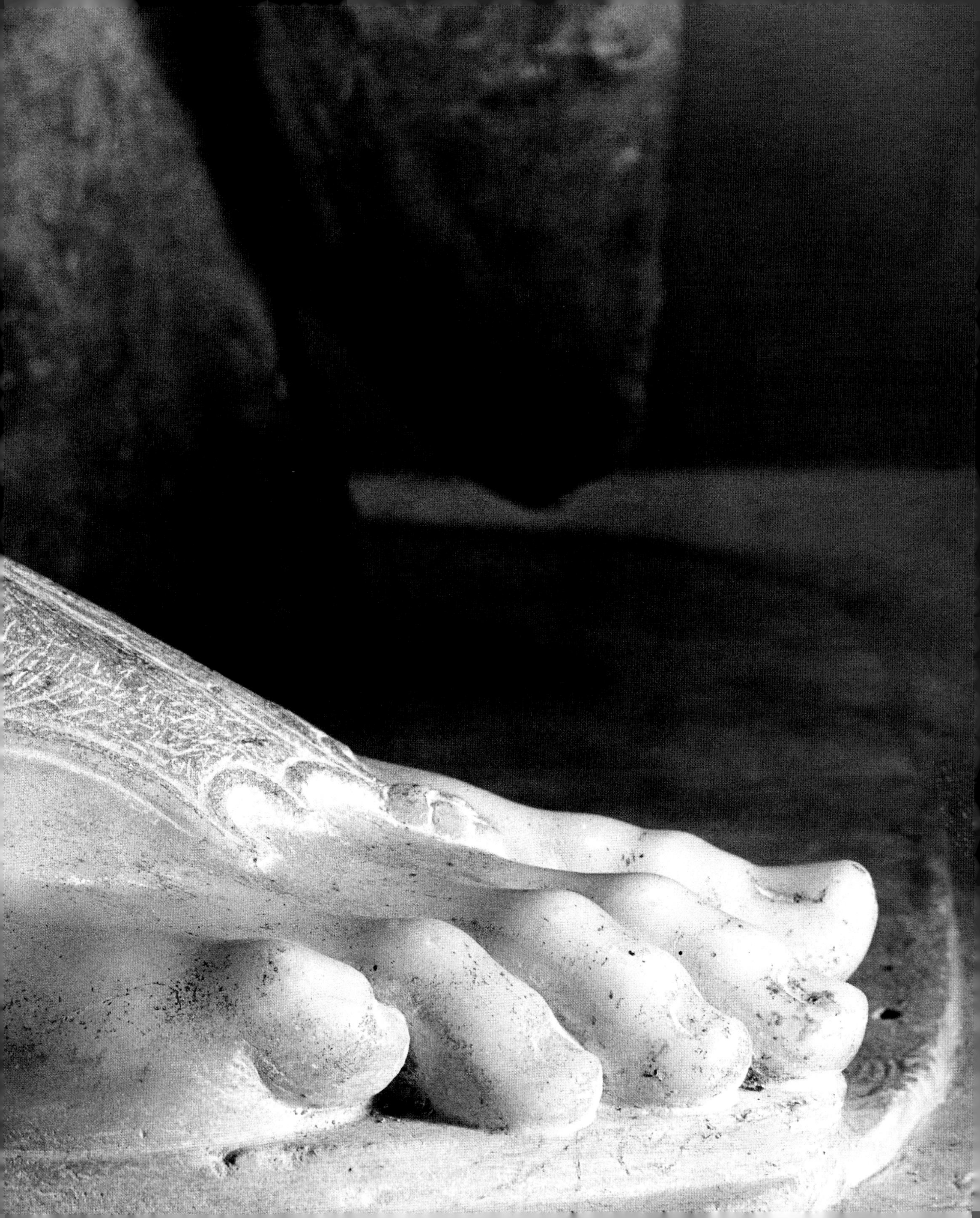

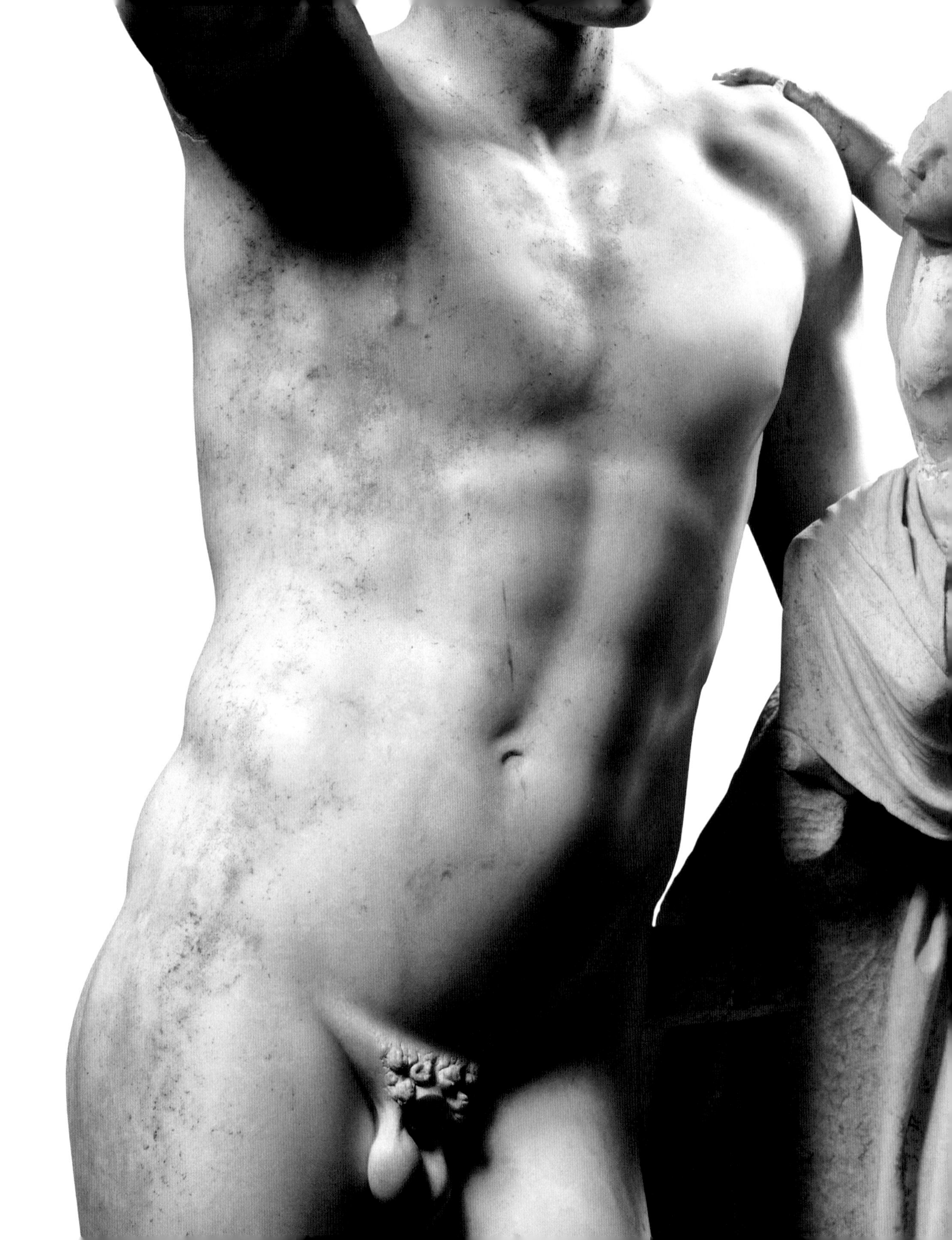

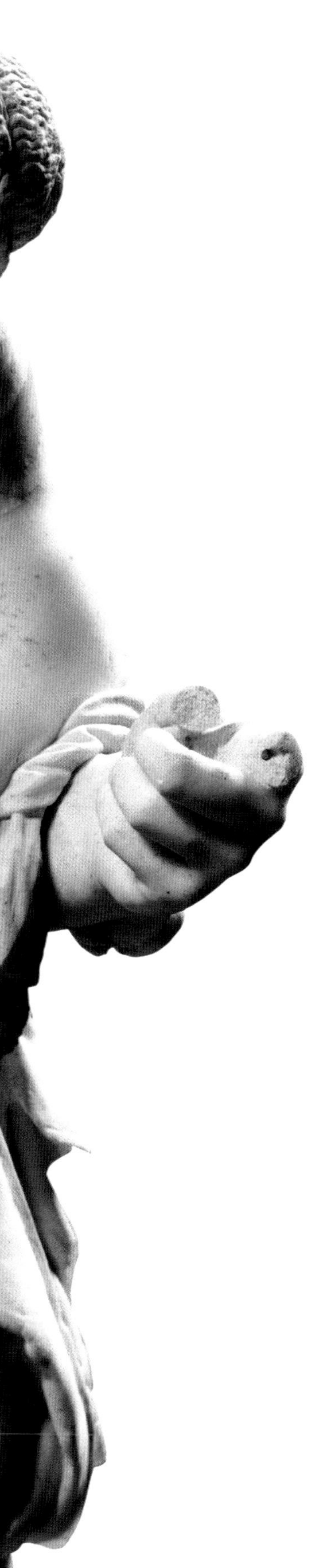

of the gods, to the mythical land of Nysa, where he was handed over to the nymphs. There, the nymphs would rear him far from the jealousy of Hera.

Hermes by Praxiteles is the sole original sculpture to have survived from antiquity that can be securely matched to its creator, an artist of unparalleled talent. This work combines the realistic trends of the age—such as the texture of the hanging textile—with an introspective idealism embodied in the figure of the god, creating an alluring effect that is unsurpassed.

NIKE OF SAMOTHRACE

SAMOTHRACE
C. EARLY SECOND CENTURY BCE (?)
PARIAN MARBLE. PRESENT HEIGHT 10.76 FEET (3.28 M)
PARIS, LOUVRE MUSEUM

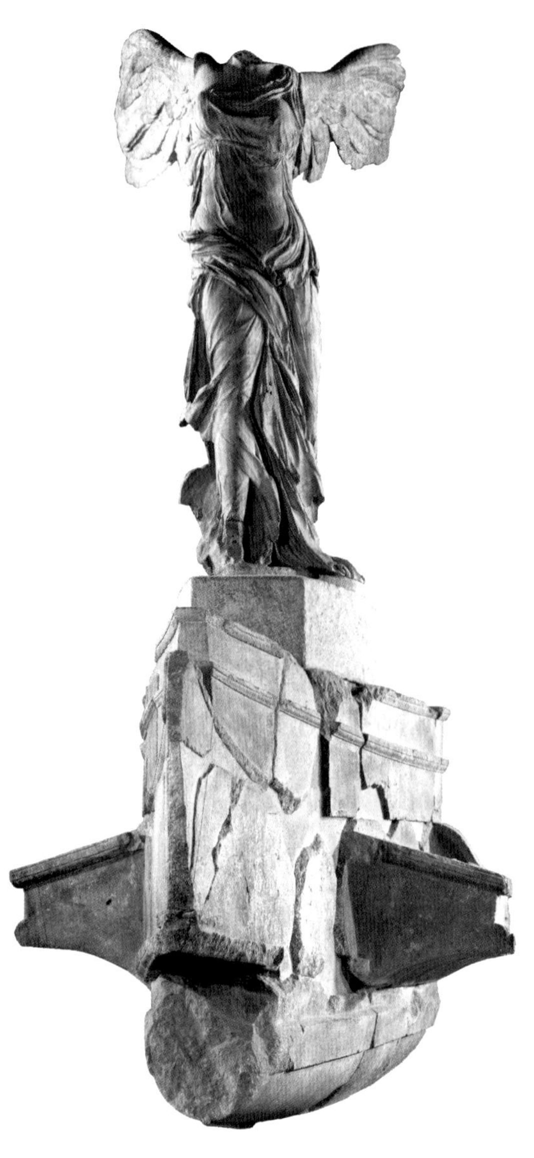

The Nike (Victory) is represented with open wings, landing on the prow of a ship. She rests on her right leg, which is placed to the fore, and draws her torso to the right, in contrast to her lower body, which turns to the left. She wears a diaphanous chiton and a himation that billows out behind her, swathing the lower back of her body, and in front doubles over in ample folds between her legs. The chiton, girdled high, just below the bosom, leaves the right shoulder bare and forms an apoptygma that falls to the thighs.

The statue together with its base stood 18.50 feet (5.64 m) high, above the theater in the sanctuary of the Great Gods, set on a terrace on the west hill of the Northeast Aegean island of Samothrace. Its materials suggest that it was an ex-voto of the Rhodians (the base is of Rhodian gray marble and is from a Rhodian workshop) after their victory at sea in 190 BCE. The Samothracian sanctuary was dedicated to the Kabeiroi, fertility daemons whose help was invoked in the event of shipwreck or for victory over the enemy. Precisely for

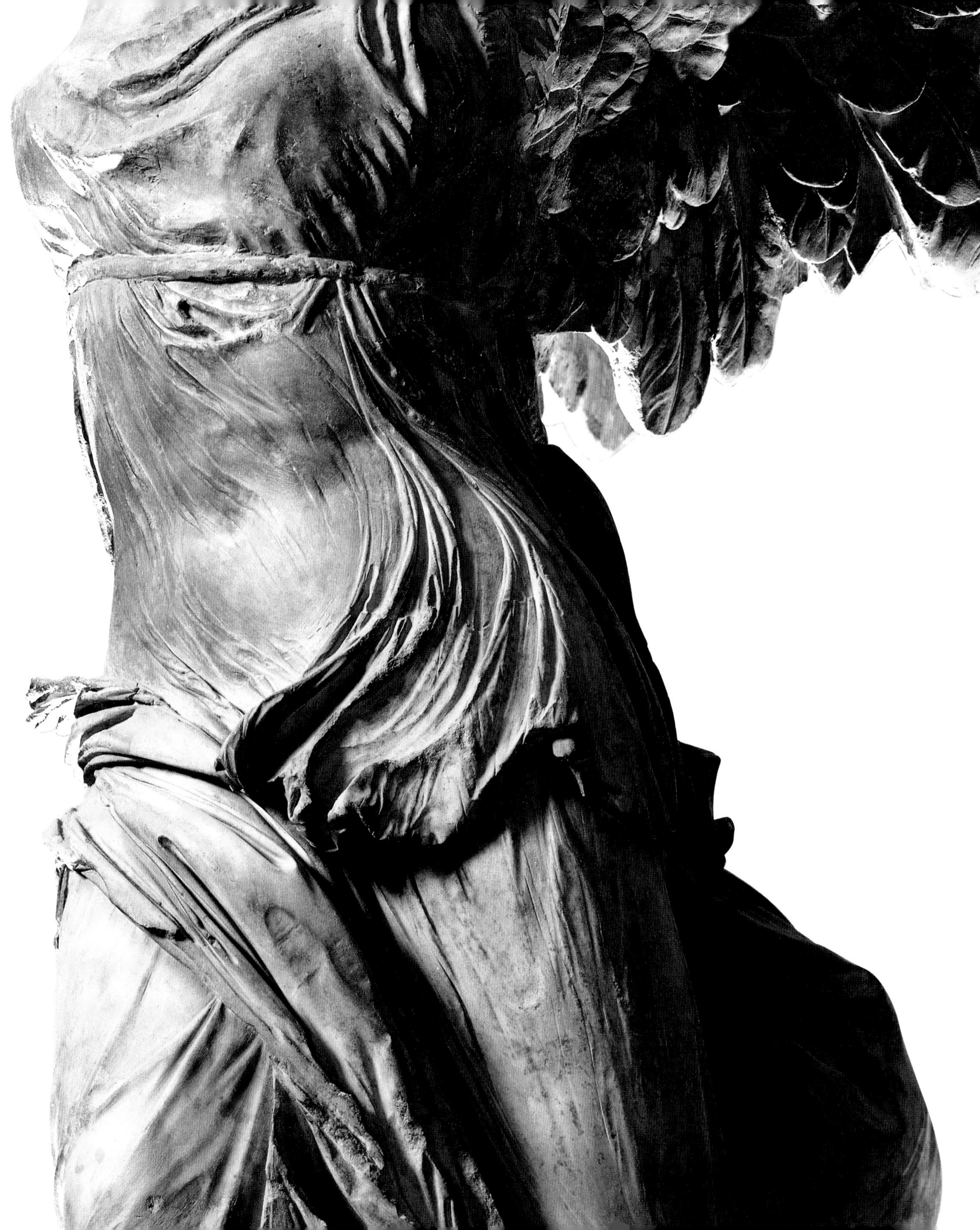

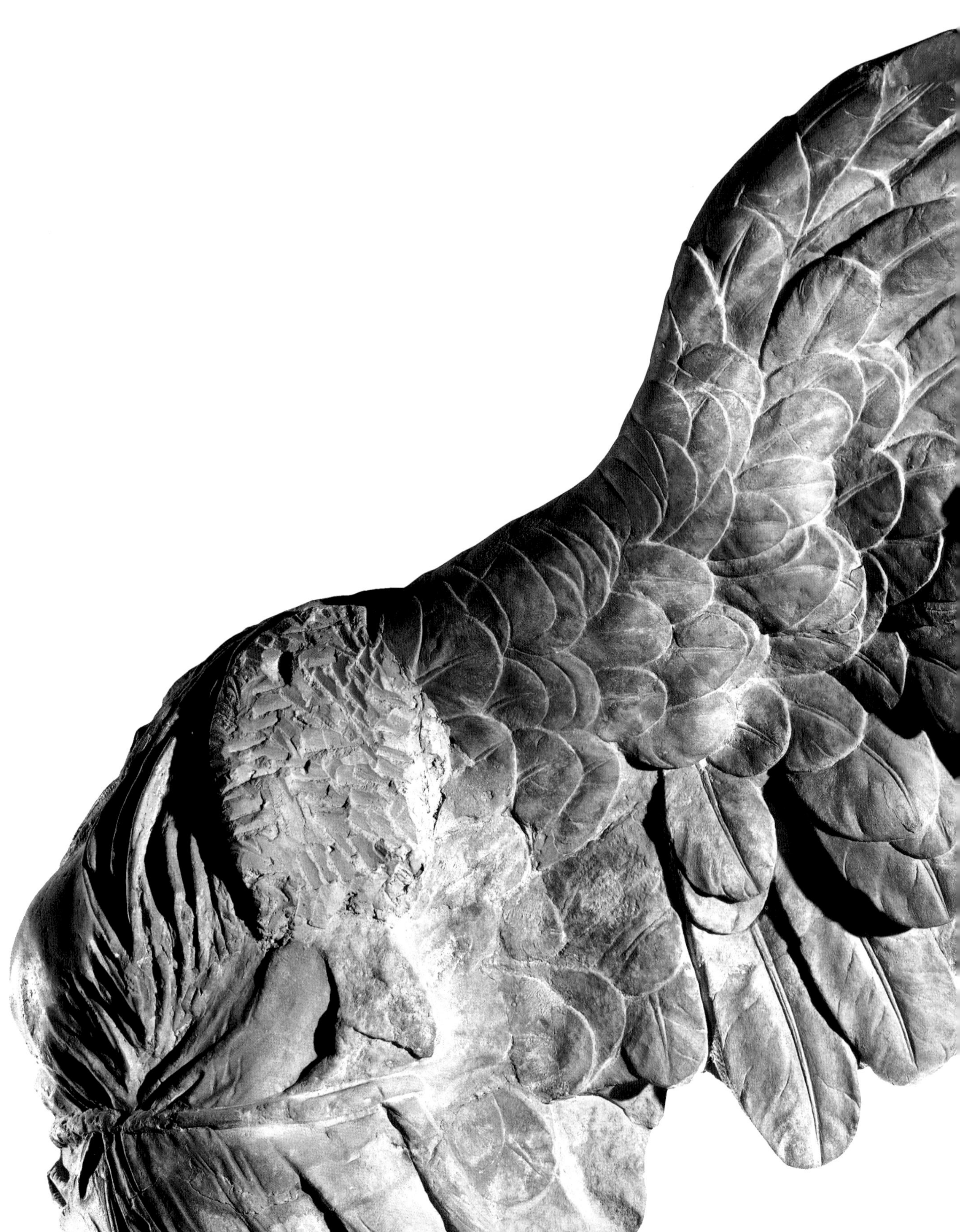

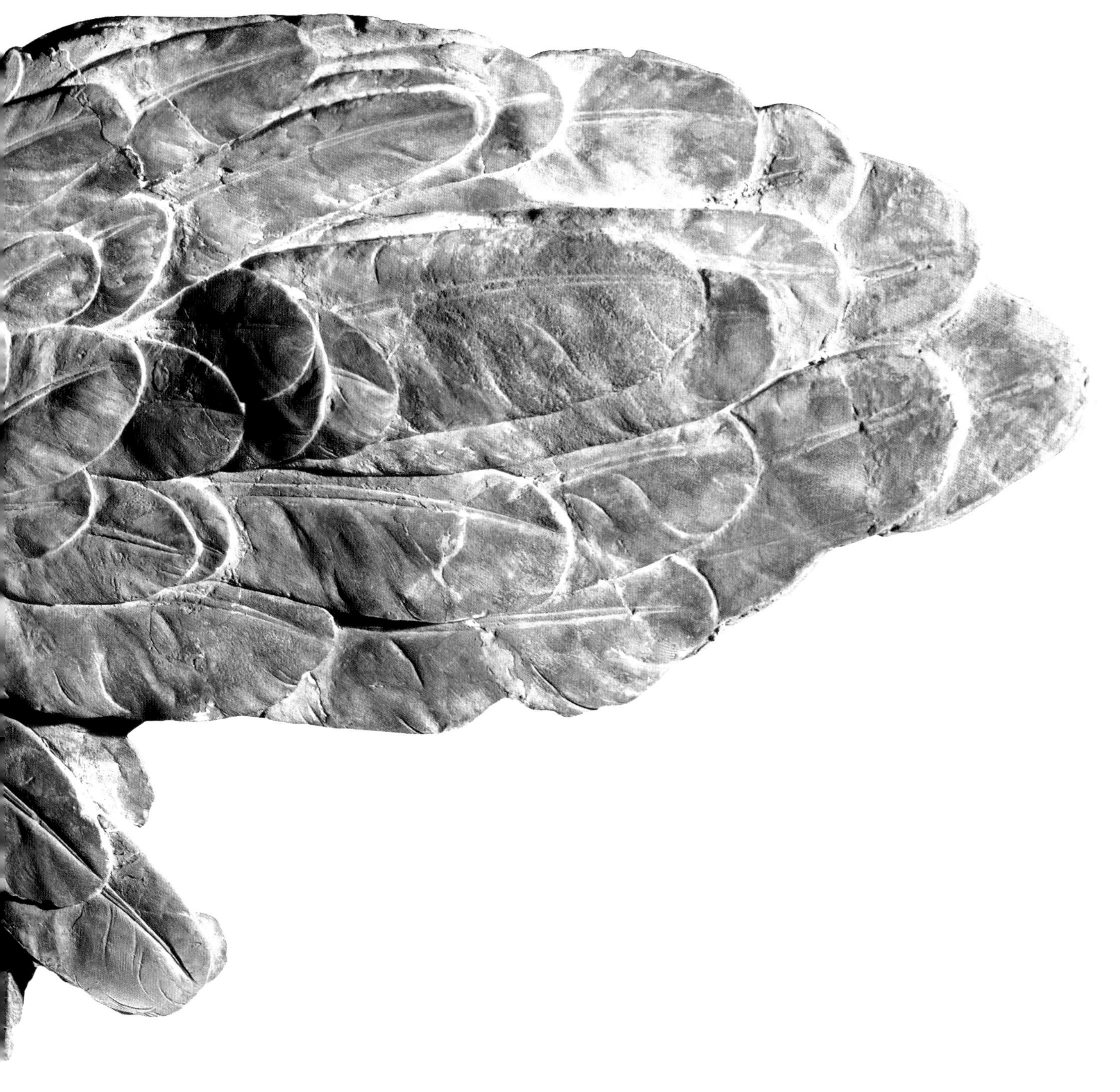

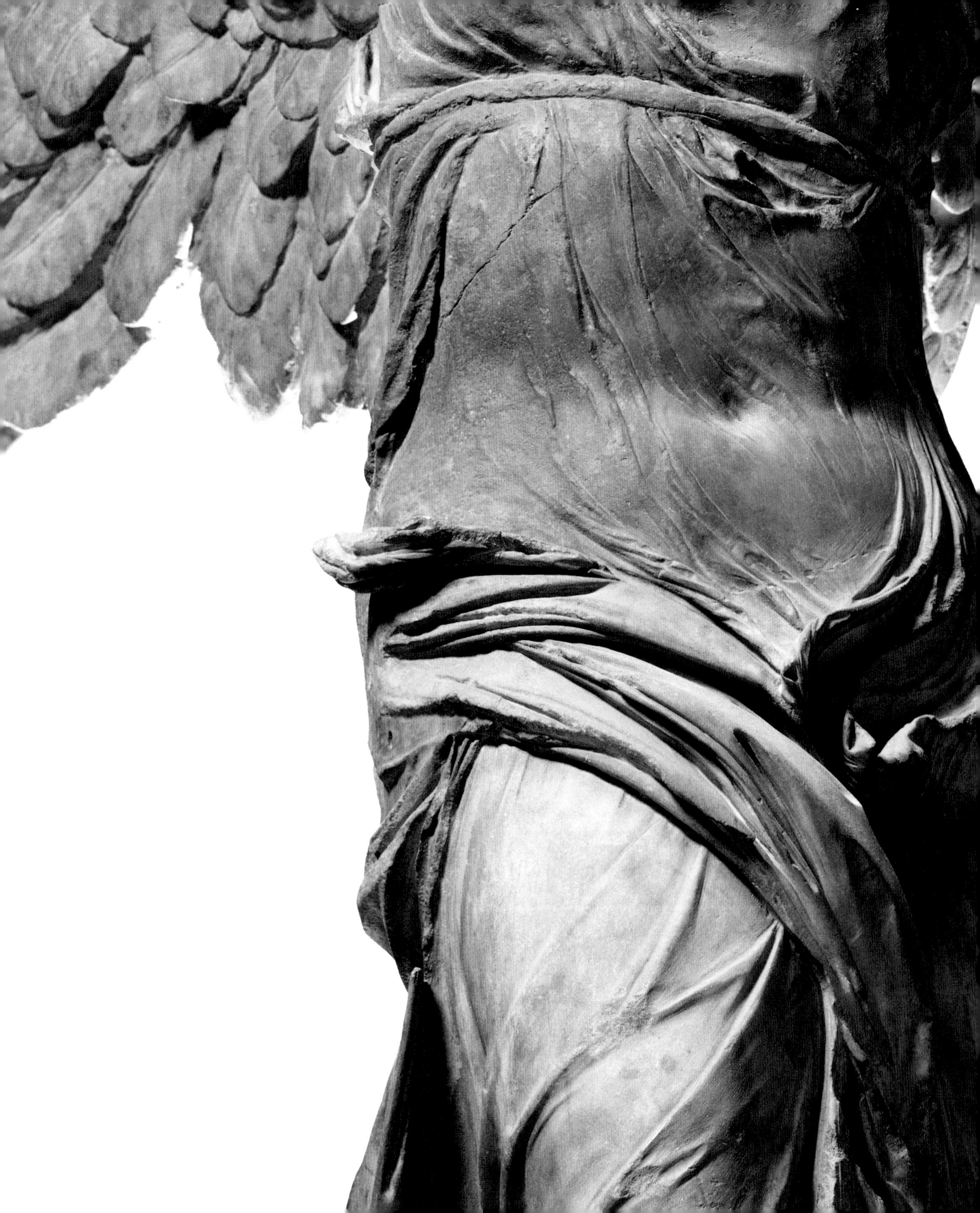

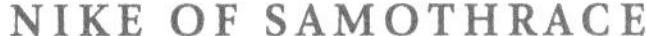

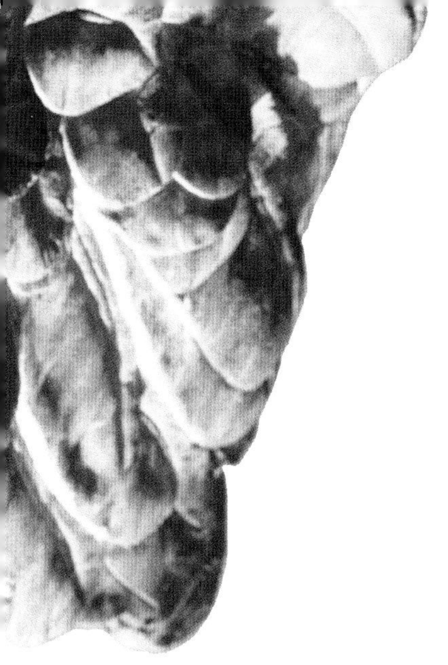

this reason, it is suggested, the Nike's right hand, now missing, was brought close to her mouth, to shout out the Rhodians' victory in a naval battle, the reason for her descent from the heavens onto the ship's prow.

This dramatic work of the mature Hellenistic period, by a Rhodian or an Asia Minor artist, matches the limpidity of the late fifth century BCE with the relatively heavy volumes of the mid-fourth century BCE in a complex creation that differentiates between individual parts: The garment displays a refined fluidity on some parts of the body, while on others it swells and acquires bulk, as happens in a strong wind. The wealth of sculptural decoration—as in the remarkable variety in the rendering of the feathers on the enormous wings, spanning out both backward and upward—the sense of volume, and the violence of intense movement are characteristic of a Rhodian style that heralds the baroque creations of the Pergamon School (c. 180–160 BCE).

THE ALTAR OF PERGAMON

ASIA MINOR, PERGAMON
164–156 BCE
BERLIN, PERGAMON MUSEUM

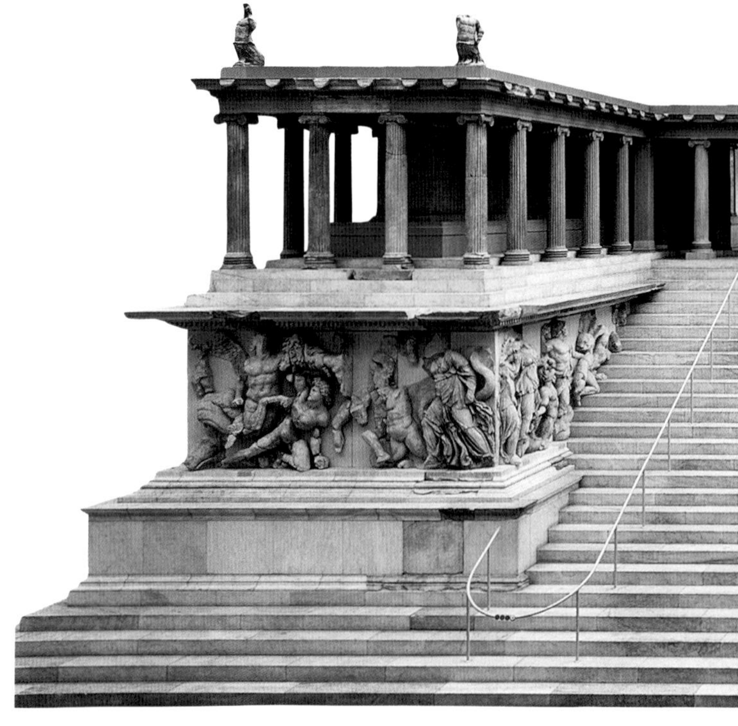

After the death of Alexander the Great in 323 BCE, there ensued ruthless struggles between his generals and co-warriors, the famous Diadochoi, or Successors. His vast empire was carved up, and the victors set up mighty kingdoms in the lands they had acquired. The Diadochos Attalos took part of the northern Ionian shores of Asia Minor, whose main city, Pergamon, was famed for her monuments throughout the Hellenistic period (third–first century BCE).

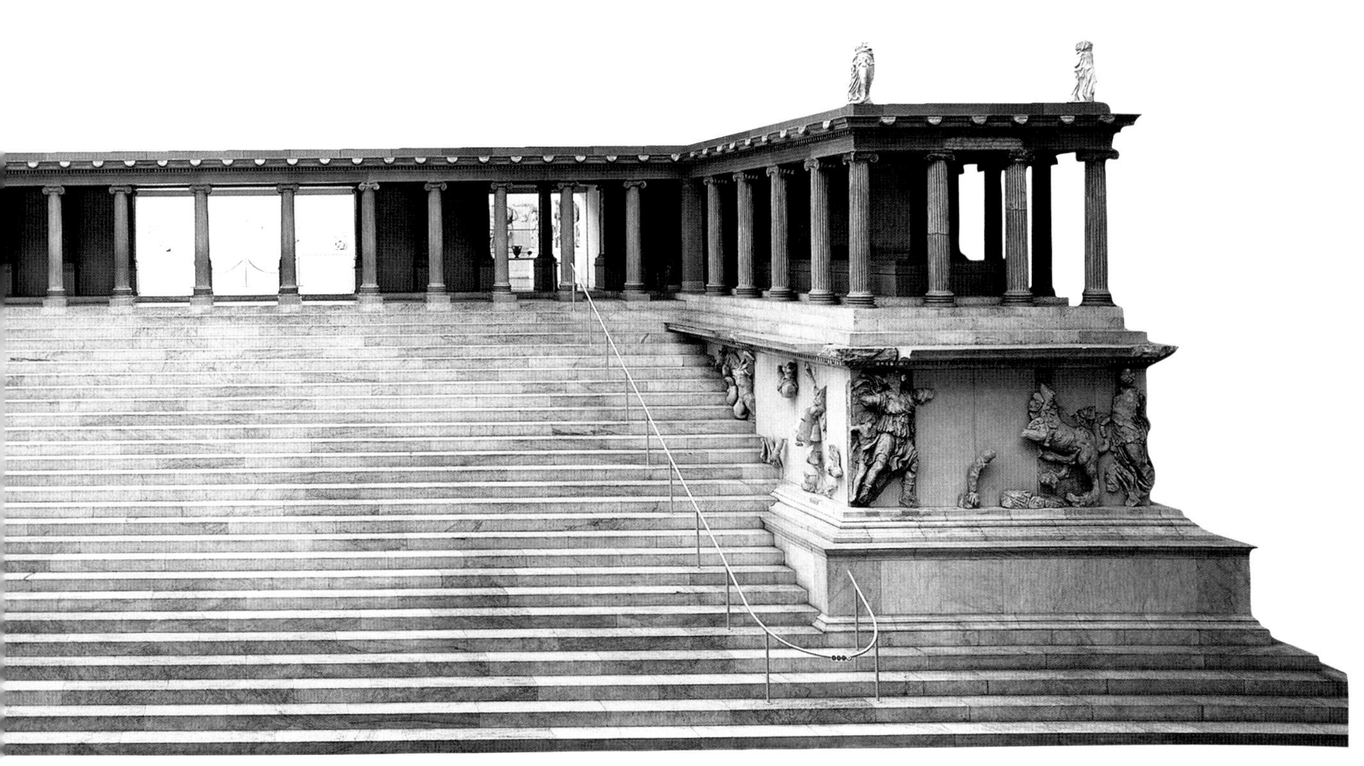

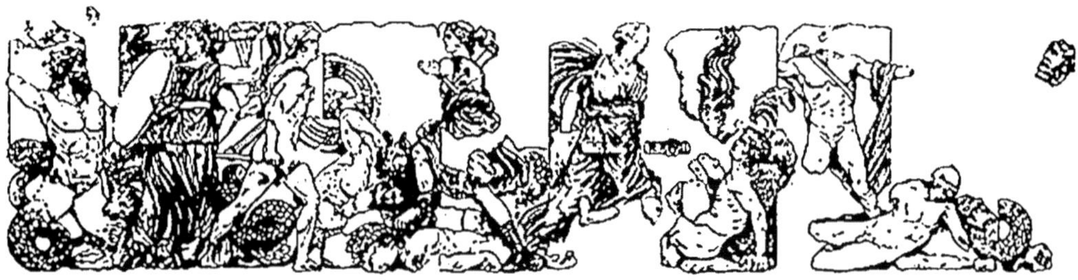
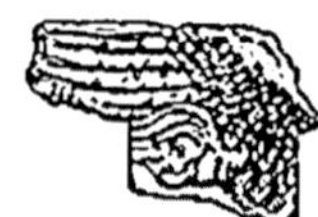

EAST FRIEZE

After the Attalid king Eumenes' various victories, c. 180 BCE, building began on an enormous altar dedicated to Zeus. The construction surrounding the altar proper was covered with sculpted decoration. This altar is one of the most famous and prominent monuments of Hellenistic architecture and sculpture.

Located in a conspicuous position on the acropolis of Pergamon, facing west on a southern terrace, below the Temple of Athena, it dominated the enormous plain spreading down to the sea: It was located in Asia but looked toward Europe. The monument comprised a court upon a high podium, which was surrounded by an Ionic colonnade and accessed via a wide staircase to the west. Its dimensions were 119.55 feet (36.44 m) on the east and west sides and 112.20 feet (34.20 m) on the north and south sides. Visitors entered the terrace through a propylon to the east, beholding first the back face, since the front face was the west. A frieze of sculpted decoration in remarkably high relief ran round the exterior of the podium, just below the colonnade. On the north, east, and south sides, the frieze ran the entire length of the building. On the west side it ran the length of the wings that projected and framed the monumental staircase. A smaller frieze (in height and length), whose sculpted decoration was in lower relief, adorned the inside wall of the elevated court. Its subject was the life of the mythical king of Pergamon and founder of the city in which he also established the worship of Athena: Telephos, son of Herakles from his secret union with the Arcadian priestess Auge, daughter of the region's king.

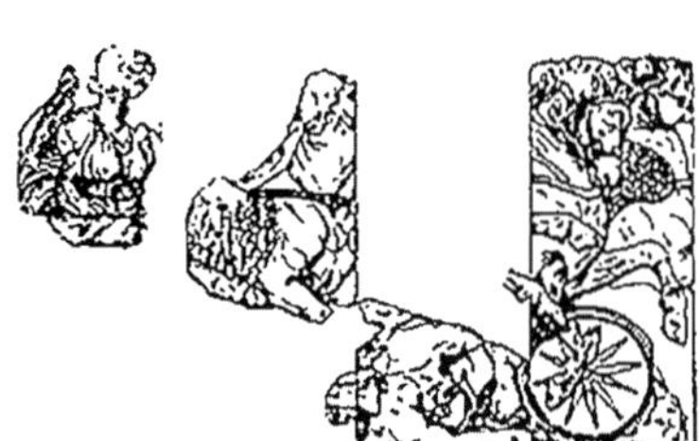
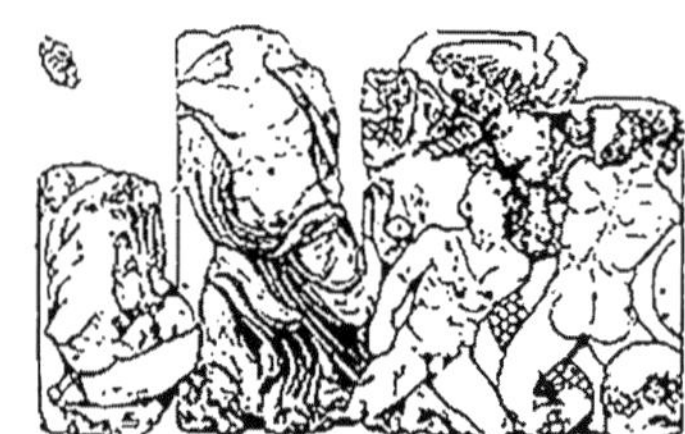
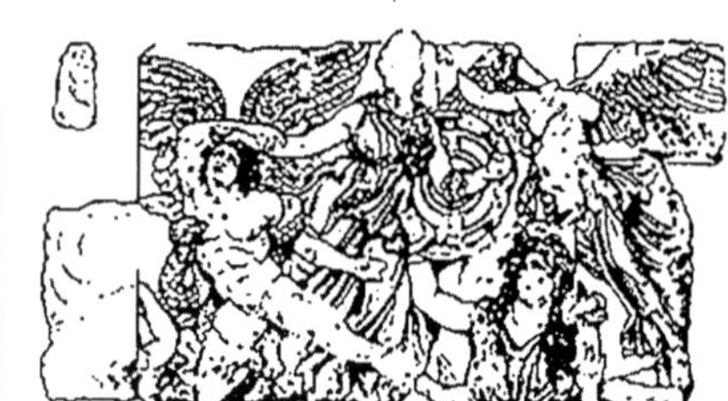
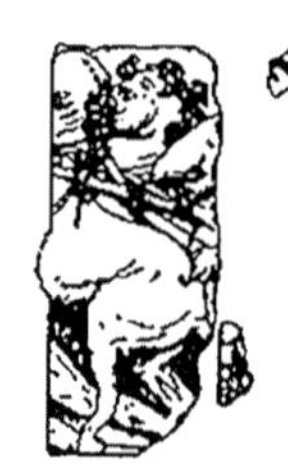

EAST FRIEZE

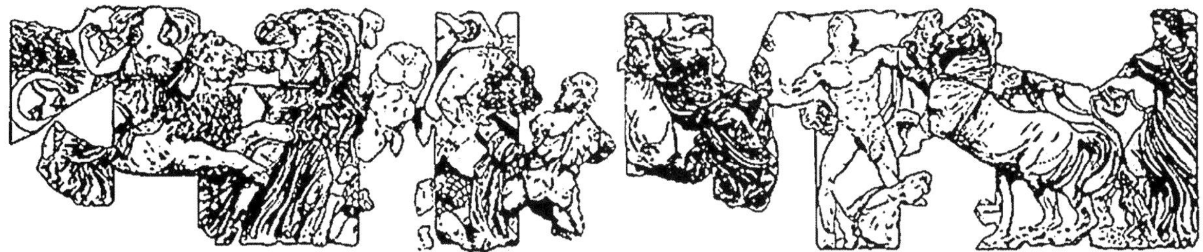

SOUTH FRIEZE

Represented on the large frieze is the Gigantomachy: the battle between the giants, the monstrous offspring of the primal deities Ge (earth) and Uranos (sky), and the victorious Olympian gods, headed by Zeus and assisted by the Titans. The giants and their half brothers—the Titans—are usually associated with pre-Hellenic cults, and their defeat by the Olympian gods may have symbolized the establishment of the basic values and institutions of Hellenic culture. That may explain why the Gigantomachy was a favorite subject of those who, like the Attalids, considered themselves fiduciaries of Greek civilization.

The frieze is 7.55 feet (2.30 m) high and 400 feet (120 m) long and must have originally included about one hundred figures; some eighty-four are preserved, not including the animals. It was executed on the basis of a program designed by not only artists but also intellectuals, such as the Stoic theoretician and critic Krates of Mallos. Nonetheless, the "key" to the iconographic program, that is, the reasoning behind the placement of each figure or group of figures, continues to elude those who study it. A complicating factor is that the entire monument was transported to Berlin, where it was reconstructed. The inscribed names of gods, Titans, and giants are of some help, but there are endless theories concerning the theme of the frieze. Some—for example, that the east frieze was dedicated to the Olympian gods, that the northwest wing featured deities associated with water and the sea, and that the southwest wing featured deities associated with earth and vegetation—have been widely accepted. The figures on the south frieze were

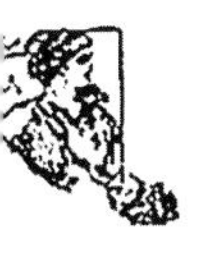

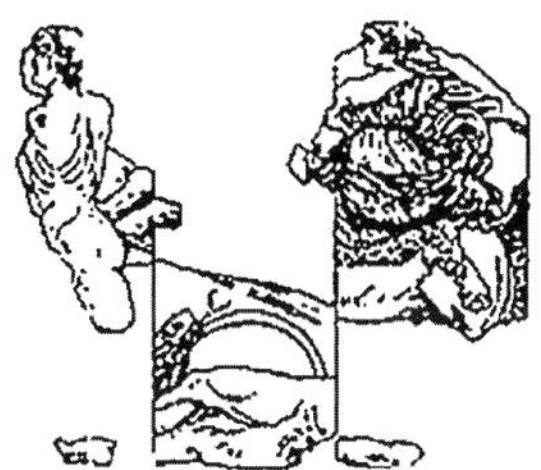

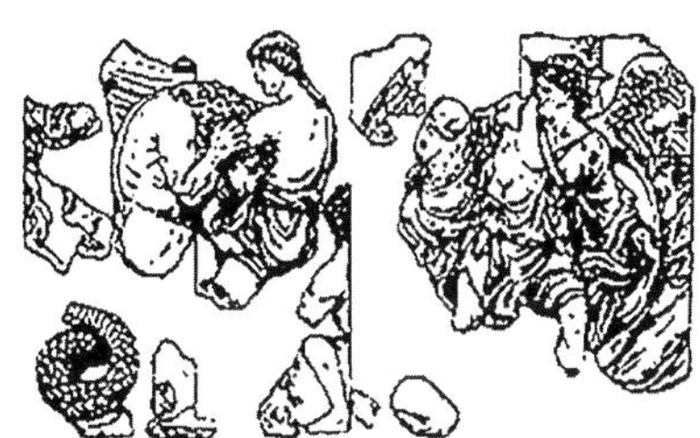

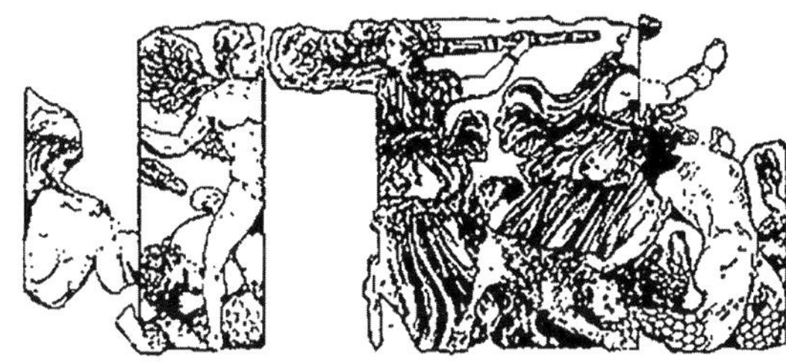

SOUTH FRIEZE

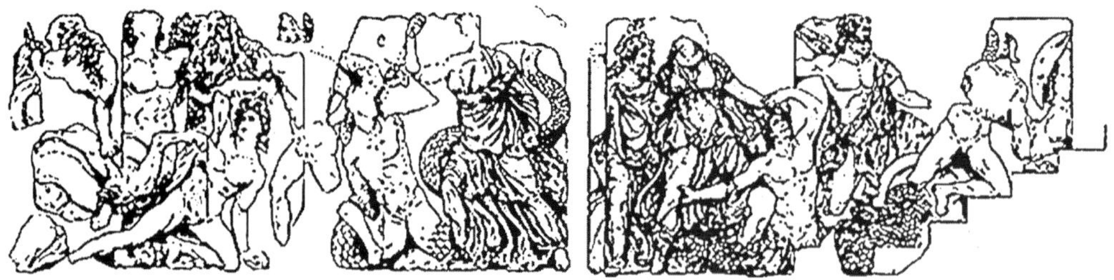

NORTH WING OF SOUTH FRIEZE

most likely deities of heaven and heavenly light. The problem lies with the north side, which is hidden from sunlight and therefore thought to depict deities of night.

Various scholars, in their efforts to identify the numerous allegorical figures, understand the spirit of the representation, and correlate elements of the frieze with Stoic cosmology, have turned mainly to texts such as Hesiod's *Theogony* and Apollodorus' *Library*, recognizing that the frieze appears to owe much to the literary and philosophical trends of the polymath intellectuals of the Hellenistic period. For example, some have observed that the position of the gods on the frieze accords in detail with a quadripartite division of the Cosmos, which was developed by Krates of Mallos on the basis of certain texts by Homer and Hesiod.

The stormy synthesis of the Pergamene Gigantomachy is unique in the history of sculpture. The drapery on the garments of the gods is rendered realistically, as if it had been whipped up by blustery winds. It moves in deep undulations, but within this agitated motion it is organized in autonomous elements, each with their own volumes in relation to the body they cover. The entire frieze presents individual scenes within a dramatic flow, capturing the viewer's interest throughout the development of the battle. Noteworthy too is an intentional classicizing element: The serene expression on the faces

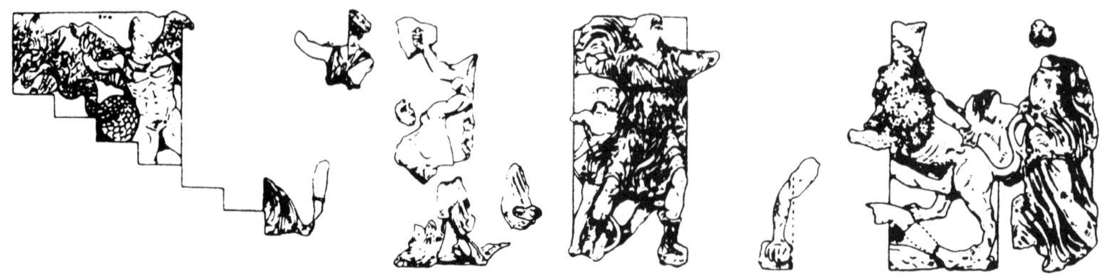

SOUTH FRIEZE

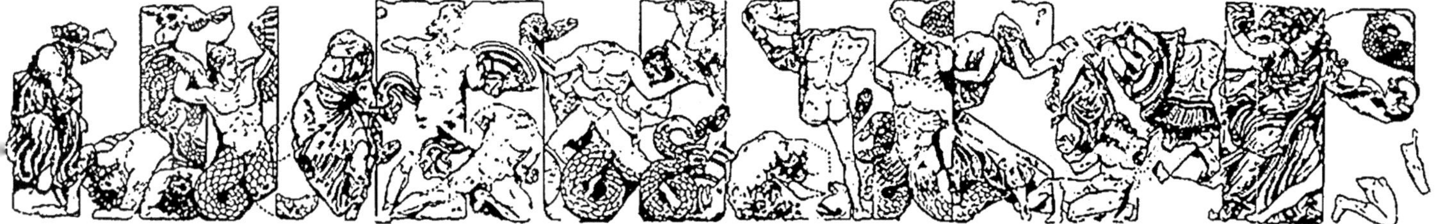

NORTH FRIEZE

of the gods enhances their divine majesty and contrasts with the passionate, violent attack of the earthly forces. This was the credo of the Stoic philosophers, who represented calm and detachment from the passions of others and the pressures of the outside world. And it was Stoic men of letters who played a part in designing the frieze.

As many as forty sculptors are thought to have worked on this monumental project, but almost nothing is known about them. Nevertheless, the input of Rhodian artists was likely significant.

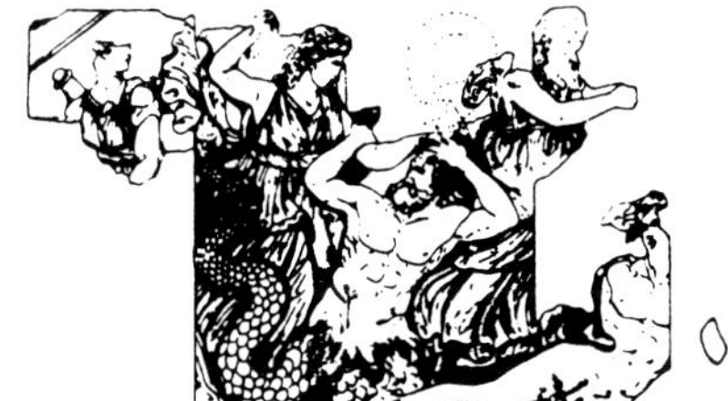

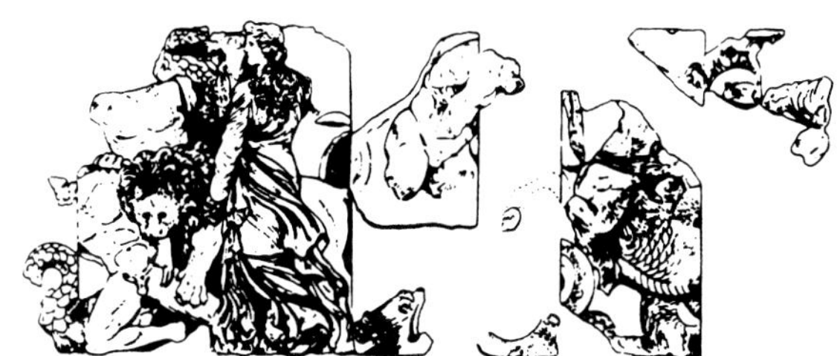

NORTH FRIEZE

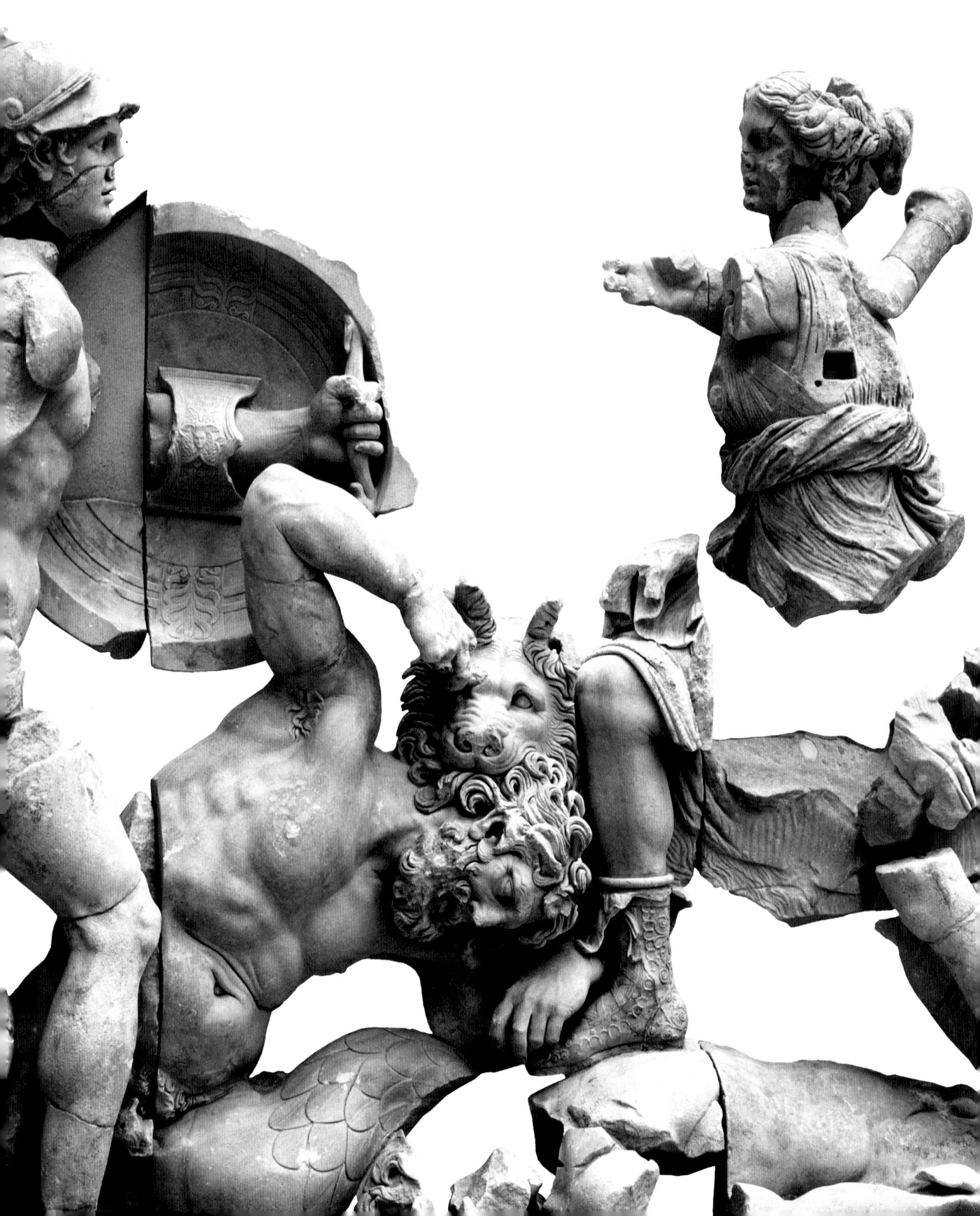

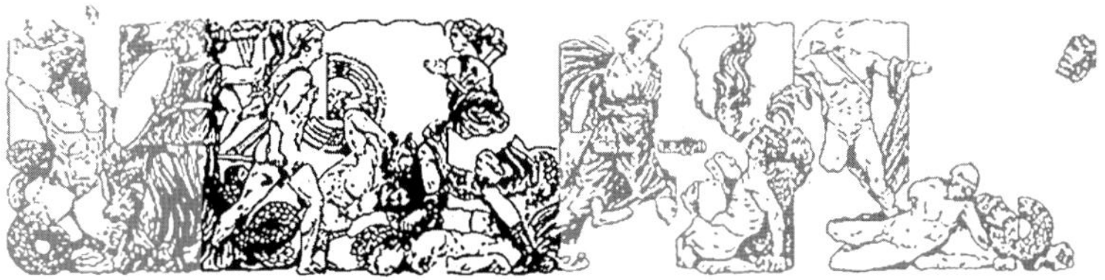

ARTEMIS AND GIANTS

ALTAR OF PERGAMON, EAST FRIEZE
164–156 BCE
BERLIN, PERGAMON MUSEUM

Artemis, goddess of hunting, wears high boots, a short chiton, and a mantle rolled in a thick pad around her waist, to prevent the upper part of her garment from blowing out and hindering her movements. She rushes to her right, aiming a bow and arrow at Otos, a fully armed giant with a shield in his left hand. Between them on the ground, another giant is in his death throes and is savaged on the back of his neck by the goddess's hound. Her right foot tramples the chest of a dead young giant lying supine.

In this three-figure scene the middle figure describes the essential diagonal axis, while the pyramidal composition enhances the dramatic intensity and pathos of the events.

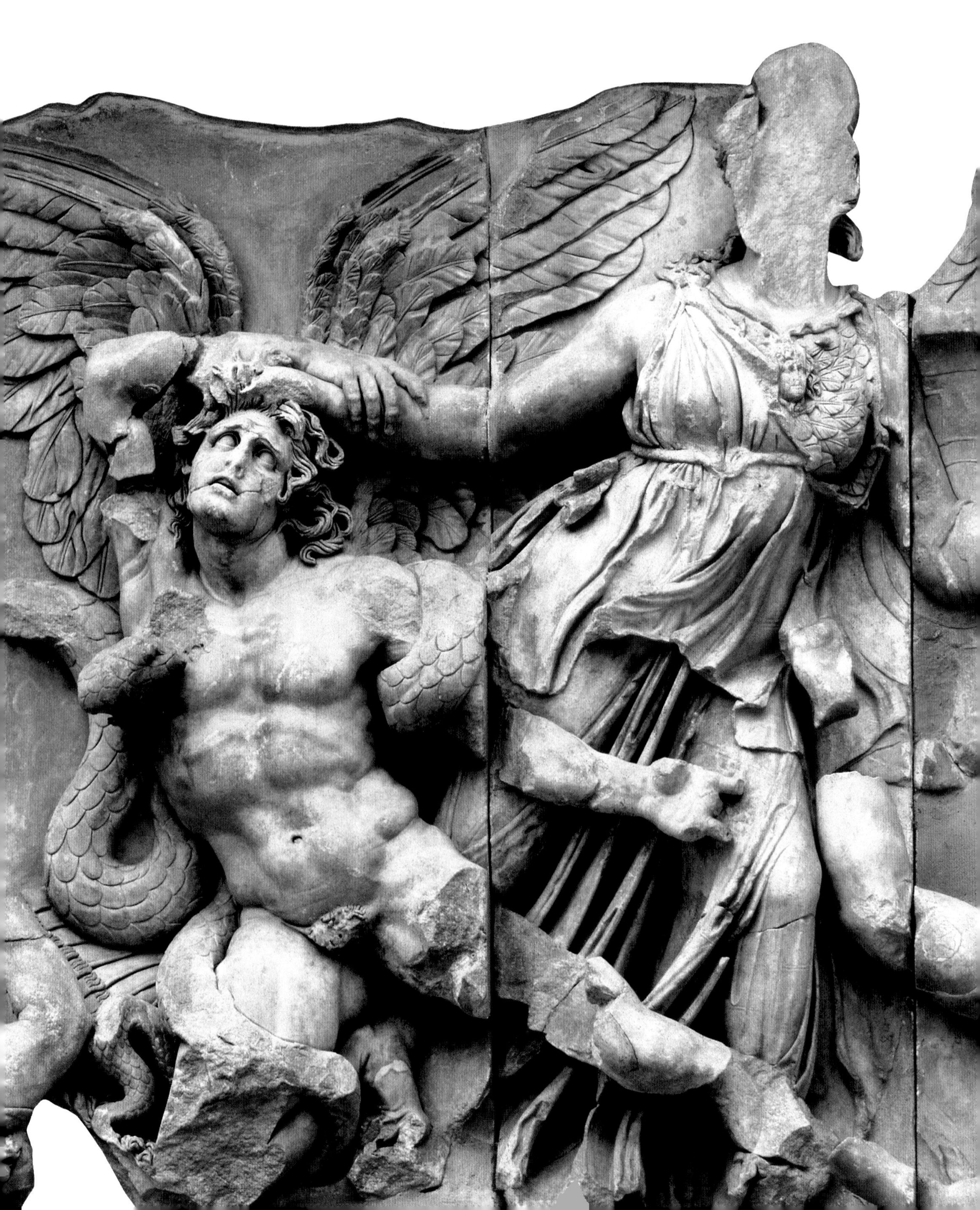

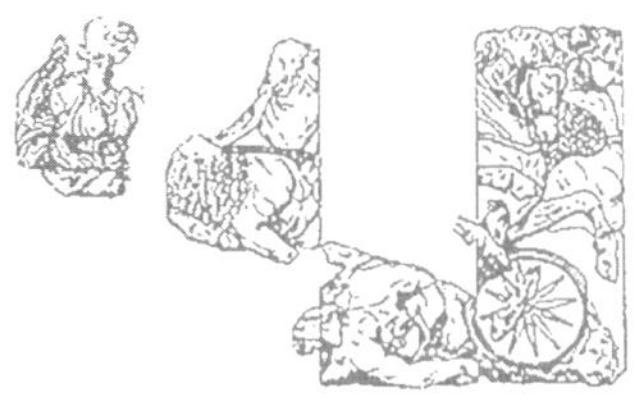
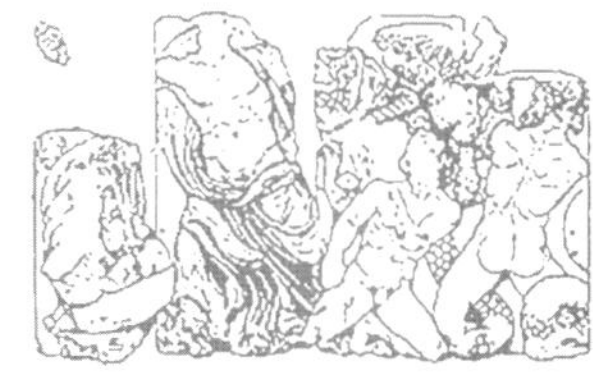
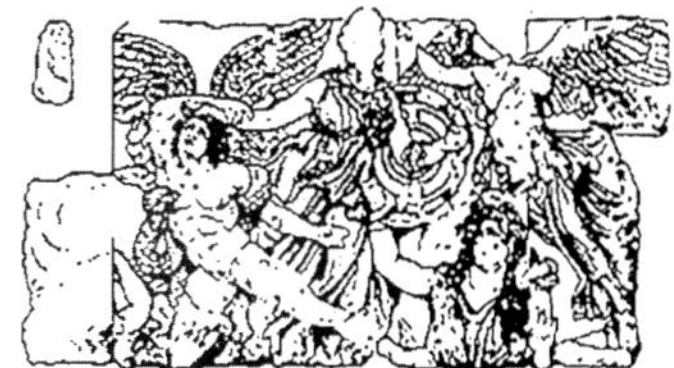
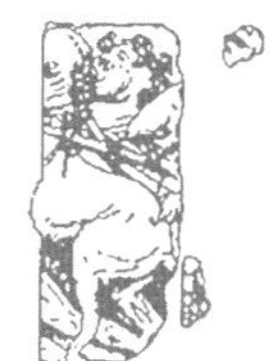

ATHENA AND GIANT

ALTAR OF PERGAMON, EAST FRIEZE
165–156 BCE
BERLIN, PERGAMON MUSEUM

Athena, in an almost frontal pose, rushes to her left, having seized by the hair, with her right hand, the giant Alcyoneus. The giant's nude body is represented in an oblique pose, forming an almost inverted triangle, which the body of the goddess extends in the opposite direction.

The goddess wears a girdled chiton with a long apoptygma and the aegis on her chest; she is holding a circular shield in her slightly bent left hand. Below and to the side of the shield, Ge (the Earth goddess) emerges from the earth. Ge is rendered on a larger scale than the other figures to enhance her supernatural power. Athena, in her effort to vanquish the giant, tugs him away from his mother, Ge, from whom he draws his strength. The Nike, flying above the head of Ge, arrives to crown Athena, thereby completing the scene. Her large open wings correspond to the enormous open wings of the giant, which beat behind him in the opposite, upper left corner of the scene.

Alcyoneus' hair frames his face in large, swirling waves, the wrinkles on his forehead are deep like scars, and his heavy eyebrows, deeply furrowed above his sunken eye sockets, give his expression an agitated pathos.

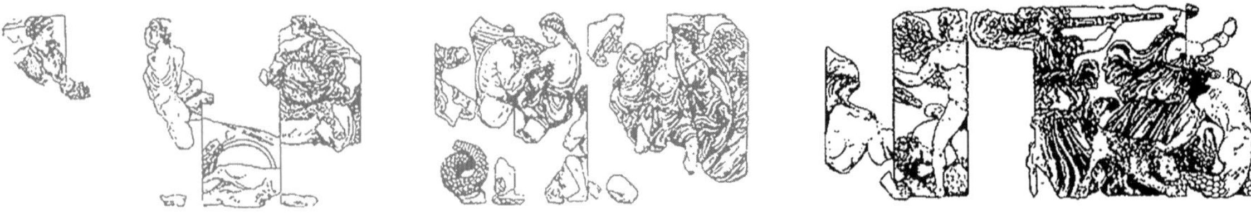

TITANESSES AND GIANT

ALTAR OF PERGAMON, SOUTH FRIEZE
165–156 BCE
BERLIN, PERGAMON MUSEUM

The Titanesses Phoebe and her daughter Asteria (sister of Leto, mother of Apollo), accompanied by a large dog, are represented in violent motion: Phoebe on the left with her back turned to the viewer, and Asteria on the right in profile. The figures are composed in an inverted triangle. Both wear a long, multipleated and girdled chiton with apoptygma; Phoebe has her mantle rolled around her waist in a thick pad, and Asteria wears a short cape, one edge of which flutters behind her back. Phoebe attacks with a large torch and Asteria with a large sword. The giant Asteria battles is represented in a complicated pose. His human torso is markedly bowed, perhaps because the leonine hound has savaged his serpentine lower body, which spreads behind him and forms almost a crescent with the upper part. The drapery of the garments of the two Titanesses has a quasi-independent existence, particularly that of Asteria, which forms an undulating cone that emphasizes the thighs and hips.

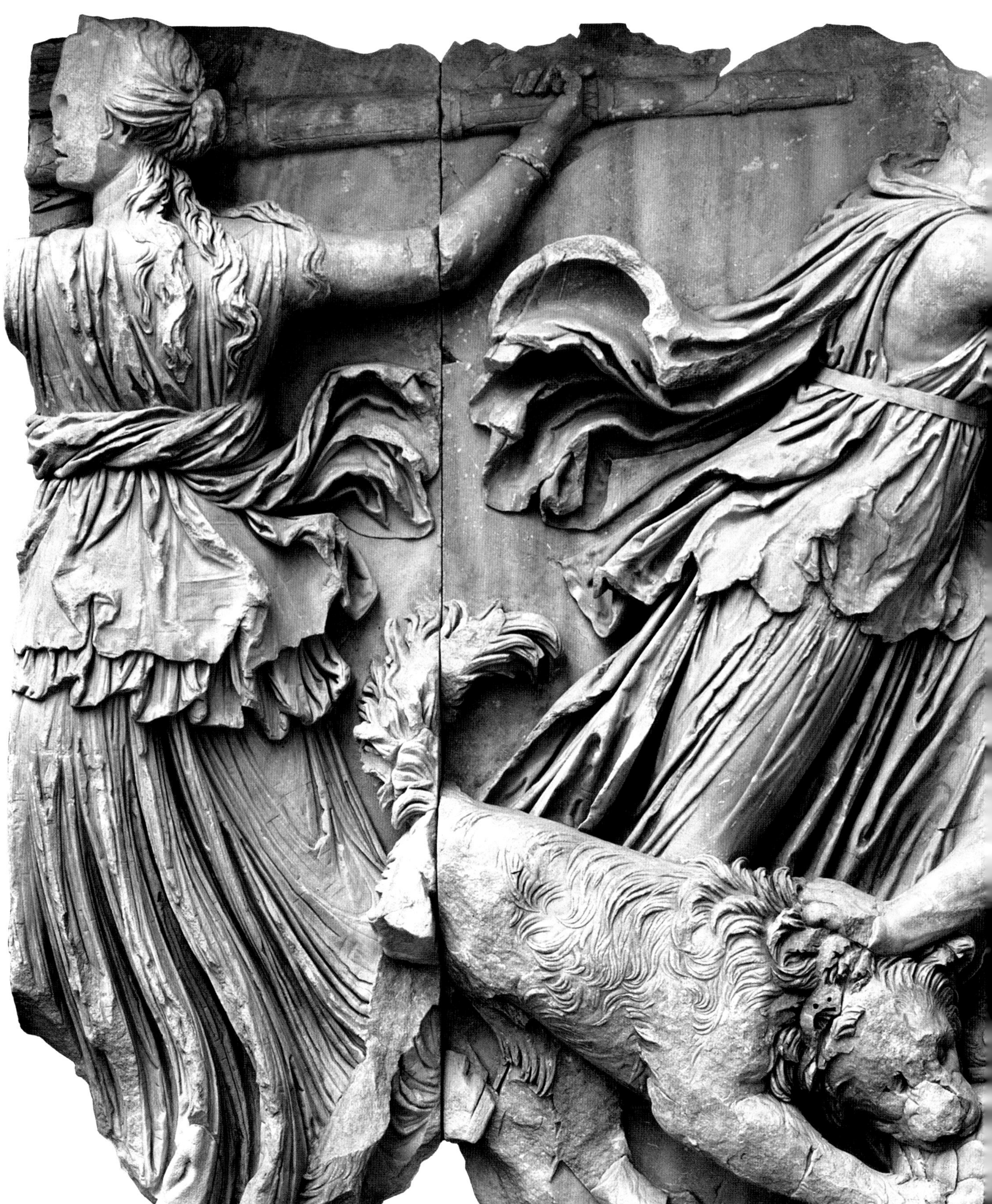

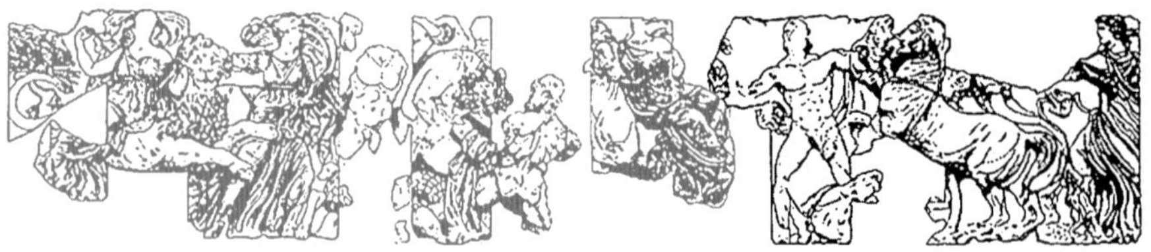

HELIOS AND GIANT

ALTAR OF PERGAMON, SOUTH FRIEZE
165–156 BCE
BERLIN, PERGAMON MUSEUM

Helios, god of light, rushes out of the sea driving his four-horse chariot and encounters a standing, nude giant. The giant is shown in a frontal pose with his legs apart and his arms in a desperate gesture to protect himself from the approaching horses. The god wears a high-girdled, multipleated chiton (characteristic of charioteers) and a himation that flutters out behind him. He carries a torch as a weapon against his adversary.

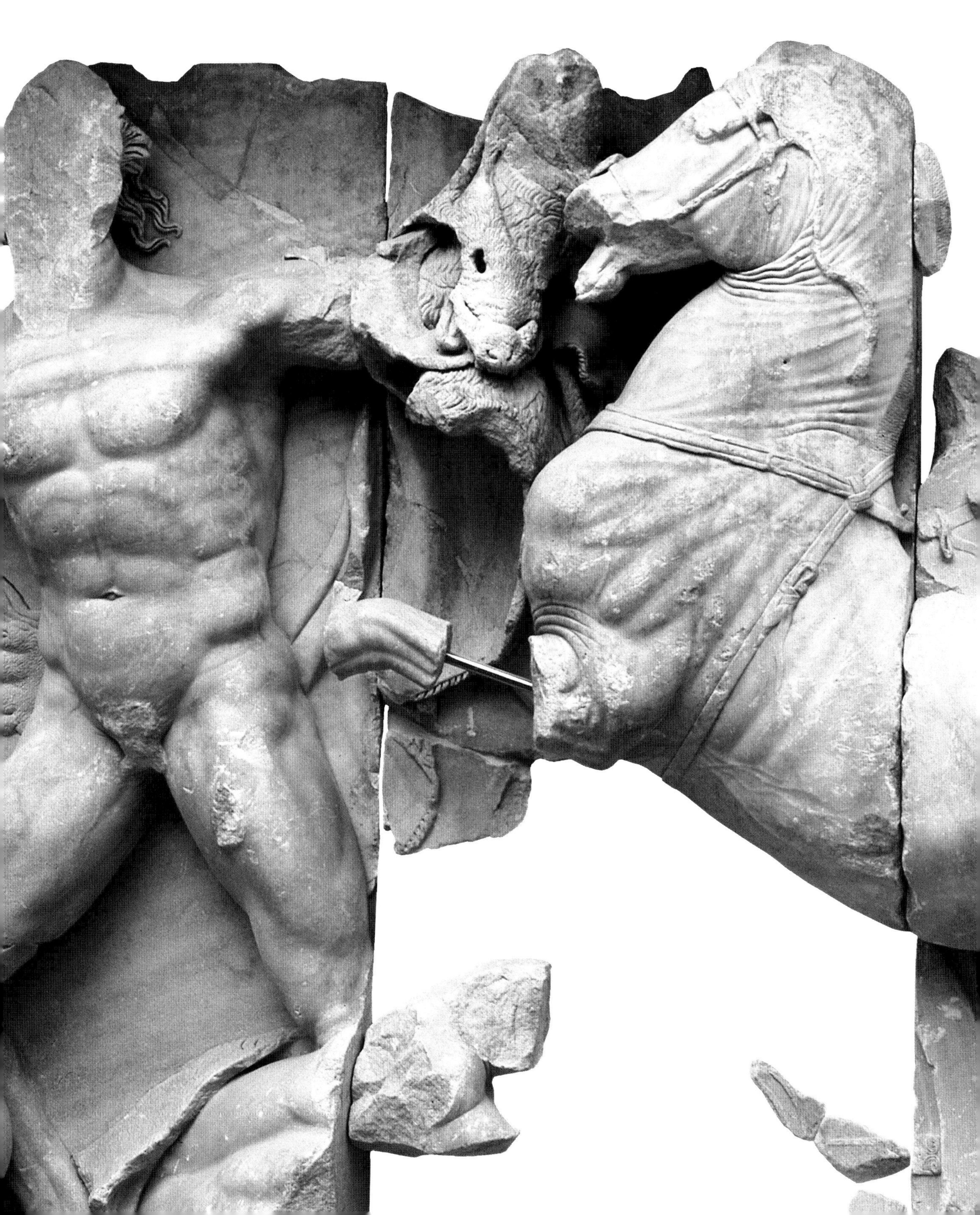

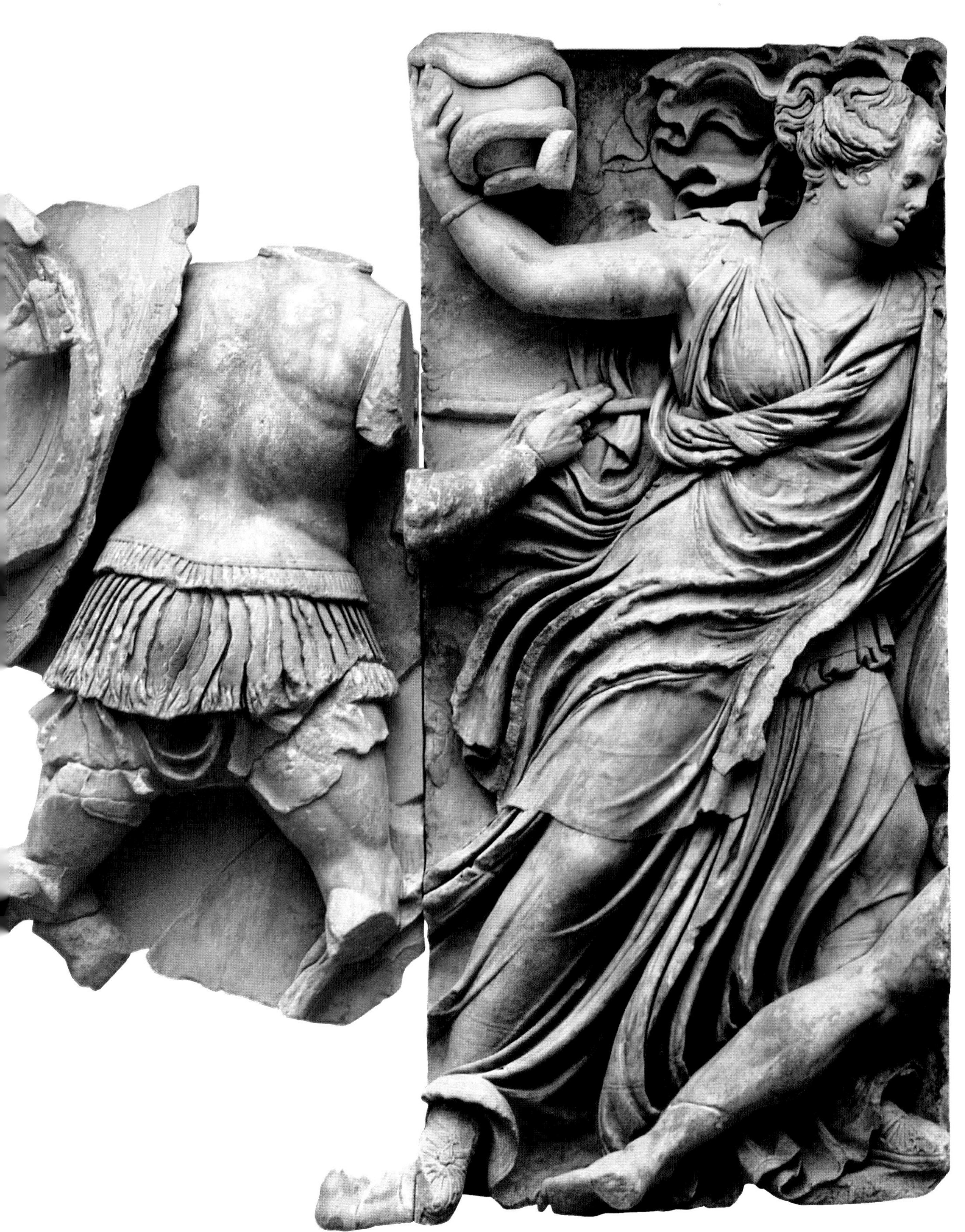

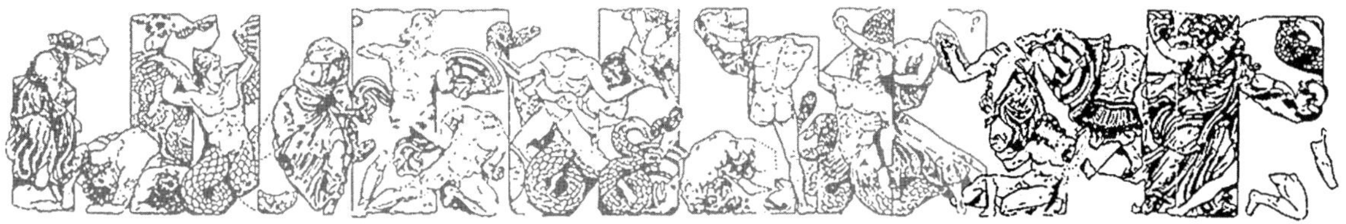

NYX AND GIANT

ALTAR OF PERGAMON, NORTH FRIEZE
164–156 BCE
BERLIN, PERGAMON MUSEUM

Nyx (the personification of Night), or Persephone according to some scholars, holds in her raised right hand a vase coiled with snakes. Poised to throw it at a half-kneeling giant, she wears a chiton and a himation diagonally laid and moves impetuously to her left, her body almost frontal and her head in profile. The giant is represented nude and with his back to the viewer. Nyx, or Persephone, is portrayed as a young woman with luxuriant, wavy hair that blows back, following her violent movement. A veil and the ends of a pearl fillet binding her hair-knot flutter around her head. The fillet falls from the back of the hairstyle to the shoulders and ends with a pomegranate flower above her left hand (the pomegranate flower, and the pomegranate in general, is an attribute of Persephone, queen of the Underworld). The classical features on the goddess's lovely face, such as the small mouth and the curvaceous outlines, mimic sculptures on the Parthenon.

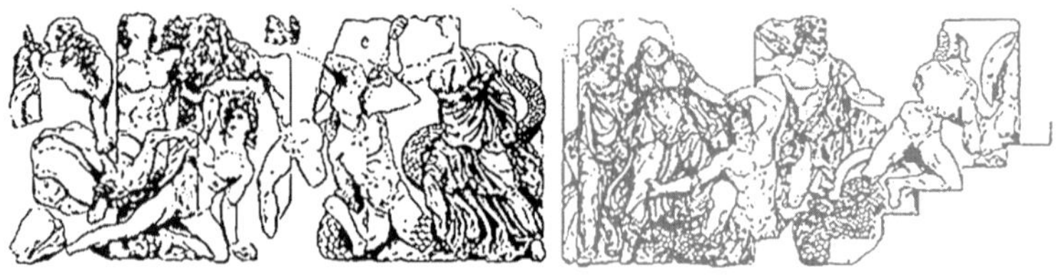

TRITON AND GIANTS

ALTAR OF PERGAMON, NORTH FRIEZE
165–156 BCE
BERLIN, PERGAMON MUSEUM

The sea god Triton, son of Poseidon, struggles alongside his mother, Amphitrite, against the giants. He is represented standing and in a frontal pose, with a naked human torso, wings, the lower body of a fish, and the forelegs of a horse. His opponents, the giants, are shown half fallen, one below and in front of him, in an oblique pose (again illustrating the triangular schema popular among the artists of the Pergamon frieze) and the other standing and attacking from his left. The figures are imbued with dynamism, tension, and pathos.

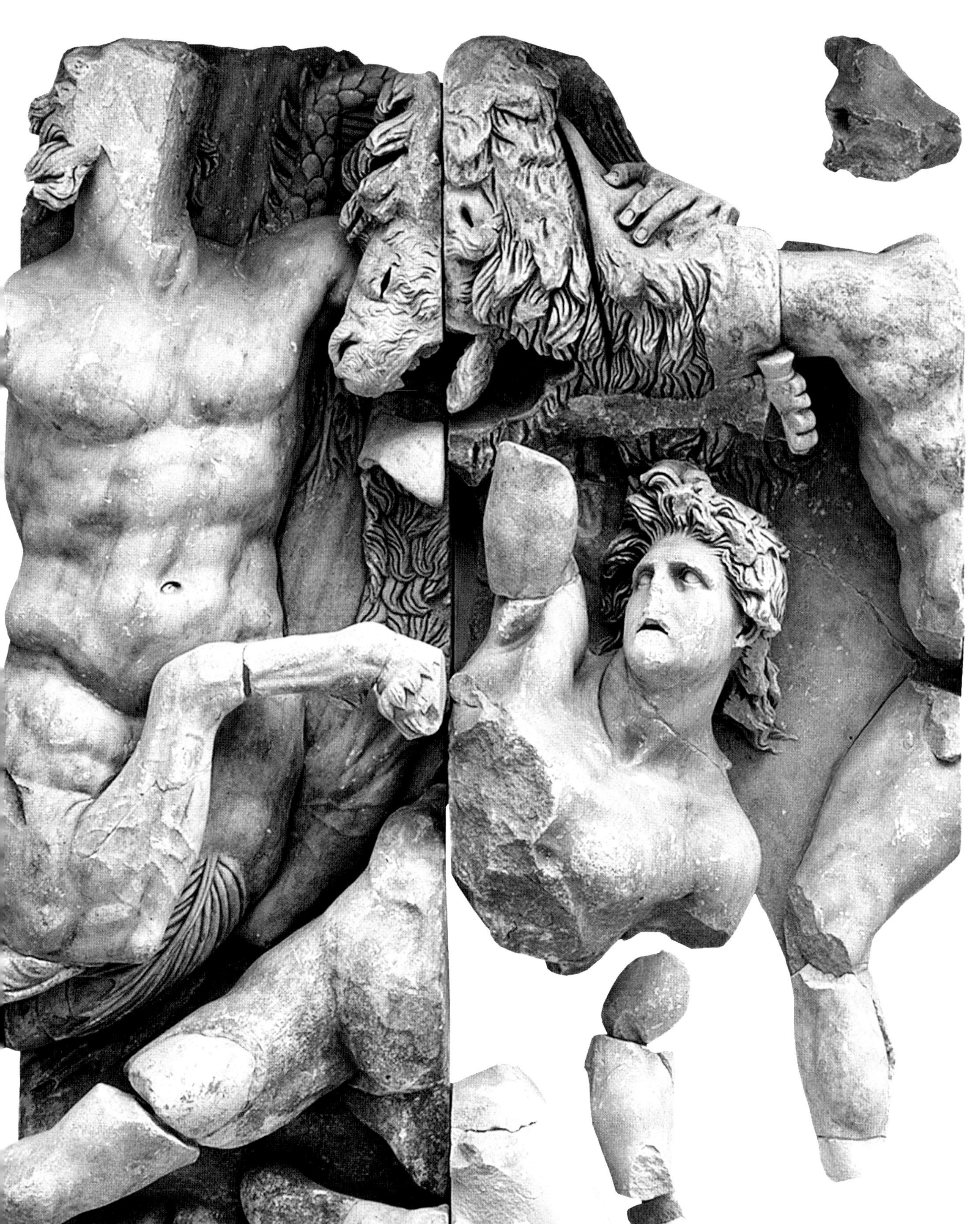

NYMPH

DELOS, LESCHE OF THE KOINON OF BERYTIAN POSEIDONIANS
HELLENISTIC PERIOD
MARBLE. PRESENT HEIGHT 2.33 FEET (0.71 M)
DELOS, ARCHAEOLOGICAL MUSEUM

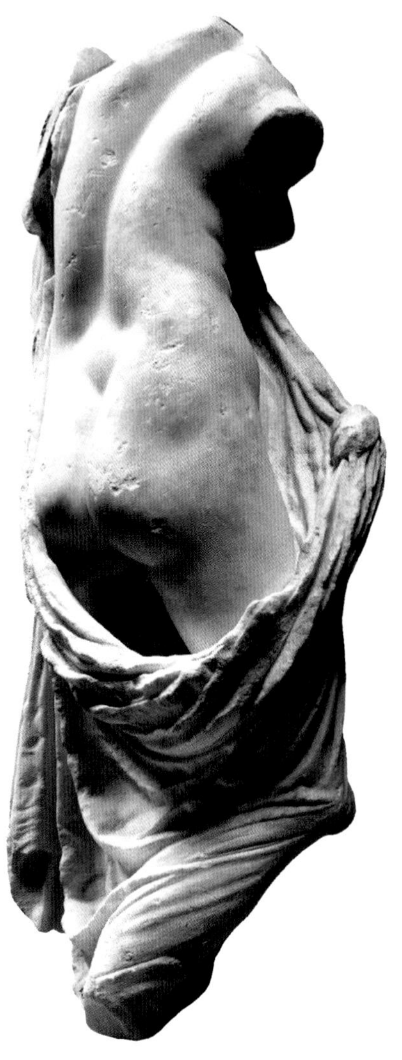

This statue of a female figure from an amorous group captures the moment of her resistance when a male figure tries to disrobe her. She attempts to distance herself from his hand, which has seized her by the himation. Portrayed from behind in three-quarter pose and naked to the thighs, her himation falls to reveal her back and buttocks and covers only her legs and part of her front. The male figure would have been represented from the front, in profile or three-quarter pose, and to the left of the female (only his hand is preserved, on the himation). The representation could be of the sacred marriage between the nymph Amymone (or Beroe), and Poseidon, in accordance with the local myth of Berytus. However, other scholars believe it to be an sexual attack on a nymph, not by a god but by someone she wishes to reject.

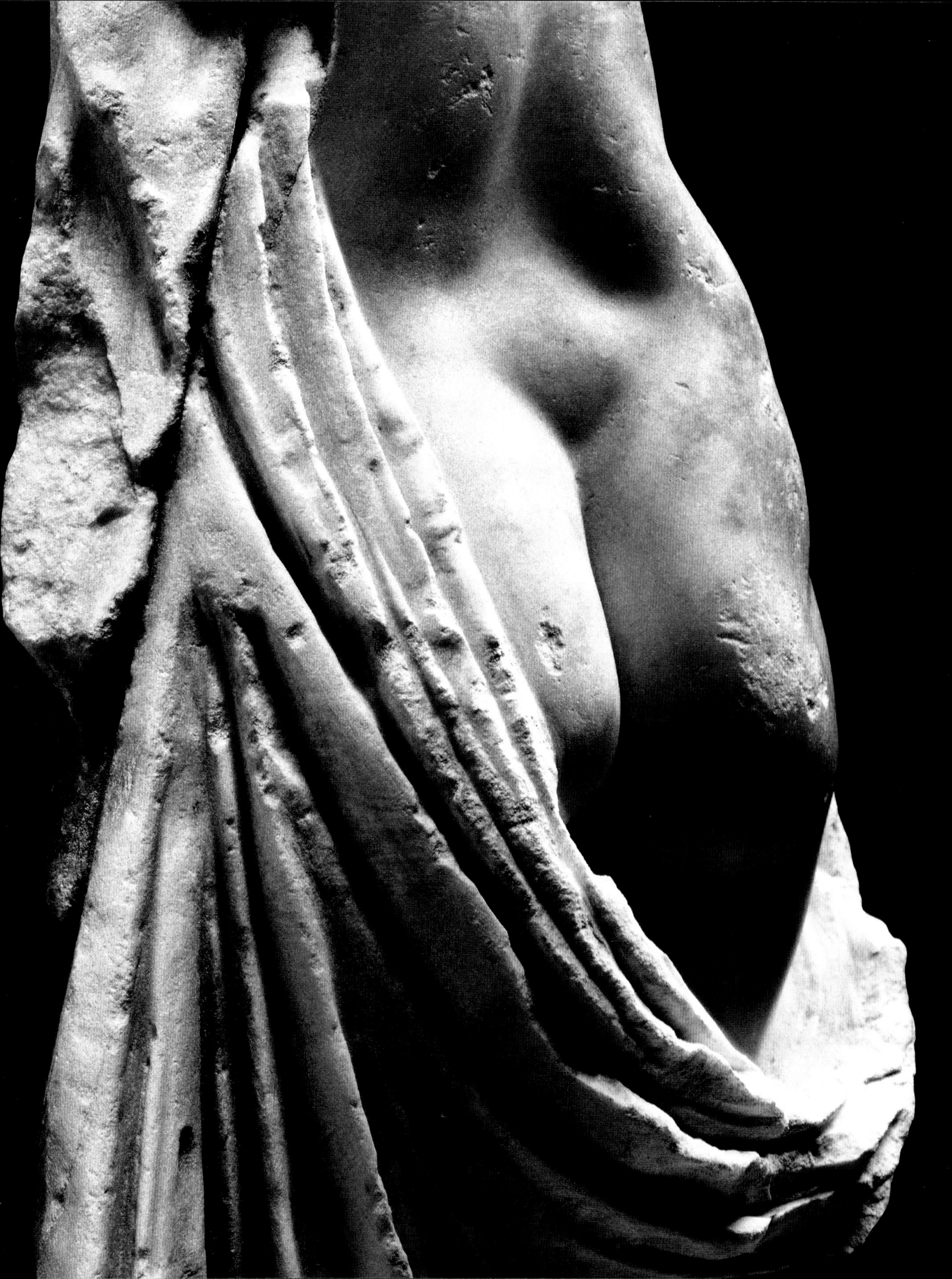

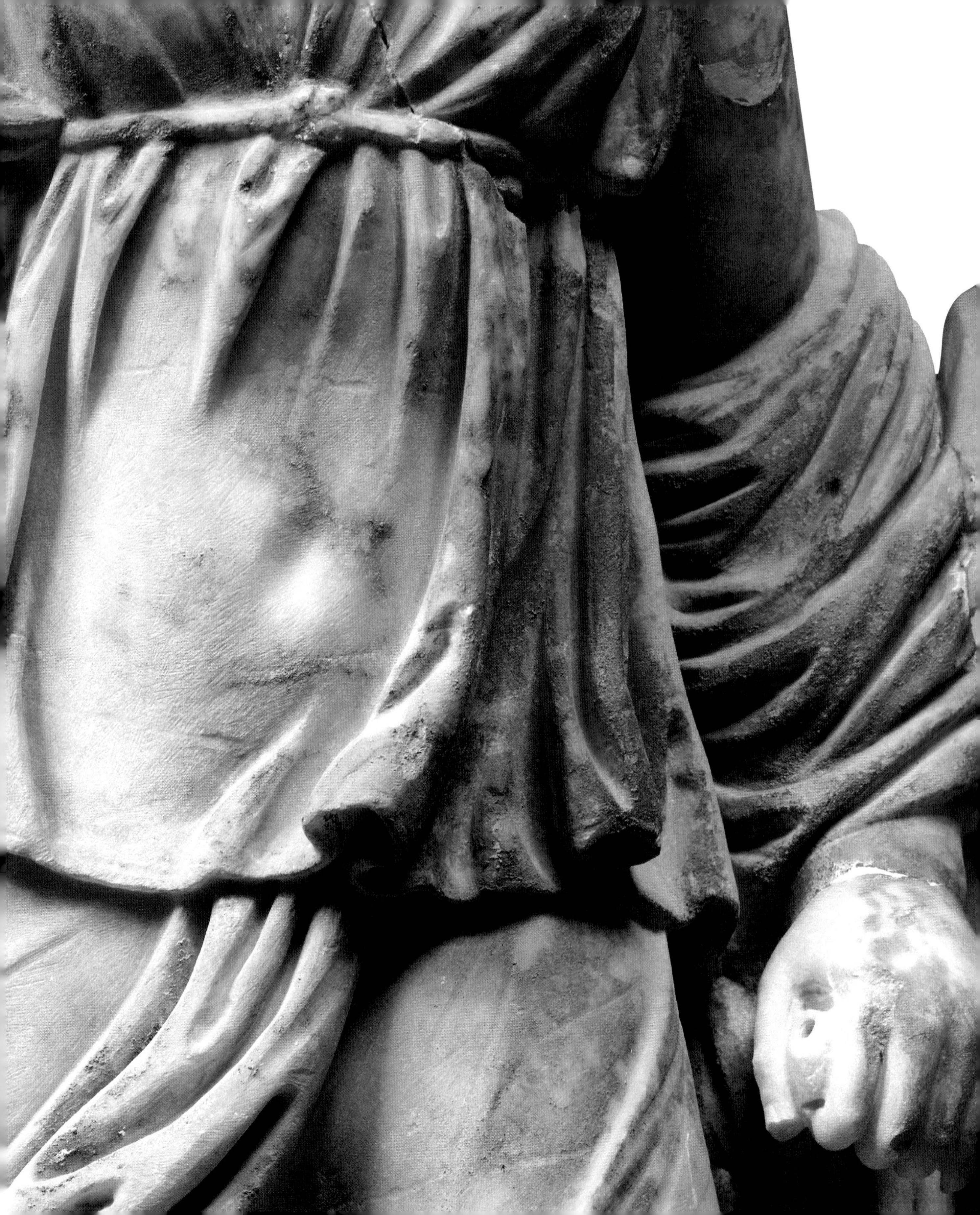

ARTEMIS ELAPHEBOLOS

DELOS, THEATER QUARTER
SECOND HALF OF SECOND CENTURY BCE
MARBLE. PRESENT HEIGHT INCLUDING BASE 4.69 FEET (1.43 M)
DELOS, ARCHAEOLOGICAL MUSEUM

In this statue group of Artemis with hind, known as Artemis Elaphebolos, the goddess wears a short chiton with apoptygma, girdled high and with painted bands on the edges of the garment. On her feet are high boots, the thongs of which were painted in red and blue. A multipleated himation is wound around and falls from her left arm, and with her left hand she grasps the deer by the antlers. She is poised to strike the final blow with her raised right hand, while she digs the knee of her bent left leg into the back of the kneeling animal. A double fillet binds her hair, which is drawn up into a krobylos on her crown.

The work conveys impulsive movement, and the anxiety of both the hunter and the prey, a popular and picturesque subject. Concurrently, however, it may have borne some relationship with the performance of a ritual. The exceptional delicacy of the goddess's facial features, with their almost dreamy look and hint of a smile, temper the ferocity of the scene.

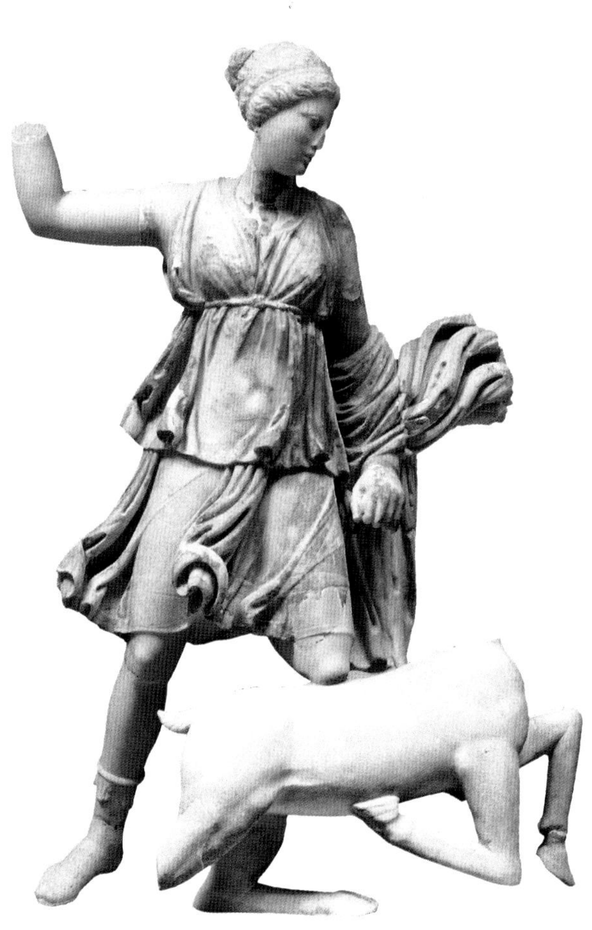

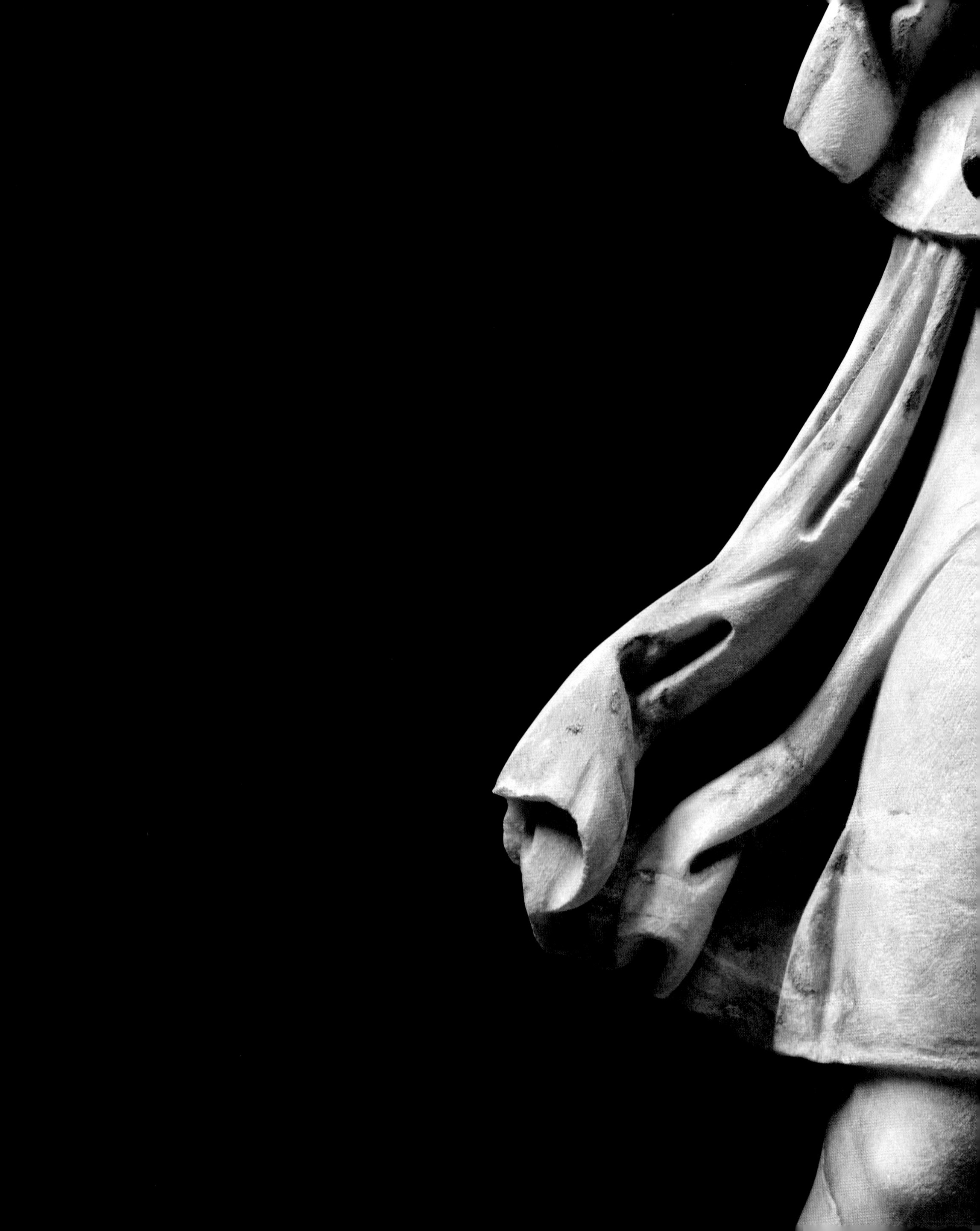

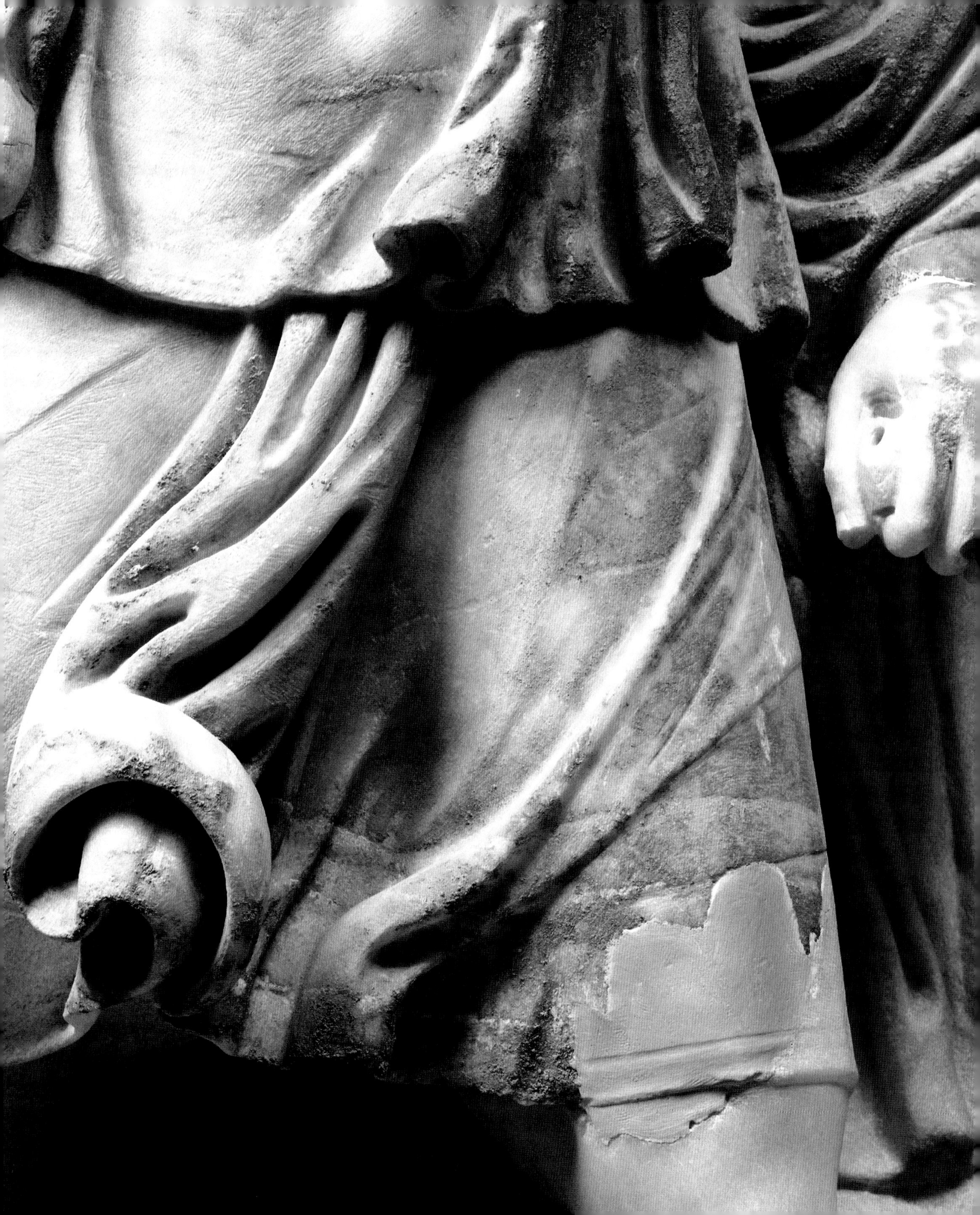

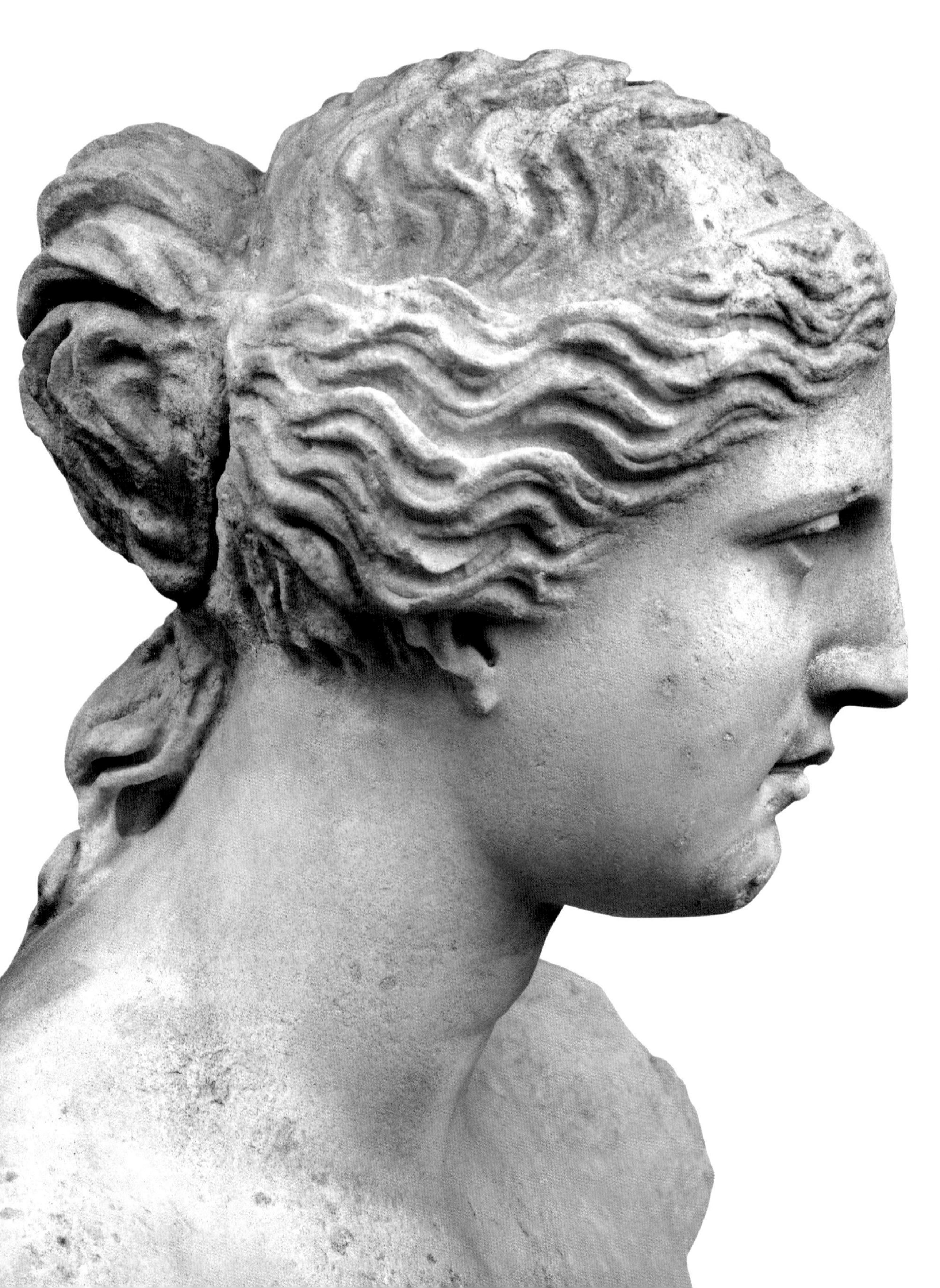

APHRODITE OF MELOS

MELOS
LATE SECOND CENTURY BCE
PARIAN MARBLE. PRESENT HEIGHT 6.63 FEET (2.02 M)
PARIS, LOUVRE MUSEUM

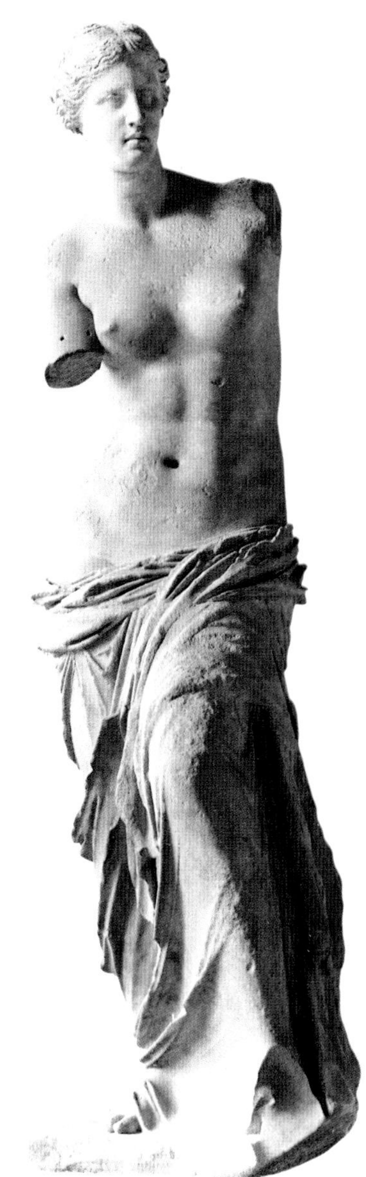

The world-famous "Venus de Milo" was found in 1820, near the theater in the ruined ancient city of Melos, which was located on the homonymous island in the southwestern Cyclades. From there it was smuggled out of Melos, to end up eventually in the Louvre Museum. It comprises two parts joined together by metal dowels at the height of the figure's hips, on which the left arm from the shoulder and the corresponding foot were inset. This manner of statue construction was common in Greece, particularly in the Cyclades.

The goddess is portrayed half-naked and resting on her right leg, while her left leg is relaxed and set forward with a slightly bent knee. A fine himation covers the lower body from the buttocks downward. The garment is folded over around the lower pelvis and held in place on the left side, falling in front between the legs. Of the pieces of metal jewelry that adorned her, only the holes for their attachment have survived: on the arm a bracelet, in the ears earrings, and on the head a diadem above the fillet that holds in place the long wavy hair. Gathered into a ***korymbos*** (a knot at the back), there are just a few curly wisps left to fall freely on the nape of the neck. The left arm is missing from the shoulder and the right from mid-upper arm; there is thus considerable debate over the identity of the figure, since no definitive attribute of a specific deity is preserved—not an apple (alluding to the Judgment of Paris), a wreath, a mirror, or even a shield (a reference to Aphrodite's relation with Ares), in which her image might have been reflected. From the outset, of course, the view that Aphrodite is represented has prevailed, because of the exquisite treatment of the marble, which exudes the sensuous tenderness of female flesh, because of the "feminine" proportions of the body, and because of the pose of the figure. Nonetheless, there are several theories about the statue's original state, prior to that in which it was found. One theory proposes that it held some objects, another that it leant on a column, or even on the shoulder of Aphrodite's erotic partner, Ares, god of war. If the figure held a bow or an amphora, then she could be Artemis

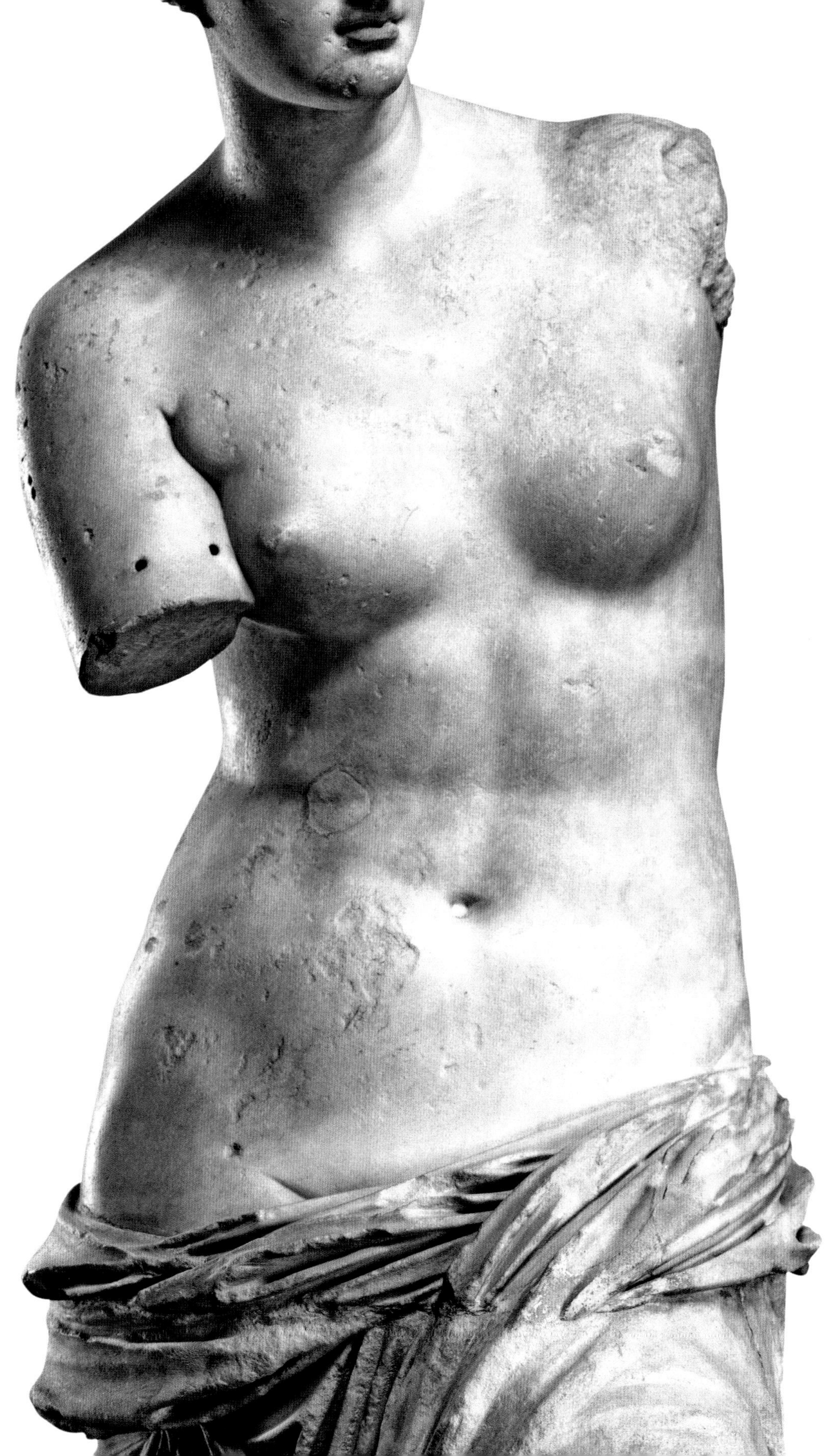

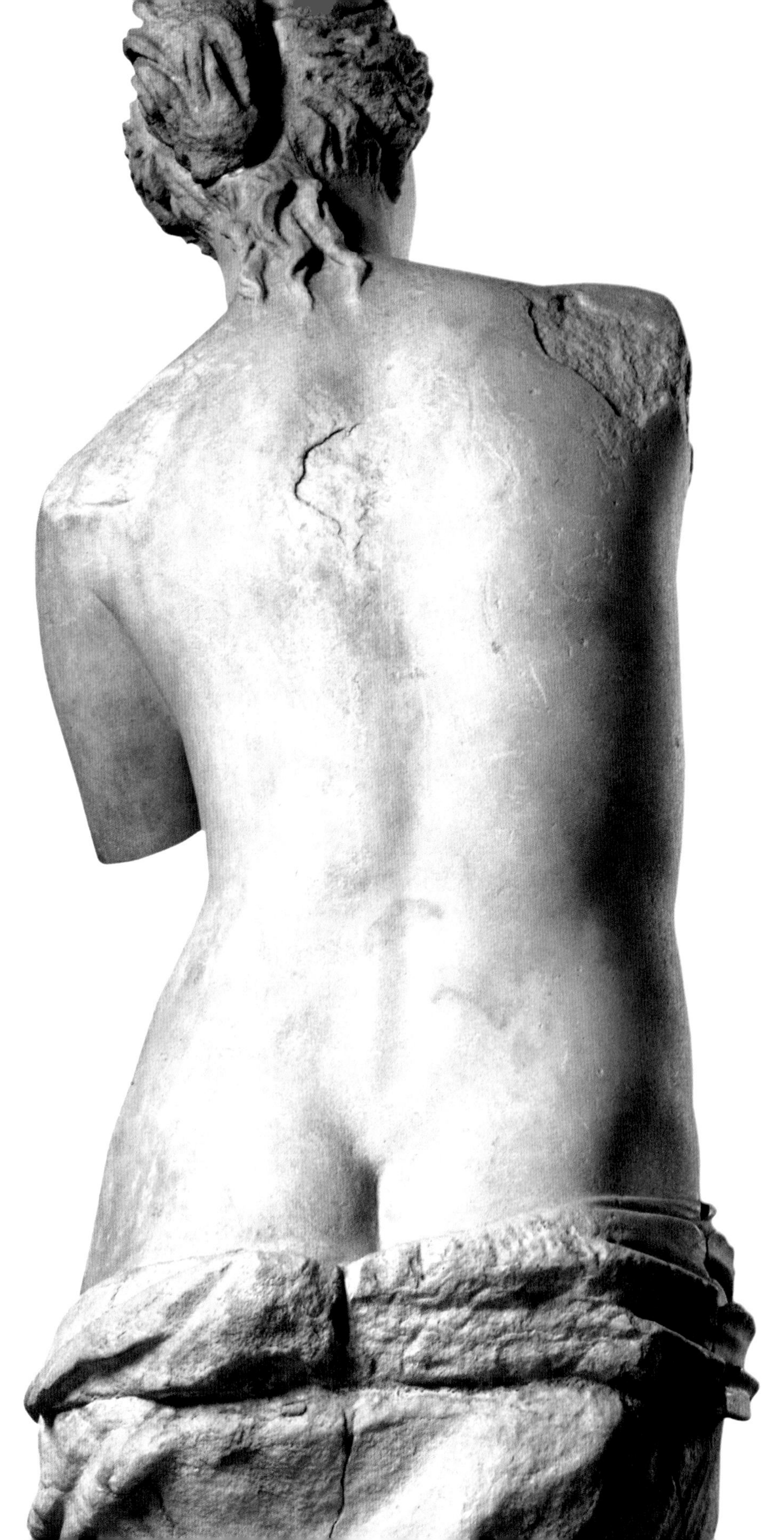

or a Danaid. The statue form combines the classical tradition with the classicistic artistic current of the late second century BCE, in which new schemas were created. The serious expression and harmonious facial features reflect the aesthetics of the fifth century BCE, whereas the hairstyle and the delicate treatment of the "skin" of the marble are consistent with Praxiteleian works of the fourth century BCE. Predominant, however, are traits of the Hellenistic period (third–first century BCE): There is the S-shaped torsion of the body, which stands freely in space. There is also the disproportionate relationship of the lower body to the upper body: The lower is more developed height-wise and holds an impressive chiaroscuro of the movement-filled drapery of the garment, while the naked torso features a small bosom and "calm" planes, though their impression may have been different if colored with pigments that are now lost.

Based on these observations, some researchers hypothesize that the statue may well be a new creation in the Hellenistic spirit, modeled on an original bronze work by Lysippos or Skopas, of the fourth century BCE.

PORTRAIT BUST

ATHENS, THEATER OF DIONYSUS
C. LATE SECOND CENTURY CE
MARBLE. PRESENT HEIGHT 1.61 FEET (0.49 M)
ATHENS, NATIONAL ARCHAEOLOGICAL MUSEUM

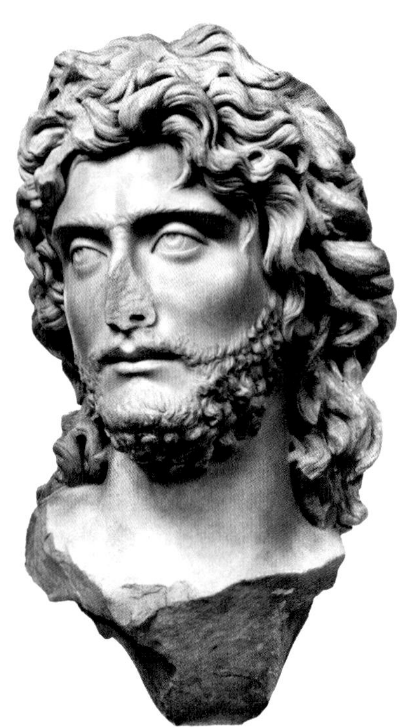

Represented is a man, his head turned three-quarters to his right, with luxuriant curly hair that is short at the top and falls to his shoulders. The figure has a short beard, mustache, thick eyebrows indicated by incisions that meet at the top of the nose, heavy eyelids, and large almond-shaped eyes, with the iris and the pupil carved and pronounced canthi. The volumes on the various planes of the face are rendered with soft transitions, while the gaze, directed slightly upward, is one of introspection and reverie, which are characteristic of Italian Renaissance figures. Preserved on the lower back surface of the bust are two leaves of an acanthus calyx, from which it projected. Any speculation about the figure's identity, including that it is the wealthy benefactor Herodes Atticus, lacks credibility.

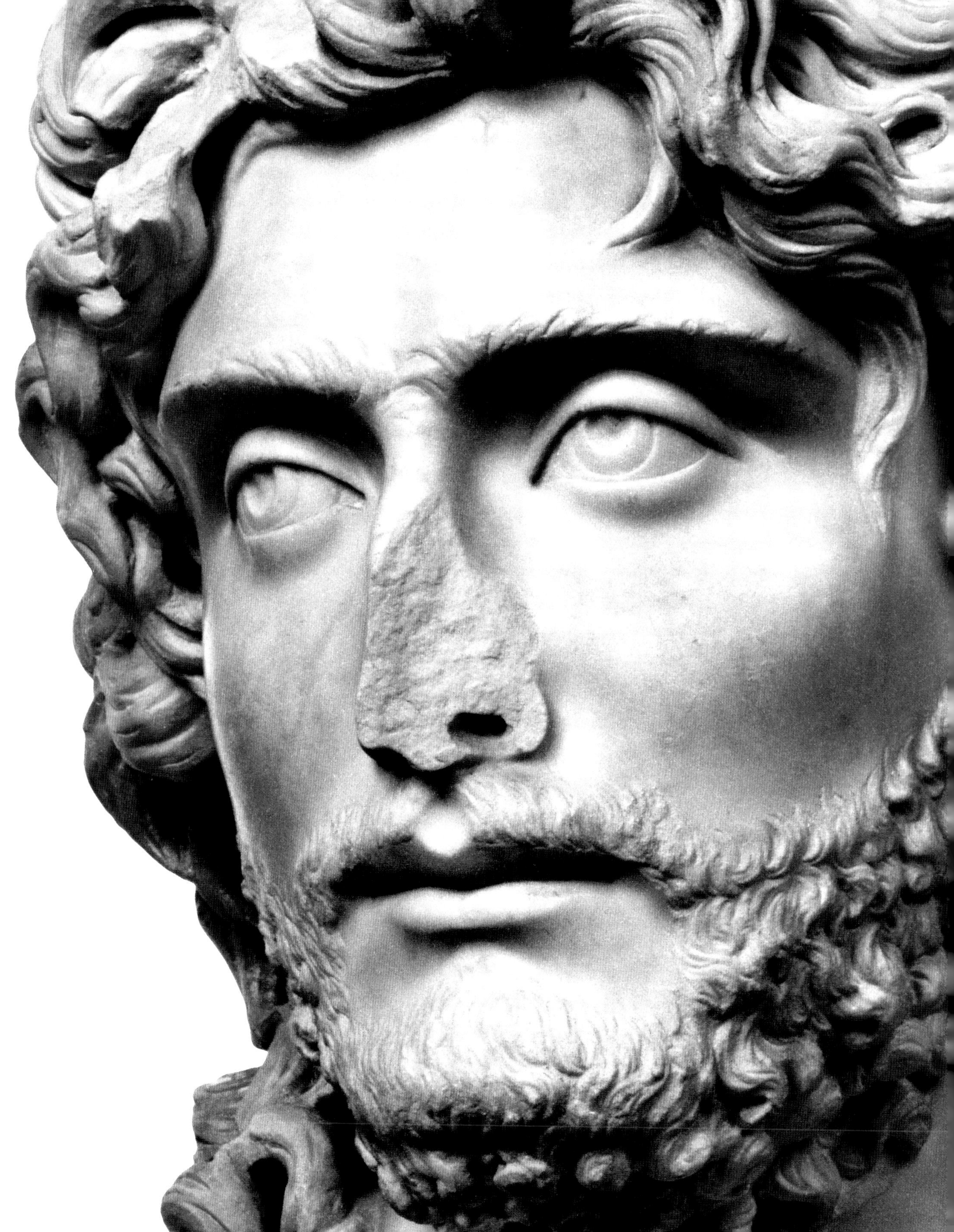

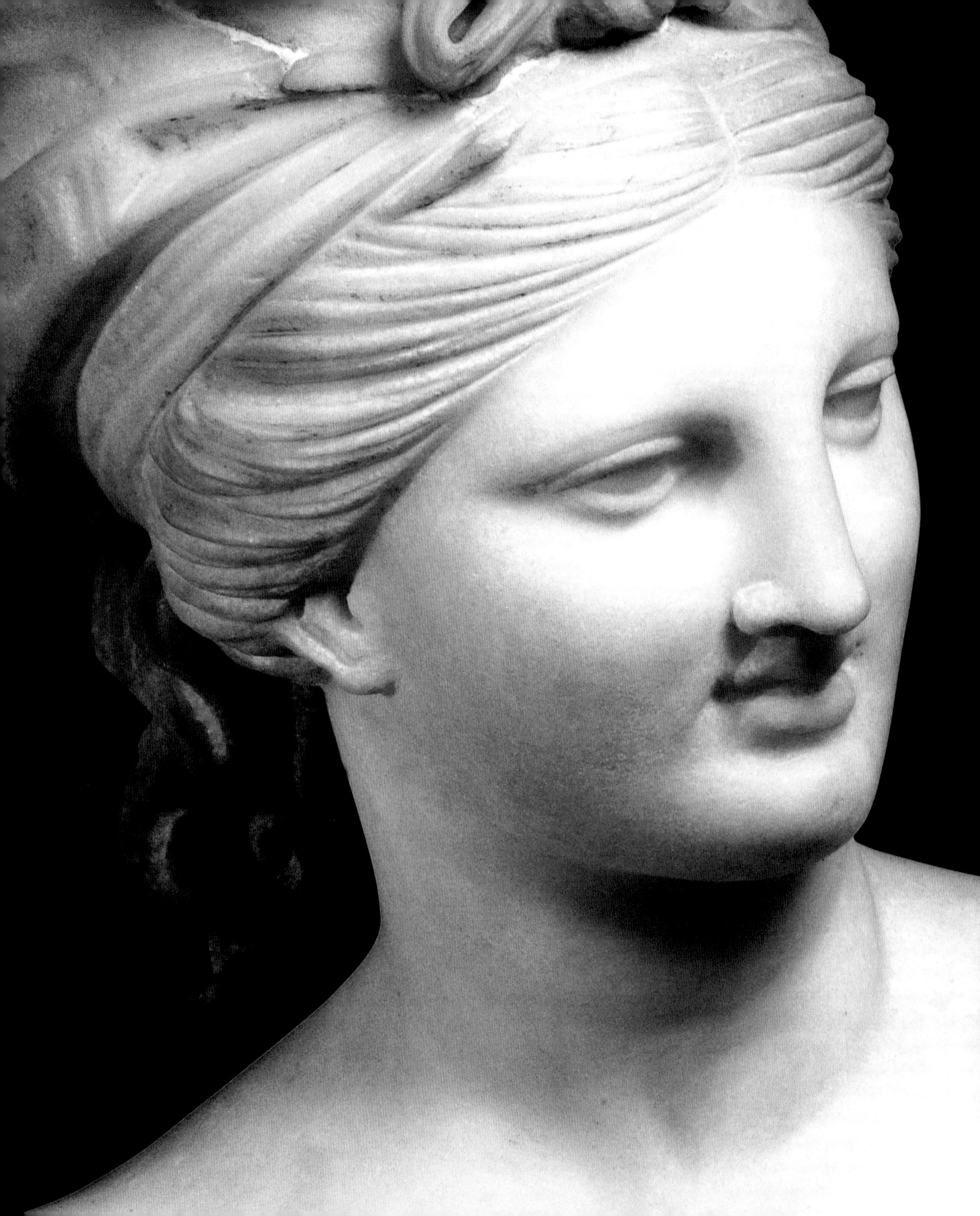

GROUP OF APHRODITE AND PAN

DELOS, LESCHE OF THE KOINON OF BERYTIAN POSEIDONIASTS
C. 100 BCE
MARBLE. HEIGHT 4.23 FEET (1.29 M)
ATHENS, NATIONAL ARCHAEOLOGICAL MUSEUM

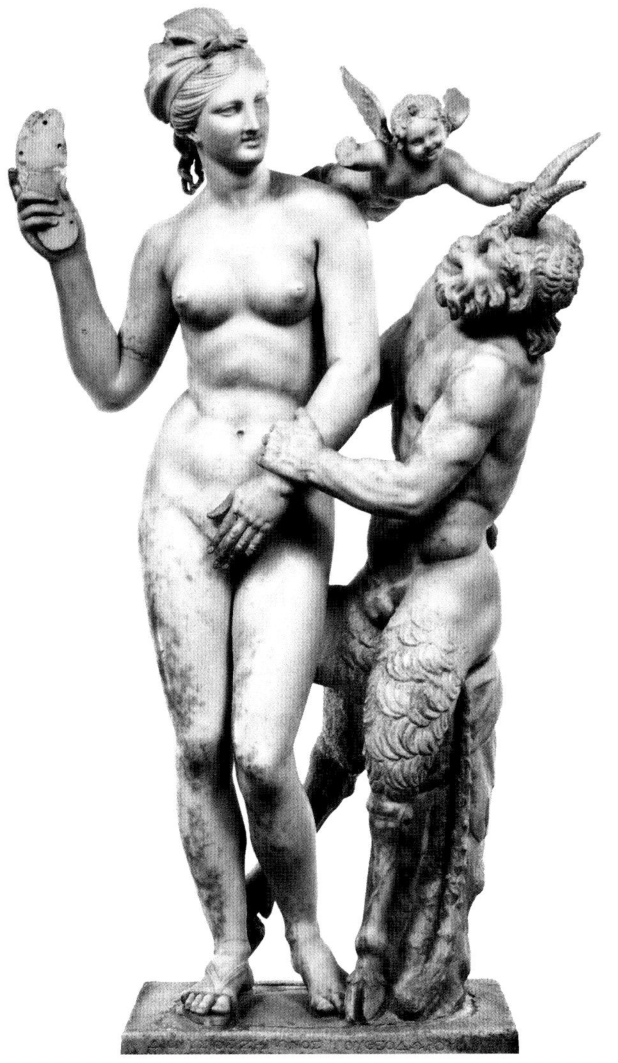

In this sculptural group of Aphrodite, Pan, and Eros, the nude sea-born goddess, having risen from the foaming waves, is attacked by the goat-legged Pan. She resists her attacker, threatening him with the sandal she holds in her raised right hand. Pan leans against a tree trunk and tries to embrace her with both hands: His right hand is on the goddess's buttocks and his left on her left arm, with which she tries to hide her pudendum. Eros flies to her aid behind her left shoulder, holding Pan at bay by grabbing his left horn with his left hand. The goddess's long hair is bound by a broad fillet and falls freely at the back. The work was commissioned by Dionysios, son of Zenon, from Berytus, one of the most important benefactors of the Lesche of Berytian Poseidoniasts. The figure of Aphrodite is in the type of the Knidian Aphrodite.

TWO RELIEF PLAQUES WITH FEMALE DANCERS

ATHENS, THEATER OF DIONYSUS
LATE FIRST CENTURY BCE
A. PENTELIC MARBLE. HEIGHT 3.51 FEET (1.07 M); WIDTH 2.17 FEET (0.66 M)
B. PENTELIC MARBLE. PRESENT HEIGHT 3.31 FEET (1.01 M); WIDTH 2.30 FEET (0.64 M)
ATHENS, NATIONAL ARCHAEOLOGICAL MUSEUM

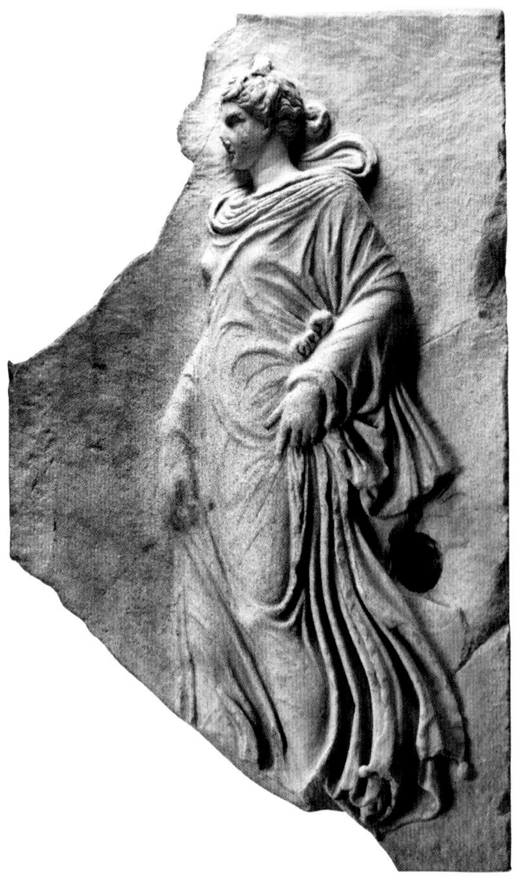

These two rectangular plaques, likely grouped together with a third, formed the revetment of a triangular base of a bronze tripod. The concave surface shows the figures in relief. Represented are two dancing girls moving left, swathed in diaphanous himations that flutter behind them. On the second dancer the himation also covers her head. The first figure is about to dance, while the second already moves to the rhythm.

These neo-Attic works of the first century BCE, whose prototypes are earlier reliefs of the fourth century BCE, are among the loveliest of their kind. They exhibit a perfect modeling of volumes through the alternation of illumined and shaded planes, endowing the figures with the freshness and grace of youth.

In all probability the Hores, or Hours, are portrayed, They are daughters of Zeus and Themis and represent the seasons of the year.

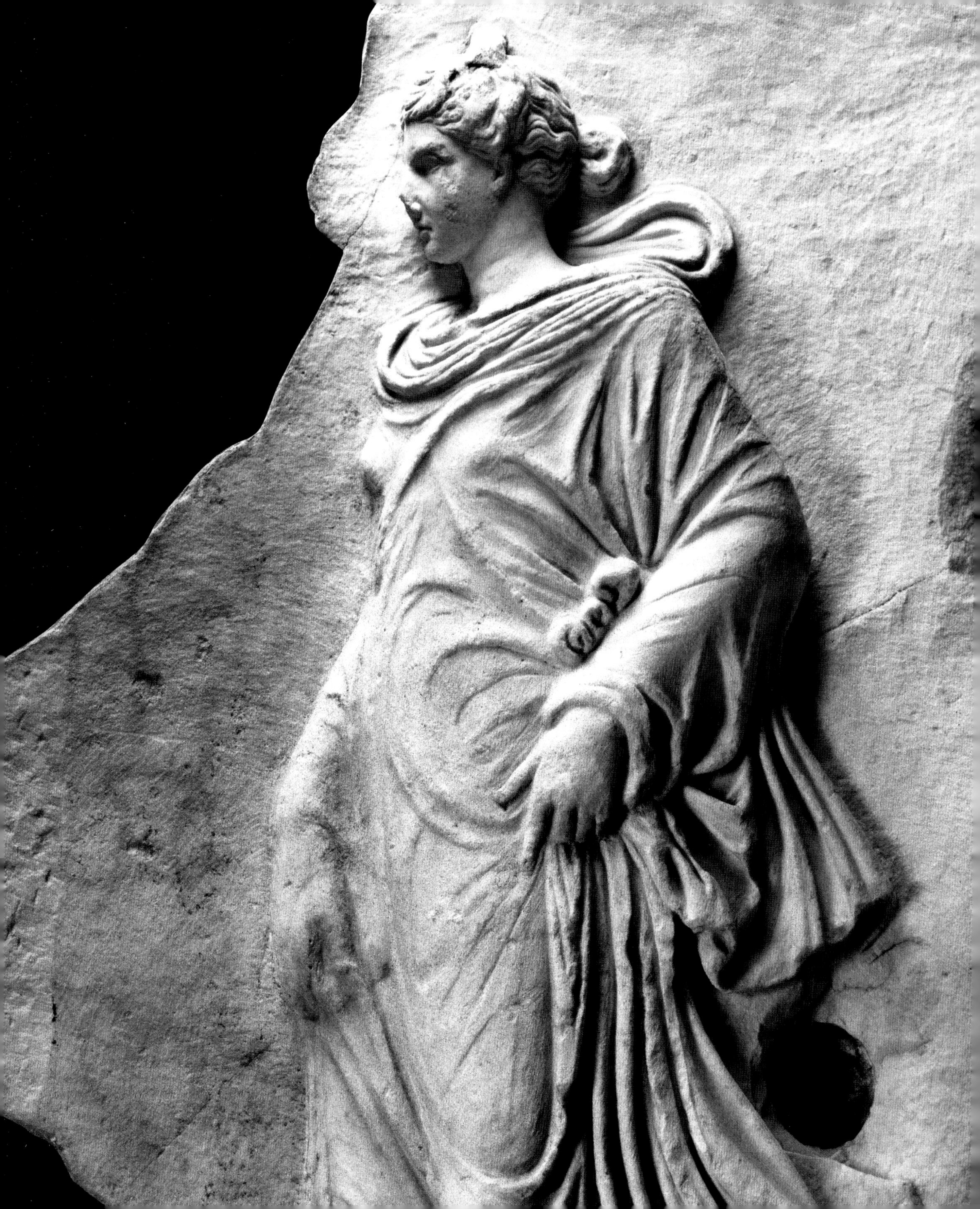

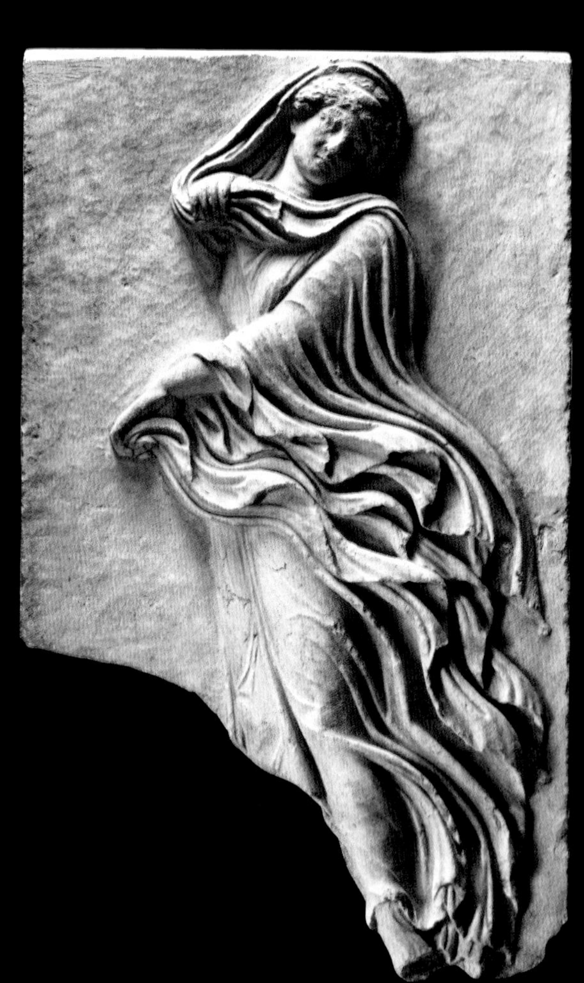

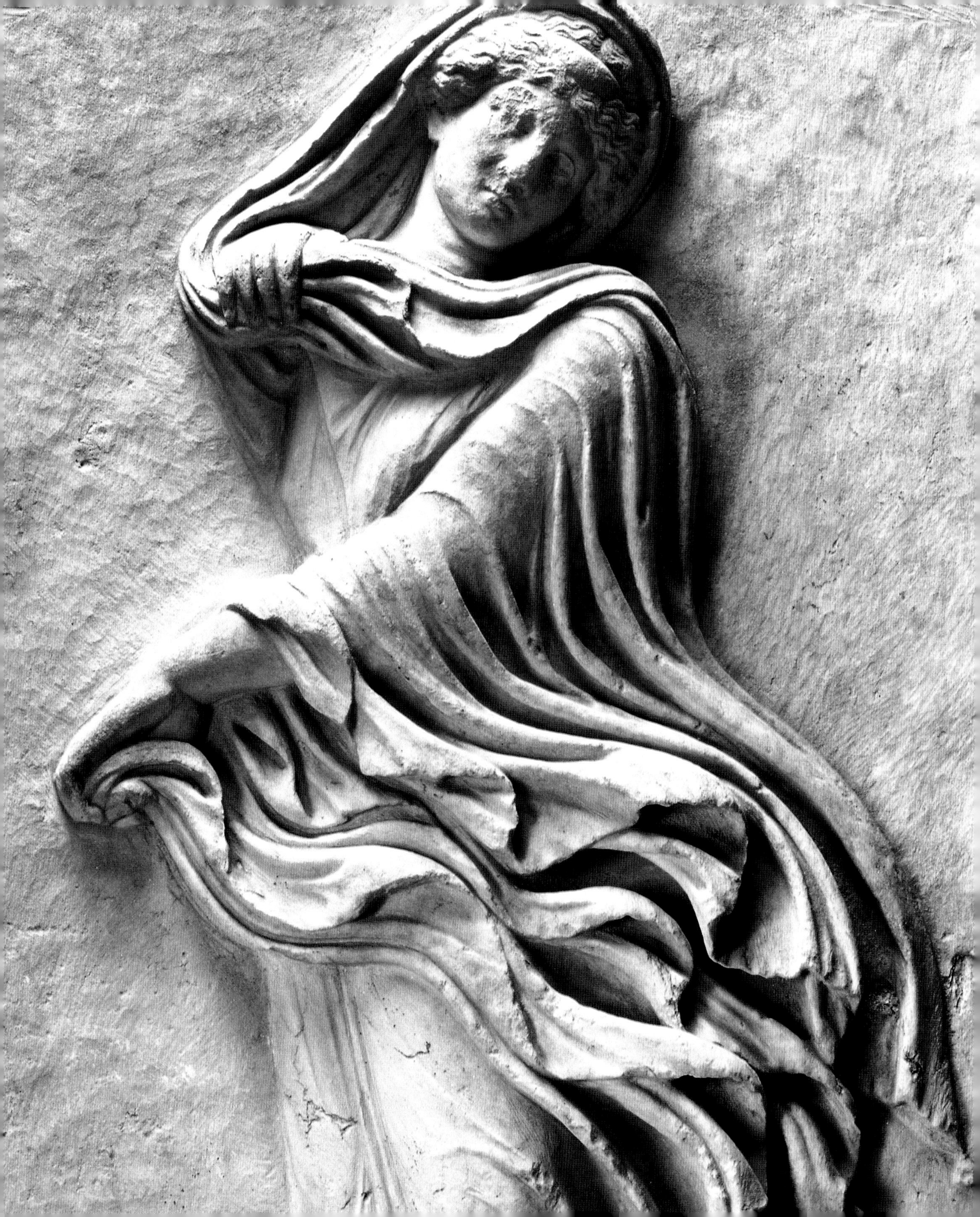

GLOSSARY

acroterion. The ornamental finial at the three angles of the pediment of an ancient temple.

aegis. A cloak with the Gorgon's head at the front and a fringe of snakes, characteristic of the goddess Athena.

apoptygma. An overfold.

cella. The inner chamber of a temple.

chiton. A garment of fine cloth.

chlamys. A short, oblong mantle worn by young men.

cire perdue. The lost-wax technique of casting bronze statues.

contrapposto. A pose in which one part of a figure twists or turns away from another part.

demos. The common people of a Greek state.

ephebe. A young man undergoing military training.

epiblema. A shawl worn by Greek women.

ex-voto. A votive offering.

himation. A mantle or wrap worn by Greek men and women.

in antis. The state of being between pillars or antae.

Ionic cymatium. An egg-and-tongue molding.

kekryphalos. A female headdress consisting of a net, or a light cloth or kerchief.

korymbos. A hairstyle worn by women, where hair is rolled into a knot behind the head.

krobylos. A hairstyle similar to the korymbos, but worn by men.

Lesbian cymatium. A leaf-and-dart molding.

loutrophoros. A ceremonial vase for water.

naiskos. A small temple.

opisthodomos. The rear porch of a temple.

pankratiast. A sporting event that combines wrestling and boxing.

peplos. A garment worn by women that hangs in loose folds at the waist.

petasos. A wide-brimmed hat.

polos. A headdress of female deities.

prodomos. An open vastibule.

quadriga. A four-horse chariot.

sakkos. A snood or kerchief.

tympanum. The recessed space enclosed by cornices of a pediment.

BIBLIOGRAPHY

Barlou, V. Die archaische Bildhauerkunst von Paros. Wiesbaden 2014.

Brouskari, M. *Μουσείον Ακροπόλεως*. Athens 1974.

Bruneau, P., and J. Ducat. *Οδηγός της Δήλου*. Athens 2010.

Cook, B. Greek and Roman Art in the British Museum. London 1976.

Delivorrias, A. The Parthenon Frieze. Athens 2004.

Despinis, G., and N. Kaltsas, eds. *Εθνικό Αρχαιολογικό Μουσείο. Κατάλογος Γλυπτών Ι.1. Γλυπτά των αρχαϊκών χρόνων από τον 7ο αι. έως τον 4ο αι. π.Χ.* Athens 2014.

Fuchs, W., and J. Floren. Die griechische Plastik. Munich 1987.

Hadjidakis, P. J. Delos. Athens 2003.

Hermary, A., P. Jockey, F. Queyrel. Sculptures déliennes. Paris 1996.

Kaltsas, N. *Εθνικό Αρχαιολογικό Μουσείο. Τα γλυπτά*. Athens 2001.

—. "Die Kore und der Kuros aus Myrrhinous." Antike Plastik 28 (2002): 7–38.

—. Olympia. Athens 2004.

—. The National Archaeological Museum. Athens 2007.

Karakasi, K. Archaische Koren. Munich 2002.

Karouzos, C. *Αριστόδικος*. Athens 1961.

—. "*Η Νίκη της Πάρου.*" *Μικρά Κείμενα* 150–153. Athens 1995.

Kostoglou-Despini, A. *Προβλήματα της παριανής πλαστικής του 5ου αι. π.Χ.* Thessaloniki 1979.

Kunze M. Die Antikensammlung Berlin. Berlin 1992.

Lanzillotta E. Paro. Dall' età arcaica all' età ellenistica. Rome 1987.

Marcadé, J., Au Musée de Délos. Paris 1965.

Masterpieces of the J. Paul Getty Museum. Los Angeles 1997.

Papachatzis, N. *Παυσανίου Ελλάδος Περιήγησις: Αττικά*. Athens 1974.

—. *Μεσσηνιακά και Ηλειακά*. Athens 1979.

—. *Βοιωτικά και Φωκικά*. Athens 1981.

Pollitt, J. Art in the Hellenistic Age. Cambridge/New York 1986.

Richter, G. The Sculpture and the Sculptors of the Greeks. New Haven 1957.

Ridgway, B. S. The Archaic Style in Greek Sculpture. Princeton 1977.

Samara-Kaufmann, A. *Ελληνικές Αρχαιότητες στο Μουσείο του Λούβρου*. Athens 2001.

Trianti, I. The Acropolis Museum. Athens 1998.

Yalouris, N. *Ελληνική Τέχνη: Αρχαία Γλυπτά*. Athens 1994.

Zapheiropoulou, P. Paros. Athens 2009.

—. Delos. Athens 1998.

—. "Parische Skulpturen." Antike Plastik 27 (2000): 7–35.

—. "Recent Finds from Paros." In Excavating Classical Culture. Ed. M. Stamatopoulou and M. Yeroulanou, 281–284. Oxford 2002.

—. "Delos." In Archaeology. Aegean Islands. Ed. A. Vlachopoulos, 232–243. Athens 2006.

—. "Paros." In Archaeology. Aegean Islands. Ed. A. Vlachopoulos, 260–268. Athens 2006.

—. "*Η Πάρος των πρώιμων χρόνων.*" In *Αμύμονα Έργα. Τιμητικός Τόμος για τον καθ. Β. Λαμπρινουδάκη*. Ed. Simantoni-Bournia et al., 109–118. Athens 2007.

—. "*Η παριανή γλυπτική και οι πρωτοπόροι δημιουργοί της.*" In La sculpture des Cyclades à l'époque archaïque. BCEH Suppl. 48. Ed. Y. Kourayos and F. Prost, 485–489. 2008.

—. "*Η Γλυπτική στην Πάρο πριν από τον Σκόπα.*" In *Ο Σκόπας και ο κόσμος του*: Skopas and his world, Paros III. Ed. D. Katsonopoulou and A. Stewart, 77–90. Athens 2013.

PROVENANCE OF ILLUSTRATIONS

Elias Eliadis
4-5, 9, 20, 27, 29, 32, 33, 35, 49, 50, 52, 55, 57, 58, 60, 70, 71, 78-84, 90-94, 96, 97, 104, 106-113, 115-118, 122, 124-126, 128-130, 132, 134, 144, 173, 180, 181, 194-202, 206, 232-235, 237, 244, 245, 248-251

Sokratis Mavrommatis
1, 6, 16, 36-39, 41-45, 62, 63, 66, 67, 73-75, 86-88, 99, 139, 141, 146, 147, 154-171, 174, 175, 177, 192, 193, 246, 247, 255

Berlin, Bildarchiv Preussischer Kulturbesitz
214-215 (16.374-1), 220 (24.982), 222 (3.964-1), 225 (26.241), 227 (10.562), 228 (19.300-1), 231 (26.237)

German Archaeological Institute, Athens
6 (NM 5059, Czako), 16 (Schrader 89, Schrader), 18, 26, 31 (1988/368, Gehnen), 22 (NM 4746, Czako), 23 (Hege 947, Hege), 24 (Hege 1276, Hege), 30 (1987/912, Koppermann), 64 (Akropolis 1783, Wagner), 68 (NM 5053, Czako), 69 (NM 5041, Czako), 72 (1972/2931, Hellner), 89 (Schrader 35/36, Schrader), 121 (Hege 445, Hege), 135 (Hege 850, Hege), 137 (NM 4537, Wagner), 190 (NM 5357a, Czako), 191 (NM 5359, Czako), 204 (Hege 472, Hege)

London, The British Museum
184-189

New York, The Metropolitan Museum of Art
142, 143 (Fletcher Fund, 1927 [27.45] ©1997 The Metropolitan Museum of Art)

Paris, the Louvre Museum © Photo RMN
208, 210 (Gerard Blot / Christian Jean), 209, 212 (Gerard Blot / Hervé Lewandowski), 238 (Daniel Arnaudet / Jean Schormans), 239, 241, 242 (Hervé Lewandowski)

Archive of the Melissa Publishing House
105, 114, 121

Restoration - Drawings
47: Hansen; 48, 51, 54, 77, 198: Fouilles de Delphes IV; 100: G. Grunauer; 102-103 (bottom), 125: True;
102-103 (top), 105, 106, 109, 110, 113, 114, 117, 121, 172: H. V. Herrmann; 149: M. Korres; 150-153: J. Boardma, D. Finn; 183: British Museum, London

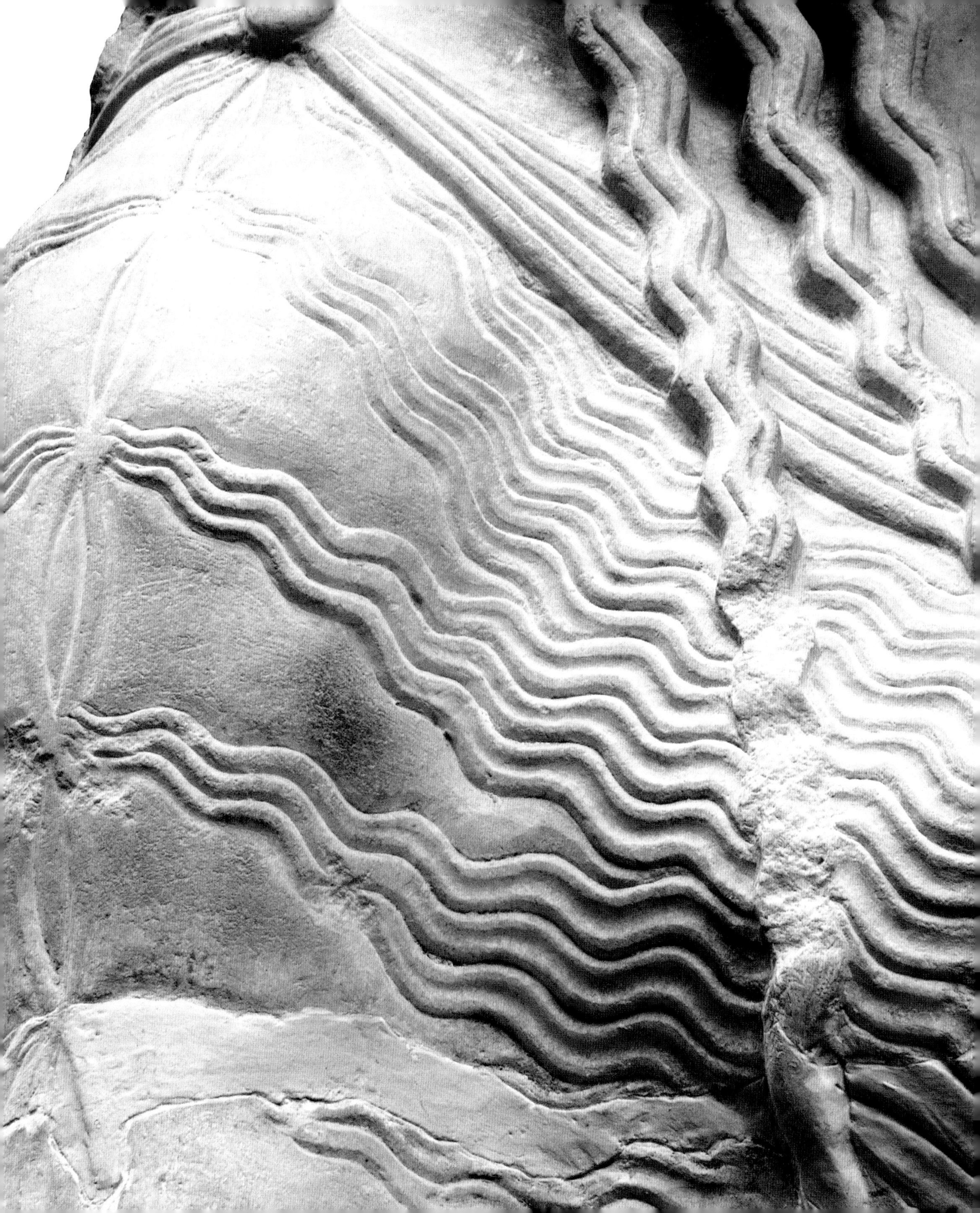

CAPTIONS

PAGE 1: The Blond Boy (see p. 86)

PAGE 6: Aristodikos (see p. 68)

PAGE 8: Grave Stele of Dexileos (see p. 180)

PAGE 14: Large relief found in Athens, in the bed of the River Ilissos (c. 340 BCE). Athens, National Archaeological Museum

PAGE 16: Kore (see p. 72)

PAGE 18: The Samos Kouros (see p. 30)

PAGE 20: The Nike of Paionios (see p. 172)

PAGE 255: The Kore of Euthydikos (see p. 88)

Originally published by MELISSA Publishing House in 2007

Original edition

PUBLICATION COORDINATOR: Athina Ragia

ENGLISH TRANSLATION: Alexandra Doumas

GRAPHIC DESIGN: metoo (Aliki Kakoulidou - Dimitra Vassilakou)

REPRODUCTION OF PHOTOGRAPHS: Nikos Alexiadis

Abrams edition

EDITOR: Sarah Massey

TYPESETTING AND COVER DESIGN: Darilyn Lowe Carnes

PRODUCTION MANAGER: Katie Gaffney

Library of Congress Control Number: 2015955484

ISBN: 978-1-4197-2229-5

Printed and bound in China
10 9 8 7 6 5 4 3 2 1

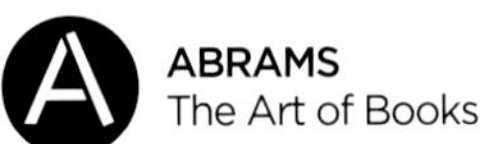

115 West 18th Street
New York, NY 10011
abramsbooks.com

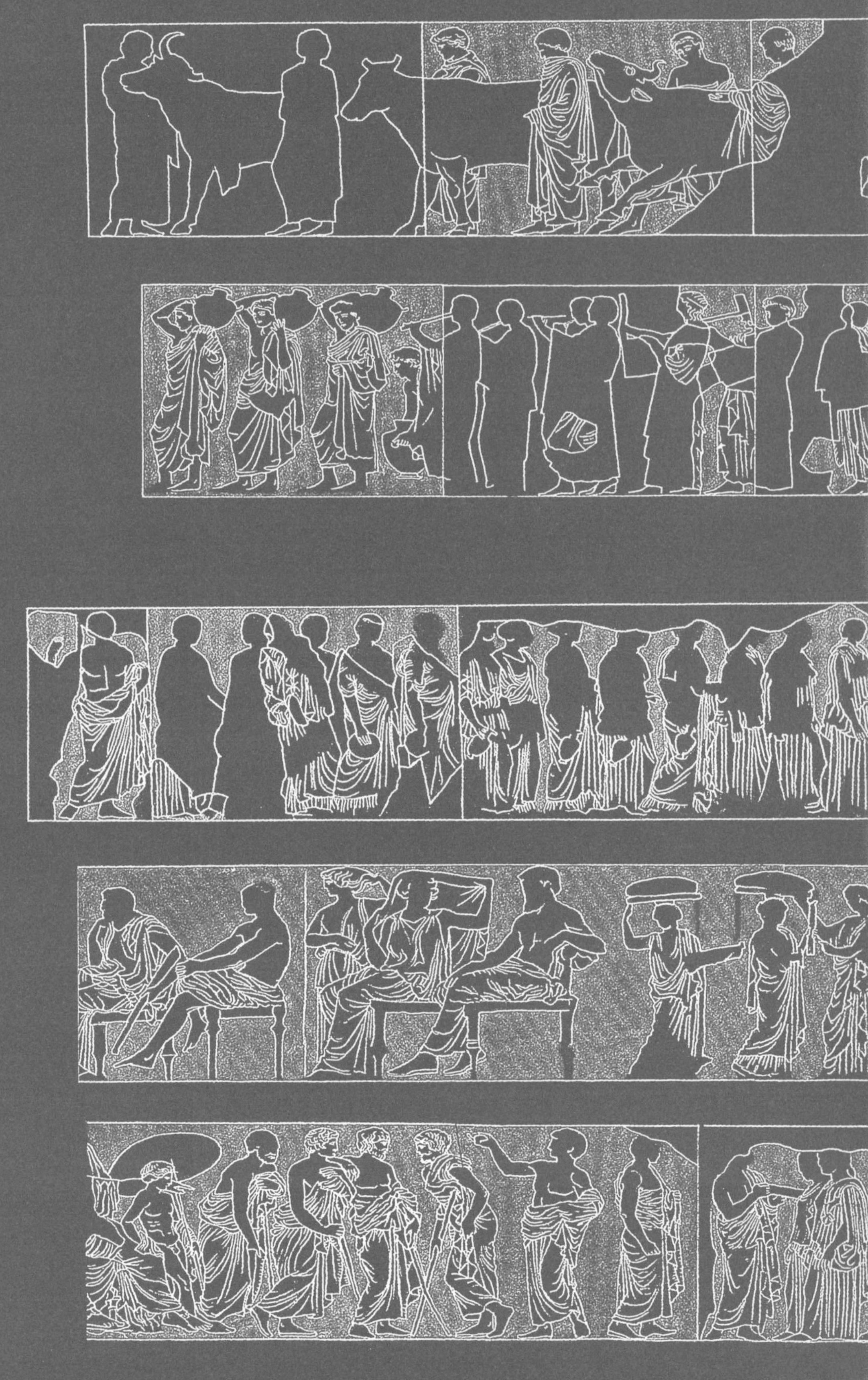